APOSTASIA

in

2nd Thess. 2:3

RAPTURE OR APOSTASY?

by

Lee W. Brainard

Soothkeep Press

APOSTASIA IN 2ND THESS. 2:3 — RAPTURE OR APOSTASY?
by Lee W. Brainard
Copyright © 2021
All rights reserved

Published by Soothkeep Press
(an "operates as" handle for the published ministry of Lee W. Brainard)

ISBN — 978-0-9987594-9-4

Cover design by Nita L. Brainard

Scripture citations are a mixture. Some are verbatim from the King James Bible, some are the author's emendations of the same, and some are the author's translations of the Greek.

The English translations in the appendices of the *apostasia* passages from the Koine and Byzantine eras are translations executed by others where such were available and my own translations where either none were available or the available translation was deemed unacceptable.

TABLE OF CONTENTS

FOREWORD

I feel honored to write a foreword for Lee Brainard's exploration into the meaning of *apostasia* in 2 Thessalonians 2:3. There is no doubt that Lee is a man after my own heart in this regard. He has provided a thorough (some could say exhaustive) examination of the linguistic background behind the differing opinions related to this topic.

One of the first subjects in training any Bible student is the foundation of proper interpretation (a.k.a. hermeneutics). This is extremely important because we all know people who have approached the Bible with their own presuppositions or allegorical methods. Ultimately, we know that where they started is most likely where they end up. They approach the Bible as a buffet and cherry pick verses or hi-jack a text to mean what it clearly does not mean.

The foundation of hermeneutics is seeking the historical, literary (including language), and theological context of any given passage of Scripture. Once these topics are explored, the student can be confident that their interpretation is probable more likely than not.

This book by Lee is not meant to be exhaustive in analyzing the history or theology of the passage itself (even though he does address these). However, if you are looking for <u>the</u> resource for understanding the linguistics of the word *apostasia*, then this book is for you. He has researched extensively to bring forth the clear usage of this key word from the period of the Koine Greek. As far as I am aware, no other study of this magnitude has ever been done with the intent of contributing to the controversy surrounding the interpretation of 2 Thessalonians 2:3.

Another element that was extremely helpful in addressing the arguments of those who see a rapture in this passage is the way in which Lee provides the background to the early English language versions of 2 Thessalonians 2:3. It is common to hear in those who see a rapture in this passage, that the King James version *began* the

3

movement away from spatial departure into a spiritual apostasy. Lee shows that this is clearly not the case.

At the end of the day, all Bible interpreters must ask if evidence matters. Lee has shown that the mistake interpreters have often made is to allow a 6th century A.D. use of the Greek word, as noted in the Liddell and Scott lexicon, to determine or shape their interpretation. This is known as the semantic anachronism exegetical fallacy and should certainly be avoided. For those that are willing to submit to the evidence as presented in this book by Lee, they will have to humbly go back and acknowledge that the rapture/departure concept is not found in 2 Thessalonians 2:3.

One final thought that Lee and I have discussed in person is that Lee is a firm believer in the pre-tribulation doctrine. Therefore, he actually could have a potential bias against his own research. Yet we know that the doctrine of the pre-tribulational rapture does not need to rest on this passage to be true. There are many other biblical passages that support such a teaching. I have already shared Lee's research with many prophecy scholars and they are having to re-examine their own theological perspectives on this passage. Integrity in scholarship will honor the Lord the most in the long run and I am thankful that Lee's research will help us with such an important passage of eschatological Scripture.

Mondo Gonzales, M.A.

Co-host at Prophecy Watchers Ministries

PREFACE

Why devote over 2000 hours to researching and writing on the interpretation of *apostasia* in 2 Thessalonians 2:3? I had two main reasons.

One, the *apostasia* question is more than a small point. It is a matter of methodology. Not so much whether or not we are following the historical-grammatical hermeneutic, but rather how consistently we apply it, and how deeply and broadly we press it.

Two, there was a lack of information available from which to make an informed decision. Yes, information was presented in the argument for the rapture understanding of *apostasia*, and it was presented in a manner that made a plausible case. But this information is both partial and misunderstood. The question of the interpretation of *apostasia* looks quite different if you examine a fuller body of evidence and understand all of the information you have garnered. My aim was to make a large body of pertinent information available to all who are interested in the subject and explain several items of information that are commonly misunderstood.

For the most part, I have presented the arguments for the rapture interpretation of *apostasia* in 2 Thessalonians 2:3 in generic form rather than quoting a plethora of passages with names and sources attached. The reason for this is straightforward. I am not trying to pick a fight with anyone on the other side of the debate. My only aim is to shed helpful light on the passage.

INTRODUCTION

In recent decades, the idea has been popularized that the Greek word ἀποστασία (apostasia) in 2 Thess. 2:3 is not a reference to apostasy in the last days but rather to the rapture. The theory claims that *apostasia* does not refer to moral departure from the Lord but physical departure from earth to meet the Lord in the clouds.

When I first heard this idea, I wanted to believe it. Were it true, it would be another powerful arrow in the quiver of arguments for the pretribulation rapture. But I was skeptical. My gut instinct, based on fairly extensive reading in Koine Greek, was that *apostasia* wasn't used for physical or spatial departure like going to the store or going on a vacation. Nor was it used in senses with neutral or positive connotations. It was used of things with negative connotations, like political sedition and religious apostasy.

But truth isn't based on feelings or instincts. It is founded on objective facts. Because of my intense love for Bible prophecy, a fire kindled in my heart to get to the bottom of this issue. I didn't care what the truth proved to be. I had no vested interest either for or against the rapture understanding. I just wanted a definitive answer. That implied extensive research.

The first step of my investigation was to read a selection of books and papers written by prominent teachers, past and present, who defend the view that *apostasia* in 2 Thessalonians 2:3 is a reference to the rapture, and take copious notes. Then I compiled a master list of the arguments that they presented in favor of this view. I wanted to have a strong grasp of the case for the position. What were the arguments for it? How strong were they? Was the case a slam dunk? Was it a toss-up? Or was it far-fetched? Ultimately, I concluded that while the position was plausible, it was not a slam dunk.

My second step was an ambitious project to examine every usage of *apostasia* in the extant Greek literature from its first appearance, whenever that was, to the end of the fifth century. I was particularly interested in the Roman era (150 BC to AD 150) and the late-Roman era (AD 150 to 250) How was the word used? What was its semantic range? What senses did it bear?

I was also interested in how the early fathers or their translators used *apostasia*, particularly how they perceived it in 2 Thessalonians 2:3. It seemed reasonable to assume that they were more likely to have a native grasp on its force than anyone in our generation. Moreover, I assumed that they would be conservative in maintaining the sense of *apostasia* which they saw in the New Testament and the Septuagint.

Did the early Fathers see a rapture or an apostasy here? If physical or spatial departure was a legitimate sense, then it could be assumed that some of the fathers who commented on the passage would offer up the rapture understanding. We would likely find evidence of an ongoing debate between the rapture school and the apostasy school.

The third step was the biblical aspect of the investigation. I labored over the context of 2 Thessalonians 2:3, wrestled with the grammar and exegesis of the passage, and pondered the relationship between 1st and 2nd Thessalonians. I took up an extensive investigation into what the Bible taught on tribulation and falling away in general in contrast to what it taught on the great tribulation and the falling away at the end of the age.

I researched the translation history of *apostasia* in the early English, German, and Latin bibles, investigated what the early translators and editors meant by *departure*, pursued the history of *falling away* in the English Bible, and delved into the history of the transliteration of the word *apostasia*.

The final step was organizing the results of my research in this volume for the benefit of all who love Bible prophecy. In the body of the book, I answer every significant argument for the *apostasia*-rapture theory that I came across in the literature. In the appendices I include all 283 instances of *apostasia* in the Thesaurus Linguae Graecae collection from its first reference in Archimedes' *The Sand Reckoner* around 250 BC to its last usage before my cut-off line—the end of the fifth century.[1] Each reference gives the Greek and an English translation with sufficient context to judge the sense intended by the author.

A large body of evidence is now available for all to examine and weigh. Nobody needs to rely on the opinions and assertions of experts or the "supposed" meaning of the *apostasia* entry in the Liddel & Scott lexicon. No scholar needs to toil away for hundreds of hours in painstaking research replicating the study. The serious student can easily peruse the information and references I have collated here in a few hours and see for himself how *apostasia* was used in the Koine era, what the translation history of *apostasia* in 2 Thessalonians 2:3 in the Latin and English Bibles really says, and how the early fathers viewed *apostasia* in 2 Thessalonians 2:3. This information will shed much light on the correct understanding of apostasia in this disputed passage.

THE APOSTASIA DEBATE

History of the Rapture Understanding

The earliest mention of the rapture interpretation of *apostasia* in 2 Thessalonians 2:3 in print appears to have been an 1895 article by J.S. Mabie in the *Morning Star*.[2] Half a century later, it was popularized by men like John Rice in *The Coming Kingdom of Christ*,[3] E. Schuyler English in *Rethinking the Rapture*,[4] and Dr. John Walvoord in *The Rapture Question*.[5] In the present day, this view is taught by numerous teachers in the dispensational camp, and it seems to be growing in popularity.

The Arguments for the Rapture Understanding

The major arguments for the rapture understanding of *apostasia* in 2 Thessalonians 2:3 can be summed up in six points.

ONE—the meaning argument. Apostasia does not mean falling away or apostasy. It means departure. Apostasia can mean either abstract departure (such as departure from the faith) or physical or spatial departure (such as departure from earth to heaven).

Greek has a unique word for *falling away*, which is *ekpiptō*. *Apostasia* and *ekpiptō* portray distinct concepts without significant overlap in meaning or sense. *Apostasia* should never be translated by terms like *falling away* or *apostasy*.

That *apostasia* can mean physical *departure* is based on two observations. The first is that the second entry in the Liddel & Scott lexicon[6] gives *departure* as one of its meanings, "2. departure, disappearance, Olymp. Mete. 320.2."

The second is that *apostasia* is the noun form of the verb *aphistemi*. This verb is a compound of the preposition *apo* "from" and *histemi* "stand," and it has the core meaning of *away from* or *departure*. *Apostasia* has the same semantic range of meanings. It should always

10

be translated by *departure*. The context will determine whether the reference is to abstract departure (rebellion, apostasy) or physical departure (leaving one location for another). The dearth of New Testament instances of *apostasia* is irrelevant. We may legitimately look to examples of *aphistemi* to ascertain the meaning of *apostasia*.

TWO—the translation argument. The view that apostasia in 2 Thessalonians 2:3 is a reference to an apostasy in the last days is a modern innovation that was initiated and perpetuated by bad Bible translations beginning with the Rheims and King James versions.

The early English translations all featured *departure*—Wycliffe (1384), Tyndale (1526), Coverdale (1535), Cranmer (1539), Breeches (1576), Beza (1583), and Geneva (1608).

Translating *apostasia* by *departure* is an ancient conviction that goes back to the earliest translations. For instance, Jerome's Latin translation (AD 405), commonly known as the Vulgate, rendered *apostasia* by *discessio*, which means *departure*.

The Rheims translation of the New Testament, a Roman Catholic production printed in 1582, was the first Bible to reject the established translation of *departure*. It rendered *apostasia* by *revolt*. The translators of the KJV, influenced by this novel rendering, followed in 1611 with the translation *falling away*. Since then the Protestant and Evangelical translations have followed the Catholic Church's lead. No good explanation or justification has ever been given for this tragic misstep.

Theodore Beza also played a significant role in polluting the translation stream. He was the first to transliterate *apostasia* rather than translating it, coining the English word *apostasy*, a mistake that plagues the church to the present day.

THREE—the theological argument. Three doctrinal problems stand in the way of the understanding that apostasia refers to a last-days apostasy.

First of all, apostasy set in while the apostles were yet alive, and there has been a continual string of apostasies since that time. This longstanding precedent militates against the idea of a special apostasy

11

in the last days. There is no reason to believe that there will be an apostasy in the last days that will differ significantly from this pattern.

Secondly, there won't be any way for the believers of the last generation to recognize that the apostasy they are facing is *the* apostasy that signals the end of the age because it isn't going to differ significantly from the apostasies that preceded it. It will not stand out in either degree or features.

Thirdly, there is no comfort to be derived from knowing that a spiritual departure (the apostasy) must precede the day of the Lord. But there is much comfort to be derived from the fact that a physical departure (the rapture) must precede the day of the Lord.

FOUR—the grammatical argument. Four grammatical considerations indicate that apostasia can't refer to a last-days apostasy.

The first is that the word *apostasia* by itself doesn't mean spiritual *departure*, it simply means *departure*. Spiritual departure is indicated by grammatical qualification such as the use of a prepositional phrase. But *apostasia* is not grammatically qualified in 2 Thessalonians 2:3, so it can't mean *apostasy*. It must mean physical *departure*.

The second is that the definite article means that the noun is an exceptional instance of something. *Apostasia* has a definite article, so whatever it refers to is an exceptional instance. This leads to the theological argument mentioned above that *apostasia* can't refer to an apostasy in the last days because the last-days apostasy will not be significantly different from the long line of apostasies that preceded it. But it can refer to an outstanding instance of physical departure— the rapture.

The third is that Greek articles often point back to and link with preceding nouns. It is noted that the feminine noun *apostasia* has the article, and it is proposed that this article looks back to and links with *coming* and *gathering* which are also feminine and have the article.

The fourth is that the definite article requires definiteness not merely in the noun itself but in the time nuance. Therefore, whatever *apostasia* refers to, it must be something that happens at a specific time—even instantaneously. This time constraint forbids the apostasy

12

understanding because apostasies develop slowly over time. But it precisely fits the rapture.

FIVE—the exegetical argument. Apostasia bears the same relationship to the revelation of the antichrist in verse three that the restraining effort bears to the revelation of the antichrist in verses six and seven. In other words, the apostasia is parallel to the restrainer.

As the restraining effort of the Holy Spirit operating through the church must be removed in verse seven (implying the rapture of the church) before the antichrist can be revealed, so the *apostasia* must happen in verse three (implying the rapture of the church) before the antichrist can be revealed.[7] This forbids the apostasy understanding of *apostasia* and requires the rapture understanding.

SIX—the contextual argument. The concept of apostasy is not found anywhere in the context of 2 Thessalonians 2:3.

The concept of apostasy does not appear anywhere in either 1st or 2nd Thessalonians. But the concept of the rapture appears in almost every chapter in both 1st and 2nd Thessalonians. This implies that *apostasia* is best understood as a reference to the rapture rather than to a reference to apostasy in the last days.

My Response to the Six Arguments

In the following chapters, each of the above arguments is addressed with a bevy of facts.

First, I address the meaning of *apostasia*, including the misuse of the Liddell & Scott lexicon, the reliance on the word-root and cognate fallacy, and the proper methodology for determining the meaning of words.

Next, I present the results of an exhaustive study of the usage of *apostasia* in the Koine era including all the church fathers of the first five centuries. This is accompanied by the results of extensive research in the usage of the entire *apostasis* family.

Usage is the heart of the question. If *apostasia* does bear the sense of physical *departure* in Koine Greek, then the interpretation of the passage will have to be decided in the trenches. But if *apostasia* never bears the sense of physical *departure* in the Koine era, then it can't bear that sense in 2 Thessalonians 2:3, and any argument that would challenge this is contrived from speculation not derived from fact.

Then I address the translation of *apostasia*, covering what the early English versions meant by *departure*, what the Latin versions meant by *discessio*, what is overlooked in the history of *falling away*, what is overlooked in the testimony of the earliest English versions, what Beza's role was in non-departure renderings, and what the real reason was for the change from translations like *discessio* and *departure* to translations like *apostasy* and *falling away*.

This is followed by examining an area that seems to have been completely ignored, which is the patristic handling of 2 Thessalonians 2:3. How do the fathers handle *apostasia*? Do any of them support the rapture interpretation?

Finally, in successive chapters, I address the various contextual, grammatical, exegetical, and theological arguments that have been made in support of the rapture understanding of *apostasia*.

It was my intention to leave no significant stone unturned and to shed light on a difficult subject, the understanding of which has been hamstrung by lack of thorough investigation. I trust that my efforts will prove a blessing to those who love the prophetic Scriptures.

THE MEANING OF APOSTASIA

The Misuse of the Liddell & Scott Lexicon

Those who hold the rapture understanding of *apostasia* in 2 Thessalonians 2:3 insist that *apostasia* can refer to the physical or spatial departure of human beings. They base this claim on the second entry given in Liddell & Scott, "2. *departure, disappearance*, Olymp. in Mete. 320.2." They see the word *departure*, pounce on it, and exploit it as the foundation of their claim that *apostasia* is a reference to the church departing this defiled earth for the courts of heaven.

But this handling is problematic. If we flesh out the second entry for *apostasia* in Liddell & Scott, using the abbreviation tables in the front of the tome, we get "2. *departure, disappearance*, Olympiadorus in *In Aristotelis Meteora commentaria* 320.2." Ten minutes of investigation reveals two things. One, Olympiadorus was a mid-sixth century philosopher (We call them scientists now.) who wrote well-known commentaries on Plato and Aristotle. Two, the Latin title *in Aristotelis meteora commentaria* rendered in English is *Commentary on Aristotle's Meteorology*. This is a scientific work. If we actually read the passage, we discover that it addresses the effects of heat and cold on solids and liquids. And we learn that *apostasia* is used for the departure of liquid from a substance when heat is applied. In other words, it is a reference to *evaporation*. These two points throw a monkey wrench into the machinery of the rapture interpretation.

In regards to the second point, *evaporation* is a technical sense which has nothing to do with the physical or spatial departure of human beings moving from point A to point B. It is not legitimate to lift the translation *departure* out of this scientific context and export it to a non-scientific context. The fact that *apostasia* can be used for liquid departing from a solid does not prove that it can be used for a human being departing on a trip or the church departing for heaven. The only possible human application of this sense would be the

15

desiccation of human bodies in some operation like mummification or burning at the stake.

Moreover, I would point out, lest anyone try to exploit the sense of *evaporation*, that the rapture is not an evaporation of the believers who will be reconstituted later. It bears no resemblance at all to getting beamed up in Star Trek. It is the simultaneous transportation and glorification of our physical bodies—from the earth and earthly to heaven and heavenly.

In regards to the first point, this sixth-century usage is the earliest instance—perhaps the only instance—of *apostasia* being used in the sense of *evaporation*. Usually, the scientific and technical senses were carried by *apostasis*. This reference is more than four centuries after the completion of the canon of the New Testament. So, even if we could somehow salvage the sense of *departure* from the wreck of *evaporation*, this usage has zero bearing on the interpretation of 2 Thessalonians 2:3. No sense that first appears four centuries after the completion of the New Testament can be considered as a potential sense for the New Testament. Selecting a sense which first appeared in the fifth or sixth century is an egregious anachronistic error that undermines the historical-grammatical hermeneutic. We are limited to senses that were current at the time of the penning of the New Testament.

Yet another place where men have stumbled in their use of Liddell & Scott is that they have somehow overlooked that the first definition opposes their rapture understanding of 2 Thessalonians 2:3. This entry fleshed out and translated into English reads, "*defection, revolt,* legal sense in Dionysius Halicarnassensis *Roman Antiquities* 7.1, Josephus *Life* 10, Plutarch *Lives* Galba 1; especially in religious sense, *rebellion against God, apostasy,* LXX Joshua 22:22, 2 Thessalonians 2:3." Notice that they cite 2 Thessalonians 2:3 as an example of *apostasia* being used in the religious sense. This is telling. This is the estimation of men who are among the foremost Greek lexicographers in history.

The Root and Cognate Fallacies

One of the main arguments presented by the advocates of the *apostasia*-rapture theory is the claim that *apostasia* is simply the noun form of the verb *aphistemi*. Based on this identity, they embrace the meaning of *aphistemi* as the meaning of *apostasia*. The verb, they point out, is a compound of the preposition *apo* "from" and *histemi* "stand" and has the core meaning of *away from* or *departure*. And so they insist that the core meaning of *apostasia* is *departure* too.

They defend turning to the meaning of *aphistemi* with the plea that *apostasia* is only used two times in the New Testament, not enough to get a feel for its meaning. Then they point out that *aphistemi* is used fifteen times in the New Testament, and only three of these instances involve departure from the faith. The others involve departure in various senses including the *departure* of individuals from one location to another.

But this argument involves both the root fallacy, the idea that the meaning of a word can be deduced from its roots, and the cognate fallacy, the idea that cognate words have the same meaning.

D.A. Carson comments on the former, "One of the most enduring of errors, the root fallacy presupposes that every word actually has a meaning bound up with its shape or its components. In this view, meaning is determined by etymology; that is, by the root or roots of a word. How many times have we been told that because the verbal cognate of ἀπόστολος (apostle) is ἀποστέλλω (I send), the root meaning of 'apostle' is 'one who is sent'?"[8]

Notice that the latter portion of his comment touches on the cognate fallacy. It is not legitimate to read the meaning of the verb ἀποστέλλω (I send) into the noun ἀπόστολος (apostle). The words are related in meaning, but not identical. The meaning of *apostle* in the New Testament is narrower than *sent one*. Every messenger is sent, but not all messengers are apostles. All believers are sent—"go ye into all the world"—but not all believers are apostles.

Likewise, in the question at hand, we have no business importing the meaning of the verb ἀφίστημι (depart) into the noun ἀποστασία (rebellion, revolt). Words must be defined by their contemporary usage, not by their word roots or the meaning of cognate words. Word roots and cognates can point us in the right general direction—usually. They can't nail down the actual uses and meanings. That we can only obtain from contemporary usage.

17

We don't have to look any farther than the English language to find examples of verb-noun pairs that have very different meanings.

The verb *desert* means "to abandon a person or cause." The noun *desert* means "a barren and arid land."

The verb *refuse* means "to decline something." The noun *refuse* means "garbage."

The verb *project* means "to throw something or cast an image on a surface." The noun *project* means "a task one is working on."

The verb *overlook* means "to fail to notice something." The noun *overlook* means "a vantage point with a great view."

The Apostasis Family

One important factor that has been overlooked by the rapture-theory advocates is the fact that there is a tight-knit family of cognates derived from *aphistemi* whose semantic ranges are all significantly narrower than *aphistemi*. This family is the *apostasis* family. It includes seven nouns, one adjective, two verbs, and one adverb.

The nouns are *apostasis* (sedition, rebellion, apostasy),[9] *apostasia* (sedition, rebellion, apostasy), *apostatēs* (rebel, apostate, deserter, runaway), *apostasion* (divorce), and three rare forms: *apostatis* (sedition, apostasy), *apostatesis* (rebellion), and *apostasēs* (rebellion, apostasy).[10] The adjective is *apostatikos* (rebellious). The family has its own verb forms: *apostateō* (rebel) and *apostasiazō* (cause to rebel). The verbs are accompanied by the gerund *apostateon* (rebelling) and the adverb *apostatikōs* (rebelliously).[11]

Just being aware of this family sheds much light on the correct interpretation of *apostasia*. If the family has its own verb forms, then *apostasia* and *apostasis* can't be regarded as identical-triplet nouns of *aphistemi* with the exact same range of meaning. They are merely cognates. We would expect their semantic range to track much more closely with the more closely related verbs *apostateō* and *apostasiazō* than with the more distantly related verb *aphistemi*. And this is exactly the case as we shall shortly demonstrate.

How to Determine the Meaning of Apostasia

Usage is the only trustworthy arbiter of the meaning of a word. Juggling word roots and cognates doesn't tell us how a word is actually used or what sense the person employing it intends to convey. An etymologist can tell us that *epic* comes from the Greek word ἔπος (word, poetry), but that has little bearing on the reason that your nephew uses *epic* in the sense of *awesome* when he talks about things like his recent snowboarding trip.

Avoiding the pitfalls of the word-root and cognate fallacies is as vital to the student of the Bible as avoiding the broken reed of Egypt was to the children of Israel. This is why the historical-grammatical hermeneutic, more commonly known as literal interpretation, insists that the vocabulary of the New Testament bears contemporary senses. Words can bear elevated senses which far transcend secular use, but they can't bear senses that didn't exist at the time. This is true even for such core Bible words as grace, love, faith, and hope.[12]

This principle has profound implications for those who seek the meaning of *apostasia* in 2 Thessalonians 2:3. When we look up *apostasia* in a lexicon, we are not free to choose from any sense we please. We are free to consider any sense which was current at the time that Paul penned the book, which was somewhere around AD 51-52. So our window would be the two centuries prior and the two centuries following. We aren't at liberty to assign a meaning which can't be attested from this era.

19

THE USAGE OF APOSTASIA

Apostasia Broken Down by Sense

So what do we discover if we examine every instance of *apostasia* from its first appearance in Archimedes around 250 BC to the end of the fifth century?

We discover that *apostasia* was never once used of the physical or spatial departure of human beings. It was never used for departing for the market or the temple, or departing on a trip or military campaign, or anything similar.

We discover that Archimedes used it once around 250 BC in the scientific sense of *distance*, a sense normally covered by *apostasis*.[13] But this usage never caught on. *Apostasis* continued to exclusively carry the workload for this sense.

We discover that Galen used it thirteen times in the late second century in the medical sense of *abscess*, a sense normally covered by *apostasis*.[14]

We discover that it was used ten times in the legal sense of *divorce*, a sense normally covered by *apostasion*.[15]

We discover that it was used once by Evagrius of Pontus late in the fourth century in the sense of *departure from sin*, which is essentially a synonym for *repentance*.[16] This is the first known use of *apostasia* with a positive connotation.

Outside of these rare or obscure senses, *apostasia* had two uses. It was used 26 times for political *sedition or rebellion* and 232 times for religious *apostasy*.[17]

This information has tremendous ramifications for the correct interpretation of *apostasia* in 2 Thessalonians 2:3. Galen's use in the sense of *abscess*, Archimedes' use in the sense of *distance*, the sense of *divorce*, and Evagrius of Pontus' use in the sense of *repentance* can be safely rejected as options. They are foreign to the context.

This means that the only two senses we can consider are political *sedition* and religious *apostasy*. And without even looking at the context, but simply weighing the probabilities based on how common these senses are, we can say that there is an 90% chance that the meaning of *apostasia* in 2 Thessalonians 2:3 is religious *apostasy*.

Apostasia Broken Down by Era and Genre

Another helpful way to examine the *apostasia* data is to break it down by era and genre. This draws our attention to some interesting facts.

Contrary to the assertions that some have made, *apostasia* was never used in the Classical era.

It first appeared about a century into the Koine era, when it was used by Archimedes around 250 BC in the technical sense of *distance*.

In the secular writings of the Roman era (150 BC to AD 150), it was used nine times in the sense of political *sedition*, including three times in Josephus, twice in Diodorus Siculus, and twice in Plutarch.

In the secular writings of the late Roman era (AD 150 to 250), it was used four times in the sense of political *sedition* and thirteen times in the medical sense of *abscess*.

In the Greek translations of the Hebrew scriptures, it was used eleven times in the sense of religious *apostasy*: three times in the Septuagint, seven times in Aquila, and once in Theodotion.

In the Jewish religious writings, it was used twice in the sense of religious *apostasy*. Once in the historical book 1 Maccabees (circa 130 BC), and once in the Book of Jubilees (written at least 100 BC).

In the lone New Testament instance outside of Paul's use in 2 Thessalonians, Acts 21:21, we find it used of religious *apostasy*.

In the Fathers through the first five centuries, it was used 246 times in 224 passages. Once late in the fourth century for *repentance*, 10 times for *divorce*, 16 times for political *sedition*, and 219 times for religious *apostasy*.

Breaking it down in this manner highlights some very interesting points. One, the sense of political *sedition* is the only sense we find in the secular historians and biographers. Two, the sense of religious *apostasy* is the only sense we find in the Greek translations of the Old Testament and the Jewish religious writings. Three, the predominant sense in the early Fathers, by far, is the sense of religious *apostasy*.

My Study on the Apostasis Family

When I first started my study on the usage of *apostasia*, I had intended to include every reference to every member of the *apostasis* family in the Roman era (150 BC to AD 150). But the vast scope of the project became apparent about one year in, and I jettisoned the idea. To find every instance of every word in the family in the TLG (Thesaurus Linguae Graecae) database, categorize and organize the copied passages, and find or execute English translations for them would have easily added another three years to the project. The appendix alone would have surpassed a thousand pages. Moreover, the conclusions from an exhaustive study of the entire family would not differ significantly from the conclusions I could obtain from an exhaustive study of *apostasia* and the large sampling that I already had from the *apostasis* family.

Despite my truncated efforts, I managed to gather 525 instances of *apostasis* from the Roman era. When I tallied them, the results were illuminating. Technical senses were common. For instance, *distance* or *separation* in scientific treatises and the discussions of battles, *asyndeton*[18] in the grammarians, and *abscess* in medical writings. There were several instances where it was used of *separation* from things or persons, a sense that seems to be a figurative use derived from the technical sense of *distance* or *separation*. These uses seem to have the sense of regret or sorrow attached to them.

The most common sense, however, and the one which dominated in historical and biographical accounts, was that of political *sedition* or *rebellion*. In this same vein of *rebellion*, there were also several instances of religious *apostasy* and one instance of medical *heresy*.

But in all of these instances, *apostasis* was not used a single time of general *departure*, i.e. the physical or spatial *departure* of an individual from one location to another. It was never once used for undertaking a jaunt, trip, journey, expedition, walk, hike, or any such thing. It was never once used of going to the market, or the temple, or the capital, or the battlefield, or a nearby city, or a neighboring land, or anything similar.

In my research of the *apostasis* family, I also managed to gather 100 instances of the noun *apostatēs* (apostate, rebel, runaway) and 20 instances of the verb *apostateō* (to rebel). Never once were either of these words used in the sense of general or physical *departure*. They were always used in the sense of *rebellion*.

These results cast a long shadow on the claim that *apostasia* can bear the sense of physical or spatial *departure*. Not only does *apostasia* never bear that sense from 250 BC to AD 500, but an examination of its three most common cognates: *apostasis*, *apostates*, and *apostateō*—totaling 645 examples—in the Roman era (150 BC to AD 150) doesn't turn up a single example where they are used for the physical or spatial *departure* of a human being from one location to another.

Paul Feinberg's Study

Paul Feinberg, who formerly taught Greek at Trinity Evangelical Divinity School, has also investigated the usage of the *apostasis* family. Here is what he had to say.

"Aphistemi and its cognates are found widely in Greek literature. … In the period from second century B.C. to first century A.D. there are at least 355 occurrences of this word group, making these rather common words in the Greek language. … If one searches for the uses of the noun "apostasy" in the 355 occurrences over the 300-year period between the second century B.C. and the first century A.D., one will not find a single instance where this word refers to a physical departure."[19]

I am assuming that by the noun *apostasy* he meant both *apostasia* and *apostasis*. I count only twelve instances of *apostasia* between 200 BC and AD 100. But there were hundreds of instances of *apostasis* in the same period. Both were used for rebellion in a fairly broad array of contexts.

While Paul Feinberg's study was not as extensive as mine, it was a broad sampling, broad enough that it would have uncovered at least a few examples of the sense of physical *departure*, if such a sense actually existed.

Negative Connotations of Apostasia

The first appearance of *apostasia* is found in Archimedes' *The Sand Reckoner* around 250 BC in the scientific sense of *distance*.[20] This sense didn't catch on, but the word did. And from that point on until Evagrius of Pontus used it late in the late fourth century in the sense of *repentance*,[21] a sense which has a positive connotation, every instance bore negative connotations. Divorce is negative. Abscesses are negative. Sedition and apostasy are negative.

This has tremendous ramifications for the understanding of *apostasia* in 2 Thessalonians 2:3. Not only was *apostasia* used only for abstract departure and never for physical departure, but it was also used only for negative departure. It was never once used of neutral departure (like going to the store, going for a walk, going to town) or positive departure (like going to my wedding, going to my reward ceremony, going to my coronation). Without the sense of physical *departure* and without the positive connotation, the ability to make *apostasia* fit the rapture mold is entirely lost. It can't mean physically leaving earth for a joyous gathering in the clouds.

Reflexive Connotations of Apostasia

Yet another aspect of the usage of *apostasia* which many have overlooked is the reflexive connotations it bears when used in association with moral beings. Universally, these instances involve severed relationships, which were severed when moral beings (human or angelic) separated themselves from other moral beings (human, angelic, or divine).

When used in political settings, it concerns men who have experienced a change of heart and breached their fealty by removing themselves from and conspiring against their erstwhile partners. This is negative self-removal.

When used in religious settings, it concerns men or angels who have experienced a change of heart and breached their fealty to God and the truth by removing themselves from and conspiring against God and those who represent him. This is negative self-removal.

Even the occasional use of *apostasia* in the sense of *divorce* bears this reflexive nuance, for divorce is instigated by someone, on their own behalf, when they give the other party the letter of divorce, formally severing the relationship. This severing is the result of the same dissatisfaction that severs political and religious relationships.

The rapture is contrary to this reflexive connotation. Bear in mind that the rapture is not men removing themselves. It is men being suddenly seized by God to be hauled to the clouds and then to heaven. This is a passive transaction, not a reflexive one. And if the rapture is contrary to the reflexive connotations of *apostasia*, then *apostasia* in 2 Thessalonians 2:3 cannot be a reference to the rapture.

The rapture needs to be represented by nouns that bear a passive connotation, like *harpagē*, which is the noun form of *harpazō*. While this particular noun doesn't appear in the New Testament in the sense of the rapture, it does appear in the fathers in this sense. It is used, for instance, five times in this sense in Ephraim of Syria's Greek works.

The Bankrupt Case for the Rapture View

By now it should be obvious that the case for the rapture view of *apostasia* in 2 Thessalonians 2:3 is bankrupt. It fails all three critical usage tests that are necessary to vindicate the rapture interpretation.

It fails the test of passive connotation. Passive uses are absent from the historical record. Everywhere *apostasia* is used in the reflexive sense of men removing or departing themselves.

It fails the test of positive connotation. Positive and neutral senses of *apostasia* were completely lacking until the fourth century when *apostasia* was first used in the sense of *repentance*.

It fails the test of physical or spatial *departure*. There is no trace of *apostasia* being used for physical *departure* before the NT era. Nor is there any trace of it for five centuries afterward.[22] It is entirely absent from the historical record during the required time frame. Reading this sense into the New Testament is like reading the modern definitions of words into Shakespeare. This wouldn't be legitimate translation, and it wouldn't be good literature. Many passages would be muddled, and some would be unintelligible.

Without proof that *apostasia* can mean physical *departure* and concurrently bear both positive and passive connotations, the whole argument for the rapture understanding of *apostasia* comes crashing to the ground. The rest of the arguments that can be brought to the table on behalf of this theory don't have the vigor to stand on their own. They are all carried on the back of the physical-departure dogma. Nonetheless, for the sake of full treatment, every significant argument will be addressed in the following pages.

Source of the Meaning of Apostasia

If we can't nail down the meaning of the noun *apostasia* by pointing to the definition "departure" in Liddel & Scott or invoking the theory that it has the same semantic range as the verb *aphistemi*, then how shall we discern its meaning? Simple. By examining its usage in the centuries before Paul penned 2 Thessalonians.

While these instances were not many, they all point to one semantic channel, that of *rebellion*. Three times it appears in the sense of political *sedition*, two of these instances in Diodorus Siculus' *Historical Library*. Three times it appears in the sense of religious *apostasy* in the Septuagint, the first Greek translation of the Old Testament. And twice the sense of *apostasy* appears in well-known Jewish religious writings, 1 Maccabees and the Book of Jubilees.

Now the Septuagint and these two religious works were part of the treasured literature that most Jews in the first century were familiar with. This literature played a major role in the cultural milieu and vocabulary of the Jews in general and the Jewish authors of the New Testament in particular.

The First Book of Maccabees details the Jewish victory in the Maccabean Revolt against the Seleucid empire. In 164 BC the Jews recaptured Jerusalem and rededicated the temple, which had been polluted by Antiochus Epiphanes. The rededication is commemorated with Hanukkah. This account resonates to this day with Jews around the world.

The Book of Jubilees was popular in the era running up to the New Testament, especially among the Essenes. More copies of it were found at Qumran than every book of the Hebrew Bible except Psalms,

Deuteronomy, Isaiah, Exodus, and Genesis. Fifteen copies each were found of the Book of Jubilees and Genesis.[23]

The influence of the Septuagint on the Jews, particularly the Jews God used to write the New Testament, was enormous. This venerable translation was the Old Testament Scriptures for many Jews, and half of the Old Testament citations in the New Testament follow its readings rather than the Hebrew of the Masoretic tradition.

Everett Harrison says, regarding the influence of the Septuagint on the New Testament, "A reader of the New Testament who approaches it by way of familiarity with the Old Testament is likely to recognize a certain similarity of structure and idiom, but he will not think of it as strange because his mind has been conditioned by the reading of the Old Testament. But if one were to come to the reading of the Greek New Testament without this background, having only an acquaintance with classical Greek, let us say, he would be impressed with certain features that would strike him as peculiar. In other words, he would discover that the New Testament, although written in a language to which he is accustomed, possesses constructions and meanings of words for which his knowledge of classical Greek provides him no preparation. These are especially marked in the quotations, but also characterize the composition of the various books to a greater or lesser degree. The technical term for these features is Semitism, a term broad enough to include both Hebraism and Aramaism (the general subject of Semitisms can be explored to good advantage in J. H. Moulton, *Grammar of New Testament Greek, II*, 411-85)."[24]

Now, these three sources (the Septuagint, 1 Maccabees, and the Book of Jubilees) were the fountain from which the Jews drew their conception of *apostasia*, and these books throw some amazing light on the understanding of 2 Thessalonians 2:3.

The reference in 1 Maccabees 2:15 concerns the occasion when the officers of Antiochus Epiphanes were forcing the Jews to commit *apostasy* by forsaking the law of God and sacrificing to Zeus. Antiochus Epiphanes had already ransacked the temple and polluted the altar by sacrificing a pig on it, fully aware that this was against the law of Moses.[25] This man and this event were predicted in the eleventh chapter of Daniel, the two being given as precursors and types of the antichrist and the abomination of desolation. No deeply religious Jew in the early church could read 2 Thessalonians 2:3 with its mention of *apostasia* and the antichrist and not think of the *apostasia* in the days of Antiochus Epiphanes, the forerunner of the antichrist.

The *apostasia* citation from the Book of Jubilees presents Nimrod leading the entire world in *apostasia*, the tower of Babel being the symbol of the world's unity in rebellion against God. Nimrod is the origin of the spirit of Babylon and the post-flood *apostasy* of mankind. It is this Babylonian or Nimrodian spirit that will be manifested in the last days in its fullest and darkest degree in the time of the antichrist. Again, no religious Jew in the early church could read 2 Thessalonians 2:3 about the *apostasia* in the last days and not have his mind turn to Nimrod's *apostasia* in the Book of Jubilees.

In 2 Chronicles 29:19 in the Septuagint, *apostasia* is used of Ahaz's *apostasy*. If we read through 2 Chronicles 28-29, we learn that Ahaz led Israel and Judah down a disastrous path, sacrificed to the gods of Damascus, cut in pieces the articles of the house of God, shut the doors of the house of God, and made altars in every corner of Jerusalem and high places in every city.

In Joshua 22:22 in the Septuagint, *apostasia* is used of the feared *apostasy* of the Transjordanian tribes who had built an altar of witness. These tribes professed their innocence and insisted that they had not built it to offer sacrifice on, but merely for a memorial. They knew full well that offering sacrifice on any altar other than God's altar in Jerusalem was *apostasy*.

In Jeremiah 2:19 *apostasia* is used for the *departure* of the entire house of Israel from the Lord. Israel had changed the glory of God, which dwelt in the temple, for gods which were not gods. They had forsaken the fountain of living waters and hewn for themselves broken cisterns which could hold no water. Rather than looking to God, they took the road to Egypt to drink the waters of Sihor and the road to Assyria to drink the waters of the river.

Notice that in all of the Septuagint passages, *apostasia* is used of men going their own way, rejecting the temple of God and the Holy One who dwelt there, and inventing their own ways of worship. While none are direct parallels to the antichrist's madness, all bear eerie echoes to the satanic incarnation and abomination. Notice further that both 1 Maccabees and the Book of Jubilees employ *apostasia* in accounts of the apostasy of men who are clear types of the antichrist. These events foreshadow the last-days *apostasia* in 2 Thessalonians 2 when the man of sin leads mankind in rebellion against God.

There is no doubt in my mind that Paul, indeed the Holy Spirit, consciously used *apostasia* in 2 Thessalonians 2:3 because it, better than any other Greek word, pointed his readers to the *apostasy* in the last days associated with the man of sin, who would fill the world with the spirit of Babel, complete what Nimrod started, and fulfill the typology of Antiochus Epiphanes.

The Accusation of Unrelated Context

Some advocates of the *apostasia*-rapture theory have attempted to muzzle the testimony of the actual usage of *apostasia* in Koine Greek with the claim that appealing to this evidence is appealing to unrelated context. They insist that Bible students should jettison all appeal to unrelated context and concern themselves only with the immediate context of 2 Thessalonians 2:3. But two problems beset this rejection of the light of Koine usage.

First of all, if appealing to the actual usage of *apostasia* in Koine Greek to obtain its meaning is appealing to unrelated context, then appealing to Liddel & Scott to obtain its meaning is appealing to unrelated context also, for guess where they got their listed meanings? That's right, from unrelated context. This accusation has hypocrisy written all over it. Advocates of the *apostasia*-rapture theory allow themselves the right to define *apostasia* by appealing to a sliver of the body of unrelated context to obtain its meaning, but they won't allow those on the other side of the question to appeal to the whole body of unrelated context to obtain its meaning. This is making selective use of the evidence while opposing a full use of the evidence with a bogus appeal to contextual integrity.

Secondly, the accusation of unrelated context attempts to limit the influence of the lexical aspect of hermeneutics on the contextual aspect of hermeneutics. Both of these aspects must be allowed to come into play with unrestricted freedom if we are going to determine the meaning of *apostasia* in 2 Thessalonians 2:3 within the confines of the historical-grammatical hermeneutic.

The lexical aspect involves determining which senses of *apostasia* are available for this passage. It involves the use of lexicons at the very least, and ideally involves the use of commentaries, technical treatises, or even personal research. The broader and deeper that we go with our research, the more likely it will be that our conclusions will be correct.

The contextual aspect involves determining which of the available senses of *apostasia* best suits the context—the sentence, the passage, the book, and the general tenor of Scripture on the subject.

Researching the meanings for a word in the New Testament is not referring to unrelated context. And limiting the potential meanings for a word in the New Testament to senses that it actually bore in Koine Greek is not referring to unrelated context. Both the research and the restriction are faithfully engaging with the well-known tenet of the historical-grammatical hermeneutic that when God wrote the New Testament, he employed Koine Greek as it was spoken and written in that era.

In regards to the meaning of *apostasia* in 2 Thessalonians 2:3, the historical-grammatical hermeneutic obligates us to determine what senses of *apostasia* were extant when Paul penned 2nd Thessalonians, limit our selection process to those senses, and then determine which of these vetted senses best fits the context.

We can't do justice to our contextual efforts until we have done justice to our lexical efforts. We must vet the senses that are listed in the lexicons or other sources to determine which ones we can legitimately choose from. If we disregard this obligation or do a haphazard job at it, we might select an impermissible sense. For example, we might select a scientific sense while the context demands a common sense, or we might select an anachronistic sense, i.e. a sense that was either long dead or didn't exist yet when the passage was penned.

Let me close with an illustration. Suppose a man owned a dog that he believed was a bulldog. He invited the experts to examine his dog, fully convinced that they would ratify his opinion. But when they

30

compared his dog to the known traits of bulldogs, they were forced to sheepishly inform him that his dog was not a bulldog but rather some kind of poodle mix. Now imagine that this man insisted that his dog was a bulldog even though it failed the bulldog test and berated those who denied his dog bulldog status, claiming they were incompetent judges who were guilty of examining unrelated dogs rather than his dog. Would this not be unfair? Yet, this is precisely what is happening with the charge of unrelated context.

THE TRANSLATION DEBATE

The Rapture Camp on Departure

The advocates of the rapture understanding of *apostasia* in 2 Thessalonians 2:3 claim that *departure* is the only correct translation and that translations like *apostasy* and *falling away* are wrong and misleading. Such translations incline readers in a doctrinal direction that neither Paul nor the early English Bible translators ever intended. They support this argument with the following line of reasoning.

The Greek language represents the concept of *departure* and the concept of *falling away* with different words: *apostasia* (departure) and *ekpiptō* (falling away). Greek users didn't confuse these words.

The early English translators, out of a sense of integrity, all translated the Greek word *apostasia* by the English word *departure*. They understood the passage to be speaking of a physical departure, not a falling away.

The history of translating *apostasia* by *departure* can be traced as far back as Jerome and the first edition of the Vulgate. He translated *apostasia* by *discessio*, which means *departure*.

The long and venerable history of translating *apostasia* in the English Bibles by *departure* was not broken until the Catholic church polluted the translation stream with the Rheims version in 1582[26], introducing the novel rendering *revolt*. The King James version, sadly, embraced this Catholic error and gave us the erroneous translation *falling away*.

Sometime prior to the Rheims version, Theodore Beza inspired the translation fiasco by transliterating *apostasia* rather than translating it, thereby coining the English word *apostasy*.

Since the dawn of the *revolt* reading in the Rheims version, the English translations have almost exclusively translated *apostasia* by such terms as *apostasy*, *falling away*, and *rebellion*. Such translations beg the question and rob the reader of the possibility to see the physical departure that Paul, indeed God himself, intended to convey.

This presentation, which seems plausible, has convinced many that the truth is being buried with a translation conspiracy. The problem is, scarcely one point in this line of reasoning is correct. In the following pages, I will address these misrepresentations at length, including the relationship between the Greek words *apostasia* (revolt) and *ekpiptō* (fall away), the meaning of the English word *departure* in the 1500s and 1600s, what the translators and editors of the early English Bibles meant by *departure*, the testimony of the early English Bibles, the source of the translation *falling away*, the meaning of the Latin word *discessio*, and the origin of the English word *apostasy*.

The Testimony of Middle English Dictionaries

Those who contend for *departure* in 2 Thessalonians 2:3 appear to operate on the assumption that *departure* was used in the 1500s and 1600s in the same way that it is used in the present day. Based on this assumption, the presence of *departure* in the early English translations is regarded as proof positive that the translators likely intended us to understand physical departure.

But if we look up *departure* in dictionaries that cover the 1500s and 1600s, we discover that it frequently bore senses that are more in line with apostasy, defection, and departure from the truth than with physical or spatial departure.

The Concise Dictionary of Middle-English[27] gives the lean entry—**Departyng,** sb. d*ivision.*

The *Online Etymology Dictionary*[28] runs—**departure (n.)**, mid-15c., "act of going away," also "deviation, divergence, a turning away," from Old French *departeure* "departure."

The Oxford English Dictionary[29] informs us that **departure** is derived from Old French *departeure* and that it commonly bore the sense of "separation, severance, parting" in the 1500s and 1600s, a sense now obsolete.

Now if *departure* bore such senses as *division, parting, separation, severance, divergence,* and *deviation* in the sixteenth and seventeenth centuries, then we are forced to conclude that *departure* in the early English versions could have meant *apostasy* or *departure* from the truth. There is certainly no ground to insist that it must mean or most likely means physical or spatial *departure*.[30]

Book Introductions and Chapter Prefaces

Thankfully, we are not obliged to settle the question of what the early translators and editors meant by *departure* with an appeal to a dictionary. That would certainly end in a stalemate. We could argue *going away* and *departying* vs. *separation* and *division* till we were blue in the face. And we could argue physical departure vs. spiritual departure until the end of the age.

The question can be settled in a matter of minutes by turning to the comments of the translators and editors themselves. In many early Bibles, the introduction for Second Thessalonians and the preface for the second chapter of the same include comments that clarify exactly what the translators and the editors meant by the word *departure*. The italics in the passages cited are my emphasis.

Geneva Bible (1560 and 1569) — The introduction to Second Thessalonians.

"Paul ... writeth unto them and exhorteth them to pacience and other frutes of faith, neither to be moued with that vaine opinion of suche as taught that the comming of Christ was at hand, forasmuche as before that day there shulde be a *falling away from true religion*, even by a great parte of the worlde, and that Antichrist shulde reigne in the Temple of God."

The Matthews Bible (1537) — The preface to the second chapter of Second Thessalonians.

"He sheweth them that the daye of the Lorde shall not come tyll *the departyng from the fayth* come fyrst: & therfore he exhorteth them not to be deceaued, but to stande stedfast in the thynges that he hath taughte them."

The Great Bible (1540) — The preface to the second chapter of Second Thessalonians.

"He sheweth them, that the daye of the Lorde shal not come, tyll *the departynge from the fayth* come first, and therefore he exhorteth them not to be disceaued, but to stande stedfast in the thynges that he hath taught them."

The 1551 Tyndale/Matthews version — The preface to the second chapter of Second Thessalonians.

"He sheweth them that the daye of the Lord shal not come, tyll *the departynge frome the faythe* come fyrst: and therefore he exhorteth them not to be disceaued, but to stand stedfast in the thinges that he hath taught them."

The Geneva NT (1557) — The preface to the second chapter of Second Thessalonians.

"He sheweth them that the day of the Lord shall not come tyl *the departing from the faith* come fyrst, and the kyngdome of Antechrist."

The Geneva Bible (1560) — The preface to the second chapter of Second Thessalonians.

"He sheweth them that the day of the Lord shal not come, til *the departing from the faith* come first, And the kingdome of Antichrist. And therefore he exhorteth them not to be deceaued, but to stand stedfast in the things that he hathe taught them."

The Bishop's Bible (1568) — The preface to the second chapter of Second Thessalonians.

"He sheweth them that the day of the Lorde shall not come tyll *the departyng of the faith* come first and the kyngdome of Antichriste."

This note is particularly helpful because the text of the Bishop's Bible reads *falling away*, so this note informs us that the translators and editors regarded *falling away* and *departing* to be synonyms.

The Geneva Bible (1569) — The preface to the second chapter of Second Thessalonians.

"He sheweth them that the day of the Lord shal not come, til *the departing from the faith* come first, And the kingdome of Antichrist. And therefore he exhorteth them not to be deceiued, but to stand stedfast in the things that he hathe taught them."

The Geneva/Thomson NT (1595) (aka Beza NT) — The preface to the second chapter of Second Thessalonians.

"He sheweth that the day of the Lord shall not come, till there be *a departure from the faith*, and that Antichrist be reveiled, whose destruction he fitteth out, and thereupon exhorteth to constauncie."

In all of these introductions and prefaces the departure is expressly stated to be a "departing from the faith," which is an allusion to 1

Timothy 4:1, "in the latter times some shall depart from the faith." This informs us, beyond all shadow of doubt, that the translators of the early English versions meant *apostasy* or spiritual *departure* when they used the translation *departure*. So translations like *revolt* and *falling away* were not departures from *departure* after all. They were merely synonyms of *departure* which enriched the translation field.

Marginal Notes in Early English Versions

The marginal notes in the early English versions are also wonderful sources for information which clarify for us what the early translators and editors meant by *departure* in 2 Thessalonians 2:3. The italics in the cited notes are my own emphasis.

Coverdale Bible (1535) — The reading in the text "departinge come fyrst" is marked with a star (*) which refers us to two texts: Dan. 9e (9:25-27) and 1 Tim. 4a (4:1-6). The first is the well-known prophetic passage that presents the seventy weeks, the seventieth week, the Roman ruler that shall come, and the abomination of desolation. The latter, which starts "in the latter times some shall depart from the faith," refers to exceptional character debasement in the last days. This demonstrates beyond all shadow of doubt that the editors of this edition identified the *departing* with the departure from the faith that shall occur in the last days in association with the antichrist.

Coverdale Bible (1553) — The reading in the text "excepte the departinge come fyrst" is marked with a dagger (†) which refers us to two texts: Dan. 9e (9:25-27) and 1 Tim. 4a (4:1-6). Again, these references demonstrate beyond all shadow of doubt that the editors of this edition identified the *departing* with the departure from the faith in the last days that shall occur in association with the antichrist.

Great Bible (1540 edition) (aka Cranmer's Bible) — The reading in the text "a departynge fyrst" is marked with a star (*). The marginal note says Dan. 9g (9:25-27) which proves that the translators regarded "a departynge fyrst" as a reference to an apostasy in the last days that would be occasioned by the antichrist.

Tyndale/Matthews 1551 — This version places a star (*) before "a departinge first" which directs our attention to Dan. 9g (9:25-27) and 1 Tim. 4*a* (4:1-3). Again, this pair of passages leaves no doubt in any candid mind that the editors of this version understood *departing* to be a reference to the departure from the faith that shall happen in the last days during the time of the antichrist.

Geneva NT (1557) — A note further down in the passage reads, "Because the false apostles had persuaded after a sort the Thessalonians that the day of the Lord was nye, and so the redemption of the Churche, S. Paul teacheth them to loke for this horrible *dissipation* before." This comment clearly associates *departure* with a distinct moral declension prior to the Lord's return.

Geneva Bible (1560) — The marginal note reads, "A wonderful *departing* of the moste parte from the faith."[31] This comment hints that the editors saw a connection with Matthew 24:12, "because iniquity shall abound, the love of many (the love of the most[32]) shall wax cold."

The Bishop's Bible (1568) — The phrase "a fallyng away first" is marked with a star (*) which directs our attention to two references: Dan. 9*g* (9:25-27) and 1 Tim. 4*a* (4:1-5). Once again, this demonstrates that the editors of this version identified the falling away with the departure from the faith that shall occur in the latter days under the watch of the antichrist.

Geneva Bible 1569 — The phrase "departing first" is marked with a superscript *c*, which takes us to the following note, "A wonderful departing of the moste parte from the faith." Once again, the editors of the Geneva Bible suggest a connection with the falling away in Matthew 24:12.

Geneva/Thomson NT (1595) — The reading in the text "except there come a departing first" is associated with a note which says, "The apostle foretelleth that before the comming of the Lord, there shall be a throne set up cleane contrary to Christs glorie, wherein that wicked man shall sit, and transferre all things that apperteine to God to himselfe, and many shall fall away from God to him." This is explicit testimony that the editors of this version regarded *departing* and *falling away* as synonyms and that they further regarded *departing* to be a reference to a falling away from the faith in the last days that is precipitated by the antichrist.

These statements are conclusive proof that *departure* in the early English Bibles was not intended to convey the idea of physical departure and cannot be used as an argument that *apostasia* is a reference to the rapture. The fact is, the early translators and editors across the board regarded *falling away* and *departure* as synonyms, and that they took *departure* as a reference to a falling away in the last days associated with the antichrist.

Testimony of Early Books and Commentaries

Commentaries and treatises published in the sixteenth and early seventeenth centuries which address 2 Thessalonians 2:3 also cast helpful light on the meaning of *apostasia* and how it should be or could be translated. The three works cited here were penned by names that most scholars will recognize. The italics are my own.

Heinrich Bullinger, *Commentary on the Second Epistle to the Thessalonians*, (1538).[33] "And first we will speak of the departing. Departing is here taken after such a manner as when a man does *slide back or fail* from his author or prince. Saint Ambrose does expound it of the dividing of the kingdom of the Romans and of the departing of other kingdoms from it. Others have interpreted if of the *departing of faith*, of the which the Apostle spoke, 1 Tim. 4, saying: The spirit speaks evidently [clearly] that in the latter days some shall depart from the faith, giving heed unto spirits of error and devilish doctrines, etc."[34]

John Calvin, *Commentary on Thessalonians*, (1550).[35] In the introduction to 2 Thessalonians he writes, "In the second, a vain and groundless fancy, which had got into circulation as to the coming of Christ being at hand, is set aside by him by means of this argument — that there must previously to that be a *revolt* in the Church, and a great part of the world must *treacherously draw back* from God, nay more, that Antichrist must reign in the temple of God."

In the body of his commentary on 2 Thessalonians he wrote, "As, however, interpreters have twisted this passage in various ways, we must first of all endeavor to ascertain Paul's true meaning. He says that the day of Christ will not come, until the world has *fallen into apostasy*, and the reign of Antichrist has obtained a footing in the

38

Church ... Paul, therefore, employs the term apostasy to mean — a *treacherous departure from God*, and that not on the part of one or a few individuals, but such as would spread itself far and wide among a large multitude of persons."[36]

Thomas Beard, *Antichrist the pope of Rome*, (early 1600s, he died 1632), Part 2, Chapter 7, Section 1[37] — "The *reuolt or falling away* mentioned by Saint Paul, 2. Thess. 2.3. which should be in the world before the comming of Christ ... that he [the Antichrist] was to be the principall and prime Apostate of the world, and as it were the Apostacy it selfe, because hee was the cause thereof; which doubtlesse was the meaning of those Fathers. But by this *Apostacy, reuolt, or falling away*, the Apostle vnderstands a famous, and as it were, a *vniuersall and generall defection from the Faith*, and from true Religion, which should be in Antichrists time; and whereof hee should bee the head and Captaine: for so the word ἀποστασία is properly and vsually taken both in holy Scripture and all holy writers, for a *defection from God, and from the Faith*."

Once again we have ample testimony that in the 1500s and 1600s those fluent in the Bible and the English language regarded *departure* in 2 Thessalonians 2:3 to be synonymous with such terms as *apostasy, falling away, defection, revolt, drawing back,* and *sliding back*.

Testimony of the Early English Bible Versions

The advocates for the rapture understanding of *apostasia* claim that the earliest English versions all rendered *apostasia* by *departure* and that non-departure translations did not appear until the Catholic Church trotted out *revolt* with the Rheims version in 1582. They insist that this change was made despite the fact that there is no justification for it. The Protestants followed with their own novel renderings. Beza introduced *apostasy*, and the King James Bible introduced *falling away*. Since then, most translations have followed the Catholic Church's lead and buried the sense of physical *departure* with renderings that allow no sense but that of *apostasy*.

But this account of translation history is pure fiction. It simply is not true that non-departure translations made their first appearance with the Rheims. The truth of the matter is, all three early editions of the Wyclif Bible featured the reading *dissencioun* (dissension), two as the reading proper and one as an alternate reading. Ultimately, the translation *dissencioun* prevailed.

Wyclif Bible (1380) — "No man disceyve you on ony maner, for but *discencioun* come first and the man of synne be schewid, the sone of perdicioun."[38]

Wyclif Bible (1382) — "That no man disceyue зou in ony maner. For no but *departyng away*, (or *dissencioun*), schal come first, and the man of synne schal be schewid, the sone of perdicioun."[39]

Wyclif Bible (1388) — "No man disseyue зou in ony manere. For but *dissencioun* come first, and the man of synne be schewid, the sonne of perdicioun."[40]

If we turn to *The Oxford English Dictionary*, we discover that the entry for *dissencioun* is "dissension, disagreement ... as produces strife or contention; discord."[41] We get more light on the sense of *discencioun* in Wyclif's day if we turn to Acts 15:39 in the Wyclif Bible where we read, "Truly dissension was made, so that they departed from each other."[42] This refers to the contention between Paul and Barnabas which led to their departing from each other.

Now, these readings demonstrate two things. One, *dissension*, not *departure* was the prevalent reading of the Wyclif Bible. Two, Wyclif regarded the rendering *departing* to mean spiritual *departure*. The departure or dissension will be man having a falling out with God.

A fascinating testimony that precedes even Wiclif's translation is the Northumbrian poem known as the *Cursor Mundi* (*The Runner of the World*) which dates around 1300. One of its lines, C.M. 22238, transposed into modern English, runs, "First shall there be *dissension* ere [before] the antichrist shall come into the land."[43]

This line obviously refers to 2 Thessalonians 2:3, and it implies a pre-Wyclif translation. Whether the author had heard the translation in a Sunday Epistle reading, or read it in an illegal manuscript, or executed it himself, we know not. But no matter the explanation, the translation *dissension* precedes the Wyclif Bible by 80 years and the Rheims Bible by nearly 300 years. So if we are going to side with the facts, we are forced to conclude that when the Rheims introduced the translation *revolt*, they were indeed introducing a new word but not a new concept. They were following an ancient tradition of translating *apostasia* by words and terms which present the concept of *dissenting from God*, i.e. *apostasy*.

Early German Translations

A significant influence on the early English translations that has been overlooked in this controversy is the early German translations. These groundbreaking works influenced a century of Bible translators in England and Europe who had been impacted by the Reformation which had started in Germany. They also cast helpful light on the translation of *apostasia* in the fifteenth and sixteenth centuries.

The Mentel Bible (20 editions between 1466 and 1518) reads, "Keiner verleyt euch in keinderweys. Wann es kum zum ersten *misshellung*; vnd der man der sunde wirt eroffent der sun des verleufes."

I translate this as follows, "Let no one deceive you in any way, for that day shall not come, unless the *dissension* come first, and the man of sin be revealed, even the son of straying [lostness]."

The German lexicons inform us that *Misshellung* is an older word, equivalent to modern Mißhelligkeit, which means *disagreement, dissen*sion, *division*.[44] Moreover, *Misshellung* was used in the Middle ages in the sense of *revolt*, particularly for the revolts and upheavals that swept across Germany.[45]

The Luther Bible (1529) reads, "Lasset euch niemand verfüren in keinerlei weise, Denn er kommt nicht, Es sei denn, das zuvor der *Abfalle* kome, und offenbaret wurde der Mensch der sunden, und das Kind des verderbens."

I translate this as follows, "Let no one deceive you in any way, for that day shall not come, unless *the falling away* come before, and the man of sin be revealed, even the son of perdition."

Cassel's German Dictionary[46] informs us that *Abfall* means *falling off, defection, secession, backsliding, revolt, rebellion*.

Both of these versions exhibited a non-departure translation of *apostasia* decades before Beza and the Rheims Bible. Because the Luther Bible was widely known and loved by the early Reformers, there is no reason to doubt that this non-departure reading influenced the later ones.

Another overlooked fact is that the first German Bible precedes Jerome's Latin translation by half a century. And this version gives us a very early instance of a rendering along the lines of *turning away* or *falling away*.

The Wulfila or Gothic Bible (ca. 350) reads, "Ni hvashun izwis usluto hvamma haidau, unte niba qimiþ *afstass* faurþis, jah andhulids wairþai manna frawaurhtais, sunus fralustais."

A stilted word for word translation, in the same order as the Gothic, runs thusly, "Not anyone you deceive any way, [*for that day shall not come,*] until except come *turning away* before and revelation become, man of sin, son of destruction."[47]

A smoother translation would run, "Let no one deceive you in any way, for that day shall not come except *the turning away* come prior and the revelation of the man of sin comes to pass, even the son of destruction."

The *Kurzgefasstes Etymologisches Wörterbuch des Gotischen Sprache* gives the following definition for *Afstass* — "severance or separation, divorce, distance oneself, turn away from, withstand."[48] In *A Comparative Glossary of the Gothic Language With Especial Reference to English and German*, we find — "f. a standing off, falling off, falling away."[49]

Latin Translations

Those who insist that we should view *apostasia* in 2 Thessalonians 2:3 as a reference to the rapture point us to the reading *discessio* in the Vulgate, a reading traced to Jerome's original edition, and insist that it means *departure*. But they have overlooked much information that is pertinent if we want to truly understand the Latin testimony.

It is not enough to inform us that the Vulgate gives us *discessio* and that this word means *depart*. There are a number of other questions that we should be asking. Does *discessio* have other meanings? What other renderings do we find in other Latin translations? Is there any information associated with the Latin editions—like book or chapter prefaces, marginal notes, footnotes, or commentaries—that will help us determine whether the translators and editors understood *discessio* in the sense of physical *departure* or in the sense of *departure* from the faith? Indeed, there is.

First of all, if we make even a cursory examination of the Latin lexicons, we discover that the rapture-interpretation camp has not given us the whole enchilada when it comes to the meaning and usage of *discessio*.

Cassel's Latin Dictionary[50] says, "**discessio.** (1) *a going separate ways, separation*; of married people; as political technical term, *voting, a division in the senate.* (2) *a going away, departure.*

Lewis and Short's Latin Lexicon[51] says, "**discessio.** I. (Very rarely), *a separation* of married persons. II. *A going away, departure, removal.* A. In general (very rarely). B. In particular. 1. **Political technical term**, a going over to any one in voting. Especially: to make a division, i.e. to get the vote of the house by dividing it. **2.** In the church, *a separation, schism* (ecclesiastical Latin), Vulgate Acts 21:21; idem 2 Thes. 2:3."

The Oxford Latin Dictionary[52] says, "**discessio.** 1. The action of going away, withdrawal, dispersal. 2. A withdrawal (for voting), division. 3. A division, schism; a divorce; a separation (from)."

Notice that all three lexicons give us apostasy-class alternatives to *departure* for our consideration as a potential sense for *discessio* in 2 Thessalonians 2:3. Notice further that Lewis and Short inform us that *discessio* is only rarely used for departure in a general sense. Typically it is used for things like political division and religious separation. This closely parallels the typical use of *apostasia* in Greek as we saw earlier in this book.

Secondly, Jerome tells us in his own words what he meant by the translation *discessio*. In his *Letter to Algasium* he wrote, answering a question on the meaning of 2 Thessalonians 2:3, "For he [Paul] says that unless the *dissension*, which is called ἀποστασία, comes first, so that all the nations who are subject to the Roman authority withdraw from them; and he will be revealed, that is, manifested, whom all the words of the prophets announced beforehand, the man of sin."[53]

Here he employs *discessio* in the sense of *dissension* or *division*. In his understanding, the nations subject to Rome will withdraw from

Rome before the antichrist is revealed. This view that the apostasy of the last days was walking away from Rome instead of walking away from God was common in the early Fathers. It coincided with the view that Rome was the restrainer.

Thirdly, in the 1965 Clementine edition of the Latin Vulgate[54], the cross-references for 2 Thessalonians 2:3 given in the footnotes are Eph. 5:6, 1 Tim. 4:1, 1 John 2:18, 1 John 4:3.

Ephesians 5:6 addresses the wrath of God that is coming upon *the children of disobedience.* 1 Timothy 4:1 addresses *the departure from the faith* in the last days. 1 John 2:18 addresses the many antichrists and *the antichrist to come.* And 1 John 4:3 addresses *the antichrist to come.* This testimony leaves no room for doubt that the editors of this edition of the Vulgate, who knew Latin like the back of their hand, understood *discessio* to be a reference to the great departure from God at the end of the age associated with the antichrist.

Fourthly, the Itala or Old Latin version that Tertullian used gives virtually the same rendering of 2 Thessalonians 2:3 as Jerome's translation except that it uses *abscessio* instead of *discessio,* and it says *man of delinquency* instead of *man of sin.*[55]

But we are not left to a lexicon debate to determine what Tertullian understood by the phrase "unless the departure come first." He makes two comments on the passage which leave no candid man with doubts: "this, of course, refers to the kingdom" and "unless the Roman state, whose separation in the dispersion of the ten kings brings forth the antichrist." It was commonly held in the early church that the antichrist would not appear until after the Roman empire had fractured into ten separate kingdoms. His comment indicates that he understood *abscessio* in the sense of political *departure* or *division.*[56]

Fifthly, some versions of the Vulgate, like the Complutensian NT (printed in 1514, published in 1522), offer *dissensio* instead of *discessio.*[57] This variation in the reading is a big heads up. While *discessio* does bear the sense of *departure, dissensio* does not. According to Cassel's Latin Dictionary[58], it means "difference in feeling or opinion, disagreement, variance." The Latin word *dissensio* is, in fact, the source of the English word *dissent.* Now the fact that *discessio* and *dissensio* are used interchangeably in the Vulgate editions indicates that the translators and editors of this version probably understood *discessio* in the sense of *division* or *separation*.

Sixthly, in the Complutensian NT (printed in 1514, published in 1522), the marginal note associated with the phrase "except there come a *dissension* first"[59] gives four references: Luke 21b (21:9-19) which addresses the signs and the persecution of the last days; Eph. 5b (5:8-19) which covers the works of darkness and the evil days; 1 Cor. 3b (3:6-11) which says there is no foundation other than Jesus Christ; and Col. 2d (2:16-23) which addresses the worship of messengers and not holding fast to the Lord. While none of these passages directly mention the departure from the faith in the last days, the mention of the last days—combined with persecution, spiritual darkness, wrong foundation, and not holding fast to the Lord—implies the apostasy of the last days.

Seventhly, in Beza's 1565 Greek New Testament (which featured the Greek, his Latin translation, and the Latin Vulgate), and in the 1598 edition of the same, he used *defectio* where the Vulgate used *discessio*.[60] This indicates that he understood *apostasia* in the Greek and *discessio* in the Vulgate to refer to division or defection or departure from the truth, not physical or spatial departure.

Departure and Falling Away Overlap in Greek

The advocates of the rapture understanding of *apostasia* in 2 Thessalonians 2:3 insist that *falling away* is a miserable translation because *apostasia* means *departure*. They bolster this with the observation that the Greek language has a unique term for *falling away* which is *ekpiptō*. The Greeks didn't confuse these terms and neither should we.

But this argument is misleading. While it is true that *apostasia* and *ekpiptō* are two different words in Greek, this does not mean that the two don't overlap in meaning. The truth is, they are synonyms with significant overlap in their semantic ranges. *Falling away* may well be a paraphrase of *apostasia*, but that does not mean that it is an inaccurate translation.

The following passages from the Fathers use *apostasia* (departure) and *ekpiptō* (fall away) as synonyms. They were found without any

45

special searching. I didn't have to ransack patristic literature to find them. They jumped off the page while I was gathering *apostasia* passages. The passages are here given in English translation with *falling away* and *apostasy* marked in bold.

Basil, *Exposition of the Prophet Isaiah*, 1.19—"He does not stand in the ranks of the believers, for he has **fallen away** ... he is lazy in prayer, thinking up fabricated excuses for those who seek [him] [to join them] ... this habit brings him to **apostasy** and leads him to utter destruction."[61]

Cyril of Alexandria, *Commentary on the Twelve Prophets*, Hosea 6:7.—"But since like the first man—Adam, that is—they slipped into **apostasy**, they too, will be completely **fallen away** from the one able to bless them."[62]

Procopius of Gaza, *Commentary on Isaiah*, (Migne 87.2).—"Or concerning those who have truly **fallen from** life. The demons for example through their **apostasy**.[63]

Eusebius of Caesarea, *Preparation for the Gospel*, 7.16.2-4 — "The leader for instance of their fall, who had been the cause both for himself and for others of their **apostasy** from, the better angels, as having **fallen down** utterly beneath the piety of the more godlike, and wrought for himself the venom of malice and impiety, and become the author of darkness and folly in consequence of his wilful departure from the light—-him the Scripture is wont to call dragon and serpent."[64]

Eusebius of Caesarea, *Commentary on Psalms*, 18:17ff (LXX 17:18) — "When I was certainly corrupted and enduring a great fall, lest after my sin I **fall away** into absolute **apostasy**, he offered support to me and became my stay. At that time he sent his prophet Nathan, who produced a rebuke of my sin and restored me."[65]

Chrysostom, *Expositions on Psalms*, 13.2-3 (LXX 12.3-4), Section 1. — "Now, this is allowed to happen for our advantage, so that through the whole of it those more indifferent people may be goaded into becoming more zealous and return to the condition from which they **fell** [fell away]. «Your **falling away** [apostasy] will instruct you, after all,» Scripture says, «and your wickedness censure you.»"[66]

Chrysostom, *Forty-Eight Excerpts from Diverse Homilies,* **Excerpt 9** — "Grief-causing things fall upon us, so that the lazy, bitten [made to feel] through all [the trials], may more diligently return from when they **fell** [fell away]. «Your **falling away** [apostasy] will instruct you,» Scripture says, «and your wickedness reprove you.»"[67]

In all of these passages *ekpiptō* (falling away) is used as a synonym of *apostasia* (apostasy), sometimes in a parallel construction. How do you avoid concluding that in the mind of the Greek speaker, the concept of *falling away* and the concept of *departure* were virtually identical? They viewed the same phenomenon (a broken relationship) from different perspectives. One viewed it from the perspective of a *falling out.* The other viewed it from the perspective of *standing aloof.*

The KJV is Not the Source of Falling Away

Those who hold the rapture understanding of *apostasia* in 2 Thessalonians 2:3 inform us that the King James Bible was the source of the translation *falling away.* This rendering is smeared as a novel gloss, inspired by the blunders of Beza and the Rheims translation, without historical background or theological justification.

But a fuller examination of the subject exposes this presentation as a house of cards and reveals that *falling away* was regarded as a legitimate translation of *apostasia* long before the King James version saw the light of day.

First of all, four Bible versions that preceded the King James Bible offer *falling away* as a translation of *apostasia* in 2 Thessalonians 2:3, either in the text itself or in a note on the text.

The Luther Bible (1529) — "Lasset euch niemand verfüren in keinerlei weise, Denn er kommt nicht, Es sei denn, das zuvor der *Abfalle*[68] kome, und offenbaret wurde der Mensch der sunden, und das Kind des verderbens."

My English translation runs, "Let no one deceive you in any way, for that day shall not come, unless *the falling away* come before, and the man of sin be revealed, even the son of perdition."

Luther's translation, executed some 80 years before the King James version, definitely belongs in the discussion of the derivation of *falling away.* It was a massive force in the Reformation, influencing not only William Tyndale's work but the entire lineage of the English Bible through the King James version.

The Geneva Bible (1560 and 1569) — The phrase *falling away* was used in the introduction to Second Thessalonians. "Paul … writeth unto them and exhorteth them to pacience and other frutes of faith, neither to be moued with that vaine opinion of suche as taught that the comming of Christ was at hand, forasmuche as before that day there shulde be a *falling away* from true religion, even by a great parte of the worlde, and that Antichrist shulde reigne in the Temple of God."

The Bishops Bible (1568) — This was the first printed version that included *falling away* in the text. "Let no man deceave you by any means for the Lorde shall not come excepte ther come a *fallyng away* first that that man of sinne be revealed, the sonne of perdition."

Not only was the Bishop's Bible published prior to both the Rheims Bible and the King James Bible, but the 1602 edition was used as the basis for the King James version. So our beloved Authorized version didn't introduce *falling away* as an innovation, it adopted it as an established translation.

The Geneva/Thomson (1595) — The phrase *falling away* was used in the footnote on 2 Thessalonians 2:3. "The apostle foretelleth that before the comming of the Lord, there shall be a throne set up cleane contrary to Christs glorie, wherein that wicked man shall sit, and transferre all things that apperteine to God to himselfe, and many shall *fall away* from God to him."

Other sources like commentaries and treatises add to the evidence that *falling away* and related phrases like *fall from* and simple *fall* were relatively widespread in the sixteenth century as translations and representations of the Greek word *apostasia* in 2 Thessalonians 2:3, indicating that it was seen as a reference to an apostasy in the last days associated with the antichrist. I will only give two here.

Thomas Tymme, *The Figure of the Antichrist*, 1586[69] —"Among these signes also those which Paul rehearseth heere in his Epistle to the Thessalonians, concerning *the falling away* from sincere doctrine, and the reuealing of antichrist, are to be reckoned which shall long before the comming of Christ to iudgment, be seene."

"He demeth that the day of Christ shall come before such time as the world shalbe *fallen* into Apostasie or defection, and the kingdome of Antichrist shall haue gotten place in the Church."

John Calvin, *Commentary on Thessalonians,* **(1550)**[70] In his introduction Calvin writes, "The day of Christ will not come, until the world has *fallen* into apostasy, and the reign of Antichrist has obtained a footing in the Church."

Theodore Beza Didn't Coin the Word Apostasy

Theodore Beza's place in this controversy has been hard to pin down. Some trace the first departure from *departure* to his reputed introduction of the word *apostasia* into the translation stream. Others trace the beginning of the translation debacle to the Rheims version, produced by the Catholic church, with its rendering *revolt*. But all seem to have Beza in the mix, guilty at the very least of helping to defile the translation stream for the English language.

But this complaint against Beza comes with a profound mystery. What exactly is the complaint that is being lodged against him? Nobody specifies what he did.

Is he guilty of introducing the transliteration *apostasia* in one of his Latin editions? If so, which one? Is he accused of introducing the anglicized transliteration *apostasy* into an English Bible version? If so, which one? Or did he merely suggest transliterating ἀποστασία into *apostasy* or *apostasia* or the French *apostasie* in one of his theological writings? Definitive answers are unlikely to be forwarded from his accusers. But even if clarifications are never forthcoming, there are several factors that we can bring to the table which will help clarify the role that Beza played in the translation changes evident in the 1500s and 1600s.

First of all, Beza didn't execute an English translation of the Bible, so there is zero chance that an English translation is the source of either the English transliteration *apostasia* or the English word *apostasy*.

Secondly, though several editions of the Geneva Bible (beginning in 1576) were occasionally associated with Beza's name because they incorporated the notes from his Greek and Latin Bible, yet the so-called Beza Bibles are not likely the solution to the mystery either. If you read his annotations on 2 Thessalonians 2:3 from his Greek and Latin editions you discover that he did not offer *apostasia* as either an alternative translation or an explanation for ἀποστασία.

Thirdly, all five major editions of his Latin translation in his Greek and Latin Bible—(1556/57, 1565, 1582, 1588/89, and 1598[71])—offer *defectio* in the text in Thessalonians 2:3. And his annotations on this verse, as mentioned above, don't suggest *apostasia* as an alternative rendering or an explanation. Further, he didn't introduce *apostasia* in either the text or the notes of Acts 21:21, the other New Testament passage featuring ἀποστασία, in any of these editions. All feature *defectio* in the text. So Beza's Latin translation must be ruled out as the source of either the pure transliteration *apostasia* or the Anglicized transliteration *apostasy*.

Fourthly, although Beza lent his hand to the revision of Olivetan's beloved French version, and the original reading of *departement* in the 1535 edition was changed to *révolte* in some of the later editions, this does not support the theory that Beza is responsible for introducing either *apostasia* or *apostasy* into the English language. For the French Bible to be legitimately regarded as the source, we would have to see *apostasie* in the later revisions.

But there is an even stronger reason why Beza can't be the source of the transliteration *apostasia* or the Anglicized transliteration *apostasy* in the English language, not through Bible translations and not through theological writings. The truth is, transliterations of the Greek word ἀποστασία had been part of the vocabulary of the English, French, and Latin languages long before Beza arrived on the scene. The word *apostasie* is attested in French as far back as 1305.[72] The word *apostasy* appears in the works of both Wyclif and Purvey in the late 1300s.[73] And the transliteration *apostasia* had been a part of the Latin language for over a thousand years already when Beza first learned Latin.[74]

So what in the world is the change that Beza introduced? Here is my theory on the mystery, for what it is worth. Beza didn't introduce either the word *apostasia* or the word *apostasy* or any cognate into any version of the Bible—not the English, not the French, not the

Latin. Nor did he coin a transliteration of ἀποστασία in any of these languages. Nor did he introduce a transliteration of ἀποστασία to the English language or any language.

He merely introduced a non-*discessio* reading (*defectio*) in his Latin version in 1556, and he was involved in revising the French version to a non-*departure* reading (*révolte*), perhaps as early as 1558. These revisions preceded the non-departure translations of the Bishops (1568), the Rheims (1582), and the KJV (1611).

So how did the story arise that Beza introduced the transliteration *apostasia* and the word *apostasy* to the English language? I suspect that once upon a time a prophecy teacher (an advocate of the physical departure theory) made the observation in his ministry (written or spoken) that Beza had introduced *apostasy* into the translation stream and defiled the formerly pure *departure* flow. He intended to convey the *concept* of apostasy. But some folks misunderstood this nugget of information, and it got garbled from the *concept* of apostasy to the *word* "apostasy." From there the story evolved into several different permutations.

But the idea that Beza introduced the concept of apostasy into the translation stream is itself a misconception. The only reason the translation change in the 16th and 17th centuries looks suspicious to anyone today is the rose-colored glasses of the modern doctrine of physical departure. These glasses paint the change as an intentional change from translations that allow physical departure to translations that exclude physical departure and beg the question for apostasy. But this was never the case.

First of all, as has already been demonstrated, the translators and editors used *departure* and *discessio* to portray spiritual departure, not physical departure. This they affirmed on many occasions. There never was a conscious change from the concept of physical departure to the concept of spiritual departure or apostasy. The concept of spiritual departure or apostasy was there the whole time. The concept of physical departure never existed in reality. It only exists in the theological imagination of men not sufficiently immersed in the facts of history.

So why did Beza and those who followed his example change from translations like *departure* and *discessio* to translations like *revolt*, *falling away*, and *defectio*? For accuracy and impact! The change was not a conspiracy instigated by the father of lies to overthrow the correct translation of *apostasia*. The change, in my opinion, is traced to the Reformation vision for an accurate and vigorous presentation of Bible truth.

Those influenced by this noble spirit rejected time-worn readings that seemed too tame for what the passage was addressing—like *departure, dissension, and discessio*. They realized that the *apostasia* of the last days mentioned in 2 Thessalonians 2 wasn't a minor case of dissension. It wasn't like Paul and Barnabas indulging in a shouting match and temporarily separating from each other. It was the whole world, under the influence of the mystery of iniquity, joining Satan and the antichrist in absolute rebellion against God. To reflect the monstrous enormity of this event they adopted translations with more punch like *falling away, rebellion, revolt, apostasy,* and *defectio*.

As for the Rheims translation, I see no reason to regard *revolt* as anything other than an honest translation. Even the papists get stuff right sometimes.

When we look at the full sweep of pertinent facts surrounding the early Bible translations, we are forced to the conclusion that there never was a tradition of physical departure. Not in the English Bibles. Not in German Bibles. Not in the Latin Bibles. Not in any Bibles.

PATRISTIC HANDLING OF 2 THESSALONIANS 2:3

Apostasia Restricted to Abstract Departure

The handling of *apostasia* by the early fathers deals a devastating blow to the theory that it can bear the sense of physical *departure*. Aside from the legal sense of *divorce*, the patristic usage during the four centuries that followed the close of the apostolic era universally falls under the umbrella of abstract departure. One of these instances, in the late fourth century, was *departure from sin*.[75] The rest of the instances can be summed up under the general heading of *revolt*. Seven percent of these instances involve political revolt. The other ninety-three percent involve religious revolt.

This restriction to abstract departure is highlighted when it comes to the patristic understanding of 2 Thessalonians 2:3. Not a single father treats *apostasia* in that passage as a reference to physical departure. This is telling. If *apostasia* bore the sense of physical *departure* in the Koine era, surely a few fathers would have proposed the rapture interpretation. But none did.

Every father treated this instance of *apostasia* as a revolt in the last days. Those who believed that the restrainer in verses 6-7 was the Roman empire regarded *apostasia* verse 3 as a political insurrection, with the subjected nations revolting against Rome. The rest regarded *apostasia* as a spiritual insurrection, with all of the world and most of the church revolting against God.

Those who held that the revolt was spiritual intimately associated this insurrection with the antichrist. Some held that it was an apostasy that will precede and prepare the way for the antichrist. Others held that the antichrist will himself be the apostasy, that is, he will be the architect of the apostasy.

Fathers Who Believed that the Apostasy Paves the Way for the Antichrist

Many of the early fathers held that a great apostasy would precede and pave the way for the revelation of the antichrist.

Basil, Letters, To the Alexandrians, 139[76] — "Is this the last hour, when *apostasy* (apostasia) uses these means to gain entrance, so that at length «the lawless one may be revealed, the son of perdition, who opposes and exalts himself above all that is called God or worshipped»?"

Basil, Letters, To Barses the Bishop of Edessa, 264[77] — "Unless indeed the *apostasy* (apostasia) is somewhere near, and what is now happening is a prelude to the entrance of the Antichrist."

Basil, Sermons on Manners, Message 12[78] — "Is it not the last hour, and the *apostasy* (apostasia) shall make its entrance through these things that the lawless one might be revealed thereafter, the son of perdition, who opposess and exalts himself against all this is called god or worship."

Athanasius, Deposition of Arius, section 1[79] — "Now there are gone forth in this diocese, at this time, certain lawless men, enemies of Christ, teaching an *apostasy* (apostasia), which one may justly suspect and designate as a forerunner of Antichrist."

Athanasius, History of Arianism, section 77[80] — "Wherefore it especially behoves us to be sober, lest this heresy which has reached such a height of impudence, and has diffused itself abroad like the poison of an adder … lest, I say, this be that *falling away* (apostasia), after which He shall be revealed, of whom Constantius is surely the forerunner."

Cyril of Jerusalem, Catechetical Lectures, 15.9[81] — "This therefore is *the falling away* (apostasia), and the enemy is soon to be looked for."

Fathers Who Believed that the Antichrist is the Architect of the Apostasy

Many of the early fathers regarded the antichrist as the architect or instigator of the apostasy that defiles the whole world at the end of the age. This identification led to the use of titles like "the man of apostasy,"[82] which is an apropos paraphrase of "the man of sin." The antichrist is, for all practical purposes, the incarnation of Satan, the source of all sin and rebellion.

The following examples demonstrate how widespread was the viewpoint that the antichrist himself is the cause of the apostasy.

Theodoret, Commentary on the Letters of Paul, 2 Thessalonians 2:3[83] — "By *defection* (apostasia) he referred to the Anti-Christ in person, making a title out of the event. For he tries to make all men apostatize from the truth."

Theodoret, Compendium of the Fables of the Heretics, 5.23[84] — "He calls the coming of the antichrist *apostasy* (apostasia) itself. For many, being deceived by the coming signs, shall apostatize from the truth and greet [welcome] the lie."

Origen, Scholia on Revelation, scholia 38[85] — "He [the Antichrist] comes, and of his own accord he recapitulates [sums up] all the *apostasy* (apostasia) in his own person, and accomplishes whatever he shall do according to his own free will, and «is seated in the temple of God», so that his dupes may adore him as the Christ [the annointed], which is why they shall deservedly «be cast into the furnace of fire»."

Justin Martyr, Dialogue with Trypho, 110[86] — "When the man of *apostasy* (apostasia), who speaks strange things against the Most High, shall venture to do unlawful deeds on the earth."

Chrysostom, Homilies on 2 Thessalonians, Homily 3[87] — "What is *the falling away* (apostasia)? He calls the antichrist himself *Apostasy* (apostasia), as one who shall destroy many, and make them fall away. So that if it were possible, he says, the very elect should be stumbled."

THE CONTEXTUAL ARGUMENT

The Claim that Apostasy is Not in the Context

The advocates of the theory that *apostasia* is a reference to the rapture often defend their position with the claim that apostasy is not found in the context: not in the near context, not in 2 Thessalonians, and not in 1 Thessalonians. In their estimation, it would be odd for *apostasia* to bear the meaning of *apostasy* when the concept of apostasy isn't addressed at all in either of these books. It is much more likely, they insist, that *apostasia* is a reference to the rapture because the rapture appears in almost every chapter in the letters to the Thessalonians.

But this argument disregards testimony in the context that calls their contention into question.

First of all, 2 Thessalonians opens with the observation that the believers were suffering persecution and tribulation for their faith (1:4-7). Later on, we read that they were treated shamefully (2:2) and persecuted by the Jews (2:14-15). Times of severe persecution are typically accompanied by men falling away from the faith, so this heavy tribulation implies, at very least, an occasion for apostasy. This tribulation is the very reason that Paul penned the first portion of the second chapter.[88]

Secondly, the connection between severe persecution and apostasy is not an ad hoc speculation on my part. Church history is filled with painful accounts which demonstrate that persecution and apostasy are frequent traveling companions. We find this connection in the Bible too. In 1 Thessalonians we read that saints in Thessalonica were suffering such severe persecution that Paul worried that his labor might be in vain (3:1-5). He knew that the church had been appointed to afflictions (3:3) and tribulations (3:4). He knew that men do get moved by these trials if they aren't properly established and comforted

(3:3). He had seen men leave the Lord in the past. Now he feared that his labor among the Thessalonians might have been for nothing (3:5).

What did Paul fear that the saints in Thessalonica might do? He feared that they might walk away from the faith they once professed. He feared their apostasy, or falling away, or spiritual departure, or whatever you want to call it. So the concept of apostasy actually is addressed in 1 Thessalonians.

Thirdly, the apostasy of the last days is addressed in the second chapter of 2 Thessalonians. The third verse transitions from the topic of the day of the Lord to the apostasy and the antichrist which precede that day. Then Paul spends nine verses (4-12) commenting on the rise and reign of this evil fiend and the powerful forces at work that force the whole world down a dark path of apostasy.

When the mystery of iniquity is finally allowed to reveal the antichrist, he will be energized by a demonstration of Satanic power that far transcends anything seen in this age (v. 9). He will have the ability to perform a broad range of miracles, signs, and wonders which authenticate his lies (v. 9). And he will exploit every kind of unrighteous deceit to promote his agenda (v. 10). On top of this, God himself will implement a strong delusion so that all who don't love the truth will believe the lie (vv. 11-12).

What is the upshot of all this? Apostasy! This deceit and delusion will deceive everyone on the planet who isn't born again. All will walk away from whatever religion they professed. Men will give up every variety of Christianity, Judaism, and Islam. They will reject all influence imbibed from Christianity, Judaism, Islam, and the Christian cults. They will abandon every vestige of patriarchal light in the world and every remnant of natural religion. They will exchange whatever feeble degree of light they had for utter darkness.

For what? For a spiritual atheism that will be even darker than materialistic atheism. They will worship the antichrist as an ascended master (an evolved god), and they will embrace the lie, "you shall be as gods."

This will be the deepest apostasy the world has ever seen. It will transcend Babel, paganism, the Vatican, and apostate Protestantism. It will transcend Sodom and the pre-flood world. It will transcend every previous manifestation of the mystery of iniquity because it will be the mystery of iniquity unleashed. The heinous heart of hell will finally be allowed to take the entire world where neither angel nor man has been allowed to go. This will be the darkest hour in the history of the world, darker even than the cross.

The Claim that the Context is the Rapture

One of the arguments for the rapture understanding of *apostasia* in 2 Thessalonians 2:3 is the claim that the context of the verse is the rapture. The advocates of this position point to the rapture mention in verse 1, "the coming of our Lord Jesus Christ and our gathering together to Him," the supposed rapture implication in verse 7, "until he is taken out of the way," the clear rapture passage in 1 Thessalonians 4:13-18, and the mentions of the coming of the Lord that appear in almost every chapter of 1st and 2nd Thessalonians. Based on the immediate rapture context and the prevalence of the rapture in both books, it is claimed that *apostasia* most likely has the sense of physical *departure* and is a reference to the rapture.

But this argument is as broken as Dagon in the presence of the ark. It has already been demonstrated that *apostasia* never bore the sense of physical *departure* during the Koine era. So no matter what the context is, *apostasia* cannot mean physical *departure* and therefore cannot be a reference to the rapture.

But beyond that, a strong argument can be made that the context of the passage overall is the day of the Lord, not the rapture.

First of all, the language of the rapture passage itself indicates that the theme is the day of the Lord. "We beseech you, brethren, by the coming of our Lord Jesus Christ and by our gathering together unto him that you be not shaken … as that the day of the Lord is at hand. Let no man deceive you by any means; for that day shall not come unless the falling away comes first and the man of sin be revealed."

Notice that the rapture is not introduced as a topic of discussion in and of itself. It is introduced as a reason not to worry about the topic of discussion, which is the day of the Lord. We are not destined for wrath. We are destined to meet the Lord in the air before the hour of trial. Not only will we miss that day of the Lord proper, which is the coming of the Son of man in glory to judge the world, we will also miss the entire time of the dawning of that day upon the world, which time we know as the tribulation. The context specifically mentions two major events which accompany the inbreaking of that day—the apostasy and the revelation of the man of sin.[89]

Secondly, the last two-thirds of the preceding chapter addresses matters pertaining to the day of the Lord. In verses 7-10 the living ungodly face temporal judgment and eternal punishment when the Lord Jesus is revealed in glory and power. In verses 5 and 7 the believers (both tribulation and church) are promised rest that will be manifested in the kingdom. In verse 6 the ungodly face a dose of tribulation as a reward for their persecution of believers. In verse 10 the Lord will be glorified on earth in the presence of every human being who has believed in him since the world began. In verses 11-12 the concern is that all who believe will live worthy of the glorious calling of the kingdom. That glorious calling, for the church, involves reigning with Christ in the kingdom. For the tribulation saints, it involves inheriting the kingdom. All of these verses address either the judgment of the day of the Lord proper, or the tribulation trials of the day of the Lord dawning on the world, or the blessings introduced on the day of the Lord proper.

Thirdly, after the reminder that the rapture will happen before the day of the Lord, chapter two continues with the theme of the day of the Lord for nine verses.

It covers events that occur during the dawning of the day: the mystery of iniquity coming to a head (2:7-8), the antichrist (2:8), the lying miracles, signs, and wonders done by the power of Satan (2:9), the unrighteous deception (2:10), the great delusion (2:11), the defilement of the temple (the abomination of desolation) (2:4), the antichrist declaring himself a god (2:4), the antichrist exalting himself above all that is called god or worshipped (2:4).

It covers the events of that day arrived: the brightness of the Lord's coming (2:8), the destruction of the antichrist (2:8), and the condemnation to hellfire of those who did not believe the truth (2:12).

To sum up the views expressed in this chapter, the context in which 2 Thessalonians 2:1-3 is set is the day of the Lord, both that day proper (the second coming) and the dawning of that day (the tribulation). The rapture is introduced as the reason we don't have to worry about that awful day. Apostasy is definitely mentioned in the context for it is alluded to in Paul's comments in 1 Thessalonians 3, and it is right at the heart of the spiritual disaster unfolding in 2 Thessalonians 2:4-12, where we see the enemy and the antichrist attempting to get every man on the planet to turn away from God.

THE GRAMMATICAL
ARGUMENT

Four Distinct Arguments

Four distinct grammatical arguments have been made as to why *apostasia* in 2 Thessalonians 2:3 should be seen as a reference to the rapture rather than a reference to apostasy in the last days.

The first is the claim that *apostasia* is not grammatically qualified and therefore can't be a reference to apostasy.

The second is the claim that *apostasia* has the definite article, which indicates an exceptional instance of something, and therefore must be a reference to the rapture.

The third is the claim that the definite article (hē) with *apostasia* points back to and links with "the coming of the Lord Jesus Christ and our gathering together unto him" and therefore *apostasia* must be a reference to the rapture.

The fourth is the claim that the definite article with *apostasia* indicates definiteness in time, even instantaneousness, and therefore *apostasia* must refer to the rapture.

But all four of these arguments flounder when subjected to deeper investigation. I will address the first, third, and fourth in this chapter, and the second in the chapter on the theological argument.

No Grammatical Qualification

The claim is made that *apostasia* by itself means generic *departure*. When abstract *departure* is meant, such as sedition or apostasy, *apostasia* will be grammatically qualified by immediately adjacent material. Where such grammatical qualification is lacking, we must defer to the sense of physical *departure*.

Grammatical qualification is illustrated with Acts 21:21, "apostasy from Moses," where *apostasy* is qualified by the prepositional phrase "from Moses." While no clear definition for grammatical qualification was given in the material that I read written on behalf of the *apostasia*-rapture theory, I suspect that those who pressed this point meant all grammatically connected qualifications of a noun—prepositional phrases, participles, relative clauses, adjectives, and nouns in the genitive.

Armed with this rule, the defenders of the rapture interpretation of *apostasia* turn to 2 Thessalonians 2:3, point out that *apostasia* has no grammatical qualification, and assert that it can't refer to spiritual departure. It can only refer to physical departure. But this argument is flawed on several levels.

First of all, it has been demonstrated that *apostasia* never bore the sense of physical *departure* in the Koine era. The only departure sense it bore from 250 BC to AD 500 was abstract departure, and every instance but one was either political departure or spiritual departure. This means that the grammatical qualification rule is bankrupt beyond bailout. No grammatical rule can indicate the presence of a sense that doesn't exist.

Secondly, grammatical qualification is not the only way to indicate which sense of *apostasia* is intended. Contextual qualification can also be employed. When a noun is qualified by information in the context, the lack of grammatical qualification is completely irrelevant.

Those who endorse the grammatical qualification rule could have and should have known better. Had they taken the time to examine a reasonable pool of *apostasia* passages in the Koine literature, they would have been forced to abandon this rule. Again and again, they would have been chagrined by instances that their rule flagged as physical departure but the context identified as either political or spiritual departure.

Here are a few examples where *apostasia* is used without grammatical qualification, yet clarification provided by the context demonstrates that they refer to religious apostasy.

Judges 19:22 (Aquila), "As they were making their hearts merry, behold, the men of the city, certain sons of *apostasia*, beset the house round about, and beat at the door." *Apostasia* has no grammatical qualification here, so the rule would claim this instance as an instance of physical departure. But we learn from the context that these "sons of *apostasia*" were not "sons of physical departure"—much less "sons of the rapture"—but "sons of Belial" who had rejected God and his morality. This instance clearly falls under the heading of religious apostasy.

Book of Jubilees, fragment z, "When they had been building for forty years, Nimrod in particular urging them into *apostasy*." There is no grammatical qualification here, so the rule would demand the sense of physical departure. But the context and parallel sources inform us that Nimrod was not urging the men to physical departure but rather to spiritual departure, and this of the deepest dye. He is the gold standard for apostasy.

Irenaeus, Against Heresies, Book 5, fragment 22, "And the number of his name, he said, among other things, is the number 666, which is six hundreds, six tens, and six ones, which summarize all the six thousand years which have passed since the *apostasy* happened." Once again we have no grammatical qualification. But this is clearly not talking about physical departure. It is not counting the time since Enoch was raptured. It is counting the time since the original apostasy of the fallen angels and mankind.

The Article Denotes a Prior Reference

Some of the rapture-theory defenders claim that the definite article with the noun *apostasia* refers back to something that was mentioned earlier. Because *apostasia* is feminine, they link it with two earlier nouns that have the same gender: *coming* and *gathering*. But this supposed grammatical insight faces four major hurdles.

First of all, the definite article, in and of itself, does not refer back to anything. It has no innate back-reference. It marks or modifies the word or phrase which follows it.

Articular back-reference in Greek is associated with well-defined grammatical patterns in which a noun, adjective, or participle preceded by an article either modifies or refers back to a preceding noun. Where one of the established patterns is present, you have a back-reference. Where no such pattern is present, there is no back-reference.

Secondly, the proposed grammatical connection linking *apostasia* with the preceding pair *coming* and *gathering* doesn't match any of the definite-article back-reference patterns in Greek which either modify or refer back to a preceding noun. These patterns can be summarized with six categories: appositional, attributive, predicate, adjunctive, attributive participles, and anaphoric.[90] While this is likely not an exhaustive treatment of the subject, it is certainly representative. Anything I missed will follow the analogy of those that I have listed.

The appositional use is when a noun with the article qualifies a preceding noun. For example, "John *the Baptist*" (Matt. 14:1) and "Herod *the king*" (Matt. 2:1).[91]

The attributive use is when an article with an adjective (in form or function) refers back to a noun that it modifies. For example, "the shepherd *the good*" (John 10:11) and "the light *the true*" (John 1:9).[92]

The predicate use has two varieties. The first marks the subject of a linking verb, distinguishing it from its predicate nominative or adjective. For instance, "God [is] *the justifier*" (Rom. 8:33) and "God was *the word*" (John 1:1). The second marks a noun that has a predicate-style relationship with the preceding adjective or participle. For instance, "with uncovered *the head*" (1 Cor. 11:5) and "hardened *the heart*" (Mark 8:17).[93]

The adjunctive use (sometimes also called attributive) connects modifying material, as a prepositional phrase, with a preceding noun. For instance, "righteousness *the of faith*" Rom.9:30) and "the powers *the in the heavens*" (Mark 13:25).[94]

The attributive participle use is when an article with a participle modifies the noun that precedes it. For example, "children *the in market sitting*" (Luke 7:32) , "gold *the perishing*" (1 Pet. 1:7), and "the fire *the eternal the prepared*" (Matt. 25:41).[95]

The anaphoric use is when a noun with an article refers back to the same noun without the article. For example, "bread" (John 6:9) and "*the bread*" (John 6:11). Another example is "Paul" (Acts 19:13) and "*the Paul*" (Acts 19:15).[96]

But none of these patterns can be exploited as an explanation for the proposed link between *apostasia* and the distant pair *coming* and *gathering*.

In the anaphoric construction, which is the only pattern that can have significant distance between the referring noun and the noun referred to (the referent), the same noun is repeated with the article. This pattern does not fit *apostasia* and the preceding nouns *coming* and *gathering*.

In the other constructions, the articulated modifier is grammatically linked (immediately adjacent) to the preceding noun that it modifies and both occur in the same clause. But there is no such proximity and no such pattern in the proposed connection between *apostasia* and the distant pair of nouns, *coming* and *gathering*.

Thirdly, the supposed grammatical link begins to look outlandish when we consider the massive jump from the proposed referring noun (*apostasia*) to the proposed referent (coming and gathering). The link must not only jump out of its own subordinated clause, but jump over the clause it is subordinated to, and then jump over two more clauses before it finally connects with the referent. This is unprecedented.

Fourthly, another discordant phenomenon that further extends the already long shadow of doubt on the purported grammatical link is that two feminine nouns stand between the supposed referring noun (*apostasia*) and the supposed referent (*coming* and *gathering*), those nouns being *the day* and *the epistle*.[97]

The standard rule of back-reference looks back from the referring noun to the first possible candidate, which is the first noun that agrees in gender, number, and case. Because *apostasia* is feminine, singular, and nominative, the standard rule would select *the day* as the referent. Yet the supposed link jumps over a noun with full agreement (day), and another noun with agreement in gender and number (epistle), and alights on a distant pair that themselves have only partial agreement (coming and gathering). How does this not seem like a stretch?

The bottom line is, there is no grammatical link between *apostasia* and the distant pair, *coming* and *gathering*. The incidental agreement in gender is meaningless. The only connection they have is that they are in the same paragraph and part of the same eschatological context.

The Article Implies Instantaneousness

The argument has been advanced by some of the advocates of the *apostasia*-rapture theory that *apostasia* has the definite article, and that this requires definiteness not merely in the noun itself but in the time nuance. Therefore, whatever *apostasia* refers to, it must be something that happens at a specific time—even instantaneously. This time constraint forbids the apostasy understanding because apostasies develop slowly over time. But it precisely fits the rapture. That wonderful event shall happen in a moment, in the twinkling of an eye—even instantaneously.

But this argument for the rapture view of *apostasia* makes two distinct blunders: one theological and one grammatical.

First of all, on a theological level, many students of prophecy from the church fathers to the present day have pointed out that while there will be a period of apostasy prior to the antichrist that primes the world to receive him as their messiah, there will be an explosion of apostasy when he sits in the temple of God, declares himself god, and requires the whole world to worship him on pain of death, this command being validated by lying miracles done in the power of Satan.

Every religion on the planet, ancient and modern, will wither and die in short order. Men will worship the antichrist to save their hide. This apostasy will be so fast and furious, and will so far outstrip all other apostasies in the history of the world, that it is regarded as *the* apostasy. The worst time of persecution in the history of the world will precipitate the worst time of apostasy in the history of the world.

It would not, in fact, be out of place to claim that the start of this apostasy will be instantaneous. It will explode on the inhabitants of earth—unforeseen and unexpected—with a definite act and a definite declaration on a definite day, the middle of the seventieth week. The Vatican (the headquarters of the one-world religion) will be burned with fire, the worldwide requirement to take the mark and bow to the image will be issued, influential men will line up to prove that they are world citizens, setting a precedent, and the executions will begin.

Because this forced apostasy by the antichrist is well known and long-established, it is completely unreasonable to reject the apostasy interpretation of *apostasia* with a cavalier wave of the hand and the smear that apostasies all unfold slowly and don't break out quickly.

Secondly, on the grammatical level, insisting that the article has reference to time is a seriously flawed notion. The article in Greek is used in many ways as making nominatives definite or turning verbals into nominatives, but it has no intrinsic reference to time. Reference to time comes from the nouns themselves and other indications of time, not from the article. The article can't define the length of the time—not long, not short, not instantaneous. The only thing the article can do is mark a stated length of time as definite.

The following examples of time periods with the article illustrate this point: *the sixty-two weeks* (Dan. 9:26), *the seventieth week* (Dan. 9:27), *the days of the prophetic ministry* of Moses and Elijah (Rev. 11:6), and *the census when Quirinius governed Syria* (Luke 2:2).[98]

There is no hint of brevity in these passages, much less the nuance of instantaneousness. All of these periods have well-defined starting and ending points. And some are quite long. The prophetic ministry of Moses and Elijah is three and a half years long. The seventieth week is seven years long. And the sixty-two weeks is 434 years long. The definite article in these passages gives us one piece of information—the mentioned periods are definite. For instance, the sixty-two weeks refers to a specific sixty-two weeks of years determined by God upon Israel, not any sixty-two weeks of years.

In John 3:19 we find a great illustration that the article itself doesn't add the connotation of definite time. "Men loved darkness rather than light." In the Greek, all three nouns have a definite article. A stilted translation would say, "the men loved the darkness rather than the light." But this is not saying that particular men at a particular point in history loved a particular darkness manifested at that particular time more than the particular display of light manifested at that same particular time. On the contrary, what we have here is the generic use of the article.[99] All three nouns are generic. This verse is simply saying that men in general love darkness more than light. This is a general principle that is not time-bound.

English uses the definite article to make generic nouns too. For instance, we might say "the mountains are better than the beach." This is not talking about a particular mountain range or a particular beach. It is speaking of mountains in general and beaches in general. But we only use the definite article with concrete nouns. We don't use it with abstract nouns. We don't say, "the love is better than the hate." We say, "love is better than hate."

One last passage illustrates that the instantaneous rule will take us places where we do not want to go. In Revelation 20:10 we read, "The devil, who deceived them, was cast into the lake of fire." In the Greek, both lake and fire have a definite article. But it provides no hint of time limitation—not for the lake or for the fire—much less limitation to an instant. The lake of fire will have already existed for seven thousand years when the adversary is cast into its bowels, and it will continue to exist forever. Moreover, it would be horrid exegesis to insist that because both lake and fire have the definite article, we are obligated to embrace annihilationism—the doctrine that the lake of fire is a momentary event that annihilates the wicked.

The above examples illustrate that we can't use the article as a lever to tip *hē apostasia* toward the instantaneous rapture view. And they illustrate that the article is perfectly compatible with long periods of time that have a definite starting point and ending point. The candid man is forced to conclude that if the article can be used for the definite three and a half year ministry of Moses and Elijah, then it can be used for the definite three and a half years of great tribulation and great falling away that are associated with the antichrist.

THE EXEGETICAL ARGUMENT

Verse 3 and Verses 6-7 are Parallel

The exegetical argument for identifying the noun *apostasia* in 2 Thessalonians 2:3 with the rapture is based on the claim that verse 3 and verses 6-7 are parallel statements of the same truth. According to the theory, *apostasia* has the same cause-and-effect relationship with the revelation of the antichrist in verse 3 that the removal of the restraining effort has with the revelation of the antichrist in verses 6-7. As the restraining Holy Spirit must be removed (implying the rapture) in the latter passage before the man of sin can be revealed, so the *apostasia* must happen (implying the rapture) in the former passage before the man of sin can be revealed. This parallel structure means that *apostasia* must be a reference to the rapture of the church, and it ought to be translated by *departure*.

Objections to the Argument

But this argument is not nearly as weighty as many have made it out to be. Observe the following points.

First of all, this argument faces the same difficulty that most of the arguments face—*apostasia* didn't bear the sense of physical or spatial *departure* during the Koine era. This sense didn't arrive on the scene until the late sixth or early seventh century (early Byzantine era). This being the case, *apostasia* can't bear the sense of physical *departure* in 2 Thessalonians 2:3. If it can't bear the sense of physical *departure*, then it can't be a reference to the rapture, and it can't imply the removal of the restrainer (the Holy Spirit) with the rapture. If it can't imply the removal of the restrainer, then there is no parallel between verse 3 and verses 6-7. This is a hurdle that no amount of exegetical gymnastics can negotiate.

Secondly, the form of the argument is problematic. The parallel between the rapture and the antichrist in verse 3 and the rapture and the antichrist in verses 6-7 is offered as proof that *apostasia* is a reference to the rapture. But this parallel assumes that *apostasia* is a reference to the rapture. (There is no parallel if you don't start with this assumption.) So this argument is either assuming the truth of the point they need to prove (begging the question), or it is arguing from the vantage point of an assumed gain (dangling a carrot). Either way, arguing with such assumptions is a counterproductive method of exegesis. This method tends to give investigators the results they desire rather than the results God intended.

Thirdly, you still have parallel accounts of the rapture and the revelation of the antichrist even if *apostasia* in verse 3 isn't a reference to the rapture. The rapture, after all, is clearly stated in verse 1, "the coming of our Lord Jesus Christ and our gathering together unto him." So we can legitimately say that the rapture and the revelation of the man of sin in verses 1-3 parallels the rapture and the revelation of the man of sin in verses 6-7. Nothing is diminished one iota because the rapture is located in verse 1 and *apostasia* in verse 3 is a reference to the apostasy associated with the antichrist.[100]

Fourthly, the argument as presented by Ken Wuest and those who have followed his lead breaks down because the parallel isn't consistent. I will let Ken speak for himself.

"But then *hee apostasia* of which Paul is speaking, precedes the revelation of Antichrist in his true identity, and is *to katechon* that which holds back his revelation (2:6). ... Furthermore, that which holds back his revelation (v. 3) is vitally connected with *hoo katechon* (v. 7), He who holds back the same event. The latter is, in my opinion, the Holy Spirit and His activities in the Church. All of which means that I am driven to the inescapable conclusion that the *hee apostasia* (v. 3) refers to the Rapture of the Church which precedes the Day of the Lord, and holds back the revelation of the Man of Sin."[101]

If you read this portion carefully, you will observe that the effort to paint a parallel between verse 3 and verses 6-7 involves a subtle sleight of hand. Most prophecy teachers regard the restrainer in verses. 6-7 to be the Holy Spirit, specifically the Holy Spirit in the church.

Ken appears to agree with this. Yet when he treats verse 3, he informs us that *apostasia* is both the rapture and the restrainer, the same restrainer as in verse 6. This treatment raises three questions.

Where is the parallel? If the restrainer in verse 6 is the Holy Spirit indwelt church and the restrainer in verse 3 is the rapture of the church, there is no parallel. There is only a superficial appearance of a parallel because the rapture, restrainer, and antichrist are either mentioned or implied in both passages.

Where is the logical consistency? If the restrainer is the Holy Spirit in the church, it can't be the rapture. If the restrainer is the rapture, it can't be the Holy Spirit in the church.

Where is the eschatological integrity? Ken claims that the rapture is the restrainer. How do folks not choke on this thought? The rapture is not the restrainer. It is the removal of the restrainer. The rapture does not hold back the man of sin. It unleashes the man of sin.

Frankly, it is unsettling that folks can read Ken's handling of the subject and not have the inconsistencies jump off the page at them. I suppose the explanation is that men are subconsciously making the necessary transposition from *apostasia* as the restrainer to *apostasia* as the removal of the restrainer, but that is certainly not what he wrote.

THE THEOLOGICAL
ARGUMENT

Argument Outlined

The theological argument for the rapture understanding of *apostasia* in 2 Thessalonians 2:3 largely revolves around the supposed theological impossibility of *apostasia* being a reference to a last-days apostasy. Three reasons are given for this supposed impossibility. One, there has always been apostasy. Two, there will be no way to distinguish a last-days apostasy from any other apostasy. Three, there is no comfort to be derived from knowing that there will be an apostasy in the last days. These reasons will be addressed in the following subsections.

Argument One:
There has Always Been Apostasy

Those who favor the rapture understanding of *apostasia* in 2 Thessalonians 2:3 often point out that the history of the church since the days of the apostles has been a continual string of apostasies. Based on this precedent, there is no reason to believe that any future apostasy will depart from this pattern.

With this groundwork laid, they trot out the observation that *apostasia* has the definite article and insist that its presence implies an exceptional instance. This is regarded as a fatal blow to the apostasy understanding. *Apostasia* can't be a reference to apostasy because no future apostasy is going to be significantly different than those over the past two thousand years. No future apostasy will stand out in any way. With the sense of exceptional spiritual *departure* in the last days ruled out, the only sense left is an exceptional physical *departure* in the last days—the rapture.

This argument, though it seems forceful and convincing to many, is a toothless dog that is all bark and no bite.

First of all, if this form of argument is legitimate, then the fact that there have always been antichrists indicates that there is no unique antichrist in the last days. How could yet one more antichrist prove anything, much less that we are in the last days? Any antichrist in the future won't be significantly different from the antichrists that have already come and gone.

Furthermore, the fact that there have always been tribulations proves that there is no unique tribulation in the last days. How could yet one more tribulation prove anything, much less that we are in the last days? Any tribulation in the future won't be significantly different from the tribulations that have already come and gone.

Can you not see that the form of this argument is unsound and militates against the literal interpretation of prophecy? Should we all embrace amillennialism and its pernicious claim that there will be no unique last days, no unique tribulation, no unique antichrist, and no unique apostasy in the last days? I think not.

For myself, I reject this argument as completely invalid in its form. The fact that there were many antichrists in the days of the apostles doesn't overthrow the clear, biblical teaching that there shall be a distinct antichrist at the end of the age. Likewise, the fact that there have been continual apostasies since the days of the apostles doesn't overthrow the biblical teaching that there will be a distinct apostasy in the last days associated with the antichrist. Events that are shadows don't disprove the existence of the shadow caster. They prove it. And the reality is always more substantial than the shadow.

Secondly, the argument for excluding spiritual departure and requiring physical departure goes belly up if *apostasia* can't mean physical *departure*. Once again, we see that the entire argument hangs on a single point—the legitimacy of the sense of physical *departure*.

But the impossibility of the physical departure understanding raises a question. Were the advocates of the *apostasia*-rapture theory sincere when they articulated their theory that the definite article means an exceptional instance of *apostasia*? If the theory be true, then we must embrace an exceptional instance of spiritual departure in the last days. For spiritual departure is the only sense left.

Thirdly, this argument depends on the assumption that there is nothing unique or outstanding about the apostasy that transpires in the last days. It is just a continuation of the string of apostasies that have occurred since the apostles with no significant difference in kind or degree. But this assumption, as will be fully demonstrated in the next subsection, is untenable.

Argument Two:
No Way to Recognize a Last Days Apostasy

The claim is frequently made by those that favor the rapture view of *apostasia* in 2 Thessalonians 2:3 that future apostasies will be indistinct from the apostasies that have continually occurred since the days of the apostles. So there will be no way to recognize a last-days apostasy. After all, an apostasy that isn't outstanding in either features or degree can't be a sign of anything, much less a sign that we are in the last days.

This point being made, they point to the fact that *apostasia* has a definite article, which implies that it is an exceptional instance. Since there can't and won't be an exceptional apostasy in the last days, this exceptional *apostasia* can't refer to an exceptional apostasy. The only option left is an exceptional physical departure—the rapture.

But this argument faces three insurmountable difficulties which have no resolution.

First of all, as the body without the spirit is dead, so the *apostasia*-rapture theory is dead if *apostasia* was never used of physical departure in the Koine era. You can't breathe life into this doctrine if the sense of physical *departure* exists only in men's imaginations.

Secondly, this argument starts with the assumption that the precedent of non-exceptional apostasy in the past forbids future exceptional apostasy. But we have already seen that we disembowel the literal interpretation of prophecy if we apply this uniformitarian principle to things like the last days, the antichrist, and tribulation, so we ought to be leary of applying it to apostasy.

Thirdly, this argument assumes and asserts that there will be no qualitative or quantitative differences between the apostasy of the last days and the apostasies of the prior two thousand years. Is this legitimate? I think not. There is plenty of material in the Bible that explodes this theory and upholds the truth of an exceptional apostasy in the last days.

The first line of argument which indicates an exceptional apostasy in the last days is the antichrist testimony of 2 Thessalonians 2:3-12. The mystery of iniquity will be amped up with the revelation of the man of sin, who will have the ability to work genuine miracles wrought by Satan's power that will authenticate his lies. On top of this, God will send a strong delusion that will persuade truth rejectors to believe the lie being propagated by the antichrist. This will be a potent one-two punch. The deception and persecution of the antichrist which are unparalleled in the annals of history coupled with God sending a great delusion which is unparalleled in the annals of history will produce an apostasy which is unparalleled in the annals of history.

The second line of argument is found in the tribulation context of Matthew 24. Verse 21 informs us that there "shall be great tribulation, such as was not since the beginning of the world to this time, nor ever shall be." Since tribulation always leads to apostasy, it is reasonable to expect that the greatest tribulation of all time will lead to the greatest apostasy of all time. And we do, in fact, read of such a great departure in Matthew 24:12, "because iniquity shall abound the love of the most shall grow cold."[102]

The third line of argument is the fact that the Bible would not use similes like "as the days of Noah" and "as it was in the days of Lot" if the moral state of the world was not going to reach a similar apex of darkness that demands absolute destruction. God didn't send the children of Israel into the Promised Land until the iniquity of the Amorites was full. He didn't flood the world until its iniquity had climaxed. He didn't send fire on Sodom until its rebellion had peaked. So we can safely conclude that the awful world-expunging judgment that falls at the second coming of Christ comes precisely because the wickedness and apostasy of mankind had reached its awful climax in the days of the antichrist.

The fourth line of argument is that the spirit of Babel, which manifested itself in succession in Babel, Assyria, Babylon, Medo-Persia, Greece, Rome, and divided Rome, will soon be manifested in the final form of the Roman empire, spiritually called Mystery Babylon in the book of Revelation. The heinous effort begun by Nimrod and squelched by God over and over again throughout the centuries will finally be allowed in the time of the antichrist to engulf the entire world with undiluted Babylonian darkness. This is, without a doubt, exceptional darkness that will surpass any of the apostasies during the church age.

The fifth line of argument is the world's rejection of God's earthly gifts in 1 Timothy 4:1-5. Here we read that deceiving spirits fabricate and propagate lies that hinder marriage and encourage men to abstain from eating foods that God gave to man.

While parts of Christendom have long hindered marriage with forced celibacy amongst the clergy, monks, and nuns, and while there has been a perversion problem since the founding of the church, these were only harbingers of the sodomite problem that is currently spreading through the world today like cancer. By the time of the end, the perversion will equal or surpass the iniquity of Sodom. This is indisputably an exceptional apostasy that goes beyond what the world has seen since the apostles.

While there have always been scattered vegetarians and vegans, the world is now being herded down a path that aims to remove meat and dairy from the human diet. Not because such foods truly are bad for our health, but because Satan is profoundly evil. When the enemy's diet-restriction platform reaches its acme at the end of the age, it will be an exceptional apostasy that will go far beyond any dietary restrictions pressed upon man in the past. It will be a worldwide opposition to two of the staple foods that God gave to mankind for health and enjoyment: meat and dairy.

The sixth line of argument is the prediction in 2 Peter 3 that the last days will be characterized by the denial of creation, the flood, and the coming judgment by fire. While there has always been unbelief in the God of the Bible, it is only in recent times that it has moved beyond such expressions as paganism, rationalism, deism, and Babylonized versions of Christianity with their watered-down versions of creation, the flood, and coming judgment. Now the world is racing down the path of atheism. It has become, for all practical purposes, the religion of our educational institutions. This religion boldly denies creation, the flood, and coming judgment. When the cancer of atheism finishes its course in the last days, it will, beyond all shadow of doubt, constitute a qualitative difference between the apostasy of the last days and the apostasies that preceded it.

The seventh line of argument is the Lord's saying in John 9:4, "I must work the works of him that sent me, while it is day: the night comes, when no man can work." Here we find a prediction that the world will be engulfed in darkness at the end of the age that exceeds the church's experience. Even in her darkest days, such as the Inquisition and the Roman persecutions, she was able to work and grow. But the dark night of the mystery of iniquity and the agenda of the antichrist will descend upon the world, bringing such deep darkness that it will be impossible to actively engage in the work of the Lord apart from supernatural empowering and protection. This special power and protection will be enjoyed by the two witnesses and the hundred and forty-four thousand, and maybe others.

The eighth line of argument is the Lord's prediction about what will happen to the Jews in Matthew 12:43-45,[103] "When the unclean spirit is gone out of a man, he walks through dry places, seeking rest, and finds none. Then he says, I will return to my house from whence I came out; and when he is come, he finds it empty, swept, and garnished. Then he goes and takes with himself seven other spirits more wicked than himself, and they enter in and dwell there: and the last state of that man is worse than the first. Even so shall it be also with this wicked generation."

During the Babylonian captivity, Israel was delivered from her idolatrous ways. In the 2500 years since, she has never gone back to classic idolatry. Undoubtedly, she is better off now than she was before the Babylonian captivity. But this will not last. The day will come when the mystery of iniquity will no longer be restrained, and two-thirds of the nation[104] will succumb to the great delusion and worship the beast and his image, leaving the nation seven times worse than she was before the captivity. When this prophecy is fulfilled, a qualitative difference between her current apostasy and her apostasy in the last days will be evident.

While this prophecy specifically applies to Israel, it is perfectly legitimate to apply the principle to the professing church. She is better off now with her tainted lip-service religion than she was in the days of her paganism. But the day will come when the church will set aside her profession of Christianity and embrace the antichrist, and she too will be seven times worse than she is now.

So you can see that the departure in the last days will go deeper and farther than any departure since the founding of the church. It will be far worse than the ancient monotheism apostatizing into paganism. It will be far worse than the early church slowly morphing into the Catholic church. It will be far worse than the Protestant churches departing from the faith into liberalism and neo-orthodoxy. It will be far worse than dead evangelicalism spawning cults like the Mormons, Jehovah's Witnesses, Seventh Day Adventists, and the like.

The antichrist will ban all religions—all that is called god or worshiped—and require the world to worship himself and his image. He will institute the emperor worship of Babylon and Rome, but it will transcend its historical precedents. In the past, the other religions were still allowed to continue. A man could bow once, get it over with, and go back to his religion. In the last days, the spiritual atheism will ban all competition. There will be one religion—the worship of the antichrist as the ascended man and the worship of his ascended master, Satan, who will pass himself off as the most advanced ascended being among all the races that have evolved in the universe.

Argument Three:
No Comfort Derived From Knowing That
There Will Be a Last Days' Apostasy

Another argument that is often leveled against *apostasia* in 2 Thessalonians 2:3 meaning *apostasy* is the claim that the church derives no comfort from knowing that there will be an apostasy before the day of the Lord, while she does derive comfort from knowing that there will be a rapture before that day. This comfort element is seen

78

as a valid reason to endorse the translation *departure* and embrace the rapture understanding of *apostasia*. But this argument is more of an emotional appeal than a theological argument.

First of all, as already pointed out numerous times on other points, if *apostasia* can't mean physical *departure*, then spiritual *departure* is the only option and the whole argument crumbles to dust.

Secondly, if comfort really is a legitimate issue in the interpretation of the events of verse three, why don't we train this gun on the revelation of the antichrist? What comfort does any believer receive from knowing that the revelation of the antichrist will happen prior to the day of the Lord?

If we reply "none" yet leave the antichrist intact though he provides no comfort, we reveal our hypocrisy. If the antichrist who doesn't provide comfort can remain, why can't we keep the apostasy which doesn't provide comfort? If the apostasy which doesn't provide comfort must go, why don't we dump the antichrist too? He doesn't provide any more comfort than the apostasy.

If we reply that the revelation of the antichrist is indirectly a comfort because he is one of the chief signs of the second coming, then we give up the *no comfort* argument. If the antichrist can be an indirect comfort, so can the apostasy.

Thirdly, this *no comfort* argument is opposed by the general prophetic principle, "When these things begin to come to pass, then look up and lift up your heads for your redemption draws near" (Luke 21:28). Every one of the things mentioned in this context is negative and tragic. None are a source of intrinsic comfort. But all of them are sources of roadsign comfort. They all indicate that the coming of the Lord is drawing nigh.

Notice that one of the negative events mentioned in Matthew's version of the Olivet Discourse is the forecast, "because iniquity shall abound, the love of most shall wax cold." This forces the candid man to conclude that if the tribulation apostasy in Matthew 24 can be a encouragement because it is a sign that points to the Lord's coming, then a tribulation apostasy in 2 Thessalonians 2 can also be a source of encouragement because it too points to the coming of the Lord.

CONCLUSION

Gullibility

After decades of watching men succumb to false teaching, on both major and minor points, I have concluded that gullibility is being observant enough to be wowed and cowed by logic but not observant enough to see the holes in the assumptions underneath the show of logic. This gullibility is the power of false doctrine.

No real Christian is gullible across the board, but most Christians are gullible in at least one area of doctrine. And all of us can be gullible on points, even within a field of strength, if we take shortcuts and don't investigate deep enough. This is especially true when defending doctrine we believe is the truth of God. May God give us all a healthy dose of holy skepticism and help us to scorn taking shortcuts in the name of truth.

Sherlock Holmes

One of my favorite quotes comes from Sherlock Holmes. "It is a capital mistake to theorize before one has data. Insensibly one begins to twist facts to suit theories, instead of theories to suit facts."

This mistake continually besets our efforts to uncover the truth. We gather information. But not enough. And not the right kind. Following an early hunch and oblivious to the lack of information, we come to wrong conclusions. All of us have had instances where we embraced positions that seemed reasonable at the time based on the information we had. But further information forced us to change our minds.

The only way to break this power of insensibly twisting facts to suit theories is to gather more light so we can make better-informed decisions on doctrinal matters. We need to make it a principled passion (or a passioned principle) to seek the whole array of pertinent information on whatever subject we are studying. Then we need to resist every solution that ignores some of the data no matter how weighty or how many the names that trumpet it as the truth. Our passion must be for the least complex solution that harmonizes ALL the data—an achievement known as Occam's razor or the elegant solution. Anything less than this is beneath the dignity of those who walk in the light.

A Summary of the Arguments for Apostasy

The arguments presented in this volume for the *apostasy* view of *apostasia* in 2 Thessalonians 2:3 are many and weighty.

ONE. The noun *apostasia* only bore the sense of abstract departure in the Koine era. It was used once for *repentance* late in the fourth century and 258 times for *rebellion*—26 times for political *sedition* and 232 times for religious *apostasy*.

TWO. The cognates in the *apostasis* family appear to have only borne the sense of *abstract departure* in the Roman era (150 BC to AD 150). I examined hundreds of instances of the nouns and verbs of this family, along with many instances of the adjective and adverb. Apart from the technical senses and the rare figurative senses of the nouns, every instance was in the vein of *rebellion*.

THREE. The only translation tradition from the church fathers to the present day in the Latin, English, and German Bibles is that of *spiritual departure*.

The introductions and marginal notes in the early English Bibles, along with commentaries on the same, indicate that the translators and editors all understood *departing* and *departure* to be references to the apostasy in the last days associated with the antichrist. They regarded these two terms to be synonymous with *revolt, falling away, apostasy, rebellion, defection, insurrection*, and the like.

The oldest English translations of 2 Thessalonians 2:3, found in Wyclif's Bible and in the *Cursor Mundi* (ca. 1300), give the reading *dissension*.

The Latin Vulgate reading *discessio* was used in the sense of *revolt* or *spiritual departure* as demonstrated by the comments of Jerome, the Vulgate editors, and commentators on the Latin Bible. This is also indicated by the alternate rendering *dissensio* (dissension) which appears in some editions.

The Old Latin (pre-Vulgate) reading *abscessio* was understood in the sense of *political departure* or *division* as evidenced by the comments of Tertullian.

For the German Bibles, the Mentel Bible (various editions 1466-1518) featured *Misshellung* (dissension, division, revolt), Luther (1529) featured *Abfalle* (falling away, apostasy), and the Wulfila or Gothic version (ca. 350) exhibited *Anstass* (standing off, falling off, falling away, turning away).

FOUR. Every church father who commented on *apostasia* in 2 Thessalonians 2:3 regarded it to have the sense of *revolt* or *rebellion*. Those who viewed the Roman empire as the restrainer regarded it as a *political revolt* from Rome. Those who viewed God as the restrainer regarded it as a *religious revolt* from God that revolved around the antichrist.

FIVE. The context defends translating *apostasia* by *apostasy* or *falling away*. The *apostasia* and the antichrist in 2 Thessalonians 2:3 are elaborated on in the following passage (verses 4-12) where we read of a time of unparalleled satanic power, unparalleled delusion, and unparalleled persecution which leads to an unparalleled apostasy. This apostasy is alluded to in the context and directly mentioned in parallel passages like Matthew 24:12.

In the face of such a wealth of evidence, theories on the meaning of *apostasia* based on the word-root and cognate fallacies, appeals to lexicon entries that are misunderstood, questionable arguments based on minutiae like the definite article, and the strained efforts of exegetical gymnastics must be abandoned as mistakes made in the pursuit of truth and light.

Morning Star Vs The Rising Sun

One of the undercurrents in modern pretribulationism is the feeling that we don't have a strong enough case for the pretribulation rapture. Many secretly hanker for a few more arguments. I suspect that this is the real motive behind such teachings as the theory that *apostasia* in 2 Thessalonians 2:3 is a reference to the rapture.

I personally do not feel a need to strengthen the argument for the pretribulation rapture. Yes, there are significantly fewer passages on the rapture than there are on the second coming. But this does not imply that the argument for a pretribulation rapture is weak. The fact is, the argument for it that can be framed from John 14:1-3, Revelation 3:10, 1 Thessalonians 4-5, 2 Thessalonians 2:1-3, and Revelation 4-5 stands like the Rock of Gibraltar.

The disparity in the number of passages is a matter of emphasis, not vagueness. Bible prophecy does not revolve around the rapture of the church but around the day of the Lord. This is why the Old Testament deals exclusively with the day of the Lord and why most of the prophetic passages in the New Testament are focused on it.

This disparity is better appreciated when we illustrate it with biblical typology. The day of the Lord is portrayed in the Bible as the sun rising in the burning heat of judgment (Mal. 4:1-3, James 1:9-11). The rapture is portrayed as the morning star (2 Pet. 2:19, Rev. 2:28). The time in between these two events is the day of the Lord dawning upon the world. Now just as the morning star is an unobtrusive phenomenon that men can easily miss if they aren't looking for it while the rising of the sun is a phenomenon that you can't miss unless you are blind, so the passages on the rapture are a small, less obtrusive group while the passages on the second coming are a large throng that dominates the prophetic message of the Bible. Nobody misses the latter. Only careful, discerning students of the Bible see the former.

APPENDIX A
Pre-Roman Era

Archimedes, Arenarius (The Sand Reckoner), 1.4-5 (Heiberg); vol. 2, p. 135 (Mugler)

— (4) Ἀρίσταρχος δὲ ὁ Σάμιος ὑποθέσιών τινων ἐξέδωκεν γραφάς, ἐν αἷς ἐκ τῶν ὑποκειμένων συμβαίνει τὸν κόσμον πολλαπλάσιον εἶμεν τοῦ νῦν εἰρημένου. (5) Ὑποτίθεται γὰρ τὰ μὲν ἀπλανέα τῶν ἄστρων καὶ τὸν ἄλιον μένειν ἀκίνητον, τὰν δὲ γᾶν περιφέρεσθαι περὶ τὸν ἄλιον κατὰ κύκλου περιφέρειαν, ὅς ἐστιν ἐν μέσῳ τῷ δρόμῳ κείμενος, τὰν δὲ τῶν ἀπλανέων ἄστρων σφαῖραν περὶ τὸ αὐτὸ κέντρον τῷ ἁλίῳ κειμέναν τῷ μεγέθει τηλικαύταν εἶμεν, ὥστε τὸν κύκλον, καθ᾽ ὃν τὰν γᾶν ὑποτίθεται περιφέρεσθαι, τοιαύταν ἔχειν ἀναλογίαν ποτὶ **τὰν** τῶν ἀπλανέων **ἀποστασίαν**, οἵαν ἔχει τὸ κέντρον τᾶς σφαίρας ποτὶ τὰν ἐπιφάνειαν.

— (4) But Aristarchus of Samos produced writings of certain hypotheses in which it follows from the suppositions that the world is many times what is now claimed. (5) For he supposes that the fixed stars and the sun remain motionless, while the earth revolves about the sun on the circumference of a circle which is placed on the middle road, but that the sphere of the fixed stars, which is placed about the same center as the sun, is so large in magnitude that the circle on which he supposes the earth to revolve has the sort of proportion to the **distance** of the fixed stars that the center of the sphere has to the surface.

— Greek Text — C. Mugler. *Archiméde, vol. 2.* Les Belles Lettres, Paris, 1971. Retrieved from *Thesaurus Linguae Graecae* (stephanus.tlg.uci.edu).

— English translation — Henry Mendell of Cal. State U, L.A., originally posted at calstatela.edu. Accessed at Internet Archive Wayback Machine (web.archive.org).

— Context compares the earth's orbit around the sun to the earth's orbit around the fixed stars. (A mistake in reasoning.)

— This is the first instance of *apostasia* in the extant literature. And it is the first and only use in Koine in the scientific sense of *distance*, a sense typically handled by *apostasis*.

— Scientific sense of DISTANCE

APPENDIX B
Roman Era

Diodorus Siculus, Library of History, Book 21, 14.1
— Ὅτι Δημήτριος ὁ βασιλεύς, τὸ δεύτερον ἀποστατησάντων Θηβαίων, πολιορκίᾳ τὰ τείχη καθελών, τὴν πόλιν κατὰ κράτος εἷλε, δέκα μόνους ἄνδρας ἀνελὼν τοὺς **τὴν ἀποστασίαν** κατεργαζομένους.
—King Demetrius laid siege to Thebes when it revolted a second time, demolished the walls with siege engines, and took the city by storm, but put to death only the ten men who were responsible for **the revolt**.
— Greek text and English Translation — *Diodorus Siculus. Library of History, Volume XI: Fragments of Books 21-32.* Translated by F. R. Walton, *Loeb Classical Library 409*, Harvard University Press, 1957. Accessed at LacusCurtius (penelope.uchicago.edu/Thayer/E/Roman/home.html).
— The context is the second Thebian revolt. Notice the association with ἀποστατέω (apostateō) *rebel, revolt.*
— POLITICAL SEDITION OR REBELLION

Diodorus Siculus, Library of History, Book 34-35, 2.44-46
— Ὅτι ἡ κατεπείγουσα χρεία καὶ σπάνις ἠνάγκαζε πάντα δοκιμάζειν τοὺς ἀποστάτας δούλους, οὐ διδοῦσα τὴν τῶν κρειττόνων ἐκλογήν. Ὅτι ὑπῆρχεν οὐ διοσημίας δεόμενον τὸ συλλογίσασθαι τῆς πόλεως τὸ εὐάλωτον. Φανερὸν γὰρ ἦν καὶ τοῖς εὐηθεστάτοις ὅτι τῶν τειχῶν διὰ τὴν πολυχρόνιον εἰρήνην κατερρυηκότων καὶ πολλῶν ἐξ αὐτῆς στρατιωτῶν ἀπολωλότων, ἔσται τῆς πόλεως εὐκατόρθωτος ἡ πολιορκία. Ὅτι ὁ εὔνους ἐκτὸς βέλους ἐπιστήσας τὴν δύναμιν ἐβλασφήμει τοὺς Ῥωμαίους, ἀποφαινόμενος οὐχ ἑαυτοὺς ἀλλ᾽ ἐκείνους εἶναι δραπέτας τῶν κινδύνων. Μίμους δὲ ἐξ ἀποστάσεως τοῖς ἔνδον ἐπεδείκνυτο, δι᾽ ὧν οἱ δοῦλοι **τὰς** ἀπὸ τῶν ἰδίων κυρίων **ἀποστασίας** ἐξεθεάτριζον, ὀνειδίζοντες αὐτῶν τὴν ὑπερηφανίαν καὶ τὴν ὑπερβολὴν τῆς εἰς τὸν ὄλεθρον προαγούσης ὕβρεως.
— Their pressing needs and lack of provisions forced the rebel slaves to risk everything because they had no opportunity to follow a better course. It did not need a revelation from God to understand how easy

86

it was to capture the city. It was obvious, even to the simplest observer, that since the walls were in disrepair due to the long time of peace, and many of the garrison had been killed, the city could not hold out for long against a siege. Eunus, keeping his army out of the range of weapons, shouted insults at the Romans, saying that it was not his men, but the Romans who were runaways from danger. He put on mimes [by some who were part of the rebellion] for those inside, in which the slaves depicted how they had **revolted** from their own masters, mocking their masters' arrogance and the excessive cruelty that led to their overthrow.

— Greek text — Ludovic Dindorf. *Diodorus Siculus: Bibliotheca Historica.* Teubner, 1886. Accessed at Attalus (attalus.org). The passage from «Ὅτι ὁ εὔνους» onward is a quotation from Posidonius.

— English translation — Produced by Andrew Smith of Attalus (attalus.org) who collated and reedited older translations. Accessed at Attalus (attalus.org).

— The context is the slave revolt.

— POLITICAL SEDITION OR REBELLION

Diogenianus, Paroemiae, Centuria 8, section 49

— Τοῦτο τὸ ὑπόδημα ἔρραψε μὲν Ἱστιαῖος, ὑπεδήσατο δὲ Ἀρισταγόρας· Ἀρταφέρνου τοῦτο τοῦ Περσῶν βασιλέως. Καὶ γὰρ Ἱστιαῖον οὗτος ᾐτιᾶτο **τῆς** Ἰώνων **ἀποστασίας**, ὁ δὲ ἠρνεῖτο, καὶ εἰς Ἀρισταγόραν μετέφερε τὴν αἰτίαν· οὗ τὸ δόλιον ἀνακαλύπτων ὁ σατράπης, εἰς αὐτὸν τοῦτο εἶπε. Λέγεται δὲ ἐπὶ τῶν τὰ ἑαυτῶν ἐγκλήματα ἄλλοις πανούργως προσαπτόντων.

— Histiaeus sewed the sandal and Aristagoras bound it. This comes from the Persian king Artaphernes. For he asked Histiaeus about the Ionian **revolt**, but he denied that he was involved and blamed Aristagoras. When the satrap uncovered the treachery, he told this to him [Histiaeus]. He confessed the charges against them for cunningly joining the others [in the rebellion fomented against Persia].

— Greek text — F.G. Schneidewin and E.L. von Leutsch. *Diogenianus: Corpus paroemiographorum Graecorum, Vol. 1.* Vandenhoeck & Ruprecht, 1839 (reprinted Hildesheim, 1965). Retrieved from Thesaurus Linguae Graecae (stephanus.tlg.uci.edu).

— English translation — The translation is my own as I could find none available.

— The context is the Ionian revolt against the Persians during the reign of Artaphernes. Notice the association with τὸ δόλιον (to dolion) *deceit* and πανούργως (panourgōs) *cunningly*.

— POLITICAL SEDITION OR REBELLION

Plutarch, Galba, 1.5

— καίτοι Διονύσιος Φεραῖον ἄρξαντα Θετταλῶν δέκα μῆνας, εἶτα εὐθὺς ἀναιρεθέντα, τὸν τραγικὸν ἀνεκάλει τύραννον, ἐπισκώπτων τὸ τάχος τῆς μεταβολῆς, ἡ δὲ τῶν Καισάρων ἑστία, τὸ Παλάτιον, ἐν ἐλάσσονι χρόνῳ τέσσαρας αὐτοκράτορας ὑπεδέξατο, τὸν μὲν εἰσαγόντων ὥσπερ διὰ σκηνῆς, τὸν δ᾽ ἐξαγόντων. ἀλλ᾽ ἦν γε παραμυθία τοῖς κακῶς πάσχουσι μία τὸ μὴ δεηθῆναι δίκης ἑτέρας ἐπὶ τοὺς αἰτίους, ἀλλ᾽ ὁρᾶν αὐτοὺς ὑφ᾽ ἑαυτῶν φονευομένους, πρῶτον δε καὶ δικαιότατα πάντων τὸν δελεάσαντα καὶ διδάξαντα τοσοῦτον ἐλπίζειν ἐπὶ μεταβολῇ Καίσαρος ὅσον αὐτὸς ὑπέσχετο, κάλλιστον ἔργον διαβαλὼν τῷ μισθῷ, **τὴν** ἀπὸ Νέρωνος **ἀποστασίαν** προδοσίαν γενομένην.

— And yet the Pheraean—who ruled Thessaly for ten months and was then promptly killed—was called the tragedy-tyrant by Dionysius, with scornful reference to the quickness of the change. But the house of the Caesars, the Palatium, in a shorter time than this received four emperors, the soldiery ushering one in and another out, as in play. But the suffering people had one consolation at least in the fact that they needed no other punishment of the authors of their sufferings, but saw them slain by one another's hands, and first and most righteously of all, the man who ensnared the soldiery and taught them to expect from the deposition of a Caesar all the good things which he promised them, thus defiling a most noble deed by the pay he offered for it, and turning **the revolt** from Nero into treachery.

— Greek text and English translation — *Plutarch Lives, Volume XI: Aratus, Artaxerxes, Galba, Otho.* Translated by Bernadotte Perrin, *Loeb Classical Library 103*, Harvard University Press, William Heinemann, 1917. Accessed in Logos in the Perseus collection. Accessed at Perseus Digital Library (perseus.tufts.edu).

— The context is the revolt from Nero. Notice the association with προδοσία (prodosia) *betrayal*, *treason*.
— POLITICAL SEDITION OR REBELLION

Plutarch, Mulierum virtutes, Pieria (Example 16)
— τῶν εἰς Μίλητον ἀφικομένων Ἰώνων στασιάσαντες ἔνιοι πρὸς τοὺς Νείλεω παῖδας, ἀπεχώρησαν εἰς Μυοῦντα κἀκεῖ κατῴκουν, πολλὰ κακὰ πάσχοντες ὑπὸ τῶν Μιλησίων: ἐπολέμουν γὰρ αὐτοῖς διὰ **τὴν ἀποστασίαν**.
— Some of the Ionians who came to dwell at Miletus, falling into contention with the sons of Neleus, departed to Myus, and there took up their situation, where they suffered many injuries from the Milesians; for they made war upon them by reason of **their revolt** from them.
— Greek text — Gregorius N. Bernardakis. *Plutarchi Chaeronensis moralia, vol. II.* Teubner, 1889. Accessed at Perseus Digital Library (perseus.tufts.edu).
— English translation — *Plutarch's Morals.* Translated from the Greek by several hands. Corrected and revised by William W. Goodwin. Little, Brown, and Company, 1874. Accessed at Perseus Digital Library (perseus.tufts.edu).
— The context is the Ionian revolt from Miletus, and Miletus' war against them. Notice the association with στἄσιάζω (stasiazō) *be at odds with*, *quarrel*.
— POLITICAL SEDITION OR REBELLION

Posidonius, Fragments, (Theiler 137, Jakoby 2a, 87, F, 108t)
— Ὅτι ὁ Εὔνους ἐκτὸς βέλους ἐπιστήσας τὴν δύναμιν ἐβλασφήμει τοὺς Ῥωμαίους, ἀποφαινόμενος οὐχ ἑαυτούς, ἀλλ᾽ ἐκείνους εἶναι δραπέτας τῶν κινδύνων. μίμους δὲ ἐξ ἀποστάσεως τοῖς ἔνδον ἐπεδείκνυτο, δι᾽ ὧν οἱ δοῦλοι **τὰς** ἀπὸ τῶν ἰδίων κυρίων **ἀποστασίας** ἐξεθεάτριζον, ὀνειδίζοντες αὐτῶν τὴν ὑπερηφανίαν καὶ τὴν ὑπερβολὴν τῆς εἰς τὸν ὄλεθρον προαγούσης ὕβρεως.
— English translation — Eunus, keeping his army out of the range of weapons, shouted insults at the Romans, saying that it was not his men, but the Romans who were runaways from danger. He put on mimes [by some who were part of the rebellion] for those inside, in

which the slaves depicted how they had **revolted** from their own masters, mocking their masters' arrogance and the excessive cruelty that led to their overthrow.

— Greek text —W. Theiler. *Posidonios: Die Fragmente, vol. 1.* De Gruyter, 1982. Retrieved from Thesaurus Linguae Graecae (stephanus.tlg.uci.edu). Also F. Jakoby. *Die Fragmente der grieschischen Historiker #87.* Brill. Series pub. 1923-1958, repr. 1954-1969). Retrieved from Thesaurus Linguae Graecae (stephanus.tlg.uci.edu).

— The context is the servants revolting from their masters.

— POLITICAL SEDITION OR REBELLION

APPENDIX C
Late Roman Era

Cassius Dio, Roman History, 16 (Zonaras)
— Ἡρρώστησε δὲ μετέπειτα ὁ Σκιπίων, κἂν τούτῳ ἐνεωτέρισαν οἱ Ἴβηρες. στράτευμα γὰρ τοῦ Σκιπίωνος περὶ Σογκρῶνα χειμάζον ἐκινήθη, καὶ πρῴην οὐκ εὐπειθὲς ὄν, οὐ μὴν φανερὰν **ἀποστασίαν** ἐπιδειξάμενον. τότε δ᾽ αἰσθόμενον τὸν Σκιπίωνα κάμνοντα, ἐπεὶ καὶ ἡ μισθοφορὰ αὐτοῖς ἐβραδύνθη, ἀναφανδὸν ἀπέστησαν, καὶ τοὺς χιλιάρχους σφῶν ἀπελάσαντες ὑπάτους ἑαυτοῖς κεχειροτονήκασιν. (Zonaras 9, 10)
— Subsequently Scipio fell sick, and thereupon the Spaniards rebelled. For one of Scipio's armies that was wintering near Sucro had become turbulent; even before this it had shown insubordination, but had not ventured upon open **rebellion**. Now, however, learning of Scipio's illness, and in view of the fact, moreover, that their pay had been delayed, they mutinied outright, drove away the tribunes, and elected consuls for themselves.
— Greek text — U.P. Boissevain. *Cassii Dionis Cocceiani historiarum Romanarum quae supersunt, Vol. 1.* Weidmann, 1895 (repr. 1955). Retrieved from Thesaurus Linguae Graecae (stephanus. tlg.uci.edu). (p. 250).
— English translation — *Dio's Roman History II: Fragments of Books 12-35 and Uncertain Reference.* Translation by Earnest Cary. *Loeb Classical Library 37*, William Heinemann, 1914. Accessed at Loebolus (ryanfb.github.io/loebolus).
— Context is the military revolt against Scipio. Notice the association with νεωτερίζω (neōterizō) *engage in revolution* and οὐκ εὐπειθὲς ὄν (ouk eupeithes on) *not being subject.*
— POLITICAL SEDITION OR REBELLION

Cassius Dio, Roman History, 63.22 (Zonaras)
— Οὐίνδιξ ὁρῶν τοὺς ὁμοφύλους Γαλάτας ὀργῶντας πρὸς **ἀποστασίαν**, δι᾽ ὧν ἐδημηγόρησεν ἠρέθισεν αὐτούς. [Zonaras 11, 13 (p. 41, 10-12 D)].

— Vindex, seeing his fellow Gauls eager for **rebellion**, aroused them by an harangue that he delivered.

— Greek text — U.P. Boissevain. *Cassii Dionis Cocceiani historiarum Romanarum quae supersunt, Vol. 3.* Weidmann, 1901 (repr. 1955). Retrieved from Thesaurus Linguae Graecae (stephanus.tlg.uci.edu).

— English translation — *Dio's Roman History VIII: Books 61-70.* Translation by Earnest Cary. *Loeb Classical Library 176*, William Heinemann, 1925. Accessed at Loebolus (ryanfb.github.io/loebolus).

— Context is the Galatians' (Gauls) frustration with Rome [Nero in particular] and their inclination to revolt.

— POLITICAL SEDITION OR REBELLION

Cassius Dio, Roman History, 63.24.4a (Zonaras)

— τῆς δ᾽ **ἀποστασίας** παρατεινομένης ὁ Οὐίνδιξ ἑαυτὸν ἀπέσφαξε, τῶν μετ᾽ αὐτοῦ στρατιωτῶν κινδυνευσάντων ὑπεραλγήσας καὶ πρὸς τὸ δαιμόνιον ἀγανακτήσας ὅτι τοσούτου πράγματος ὀριγνηθείς, τοῦ τὸν Νέρωνα καθελεῖν καὶ τοὺς Ῥωμαίους ἐλευθερῶσαι, οὐκ ἐξετέλεσεν αὐτό. [Zonaras 11, 13 (p. 41, 19-24 D)].

— As **the revolt** continued, Vindex slew himself; for he felt exceedingly grieved because of the peril of his soldiers and was vexed at Fate because he had not been able to attain his goal in an undertaking of so great magnitude, namely the overthrow of Nero and the liberation of the Romans.

— Greek text — U.P. Boissevain. *Cassii Dionis Cocceiani historiarum Romanarum quae supersunt, Vol. 3.* Weidmann, 1901 (repr. 1955). Retrieved from Thesaurus Linguae Graecae (stephanus. tlg.uci.edu).

— English translation — *Dio's Roman History VIII: Books 61-70.* Translation by Earnest Cary. *Loeb Classical Library 176*, William Heinemann, 1925. Accessed at LacusCurtius (penelope.uchicago.edu/ Thayer/E/Roman/home.html) and at Loebolus (ryanfb.github.io/ loebolus).

— Context is Vindex's sedition against Nero. Notice the association with the verb καθαιρέω (kathaireō) *overthrow*.

— POLITICAL SEDITION OR REBELLION

Cassius Dio, Roman History, 65.8.3 (Zonaras)
— ἐπράχθη δὲ τὰ τῆς ἐπαναστάσεως ὧδε. Οὐεσπασιανὸς ἐν Ἰουδαίᾳ διατρίβων (ὡς γὰρ ἤδη ἱστόρηται, παρὰ Νέρωνος ἦν ἐκεῖσε σταλεὶς διὰ **τὴν** τῶν Ἰουδαίων **ἀποστασίαν**) τῷ μὲν Γάλβᾳ αὐταρχήσαντι τὸν υἱὸν ἔπεμψε Τίτον προσεροῦντα αὐτόν, ἐπανελθόντος δὲ Τίτου ἐπεὶ καθ᾽ ὁδὸν ἐμεμαθήκει τὴν τοῦ Οὐιτελλίου καὶ τοῦ Ὄθωνος ἐπανάστασιν, πρὸς μοναρχίαν καὶ αὐτὸς ὡρμήθη.
[Zonaras 11, 16 (p. 489, 5-11 B) (p. 49, 1–8 D)].
— The matters of the insurrection came about in this manner. Vespasian was stationed in Judaea (as already reported, he had been sent there by Nero because of **the rebellion** of the Jews). When Galba was acting independently, he sent his son Titus to talk to him, but while he was on his journey, he learned about the insurrection of Vitellius and Otho for the monarchy, and he hastened on.
— Greek text — U.P. Boissevain. *Cassii Dionis Cocceiani historiarum Romanarum quae supersunt, Vol. 3.* Weidmann, 1901, (repr. 1955). Retrieved from Thesaurus Linguae Graecae (stephanus. tlg.uci.edu).
— English translation — The translation is my own as I could find none available.
— Context is the rebellion of the Jews against Rome, which ultimately led to the destruction of Jerusalem. Notice the association with ἐπανάστασις (epanastasis) *insurrection*.
— POLITICAL SEDITION OR REBELLION

Galen, On the Constitution of the Art of Medicine, chapter 17, (Kuhn 1.295)
— κοινὸν δ᾽ ἐπὶ πάντων, ὡς οὐχ οἷόν τε διαλυθῆναι τὸ νόσημα, πρὶν ἐν τοῖς ἀπιοῦσι περιττώμασιν ὀφθῆναι πέψεως γνωρίσματα. οὕτω κἂν ὦτα κακῶς ἔχῃ, κἂν ὀφθαλμοὶ, κἂν φάρυγξ, κἂν μόριόν τι ἑλκωθὲν ᾖ, ἢ συλλήβδην εἰπεῖν ἅπαντες πεπασμοὶ ταχυτῆτα κρίσεως καὶ ἀσφάλειαν ὑγιεινὴν σημαίνουσιν. ὠμὰ δὲ καὶ ἄπεπτα, καὶ εἰς κακὰς **ἀποστασίας** ἐκτρεπόμενα, ἀκρισίας, ἢ πόνους, ἢ χρόνους, ἢ θανάτους, ἢ τῶν αὐτῶν ὑποστροφάς.
— Common in all these cases is that it is not possible for the disease to be resolved before the signs of concoction are seen in the outgoing superfluities, if the ears, eyes and pharynx are bad (adversely affected)

or if some part is ulcerated. In short, concoctions mean the swift onset of a crisis and signify certain health, whereas raw and unconcocted [superfluities], which also turn into bad **abscesses**, mean no crisis, pains, chronicity, and death, or a return of the same symptoms.
— Greek text —C.G. Kühn. *Claudii Galeni opera omnia, Vol. 1.* Knobloch, 1821, (repr. Hildesheim, 1964). Retrieved from Thesaurus Linguae Graecae (stephanus.tlg.uci.edu).
— English translation — *Galen: On the Constitution of the Art of Medicine, The Art of Medicine, A Method of Medicine to Glaucon.* Editing and Translation by Ian Johnston. *Loeb Classical Library 523,* Harvard University Press, 2016.
— Used here in the medical sense of *abscess*. Typically, the term used for this sense is ἀπόστᾰσις (apostasis).
— Medical sense of ABSCESS

Galen uses this same sense twelve further times in his medical writings.
— The instances are found at: *De crisibus libri iii*, Kühn 9.563; *De crisibus libri iii*, Kühn 9.616; *De crisibus libri iii*, Kühn 9.754; *De crisibus libri iii*, Kühn 9.757; *In Hippocratis librum primum epidemiarum commentarii iii*, Kühn 17a.139 (2X); *In Hippocratis librum primum epidemiarum commentarii iii*, Kühn 17a.144; *In Hippocratis aphorismos commentarii vii*, Kühn 17b.685; *In Hippocratis prognosticum commentaria iii*, Kühn 18b.100; *In Hippocratis prognosticum commentaria iii*, Kühn 18b.210; *In Hippocratis prognosticum commentaria iii*, Kühn 18b.283; and *In Hippocratis prognosticum commentaria iii*, Kühn 18b.312.

APPENDIX D
OT Translations

SEPTUAGINT

Septuagint, Joshua 22:22 (with context)

— (16) Τάδε λέγει πᾶσα ἡ συναγωγὴ κυρίου Τίς ἡ πλημμέλεια αὕτη, ἣν ἐπλημμελήσατε ἐναντίον τοῦ θεοῦ Ισραηλ, ἀποστραφῆναι σήμερον ἀπὸ κυρίου οἰκοδομήσαντες ὑμῖν ἑαυτοῖς βωμὸν ἀποστάτας ὑμᾶς γενέσθαι ἀπὸ κυρίου; ... (22) Ὁ θεὸς θεός ἐστιν κύριος, καὶ ὁ θεὸς θεὸς κύριος αὐτὸς οἶδεν, καὶ Ισραηλ αὐτὸς γνώσεται· εἰ ἐν **ἀποστασίᾳ** ἐπλημμελήσαμεν ἔναντι τοῦ κυρίου, μὴ ῥύσαιτο ἡμᾶς ἐν ταύτῃ·(23) καὶ εἰ ᾠκοδομήσαμεν αὐτοῖς βωμὸν ὥστε ἀποστῆναι ἀπὸ κυρίου τοῦ θεοῦ ἡμῶν ὥστε ἀναβιβάσαι ἐπ᾽ αὐτὸν θυσίαν ὁλοκαυτωμάτων ἢ ὥστε ποιῆσαι ἐπ᾽ αὐτοῦ θυσίαν σωτηρίου, κύριος ἐκζητήσει.

— (16) Thus says the whole congregation of the Lord, What is this transgression that ye have transgressed before the Lord God of Israel, to turn away today from the Lord, in that ye have built for yourselves an altar, so that ye should be apostates from the Lord? ... (22) God even God, is the Lord, and God even God himself knows, and Israel he shall know. If we have transgressed before the Lord by **apostasy**, let him not deliver us this day. (23) And if we have built to ourselves an altar, so as to apostatize from the Lord our God, so as to offer upon it a sacrifice of whole-burnt offerings, so as to offer upon it a sacrifice of peace-offering, the Lord shall require it.

— Greek text — A. Rahlfs. *Septuaginta, vol. 1, 9th ed.* Württemberg Bible Society, 1935 (repr. 1971). Retrieved from Thesaurus Linguae Graecae (stephanus.tlg.uci.edu).

— English translation — Lancelot Brenton. *The Septuagint Version: Greek and English.* Zondervan, 14th print, 1983, orig. Samuel Bagster and Sons.

— The context is the Transjordanian tribes building an altar for a witness and being misunderstood. Notice the association with πλημμέλεια (plēmmeleia) *discordant note, error.* Notice that

ἀποστῆναι ἀπὸ κυρίου τοῦ θεοῦ ἡμῶν "to apostatize from the Lord our God" and ἀποστραφῆναι σήμερον ἀπὸ κυρίου "to turn away today from the Lord" are used to illustrate ἀποστασία (apostasia).
— RELIGIOUS APOSTASY

Septuagint, 2 Chronicles 29:19, (Paralipomenon ii 29:19) (with context)
— (18) καὶ εἰσῆλθαν ἔσω πρὸς Εζεκιαν τὸν βασιλέα καὶ εἶπαν Ἡγνίσαμεν πάντα τὰ ἐν οἴκῳ κυρίου, τὸ θυσιαστήριον τῆς ὁλοκαυτώσεως καὶ τὰ σκεύη αὐτοῦ καὶ τὴν τράπεζαν τῆς προθέσεως καὶ τὰ σκεύη αὐτῆς·(19) καὶ πάντα τὰ σκεύη, ἃ ἐμίανεν Αχαζ ὁ βασιλεὺς ἐν τῇ βασιλείᾳ αὐτοῦ ἐν **τῇ ἀποστασίᾳ** αὐτοῦ, ἡτοιμάκαμεν καὶ ἡγνίκαμεν, ἰδού ἐστιν ἐναντίον τοῦ θυσιαστηρίου κυρίου.
— (18) And they went in to king Ezekias and said, We have purified all the things in the house of the Lord, the altar of whole-burnt offering, and its vessels, and the table of shew-bread, and its vessels. (19) And all the vessels which king Achaz polluted in his reign, in his **apostacy**, we have prepared and purified. Behold, they are before the altar of the Lord.
— Greek text — A. Rahlfs. *Septuaginta, vol. 1, 9th ed.* Württemberg Bible Society, 1935 (repr. 1971). Retrieved from Thesaurus Linguae Graecae (stephanus.tlg.uci.edu).
— English translation — Lancelot Brenton. *The Septuagint Version: Greek and English.* Zondervan, 14th print, 1983, orig. Samuel Bagster and Sons.
— The context is the apostasy during the reign of Ahaz and the restoration in the reign of Hezekiah. Notice the association with μιαίνω (miainō) *stain, defile, pollute.*
— RELIGIOUS APOSTASY

Septuagint, Jeremiah 2:19 (with context)
— (18) καὶ νῦν τί σοι καὶ τῇ ὁδῷ Αἰγύπτου τοῦ πιεῖν ὕδωρ Γηων; καὶ τί σοι καὶ τῇ ὁδῷ Ἀσσυρίων τοῦ πιεῖν ὕδωρ ποταμῶν; (19) παιδεύσει σε **ἡ ἀποστασία** σου, καὶ ἡ κακία σου ἐλέγξει σε·καὶ γνῶθι καὶ ἰδὲ ὅτι πικρόν σοι τὸ καταλιπεῖν σε ἐμέ, λέγει κύριος ὁ θεός σου·καὶ οὐκ εὐδόκησα ἐπὶ σοί, λέγει κύριος ὁ θεός σου.

— (18) And now what hast thou to do with the way of Egypt to drink the waters of Geon? And what hast thou to do with the way of the Assyrians to drink the water of rivers? (19) Thine **apostasy** shall correct thee, and thy wickedness shall reprove thee. Know then and see that thy forsaking me has been bitter to thee saith the Lord thy God. And I have taken no pleasure in thee saith the Lord thy God.

— Greek text — A. Rahlfs. *Septuaginta, vol. 1, 9th ed.* Württemberg Bible Society, 1935 (repr. 1971). Retrieved from Thesaurus Linguae Graecae (stephanus.tlg.uci.edu).

— English translation — Lancelot Brenton. *The Septuagint Version: Greek and English.* Zondervan, 14th print, 1983, orig. Samuel Bagster and Sons.

— Context is Judah's propensity to look to Egypt and Assyria for help. Notice the association with κακία (kakia) *wickedness, evil* and καταλείπω (kataleipō) *leave, abandon, forsake.*

— RELIGIOUS APOSTASY

AQUILA

In the following passages, I use the Septuagint and the KJV to provide the context in the Greek and the English. The words where Aquila employs ἀποστασία (apostasia) instead of the Septuagint rendering are given in brackets and bold.

Aquila, Deuteronomy 15:9

— πρόσεχε σεαυτῷ μὴ γένηται ῥῆμα κρυπτὸν ἐν τῇ καρδίᾳ σου **[ἀνόμημα]**, λέγων Ἐγγίζει τὸ ἔτος τὸ ἕβδομον, ἔτος τῆς ἀφέσεως, καὶ πονηρεύσηται ὁ ὀφθαλμός σου τῷ ἀδελφῷ σου τῷ ἐπιδεομένῳ, καὶ οὐ δώσεις αὐτῷ, καὶ καταβοήσεται κατὰ σοῦ πρὸς Κύριον, καὶ ἔσται ἐν σοὶ ἁμαρτία μεγάλη.

— Beware that there be not a thought in thy **[wicked]** heart, saying, the seventh year, the year of release, is at hand; and thine eye be evil against thy poor brother, and thou givest him nought; and he cry unto the LORD against thee, and it be sin unto thee.

— Greek text — H.B. Swete. *The Old Testament in Greek: According to the Septuagint.* Cambridge University Press, 1909. Accessed in Logos Bible Software.

— English translation — KJV

— Aquila notes — The Hebrew phrase under consideration is בליעל (bəliyya'al) *Belial, evil, wickedness.* The Septuagint translates it with ἀνόμημα (anonēma) *iniquity, lawlessness.* Aquila translates it with ἀποστασία (apostasia) *apostasy.*

— Heads up for ἀποστασία (apostasia) in Aquila — Edwin Hatch, Henry Redpath. *A Concordance to the Septuagint and the Other Greek Versions of the Old Testament (Including the Apocryphal Books).* Baker Book House, 5th print. 1991, reprod. Clarendon Press, 1897.

— Aquila reading — Fridericus Field. *Origenis hexaplorum quae supersunt; sive veterum interpretum graecorum in totum vetus testamentum fragmenta, Vol. 1, Prolegomena, Genesis - Esther.* Oxford University Press, 1875. Downloaded from Internet Archive (archive.org).

— Other notes — I would translate the phrase under consideration as follows, "lest there be a Belial thought (wicked thought) in your heart."

— Context is ignoring the Bible's teaching on the year of release and doing evil against your brother. Notice the association with חטא (chata), ἁμαρτία (hamartia), *sin.*

— RELIGIOUS APOSTASY

Aquila, Judges 19:22 (with context)

— (22) αὐτοὶ δ' ἀγαθύνοντες καρδίαν αὐτῶν, καὶ ἰδοὺ ἄνδρες τῆς πόλεως υἱοὶ **[παρανόμων]** ἐκύκλωσαν τὴν οἰκίαν κρούοντες ἐπὶ τὴν θύραν, καὶ εἶπον πρὸς τὸν ἄνδρα τὸν κύριον τοῦ οἴκου τὸν πρεσβύτην λέγοντες Ἐξένεγκε τὸν ἄνδρα ὃς εἰσῆλθεν εἰς τὴν οἰκίαν σου, ἵνα γνῶμεν αὐτόν. (23) καὶ ἐξῆλθεν πρὸς αὐτοὺς ὁ ἀνὴρ ὁ κύριος τοῦ οἴκου καὶ εἶπεν Μή, ἀδελφοί, μὴ κακοποιήσητε δὴ μετὰ τὸ εἰσελθεῖν τὸν ἄνδρα τοῦτον εἰς τὴν οἰκίαν μου· μὴ ποιήσητε τὴν ἀφροσύνην ταύτην.

— (22) Now as they were making their hearts merry, behold, the men of the city, certain sons **[of Belial]**, beset the house round about, and beat at the door, and spake to the master of the house, the old man, saying, Bring forth the man that came into thine house, that we may know him. (23) And the man, the master of the house, went out unto

98

them, and said unto them, Nay, my brethren, nay, I pray you, do not so wickedly; seeing that this man is come into mine house, do not this folly.

— Greek text — H.B. Swete. *The Old Testament in Greek: According to the Septuagint*. Cambridge University Press, 1909. Accessed in Logos Bible Software.

— English translation — KJV

— Aquila note — The Hebrew phrase under consideration is בני בליעל (bənē bəliyya'al) *sons of Belial* or *sons of wickedness*. The Septuagint translates this phrase υἱοὶ παρανόμων (huioi paranomōn) *sons of transgression*, Aquila renders it υἱοὶ ἀποστασίας (huioi apostasias) *sons of apostasy*, Theodotion translates it υἱοὶ Βελιάλ (huioi belial) *sons of Belial*, and Symmachus renders it υἱοὶ ἀπαίδευτοι (huioi apaideutoi) *undisciplined* or *uneducated sons*.

— Heads up for ἀποστασία (apostasia) in Aquila — Edwin Hatch, Henry Redpath. *A Concordance to the Septuagint and the Other Greek Versions of the Old Testament (Including the Apocryphal Books)*. Baker Book House, 5th print. 1991, reprod. Clarendon Press, 1897.

— Readings in Aquila, Theodotion, and Symmachus — Fridericus Field. *Origenis hexaplorum quae supersunt; sive veterum interpretum graecorum in totum vetus testamentum fragmenta, Vol. 1, Prolegomena, Genesis - Esther*. Oxford University Press, 1875. Downloaded from Internet Archive (archive.org).

— Context is the Levite who spent the night with an old man in Gibeah, and the men of the city assaulted the old man's house and demanded that he turn over his guest so they could carnally know him. Notice the association with נבלה (nəbilah), ἀφροσύνη (aphrosunē), *foolishness* and with הרע (hara'), κακοποιέω (kakopoieō), *do evil* in verse 23.

— RELIGIOUS APOSTASY

Aquila, 1 Kings 2:12 (1 Samuel 2:12) (with context)

— (12) Καὶ υἱοὶ Ἠλεὶ τοῦ ἱερέως υἱοὶ **[λοιμοί]**, οὐκ εἰδότες τὸν κύριον. (17) καὶ ἦν ἡ ἁμαρτία ἐνώπιον Κυρίου τῶν παιδαρίων μεγάλη σφόδρα, ὅτι ἠθέτουν τὴν θυσίαν Κυρίου.

— (12) Now the sons of Eli were sons of **[Belial]**; they knew not the LORD. (17) Wherefore the sin of the young men was very great before the LORD for men abhorred the offering of the LORD.

— Greek text — H.B. Swete. *The Old Testament in Greek: According to the Septuagint.* Cambridge University Press, 1909. Accessed in Logos Bible Software.

— English translation — KJV

— Aquila note — The Hebrew phrase under consideration is בליעל בני (bənē bəliyya'al) *sons of Belial* or s*ons of wickedness.* The Septuagint translates this phrase υἱοὶ λοιμοὶ (huioi loimoi) *pestilent sons.* Aquila translates it υἱοὶ ἀποστασίας (huioi apostasias) *sons of apostasy.* Symmachus translates it υἱοὶ ἀνυπότακτοι (huioi anupotaktoi) *insubordinate sons.*

— Heads up for ἀποστασία (apostasia) in Aquila — Edwin Hatch, Henry Redpath. *A Concordance to the Septuagint and the Other Greek Versions of the Old Testament (Including the Apocryphal Books).* Baker Book House, 5th print. 1991, reprod. Clarendon Press, 1897.

— Readings in Aquila and Symmachus — Fridericus Field. *Origenis hexaplorum quae supersunt; sive veterum interpretum graecorum in totum vetus testamentum fragmenta, Vol. 1, Prolegomena, Genesis - Esther.* Oxford University Press, 1875. Downloaded from Internet Archive (archive.org).

— Context is the sons of Eli departing from the ways of the Lord by forcibly stealing meat from those offering sacrifice. Notice the association with חטא (chata), ἁμαρτία (hamartia), *sin* and נאץ (naats) *scorn, despise,* ἀθετέω (atheteō) *reject* or *set aside,* here employed of abhorring the offering of the Lord. The foundation of their departure was that they did not know the Lord.

— RELIGIOUS APOSTASY

Aquila, 1 Kings 10:27 (1 Samuel 10:27) (with context)

— (26) καὶ Σαοὺλ ἀπῆλθεν εἰς τὸν οἶκον αὐτοῦ εἰς Γαβαά· καὶ ἐπορεύθησαν υἱοὶ δυνάμεων ὧν ἥψατο Κύριος καρδίας αὐτῶν μετὰ Σαούλ. (27) καὶ υἱοὶ **[λοιμοὶ]** εἶπαν Τίς σώσει ἡμᾶς οὗτος; καὶ ἠτίμασαν αὐτόν, καὶ οὐκ ἤνεγκαν αὐτῷ δῶρα.

— (26) And Saul also went home to Gibeah; and there went with him a band of men, whose hearts God had touched. (27) But the children of **[Belial]** said, How shall this man save us? And they despised him, and brought him no presents. But he held his peace.

— Greek text — H.B. Swete. *The Old Testament in Greek: According to the Septuagint*. Cambridge University Press, 1909. Accessed in Logos Bible Software.

— English translation — KJV

— Aquila note — The Hebrew phrase under consideration is בליעל בני (bənē bəliyya'al *sons of Belial* or *sons of wickedness*. The Septuagint translates this phrase υἱοὶ λοιμοὶ (huioi loimoi) *pestilent sons*. Aquila translates it υἱοὶ ἀποστασίας (huioi apostasias) *sons of apostasy*.

— Heads up for ἀποστασία (apostasia) in Aquila — Edwin Hatch, Henry Redpath. *A Concordance to the Septuagint and the Other Greek Versions of the Old Testament (Including the Apocryphal Books)*. Baker Book House, 5th print. 1991, reprod. Clarendon Press, 1897.

— Aquila reading — Fridericus Field. *Origenis hexaplorum quae supersunt; sive veterum interpretum graecorum in totum vetus testamentum fragmenta, Vol. 1, Prolegomena, Genesis - Esther*. Oxford University Press, 1875. Downloaded from Internet Archive (archive.org).

— Context is Samuel's — indeed God's — selection of Saul as king and the fact that some despised God's chosen man. Notice the association with בזה (bazah), ἀτιμάω (atimaō), *dishonor*, *despise*, here used of despising someone whom God has chosen.

— The context is religious apostasy, which manifested itself in the rejection of the will of God revealed through the prophet.

— RELIGIOUS APOSTASY

Aquila, 1 Kings 25:17 (1 Samuel 25:17)

— καὶ νῦν γνῶθι καὶ ἴδε τί σὺ ποιήσεις, ὅτι συντετέλεσται ἡ κακία εἰς τὸν κύριον ἡμῶν καὶ εἰς τὸν οἶκον αὐτοῦ· καὶ οὗτος υἱὸς **[λοιμὸς]** καὶ οὐκ ἔστιν λαλῆσαι πρὸς αὐτόν.

— Now therefore know and consider what thou wilt do; for evil is determined against our master, and against all his household: for he is such a son of **[Belial]**, that a man cannot speak to him.

— Greek text — H.B. Swete. *The Old Testament in Greek: According to the Septuagint.* Cambridge University Press, 1909. Accessed in Logos Bible Software.

— English translation — KJV

— Aquila note — The Hebrew phrase under consideration is בליעל בן (ben bəliyya'al) son of Belial or wickedness. The Septuagint translates this phrase υἱὸς λοιμός (huios loimos) *pestilent son.* Aquila translates it υἱὸς ἀποστασίας (huios apostasias) *son of apostasy.*

— Heads up for ἀποστασία (apostasia) in Aquila — Edwin Hatch, Henry Redpath. *A Concordance to the Septuagint and the Other Greek Versions of the Old Testament (Including the Apocryphal Books).* Baker Book House, 5th print. 1991, reprod. Clarendon Press, 1897.

— Aquila reading — Fridericus Field. *Origenis hexaplorum quae supersunt; sive veterum interpretum graecorum in totum vetus testamentum fragmenta, Vol. 1, Prolegomena, Genesis - Esther.* Oxford University Press, 1875. Downloaded from Internet Archive (archive.org).

— The context is Nabal's servants warning Abigail about the danger they faced because their wicked master had offended David.

— RELIGIOUS APOSTASY

Aquila, Proverbs 16:27

— ἀνὴρ [ἄφρων] ὀρύσσει ἑαυτῷ κακά, ἐπὶ δὲ τῶν ἑαυτοῦ χειλέων θησαυρίζει πῦρ.

— An [ungodly] man diggeth up evil: and in his lips there is as a burning fire.

— Greek text — H.B. Swete. *The Old Testament in Greek: According to the Septuagint.* Cambridge University Press, 1909. Accessed in Logos Bible Software.

— English translation — KJV

— Aquila note — The Hebrew phrase under consideration is בליעל איש (ish bəliyya'al) *man of Belial* or *wickedness.* The Septuagint translates this phrase ἀνὴρ ἄφρων (anēr aphrōn) *foolish man.* Aquila translates it ἀνὴρ ἀποστασίας (anēr apostasias) *man of apostasy.* Symmachus renders it ἀνὴρ ἀνυπόστατος (anēr anupostatos) *man without foundation* or *ungrounded man.*

— Heads up for ἀποστασία (apostasia) in Aquila — Edwin Hatch, Henry Redpath. *A Concordance to the Septuagint and the Other Greek Versions of the Old Testament (Including the Apocryphal Books)*. Baker Book House, 5th print. 1991, reprod. Clarendon Press, 1897.

— Readings in Aquila and Symmachus — Fridericus Field. *Origenis hexaplorum quae supersunt; sive veterum interpretum graecorum in totum vetus testamentum fragmenta, Vol. 2, Jobus - Malachias. Auctarium et indices*. Oxford University Press, 1875. Downloaded from Internet Archive (archive.org).

— The context is evil men going out of their way to indulge evil. Notice the association with רעה (ra'ah), κακία (kakia) *wickedness*, *evil*.

— RELIGIOUS APOSTASY

Aquila, Nahum 1.11

— ἐκ σοῦ ἐξελεύσεται λογισμὸς κατὰ τοῦ κυρίου, **[πονηρὰ]** βουλευόμενος ἐναντία.

— There is one come out of thee, that imagineth evil against the LORD, a **[wicked]** counselor.

— Greek text — H.B. Swete. *The Old Testament in Greek: According to the Septuagint*. Cambridge University Press, 1909. Accessed in Logos Bible Software.

— English translation — KJV

— Aquila note — The Hebrew phrase under consideration is בליעל יעץ רעה (ra'ah yōēts bəliyya'al) *evil Belial counselor* or *wicked Belial counselor*. The Septuagint translates this phrase πονηρὰ βουλευόμενος ἐναντία (ponēra bouleumenos enantia) *counseling evil opposition*. Aquila translates it κακίαν βουλευόμενος ἀποστασίαν (kakian bouleumenos apostasian) *counseling wicked apostasy*.

— Heads up for ἀποστασία (apostasia) in Aquila — Edwin Hatch, Henry Redpath. *A Concordance to the Septuagint and the Other Greek Versions of the Old Testament (Including the Apocryphal Books)*. Baker Book House, 5th print. 1991, reprod. Clarendon Press, 1897.

— Aquila reading — Fridericus Field. *Origenis hexaplorum quae supersunt; sive veterum interpretum graecorum in totum vetus testamentum fragmenta, Vol. 2, Jobus - Malachias. Auctarium et*

indices. Oxford University Press, 1875. Downloaded from Internet Archive (archive.org).
— Context is a man who offers evil counsel against the Lord.
— RELIGIOUS APOSTASY

THEODOTION

In the following passage, I use the Septuagint and the KJV to provide the context in the Greek and the English. The word where Theodotion employs ἀποστασία (apostasia) is given in brackets and bold.

Theodotion, 3 Kings 20:13, (1 Kings 21:13)

— καὶ ἦλθον δύο ἄνδρες υἱοὶ **[παρανόμων]** καὶ ἐκάθισαν ἐξ ἐναντίας αὐτοῦ καὶ κατεμαρτύρησαν αὐτοῦ λέγοντες Ηὐλόγησεν θεὸν καὶ βασιλέα· καὶ ἐξαγαγέτωσαν αὐτὸν καὶ λιθοβολησάτωσαν αὐτόν, καὶ ἀποθανέτω.

— And there came in two men, children **[of Belial]**, and sat before him: and the men of Belial witnessed against him, even against Naboth, in the presence of the people, saying, Naboth did blaspheme God and the king. Then they carried him forth out of the city, and stoned him with stones, that he died.

— Greek text — H.B. Swete. *The Old Testament in Greek: According to the Septuagint*. Cambridge University Press, 1909. Accessed in Logos Bible Software.

— English translation — KJV

— Theodotion note — The Hebrew phrase under consideration is בְלִיַּעַל בְּנֵי (bənē bəliyya'al) **sons of Belial** or **wickedness**. The Septuagint translates this phrase υἱοὶ παρανόμων (huioi paranomōn) *sons of transgression*, while Theodotion renders it ἄνδρες τῆς ἀποστασίας (andres tēs apostasias) **men of apostasy**.

— Heads up for ἀποστασία (apostasia) in Theodotion — Edwin Hatch, Henry Redpath. *A Concordance to the Septuagint and the Other Greek Versions of the Old Testament (Including the Apocryphal Books)*. Baker Book House, 5th print. 1991, reprod. Clarendon Press, 1897.

— Reading in Theodotion — Fridericus Field. *Origenis hexaplorum quae supersunt; sive veterum interpretum graecorum in totum vetus testamentum fragmenta, Vol. 2, Jobus - Malachias. Auctarium et indices.* Oxford University Press, 1875. Downloaded from Internet Archive (archive.org).

— The context is Jezebel arranging for evil men to bear false witness of blasphemy against Naboth so he would be stoned and Ahab could seize his vineyard.

— RELIGIOUS APOSTASY

APPENDIX E
Jewish Religious Writings

1 Maccabees 2:15 (with context)

— (15) Καὶ ἦλθον οἱ παρὰ τοῦ βασιλέως οἱ καταναγκάζοντες **τὴν ἀποστασίαν** εἰς Μωδεῖν τὴν πόλιν, ἵνα θυσιάσωσιν. (16) καὶ πολλοὶ ἀπὸ Ισραηλ πρὸς αὐτοὺς προσῆλθον·καὶ Ματταθιας καὶ οἱ υἱοὶ αὐτοῦ συνήχθησαν. (17) καὶ ἀπεκρίθησαν οἱ παρὰ τοῦ βασιλέως καὶ εἶπον τῷ Ματταθια λέγοντες Ἄρχων καὶ ἔνδοξος καὶ μέγας εἶ ἐν τῇ πόλει ταύτῃ καὶ ἐστηρισμένος υἱοῖς καὶ ἀδελφοῖς· (18) νῦν πρόσελθε πρῶτος καὶ ποίησον τὸ πρόσταγμα τοῦ βασιλέως, ὡς ἐποίησαν πάντα τὰ ἔθνη καὶ οἱ ἄνδρες Ιουδα καὶ οἱ καταλειφθέντες ἐν Ιερουσαλημ, καὶ ἔσῃ σὺ καὶ οἱ υἱοί σου τῶν φίλων τοῦ βασιλέως, καὶ σὺ καὶ οἱ υἱοί σου δοξασθήσεσθε ἀργυρίῳ καὶ χρυσίῳ καὶ ἀποστολαῖς πολλαῖς. (19) καὶ ἀπεκρίθη Ματταθιας καὶ εἶπεν φωνῇ μεγάλῃ Εἰ πάντα τὰ ἔθνη τὰ ἐν οἴκῳ τῆς βασιλείας τοῦ βασιλέως ἀκούουσιν αὐτοῦ ἀποστῆναι ἕκαστος ἀπὸ λατρείας πατέρων αὐτοῦ καὶ ἡρετίσαντο ἐν ταῖς ἐντολαῖς αὐτοῦ, (20) κἀγὼ καὶ οἱ υἱοί μου καὶ οἱ ἀδελφοί μου πορευσόμεθα ἐν διαθήκῃ πατέρων ἡμῶν·(21) ἵλεως ἡμῖν καταλιπεῖν νόμον καὶ δικαιώματα· (22) τῶν λόγων τοῦ βασιλέως οὐκ ἀκουσόμεθα παρελθεῖν τὴν λατρείαν ἡμῶν δεξιὰν ἢ ἀριστεράν.

— (15) And the king's officers who were enforcing **the apostasy** came to the city of Modin to make them sacrifice. (16) And many from Israel went unto them; but Mattathias and his sons gathered themselves together. (17) Then the king's officers answered and spake unto Mattathias, saying: "A ruler art thou, and illustrious and great in this city, and upheld by sons and brothers. (18) Do thou, therefore, come first, and carry out the king's command, as all the nations have done, and all the people of Judah, and they that have remained in Jerusalem; then shalt thou and thy house be (numbered among) the friends of the king, and thou and thy sons shall be honoured with silver and gold, and with many gifts." (19) Thereupon Mattathias answered and said with a loud voice: "If all the nations that are within the king's dominions obey him by forsaking, every one of them, the worship of their fathers, (20) and have chosen for themselves to follow his commands, yet will I and my sons and my brethren walk in the covenant of our fathers. (21) Heaven forbid that we should forsake the Law and the ordinances; (22) (but) the law of the king we will not obey by departing from our worship either to the right hand or to the left."

— Greek text — A. Rahlfs. *Septuaginta, vol. 1, 9th ed.* Württemberg Bible Society, 1935 (repr. 1971). Retrieved from Thesaurus Linguae Graecae (stephanus.tlg.uci.edu).

— English translation — R. H. Charles (Ed.). *Apocrypha of the Old Testament*. Clarendon Press, 1913.

— Context is the Maccabaean revolt. Mattathias was commanded to offer a sacrifice according to the Roman emperor's demand, and he refused to depart from the Jewish law and worship. Notice that he regarded obeying this command as departing (ἀποστῆναι) from the worship of his fathers and forsaking (καταλιπεῖν) the law.

— RELIGIOUS APOSTASY

Book of Jubilees, fragment z, (10.21 and 10.24)

— (10.21) ἐπὶ γὰρ ἔτη τεσσαράκοντα οἰκοδομήσαντες, ἐκείνου (Νεβρὼδ) μάλιστα παρορμῶντος αὐτοὺς εἰς **ἀποστασίαν** ... (10.24) συνεχύθησαν διαιρεθέντες εἰς πολυγλωσσίαν ὑπὸ τοῦ θεοῦ. ἐκεῖνος (Νεβρὼδ) δὲ ἔμεινεν ἐκεῖ κατοικῶν καὶ μὴ ἀφιστάμενος τοῦ πύργου, βασιλεύων μερικοῦ τινος πλήθους.

— When they had been building for forty years, Nimrod in particular urging them into **apostasy** ... they were confounded, being divided into many tongues by God. Nimrod continued dwelling there and didn't give up on the tower, ruling over a portion of the multitude.

— Greek text – A.M. Denis, *Fragmenta pseudepigraphorum quae supersunt Graeca* [Pseudepigrapha Veteris Testamenti Graece 3. Brill, 1970]. Retrieved from Thesaurus Linguae Graecae (stephanus. tlg.uci.edu).

— English translation – The translation is my own as I could find none available.

— Context is the apostasy of Nimrod when he led the world in rebellion against God to build the tower of Babel.

— RELIGIOUS APOSTASY

APPENDIX F
Church Fathers

(1) Acts of Xanthippe and Polyxena, Section 6

— τούτων λεγομένων ὑπ' αὐτῆς, ἐπανῆλθεν καὶ ὁ Πρόβος ἀπὸ τῆς πλατείας πρὸς τὸ ἄριστον, καὶ ὡς εἶδεν τὸ πρόσωπον αὐτῆς ἠλλοιωμένον ἀπὸ τῶν δακρύων, ἤρξατο ἐκτίλλειν τὰς τρίχας τῆς κεφαλῆς αὐτοῦ, εἰπεῖν δὲ αὐτῇ τέως τι οὐκ ἐτόλμησεν διὰ τὸ μὴ ἐπικερασθῆναι ἐν τῇ θλίψει αὐτῆς ἑτέραν θλῖψιν. πορευθεὶς δὲ ἀνέπεσεν ἐπὶ τῆς κλίνης αὐτοῦ, καὶ στενάξας εἶπεν· Οἴμοι, ὅτι οὔτε κἂν τέκνου παραμυθίαν ἔσχον ἐξ αὐτῆς, ἀλλ' ὀδύνην μόνον ἐπ' ὀδύνην κερδαίνω· οὐ πλήρεις εἰσιν δύο ἐνιαυτοὶ ἀφ' οὗ συνεζεύχθην αὐτῇ, καὶ ἤδη **ἀποστασίαν** μελετᾷ.

— And again she said, God to whom praise is sung by all, give me peace and comfort. As she said these things, Probus also came up from the street to break his fast, and when he saw her countenance altered by tears, he began to pull out the hairs of his head, but he dared not speak to her then so as not to mingle other trouble with her trouble. So he went and fell upon his couch, and said, groaning, Alas, that I had not even the consolation of a child from her, but only acquire grief upon grief. Two years are not yet full since I was wedded to her, and already she meditates **divorce**.

— Greek text — M.R. James. *Apocrypha anecdota* [*Texts and Studies 2.3.*] Cambridge University Press, 1893. Retrieved from Thesaurus Linguae Graecae (stephanus.tlg.uci.edu).

— English translation —W.A. Craigie. *Ante-Nicene Fathers, Vol. 9.* Ed. A. Menzies. Christian Literature Publishing, 1896. Revised and edited for New Advent by Kevin Knight. Accessed at New Advent (newadvent.org/fathers).

— Context is a man grieved because his wife is contemplating divorce.

— DIVORCE

(2) Agathangelus, Ecclesiastical History of Armenia, chapter 51

— Καὶ τῇ ἐπιούσῃ ἡμέρᾳ ἤνεγκαν αὐτὸν ἐπὶ τοῦ βασιλέως. Ἡρώτα δὲ αὐτὸν καὶ ἔλεγεν· «Θαυμάζω, θαυμάζω σφόδρα πῶς ἔμεινας ζῶν καὶ οὐδὲν ἐλογίσω τοὺς πόνους, ἀλλὰ καὶ λαλεῖς. Ἔδει γὰρ σὲ πάλαι τεθνάναι ἀπὸ τοσούτων βασάνων». Ἀποκριθεὶς δὲ ὁ ἅγιος Γρηγόριος εἶπεν· «Οὐκ ἔστιν ἐμὸν τὸ ὑπομεῖναι τῇ ἐμῇ δυνάμει, ἀλλὰ διὰ τῆς ἰσχύος καὶ χάριτος τοῦ ἐμοῦ δεσπότου καὶ τῆς ἐμῆς προαιρέσεως αἰτούσης αὐτόν, ἵνα καὶ σὺ πεῖραν λάβῃς τοῦ δούλου τοῦ Θεοῦ ὅπως γνῷς ὡς οὐδεὶς δύναται ἀποχωρίσαι τῆς ἀγάπης αὐτοῦ τοὺς ἠλπικότας ἐπ' αὐτόν. Αὐτὸς γὰρ δίδωσι δύναμιν καὶ ὑπομονὴν βαστάζειν τὰς θλίψεις τῶν πειρασμῶν ἵνα καταισχυνθῶσιν οἱ ἄνομοι ἐν τῇ ματαιότητι αὐτῶν καὶ ἐν **τῇ** ἀσεβείᾳ καὶ **ἀποστασίᾳ** οἱ κατὰ σὲ ὑπάρχοντες καὶ σταθῶσι μετ' αἰσχύνης ἐν ἡμέρᾳ ἐπισκοπῆς καὶ ἐλεγμοῦ αὐτῶν». Καὶ ἐκέλευσεν περικνημῖδας σιδηρᾶς γενέσθαι εἰς τὰ γόνατα αὐτοῦ καὶ πῆξαι παχεῖς σφῆνας καὶ ἀνακρεμάσαι αὐτὸν ἕως οὗ διασπασθῇ τὰ γόνατα αὐτοῦ.

— And in the following day, they brought him to the king. He inquired of him and said, "I am amazed, I am greatly amazed how you have remained alive and you regard the sufferings as nothing, indeed you are even talking. For you ought to have already been dead from these tortures." Saint Gregory answered, "it is not in my own strength that I am able to endure, but through the strength and grace of my Master and my purposeful petitioning of him that you might take trial of the servant of God and that you might know how that not one of those who hope on him are able to be separated from his love. For he gives strength and patience to bear the tribulations of the trials that the lawless might be ashamed in their vanity and in their ungodliness and **apostasy**, those living like you, and they shall stand with shame in the day of their visitation and reproof." And the king commanded leg irons to be put on his knees and fasten thick wedges and hang him up until his knees separated.

— Greek text — G. Lafontaine. *La version grecque ancienne du livre Arménien d'Agathange* [*Publications de l'institut orientaliste de Louvain 7*]. Louvain-la-Neuve, 1973. Retrieved from Thesaurus Linguae Graecae (stephanus.tlg.uci.edu).

— English translation — The translation is my own by necessity. Robert W. Thomson's translation, *Agathangelos: History of the Armenians*, publ. by State Univ. of New York Press, 1976, is out of print, and used copies are in the $200 range.

— The context is apostasy from the true God in heaven. King Tiridates, Gregory's king, worshipped the pagan goddess Anahid. Notice that apostasy is associated with lawlessness, vanity, and ungodliness.

— RELIGIOUS APOSTASY

(3) Alexander, Invention of the Cross, (Migne, p. 4041)

— Τότε ὅλον τὸ ἔθνος τὴν πρὸς Ῥωμαίους **ἀποστασίαν** εἰργάσαντο. Ἀγρίππας δὲ φυγὰς ᾤχετο ἐπὶ τὴν Ῥώμην. Τότε Νέρων ἐν ὀργῇ καὶ θυμῷ ἔγραψε τῷ τῆς Ἑῴας στρατηγῷ (Οὐεσπασιανὸς δὲ ἦν τὸ τηνικαῦτα) κελεύων αὐτὸν συνεγείρειν πᾶσαν τὴν ὑπ' αὐτῷ στρατιὰν, καταλαμβάνειν τὴν Ἰουδαίαν γῆν, καὶ ἄρδην ἀπολέσαι αὐτήν.

— Then the whole nation fomented **rebellion** against the Romans. Agrippa departed in flight to Rome. Then Nero in wrath and fury wrote to the general of the East (which was Vespasian at that time), commanding him to gather his entire force under him, sieze the entire land of Judah, and utterly destroy it.

— Greek Text — J.P. Migne. *Patrologiae cursus completus (series Graeca 87.3)*. Migne, 1857-1866. Retrieved from Thesaurus Linguae Graecae (stephanus.tlg.uci.edu).

— English translation — The English translation is my own as I could find none readily available.

— Context is the Jewish rebellion against the Romans which began while Nero was emperor and Vespasian was the general over the East.

— POLITICAL SEDITION OR REBELLION

(4) Ammonius, Fragments in John, John 13:27, section 460

— (John 13: 27) Οὐκ αἴτιον **τῆς ἀποστασίας** Ἰούδα τὸ ἐν τάξει εὐλογίας δοθὲν αὐτῷ ψωμίον, ἀλλ' ἡ μετὰ τὸν ἔλεγχον ἀμετάθετος κακία. διὸ καὶ ὡς εἰς ἀθύρωτον πόλιν εἰσεπήδησεν ὁ ἐχθρός

— The cause of Judas' **apostasy** was not the piece of bread given to him in the appointment of blessing, but the unreformable evil after the reproof. Therefore the enemy burst in as into an unwalled city.

110

— Greek text — J. Reuss. *Johannes-Kommentare aus der griechischen Kirche* [*Texte und Untersuchungen 89*]. Akademie Verlag, 1966. Retrieved from Thesaurus Linguae Graecae (stephanus.tlg.uci.edu).
— English translation — The translation is my own as I could find none readily available.
— Context is Judas' apostasy.
— RELIGIOUS APOSTASY

(5) Amphilochius, Against the Heretics (Against False Asceticism), [p. 197 Datema; p. 45 Ficker]
—Καὶ ἄνω δὲ τοῦτο ἐδείξαμεν ὅτι αὐτὸς ὁ Σίμων ἀπὸ τῶν ἀποστόλων ἀποστατήσας ἔλεγεν ἑαυτὸν τὴν δύναμιν τοῦ θεοῦ. Βλέπε πῶς ἐν συντόμῳ εὗρεν ἑαυτῷ ὄνομα δυνάμενον καταπλῆξαι τοὺς νηπιάζοντας. Καὶ ὁ τούτου δὲ μαθητὴς Γέμελλος ἀπόταξιν κηρύξας **ἀποστασίαν** ἐποίησεν.
— We demonstrated above that Simon himself apostatized from the apostles when he called himself the power of God. See how in a short time he made a name for himself, able to amaze the immature (gullible). And his disciple Gemellos commit **apostasy** [too] when he preached [false] renunciation.
— Greek text — C. Datema. *Amphilochii Iconiensis opera*. Brepols, 1978. Retrieved from Thesaurus Linguae Graecae (stephanus. tlg.uci.edu).
— English translation — The English translation is my own. For comparison, see the translation of Andrew Jacobs, professor of Greek at Harvard Divinity School, publ. under Creative Commons Attribution-Non-Commercial 4.0 International, available at andrewjacobs.org/translations/asceticism.
— The context is the apostasy of Simon Magus after he had been baptized and the later apostasy of his disciple Gemellos.
— RELIGIOUS APOSTASY

(6) Amphilochius, Against the Heretics (Against False Ascetiscism), [p. 199 Datema; pgg. 50-51 Ficker]
— Πλὴν ἀλλ᾽ εἰ καὶ Μωϋσῆς πολλάκις τὰ αὐτὰ ἔγραψεν ἀλλαχοῦ μὴ ἀνενεγκεῖν θυσίαν, ἀλλ᾽ Ἱεροβοὰμ ὁ υἱὸς Ναβάτ, ὁ ἀγενής, ὁ μὴ

φοβούμενος τὸν θεόν, ὁ τοῦ νόμου καὶ τῶν προφητῶν ἐπιλαθόμενος, ἀποσχίζει τὸν λαὸν ἀπὸ Ἱερουσαλὴμ καὶ **ἀποστασίαν** διδάξας νομοθέτησεν ἐν αὐτοῖς μὴ ἀναβαίνειν εἰς Ἱερουσαλὴμ μηδὲ ἐκεῖ ἀναφέρειν τὰς λατρείας ἃς προσέταξεν ὁ νόμος, μηδὲ ἐπακούειν τῶν γραφῶν, μηδὲ ὅλως βλέπειν τὸν οἶκον τοῦ θεοῦ, λογιζόμενος τοῦτο, ὅτι ἐὰν ὁ λαὸς ἔρχηται εἰς Ἱερουσαλὴμ καὶ ἐπακούῃ τῶν ἐντολῶν τοῦ θεοῦ, προστεθήσεται τῷ οἴκῳ τοῦ θεοῦ καὶ τιμήσει τὸν ἔννομον βασιλέα καὶ αὐτὸν καταλείψει.

— But even though Moses had many times written the same things, not to offer sacrifice anywhere else, nonetheless ignoble Jeroboam, the son of Nebat, who didn't fear God, who disregarded the Law and the Prophets, separated the people from Jerusalem and taught **apostasy**. He made it a law for them not to go up to Jerusalem, nor offer there the worship which the Law commanded, nor heed the Scriptures, nor even to look upon the house of God at all, figuring that if the people went to Jerusalem and obeyed the commands of God, they would associate themselves with the house of God and honor the lawful king and forsake him.

— Greek text — C. Datema. *Amphilochii Iconiensis opera.* Brepols, 1978. Retrieved from Thesaurus Linguae Graecae (stephanus. tlg.uci.edu).

— English translation — The English translation is my own. For comparison, see the translation of Andrew Jacobs, published under Creative Commons Attribution-Non-Commercial 4.0 International, available at andrewjacobs.org/translations/asceticism.

— The context is Jeroboam, the son of Nebat teaching Israel apostasy. Notice that apostasy is associated with not fearing God, forgetting the law and the prophets, and separating from God's people.

— RELIGIOUS APOSTASY

(7) Amphilochius, Against the Heretics (Against False Asceticism), [p. 202 Datema; p. 55 Ficker]

— Καὶ ὥσπερ ὁ Σαμαρείτης διὰ τοῦ σχήματος **τὴν ἀποστασίαν** ἐποίησε καὶ ὑπὸ τῆς περιτομῆς ἐλέγχεται ὅτι ποτὲ Ἰσραηλίτης ἦν, οὕτως καὶ σύ, εἰ καὶ ἀπέσχισας ἀπὸ τῆς ἐκκλησίας ἢ ἐκαινοτόμησας παράβασιν, ἀλλ' ὅμως ὑπὸ τῆς σφραγίδος ἐλέγχῃ· τὸ γὰρ βάπτισμα ἐν τῇ ἐκκλησίᾳ τοῦ Χριστοῦ ὑπεδέξω.

— Just as the Samaritans caused **apostasy** through their form (customs) and were reproved by circumcision as having once been Israelites, so you will too, if you separate from the church or introduce transgression, but are nonetheless reproved by the seal, for you have received baptism in the church of Christ.

— Greek text — C. Datema. *Amphilochii Iconiensis opera.* Brepols, 1978. Retrieved from Thesaurus Linguae Graecae (stephanus. tlg.uci.edu).

— English translation — The English translation is my own. For comparison, see the translation of Andrew Jacobs, published under Creative Commons Attribution-Non-Commercial 4.0 International, available at andrewjacobs.org/translations/asceticism.

— The context compares schism from the church with the apostasy of the Samaritans. Apostasy is associated with schism and transgression.

— RELIGIOUS APOSTASY

(8) Apophthegms of the Fathers (alphabetical collection), About Gelasius, section 4 — (Migne 65.149)

— Ὁ δὲ ἐκ τῆς τοῦ ἀνδρὸς καταστάσεως, καὶ ἐκ τῆς προσούσης αὐτῷ θεόθεν συνέσεως, τὸ διεφθαρμένον τῆς αὐτοῦ γνώμης καταλαβὼν, οὐ συναπήχθη **τῇ** αὐτοῦ **ἀποστασίᾳ**, ὡς οἱ τότε σχεδὸν πάντες, ἀλλ᾽ ἀξίως αὐτὸν ἀτιμάσας ἀπέπεμψεν.

— When he perceived, from the man's settled conviction and his advanced, God-given understanding, that the man had a corrupt mind, he was not carried away in his **apostasy**, as nearly all were at the time, but sent him away notably shamed.

— Greek text — J.P. Migne. *Patrologiae cursus completus* (*series Graeca 65*). Migne, 1857-1866.

— English translation — Translation is my own as I could find none readily available.

— The context is a meeting between Gelasius and Theodosius when the latter defended the Nestorian error, and the former, perceiving the corruption of Theodosius' mind was not carried away by his apostasy, as were nearly all, but sent him away notably shamed.

— RELIGIOUS APOSTASY

(9) Apophthegms of the Fathers (alphabetical collection), Chapter Ten - Concerning Discernment, Paragraph 96

— Εἶπεν ἀββᾶ Παλλάδιος· Δεῖ τὴν κατὰ Θεὸν ἀσκουμένην ψυχὴν ἢ μανθάνειν πιστῶς ἃ οὐκ οἶδεν ἢ διδάσκειν σαφῶς ἃ ἔγνω. Εἰ δὲ ὁπότερον μὴ βούλεται μανίαν νοσεῖ. Ἀρχὴ γὰρ **ἀποστασίας** διδασκαλίας κόρος καὶ ἀνορεξία λόγου, ὧν ἀεὶ πεινᾷ ἡ ψυχὴ τοῦ φιλοθέου.

— Abbot Galladios said the exercised soul seeking God should be either faithfully learning what he doesn't know or clearly teaching what he does know. The beginning of **apostasy** is feeling satisfied with teaching (you have eaten enough) and lack of appetite for the word, for which things the soul of the God-lover is always hungering.

— Greek text — J.-C. Guy. *Les apophtegmes des pères: Collection systématique, chapitres x-xvi*; [*Sources chrétiennes 474*]. Éditions du Cerf, 2003. Retrieved from Thesaurus Linguae Graecae (stephanus.tlg.uci.edu).

— English translation — Translation is my own as I could find none readily available.

— Context is Galladios' observation on the beginning of apostasy.

— RELIGIOUS APOSTASY

(10) Ariston of Pella, Fragments (cited in Eusebius)

— Καὶ δῆτα τῆς Ἰουδαίων **ἀποστασίας** αὖθις εἰς μέγα καὶ πολὺ προελθούσης, Ῥοῦφος ἐπάρχων τῆς Ἰουδαίας, στρατιωτικῆς αὐτῷ συμμαχίας ὑπὸ βασιλέως πεμφθείσης, ταῖς ἀπονοίαις αὐτῶν ἀφειδῶς χρώμενος ἐπεξήει, μυριάδας ἀθρόως ἀνδρῶν ὁμοῦ καὶ παίδων καὶ γυναικῶν διαφθείρων, πολέμου δὲ νόμῳ τὰς χώρας αὐτῶν ἐξανδραποδιζόμενος.

— The **rebellion** of the Jews once more progressed in character and extent, and Rufuf, the governor of Judaea, when military aid had been sent him by the Emperor, moved out against them, treating their madness without mercy. He destroyed in heaps thousands of men, women, and children, and under the law of war, enslaved their land.

— Greek text and English translation — Eusebius of Caesarea, *Historia ecclesiastica*, with English translation by Kirsopp Lake, *The Loeb Classical Library*; Harvard University Press; William

Heinemann; 1926. Accessed at Perseus Digital Library (perseus. tufts.edu) and Internet Archive Wayback Machine (web.archive.org).
— The context is the rebellion of the Jews against the Romans.
— POLITICAL SEDITION OR REBELLION

(11) Asterius the Sophist, Commentary on the Psalms (31 Homilies), 11.2

— Οὐκέτι αὐλοὶ τῇ χρυσῇ εἰκόνι προσκυνεῖν ἀναγκάζουσιν, ἀλλὰ ψαλμοὶ τῷ θεῷ προσκυνεῖν διδάσκουσιν. Οὐκέτι πόδες πόρνης ὀρχοῦνται Ἰωάννου θάνατον, ἀλλὰ πόδες ἐκκλησίας πατοῦσι τὸν θάνατον. Ἐπαύσαντο **αἱ ἀποστασίαι** καὶ ἤκμασαν αἱ γονυκλισίαι· ἤργησαν αἱ τραγῳδίαι καὶ ἤνθησαν αἱ ψαλμῳδίαι. Οὐκ ἀναβαίνει καπνὸς ἀπὸ κνίσης, ἀλλὰ τῶν προσευχῶν τὸ θυμίαμα·

— No longer do pipes force men to worship the golden image, but Psalms teach us to worship God. No longer do the feet of a harlot dance the death of John (the Baptist), but the feet of the church tread the way of death. **Apostasie**s cease and knee-bending reaches its heights. The Tragedians have ceased, and the Psalmists have blossomed. No longer does smoke ascend from sacrifice, but the incense of prayers ascends.

— Greek text — M. Richard. *Asterii sophistae commentariorum in Psalmos quae supersunt [Symbolae Osloenses fasc. suppl. 16.]* Brogger, 1956. Retrieved from Thesaurus Linguae Graecae (stephanus.tlg.uci.edu).

— English translation — Translation is my own as I could find none readily available.

— The context contrasts apostasy with bending the knee to Christ. It associates apostasy with things like worshiping the golden image and dancing for the death of John the Baptist.
— RELIGIOUS APOSTASY

(12) Asterius the Sophist, Commentary on the Psalms (31 Homilies), 21.16

— «Σῶσόν με, κύριε, ὅτι ἐκλέλοιπεν ὅσιος». Καὶ διὰ τί τὸν ὑπὲρ τῆς ὀγδόης ψάλλων τὴν ἔκλειψιν τῶν ὁσίων ὠλοφύρετο; Ἀλλὰ καὶ σφόδρα καλῶς· ἐπειδὴ γὰρ ἡ ὀγδόη καὶ ἡ τῶν νεκρῶν ἔγερσις βοᾷ τὴν τοῦ κόσμου συντέλειαν, τότε δὲ γίνεται ἡ κόσμου συντέλεια ὅτε οἱ ὅσιοι καὶ οἱ εὐσεβεῖς ἐκλείψουσι. Καὶ τούτου μάρτυς ὁ Χριστὸς εἰπών· Ἄρα «ἐλθὼν ὁ υἱὸς τοῦ ἀνθρώπου εὑρήσει τὴν πίστιν ἐπὶ τῆς γῆς;» Καὶ ὁ ἀπόστολος· Ὅτι «ἐὰν μὴ ἔλθῃ **ἡ ἀποστασία** πρῶτον, ὅτε ἀποστήσονται τῆς πίστεως προσέχοντες πνεύμασι πλάνης καὶ διδασκαλίαις δαιμονίων.»

— «Help, Lord because the godly man has ceased.» And why lament the eclipse of godly men on an eight-stringed harp--Indeed, exceedingly well done? Because the eighth day and the resurrection of the dead testify of the end of the world. Then comes the end of the world when the holy men and the godly men shall cease. And Christ himself is a witness of this, for he said, «when the Son of man comes, shall he find faith on the earth?» And the apostle said, «unless **the apostasy** comes first,» when men shall depart from the faith and give heed to deceiving spirits and doctrines of devils.

— Greet text — M. Richard. *Asterii sophistae commentariorum in Psalmos quae supersunt* [*Symbolae Osloenses fasc. suppl. 16.*] Brogger, 1956. Retrieved from Thesaurus Linguae Graecae (stephanus.tlg.uci.edu).

— English translation — Translation is my own as I could find none readily available.

— Context is the apostasy of the last days. Notice the explanation given: when men shall depart from the faith and adhere to deceiving spirits and demonic teaching.

— RELIGIOUS APOSTASY

(13) Athanasius, Against Sabellian, (Migne 28.101)

— Πῶς δὲ τὰς τοῦ δεσπότου δέξῃ φωνάς, «Ἐγώ,» φησί, «καὶ ὁ Πατὴρ ἕν ἐσμεν;» Καὶ πάλιν περὶ τοῦ Πατρὸς διαλεγόμενος, «Παρ' αὐτοῦ εἰμι,» φησί, «κἀκεῖνος ἐμὲ ἀπέστειλε·» προστίθησι δὲ καὶ τὸ τρίτον· «Ἐγώ,» φησί, «παρακαλέσω τὸν Πατέρα μου, καὶ ἄλλον Παράκλητον δώσει ὑμῖν.» Ὅταν οὖν περὶ μὲν ἑαυτοῦ λέγῃ τὸ, «Ἐγώ,» περὶ δὲ τοῦ Πατρὸς, «Ἐκεῖνος,» περὶ δὲ τοῦ Πνεύματος, «ἄλλος·» πῶς οὐκ **ἀποστασία** σαφὴς ἀρνεῖσθαι τὰ τρία, καὶ μόνον εἶναι λέγειν τὸν φάσκοντα· «Οὐκ εἰμὶ μόνος, ὅτι ὁ πέμψας με Πατὴρ μετ' ἐμοῦ ἐστι.» Χρῆται δὲ καὶ νομικῇ φωνῇ, καὶ διὰ ταύτης δύο παρίστησιν ὄντας αὐτόν τε καὶ τὸν Πατέρα·

116

— How shall you handle the saying of the Master, «I,» he says, «and the Father are one»? And again, conversing on the Father, «am from Him,» he says, «He sent me.» And he adds a third [testimony]. «I,» he says, «shall ask my Father and he shall give you another Comforter.» When he speaks about himself he says «I,» when he speaks of the Father he says «He,» and when he speaks of the Spirit he says «Another.» How is it not **apostasy** to openly deny the trinity and say it only appears to be so? «I am not alone because the Father who sent me is with me.» He uses the legal voice, and through it presents two beings—himself and the Father.

— Greek text — J.P. Migne. *Patrologiae cursus completus* (*series Graeca 28*). Migne, 1857-1866. Retrieved from Thesaurus Linguae Graecae (stephanus.tlg.uci.edu).

— English translation— The translation is my own as I could find none readily available.

— The context is a denial of the trinity, which denial Athanasius regards as apostasy.

— RELIGIOUS APOSTASY

(14) Athanasius, The Decisions of the Synod of Nicea, section 27

— Ἰδοὺ ἡμεῖς μὲν ἐκ πατέρων εἰς πατέρας διαβεβηκέναι τὴν τοιαύτην διάνοιαν ἀποδεικνύομεν, ὑμεῖς δέ, ὦ νέοι Ἰουδαῖοι καὶ τοῦ Καιάφα μαθηταί, τίνας ἄρα τῶν ῥημάτων ὑμῶν ἔχετε δεῖξαι πατέρας; ἀλλ' οὐδένα τῶν φρονίμων καὶ σοφῶν ἂν εἴποιτε· πάντες γὰρ ὑμᾶς ἀποστρέφονται, πλὴν μόνου τοῦ διαβόλου. μόνος γὰρ ὑμῖν οὗτος **τῆς** τοιαύτης **ἀποστασίας** πατὴρ γέγονεν, ὁ καὶ κατὰ τὴν ἀρχὴν ὑμῖν ἐπισπείρας τὴν ἀσέβειαν ταύτην καὶ νῦν λοιδορεῖν τὴν οἰκουμενικὴν σύνοδον πείσας ὑμᾶς, ὅτι μὴ τὰ ὑμέτερα ἀλλὰ ταῦτα γεγράφασιν, ἅπερ οἱ ἀπ' ἀρχῆς αὐτόπται καὶ ὑπηρέται τοῦ λόγου γενόμενοι παρα δεδώκασιν. ἣν γὰρ ἡ σύνοδος ἐγγράφως ὡμολόγησε πίστιν, αὕτη τῆς καθολικῆς ἐκκλησίας ἐστί. ταύτην ἐκδικοῦντες οἱ μακάριοι πατέρες οὕτως ἔγραψαν καὶ κατέκριναν τὴν ἀρειανὴν αἵρεσιν·

— See, we are proving that this view has been transmitted from father to father; but you, O modern Jews and disciples of Caiaphas, how many fathers can you assign to your phrases? Not one of the understanding and wise; for all abhor you, but the devil alone ; none but he is your father in this **apostasy**, who both in the beginning sowed you with the seed of this irreligion, and now persuades you to slander the Ecumenical Council , for committing to writing, not your doctrines, but that which from the beginning those who were eye-witnesses and ministers of the Word have handed down to us. For the faith which the Council has confessed in writing, that is the faith of the Catholic Church; to assert this, the blessed Fathers so expressed themselves while condemning the Arian heresy.

— Greek text — H.G. Opitz, *Athanasius Werke*, vol. 2.1. De Gruyter, 1940. Retrieved from Thesaurus Linguae Graecae (stephanus. tlg.uci.edu).

— English translation — John Henry Newman. *Nicene and Post-Nicene Fathers, Second Series, Vol. 4*. Ed. Philip Schaff and H. Wace, Christian Literature Publishing, 1892. Revised and edited for New Advent by Kevin Knight. Accessed at New Advent (newadvent. org/fathers).

— The context is the Arian heresy which Athanasius attributes to Satan.

— RELIGIOUS APOSTASY

(15) Athanasius, Deposition of Arius, section 1, [The Decisions of the Synod of Nicea, section 35, Opitz]

— Ἑνὸς σώματος ὄντος τῆς καθολικῆς ἐκκλησίας ἐντολῆς τε οὔσης ἐν ταῖς θείαις γραφαῖς τηρεῖν τὸν σύνδεσμον τῆς ὁμονοίας καὶ εἰρήνης ἀκόλουθόν ἐστι γράφειν ἡμᾶς καὶ σημαίνειν ἀλλήλοις τὰ παρ' ἑκάστου γινόμενα, ἵνα εἴτε πάσχει εἴτε χαίρει ἓν μέλος ἢ συμπάσχωμεν ἢ συγχαίρωμεν ἀλλήλοις. ἐν τῇ ἡμετέρᾳ τοίνυν παροικίᾳ ἐξῆλθον νῦν ἄνδρες παράνομοι καὶ χριστομάχοι διδάσκοντες **ἀποστασίαν**, ἣν εἰκότως ἄν τις πρόδρομον τοῦ ἀντιχρίστου ὑπονοήσειε καὶ καλέσειεν.

— As there is one body of the Catholic Church, and a command is given us in the sacred Scriptures to preserve the bond of unity and peace, it is agreeable thereto that we should write and signify to one another whatever is done by each of us individually; so that whether one member suffer or rejoice, we may either suffer or rejoice with one another. Now there are gone forth in this diocese, at this time, certain lawless men, enemies of Christ, teaching an **apostasy**, which one may justly suspect and designate as a forerunner of Antichrist.

— Greek text — H.G. Opitz, *Athanasius Werke*, vol. 2.1. De Gruyter, 1940. Retrieved from Thesaurus Linguae Graecae (stephanus. tlg.uci.edu).

— English translation — M. Atkinson and A. Robertson, *Nicene and Post-Nicene Fathers, Second Series, Vol. 4.* Ed. Philip Schaff and H. Wace, Christian Literature Publishing, 1892.

— NOTE. The *Deposition of Arius* was appended to the *Definition of Nicaea* in the collected works of Athanasius, but it stands on its own in *Nicene and Post-Nicene Fathers, Second Series, Vol. 4.*

— The context is the Arians, who are regarded as lawless, Christ-fighting men teaching apostasy, rightly called forerunners of the antichrist.

— RELIGIOUS APOSTASY

(16) Athanasius, Disputation Against Arius, (Migne 28.500)

— Ἀθ. εἶπεν· Ἀκμὴν ἔτι ἔνδυμα φορεῖς τῆς πλάνης συνευγνωμονήσαις ῥίψεις καὶ αὐτὸ πρὸς τοῖς λοιποῖς **τῆς ἀποστασίας** πράγμασι, καὶ δυνησόμεθα ἐπὶ τὸ αὐτὸ εὔξασθαι.

— Athanasius said, even now, you are still wearing the garment of deception. Cast aside your sympathies for such things and ditto for your other **apostate** practices, and we shall be able to pray on common ground.

— Greek text — J.P. Migne. *Patrologiae cursus completus* (*series Graeca 28*). Migne, 1857-1866. Retrieved from Thesaurus Linguae Graecae (stephanus.tlg.uci.edu).

— English translation — The translation is my own as I could find none readily available.

— The context is apostate teachings and practices of the Arius and his disciples.

— RELIGIOUS APOSTASY

(17) Athanasius, Expositions in Psalms, 18:17, (Migne 27.113)

— «Ῥύσεταί με ἐκ τῶν ἐχθρῶν μου δυνατῶν, καὶ ἐκ τῶν μισούντων με.» Εἰς τὰ πεπραγμένα αὐτῷ ἐπὶ τῇ ἁμαρτίᾳ καὶ τῇ μετανοίᾳ μετέβη. Ὃ δὲ λέγει τοιοῦτόν ἐστιν. Ἤδη μὲν, τῆς ἐξομολογήσεώς μου ἐπακούσας ὁ Κύριος, γέγονέ μοι ἀντιστήριγμα, μέλλοντός μου περιτρέπεσθαι καὶ μέγα πτῶμα ὑπομένειν, εἰ μετὰ τὴν ἁμαρτίαν εἰς παντελῇ ἐξέπιπτον **ἀποστασίαν**. Πλὴν ἀλλὰ καὶ παντελῶς ῥύσεταί με διδοὺς ἄφεσιν τῆς ἁμαρτίας κατὰ τὸν προφητευόμενον καιρὸν τῆς αὐτοῦ παρουσίας, καὶ τοῦτο ποιήσει εὐεργετῶν με ὁ Κύριος, Ὅτι ἠθέλησέ με. Εἰ μὴ γὰρ ἠθέλησέ με, οὐκ ἂν τὸν προφήτην αὐτοῦ πρὸς μὲ ἀπέστειλε.

— «Deliver me from my mighty enemies and those who hate me.» This regards the things that happened to him when he passed from sin to repentance. This is what he says. Now the Lord has heard my confession. He has become my support when I am about to turn from and survive a great fall, lest after the sin I might fall into complete **apostasy**. Moreover, he shall completely deliver me and grant me forgiveness of sin in the prophesied time of his coming, and this he shall do blessing me because he chose me. For if he hadn't chosen me, he would not have sent his prophet to me.

— Greek text — J.P. Migne. *Patrologiae cursus completus* (*series Graeca 27*). Migne, 1857-1866. Retrieved from Thesaurus Linguae Graecae (stephanus.tlg.uci.edu).

— English translation — The translation is my own as I could find none readily available.

— The context is David seeking God for help lest after sin he falls into everlasting apostasy. Athanasius regards apostasy as a step beyond backsliding.

— RELIGIOUS APOSTASY

(18) Athanasius, History of Arianism, section 77

— Δεινὰ μὲν οὖν καὶ πέρα δεινῶν τὰ τοιαῦτα, πρέπουσα δὲ πρᾶξις ὅμως τῷ σχηματιζομένῳ τὰ τοῦ ἀντιχρίστου. τίς γὰρ βλέπων αὐτὸν ἐξάρχοντα τῶν νομιζομένων ἐπισκόπων καὶ προκαθήμενον τῶν ἐκκλησιαστικῶν κρίσεων οὐκ ἀκολούθως ἂν εἴποι τοῦτ' εἶναι τὸ διὰ τοῦ Δανιὴλ εἰρημένον «βδέλυγμα τῆς ἐρημώσεως»; τὸν γὰρ Χριστιανισμὸν περιβεβλημένος καὶ εἰς τοὺς ἁγίους τόπους εἰσερχόμενος ἑστηκώς τε ἐν αὐτοῖς ἐρημοῖ τὰς ἐκκλησίας, παραλύων τοὺς τούτων κανόνας καὶ τὰ ἴδια κρατεῖν βιαζόμενος. ἆρα τίς ἔτι τολμᾷ λέγειν τὸν καιρὸν τοῦτον εἰρηνικὸν εἶναι Χριστιανῶν καὶ οὐ μᾶλλον διωγμόν; καὶ διωγμόν, οἷος οὔτε πώποτε γέγονεν οὔτε τάχα τις ποιήσει ποτὲ τοιοῦτον εἰ μὴ ἄρα «ὁ υἱὸς τῆς ἀνομίας», ὃν οἱ χριστομάχοι δεικνύουσιν ἀναζωγραφοῦντες ἐν αὐτοῖς ἤδη. διὸ καὶ μάλιστα προσήκει νήφειν, μήπως ἡ αἵρεσις αὕτη πολλὴν ἀναισχυντίαν ἔχουσα καὶ διαχυνομένη ὡς «ἰὸς κεράστου», καθὼς ἐν ταῖς Παροιμίαις γέγραπται, διδάσκουσά τε κατὰ τοῦ σωτῆρος φρονεῖν, αὕτη ἂν εἴη «**ἡ ἀποστασία**», μεθ᾽ ἣν ἐκεῖνος ἀποκαλυφθήσεται πάντως ἔχων τὸν πρόδρομον ἑαυτοῦ Κωνστάντιον.

— Terrible indeed, and worse than terrible are such proceedings; yet conduct suitable to him who assumes the character of Antichrist. Who that beheld him taking the lead of his pretended Bishops, and presiding in Ecclesiastical causes, would not justly exclaim that this was «the abomination of desolation» spoken of by Daniel? For having put on the profession of Christianity, and entering into the holy places, and standing therein, he lays waste the Churches, transgressing their Canons, and enforcing the observance of his own decrees. Will any one now venture to say that this is a peaceful time with Christians, and not a time of persecution? A persecution indeed, such as never arose before, and such as no one perhaps will again stir up, except «the son of lawlessness», do these enemies of Christ exhibit, who already present a picture of him in their own persons. Wherefore it especially behoves us to be sober, lest this heresy which has reached such a height of impudence, and has diffused itself abroad like the «poison of an adder» as it is written in the Proverbs, and which teaches doctrines contrary to the Saviour; lest, I say, this be that «**falling away**», after which He shall be revealed, of whom Constantius is surely the forerunner.

— Greek text — H.G. Opitz, *Athanasius Werke, vol. 2.1.* De Gruyter, 1940. Retrieved from Thesaurus Linguae Graecae (stephanus. tlg.uci.edu).

— English translation — M. Atkinson and A. Robertson, *Nicene and Post-Nicene Fathers, Second Series, Vol. 4*. Ed. Philip Schaff and H. Wace, Christian Literature Publishing, 1892.

— The context is Athanasius pointing out the likeness of Constantine to the antichrist and regarding him as the forerunner of the same. Notice that he correlates the diffusion of heresy (ἡ αἵρεσις) through Constantine with the falling away (ἡ ἀποστασία) in the days of the antichrist. This implies that he sees the apostasy as sponsored and caused by the antichrist.

— RELIGIOUS APOSTASY

(19) Athanasius, On the Holy Trinity, dialogue 1.3.5, (Migne 28.1124)

— Ἀνόμ. Ποῦ γέγραπται, ὅτι χαρακτήρ ἐστι τῆς ὑποστάσεως ὁ Υἱός; Ὀρθ. Παρὰ τῷ ἀποστόλῳ Παύλῳ ἐν τῇ πρὸς Ἑβραίους. Ἀνόμ. Οὐκ ἐκκλησιάζεται; Ὀρθ. Ἀφ' οὗ κατηγγέλη τὸ Εὐαγγέλιον Χριστοῦ, Παύλου εἶναι πεπίστευται ἡ ἐπιστολή· καὶ μετ' αὐτῆς εἰσιν ἐπιστολαὶ ιδ΄ αἱ πᾶσαι τοῦ Παύλου. Ἀνόμ. Ἀνέγνως, ὅτι ἐν μὲν πάσαις τὸ ὄνομα αὐτοῦ ἐμφέρεται, ἐν δὲ ταύτῃ οὔ; Ὀρθ. Ὅτι Ἑβραίοις ἔγραφεν· ἦσαν δὲ κατηχηθέντες περὶ αὐτοῦ, ὅτι **ἀποστασίαν** διδάσκει· καὶ ἵνα μὴ, σειριάσαντες αὐτοῦ τὸ ὄνομα, κλείσωσι τὴν ἀκοήν· διὰ τοῦτο ἀπὸ τῶν πατέρων ἤρξατο, λέγων· «Πολυμερῶς καὶ πολυτρόπως πάλαι ὁ Θεὸς λαλήσας τοῖς πατράσιν ἡμῶν ἐν τοῖς προφήταις, ἐπ' ἐσχάτου τῶν ἡμερῶν ἐλάλησεν ἡμῖν ἐν Υἱῷ.»

— Contrary— Where is it written that the Son is the exact image of the essence [of God]? Orthodoxy—In the apostle Paul in his letter to the Hebrews. Contrary—It is not approved (proved) by the church. Orthodoxy—From the fact that the gospel of Christ is proclaimed, the epistle is believed to be from Paul. And with it, there are fourteen further epistles which are all from Paul. Contrary—It is readily seen that his name appears in all his letters, but in this one [Hebrews] it doesn't appear. Orthodoxy—Because it was written to the Hebrews. They had all been instructed about him that he taught **apostasy**, and therefore [his name was not appended] lest they stop their ears when they made a connection with his name. Therefore he began from the fathers saying, «In various times and various ways God spoke in time past to the fathers by the prophets, but in these last days he has spoken to us by His Son.»

— Greek text — J.P. Migne. *Patrologiae cursus completus* (*series Graeca 28*). Migne, 1857-1866. Retrieved from Thesaurus Linguae Graecae (stephanus.tlg.uci.edu).

— English translation — The translation is my own as I could find none readily available.

— The context is the observation that the Jews had been instructed about Paul that he taught apostasy from Moses, and therefore Paul did not append his name to the epistle to the Hebrews lest they be stumbled at the gate.

— RELIGIOUS APOSTASY

(20) Athanasius, Synopsis of Sacred Scripture, (Migne 28.380)

— Περὶ αὐτεξουσίου, ὅτι περὶ **ἀποστασίας** μὴ αἰτιῶ τὸν Κύριον· πάντα γάρ σοι παρέθετο.

— Concerning free will, that we can't blame the Lord for **apostasy**, for all things [necessary for living right] have been given.

— Greek text — J.P. Migne. *Patrologiae cursus completus (series Graeca 28)*. Migne, 1857-1866. Retrieved from Thesaurus Linguae Graecae (stephanus.tlg.uci.edu).

— English translation — The translation is my own as I could find none readily available.

— The context is the relationship between free will and apostasy.

— RELIGIOUS APOSTASY

(21) Athanasius, Synopsis of Sacred Scripture, (Migne 28.424)

— ἔπειτα δὲ καὶ περὶ τῆς παρουσίας τοῦ Σωτῆρος διδάσκει, «μηδενὶ αὐτοὺς πείθεσθαι, μηδὲ θροεῖσθαι, μήτε διὰ Πνεύματος, μήτε ὡς αὐτοῦ γράψαντος, μηδὲ ὅλως νομίζειν ἤδη παρεῖναι αὐτὴν, μηδὲ πρότερον ἔσεσθαι ταύτην, ἐὰν μὴ **ἡ ἀποστασία** πρότερον ἔλθῃ, καὶ μετ᾽ αὐτὴν ὁ Ἀντίχριστος, ὁ υἱὸς τῆς ἀπωλείας, οὗ τὴν παρουσίαν ἐν σημείοις καὶ τέρασι ψεύδους κατ᾽ ἐνέργειαν τοῦ Σατανᾶ ἔσεσθαι σημαίνει.»

— Later he teaches concerning the coming of the Saviour «not to let anyone persuade them nor disturb them, not through the Spirit, not as written from him, absolutely not to suppose that the coming is already here, nor that this day will come first, for it shall not come unless **the apostasy** comes first and with it the antichrist, the son of perdition, whose coming shall be signified with lying signs and wonders in the power of Satan.»

— Greek text — J.P. Migne. *Patrologiae cursus completus (series Graeca 28)*. Migne, 1857-1866. Retrieved from Thesaurus Linguae Graecae (stephanus.tlg.uci.edu).

— English translation — The translation is my own as I could find none readily available.

— The context is essentially a paraphrase of the first portion of 2 Thessalonians 2 with some interpretive remarks. Notice that he associates the apostasy with the antichrist.

— RELIGIOUS APOSTASY

(22) Athanasius, Life of Anthony, section 68, (Migne 26.940)

— Καὶ τῇ πίστει δὲ πάνυ θαυμαστὸς ἦν καὶ εὐσεβής. Οὔτε γὰρ Μελετιανοῖς τοῖς σχισματικοῖς ποτε κεκοινώνηκεν, εἰδὼς αὐτῶν τὴν ἐξ ἀρχῆς πονηρίαν καὶ **ἀποστασίαν**. Οὔτε Μανιχαίοις ἢ ἄλλοις τισὶν αἱρετικοῖς ὡμίλησε φιλικὰ ἢ μόνον ἄχρι νουθεσίας τῆς εἰς εὐσέβειαν μεταβολῆς,

— And he was altogether wonderful in faith and religious, for he never held communion with the Meletian schismatics, knowing their wickedness and **apostasy** from the beginning; nor had he friendly dealings with the Manichæans or any other heretics; or, if he had, only as far as advice that they should change to piety.

— Greek text — G.J.M. Bartelink, *Athanase d'Alexandrie, Vie d'Antoine; [Sources chrétiennes 400]*. Éditions du Cerf, 2004.

— English translation — H. Ellershaw, *Nicene and Post-Nicene Fathers, Second Series*, Vol. 4. Ed. by P. Schaff and H. Wace, Christian Literature Publishing, 1892. Revised and edited for New Advent by Kevin Knight. Accessed at New Advent (newadvent. org/fathers).

— Context is the Meletian, Manichaean, and other heresies which were characterized by bad doctrine and apostasy.

— RELIGIOUS APOSTASY

(23) Basil of Caesarea, The Great Asceticon (Περὶ τάξεως καὶ ἀκολουθίας), Question 2, (Migne 31.916)

— Ὁ γὰρ νῦν ἀπατῶν ἡμᾶς, καὶ διὰ τῶν κοσμικῶν δελεασμάτων λήθην ἐμποιεῖν ἡμῖν τοῦ εὐεργέτου μηχανῇ πάσῃ σπουδάζων, ἐπ' ὀλέθρῳ τῶν ψυχῶν ἡμῶν ἐναλλόμενος ἡμῖν, καὶ ἐπεμβαίνων, εἰς ὀνειδισμὸν τότε προσοίσει τῷ Κυρίῳ τὴν ἡμετέραν καταφρόνησιν, καὶ ἐγκαυχήσεται τῇ ἀπειθείᾳ καὶ **ἀποστασίᾳ** ἡμῶν· ὅς γε οὔτε κτίσας ἡμᾶς, οὔτε ἀποθανὼν ὑπὲρ ἡμῶν, ἀλλ' ὅμως ἔσχεν ἡμᾶς ἀκολουθοῦντας αὐτῷ ἐν τῇ ἀπειθείᾳ καὶ ἐν τῇ ἀμελείᾳ τῶν ἐντολῶν τοῦ Θεοῦ.

— For he that now deceives us, and does his best through worldly bait in every conceived kind to make us forget our benefactor, and lunges after the destruction of our souls, and attacks [us] that he might with reproach present to the Lord our contemptible failures and boast (glory in) our insubordination and **departure**, who neither created us, nor died for us, but only wants us to follow him in unbelief and disregard for the commands of God.

— Greek text — J.P. Migne. *Patrologiae cursus completus* (*series Graeca 31*). Migne, 1857-1866. Retrieved from Thesaurus Linguae Graecae (stephanus.tlg.uci.edu).

— English translation — The translation is my own.

— The context associates apostasy with unbelief and following Satan rather than the one who created us and died for us.

— RELIGIOUS APOSTASY

(24) Basil of Caesarea, The Great Asceticon (Περὶ τάξεως καὶ ἀκολουθίας), Question 15, (Migne 31.957)

— Ὅπως δὲ φοβερὸν ἡ ἀκρασία, καὶ ὁ Ἀπόστολος ἔδειξεν, ἐν τοῖς ἰδιώμασι **τῆς ἀποστασίας** καταριθμήσας αὐτὴν, καὶ εἰπών·«Ἐν ἐσχάταις ἡμέραις ἐνστήσονται καιροὶ χαλεποί. Ἔσονται γὰρ ἄνθρωποι φίλαυτοι.» Καὶ πλείονα ἀπαριθμησάμενος τῆς κακίας εἴδη, ἐπήγαγε· «Διάβολοι, ἀκρατεῖς.»

— That there would be a terrible lack of self-control the apostle also showed when he enumerated it with the characteristics of **apostasy** and said, «In the last days perilous times will come, for men will be lovers of themselves.» And after he had enumerated many forms of evil, he appended «slanderers, without self-control.»

— Greek text — J.P. Migne. *Patrologiae cursus completus* (*series Graeca 31*). Migne, 1857-1866. Retrieved from Thesaurus Linguae Graecae (stephanus.tlg.uci.edu).

— English translation — The translation is my own.

— The context here is the perilous times that shall happen in the last days. Note that Paul's enumeration of last days' evils is expressly called expressions of apostasy. Note that the same list is called "forms of evil."

— RELIGIOUS APOSTASY

(25) Basil of Caesarea, The Great Asceticon (Περὶ τάξεως καὶ ἀκολουθίας), Question 42, (Migne 31.1025)

— καθόσον ἐπ' ἄνθρωπον τὴν ἐλπίδα ἔθετο, κίνδυνον ἔχει ὑποπεσεῖν τῇ κατάρα τῇ λεγούσῃ·«Ἐπικατάρατος ἄνθρωπος ὃς τὴν ἐλπίδα ἔχει ἐπ' ἄνθρωπον, καὶ στηρίξει σάρκα βραχίονος αὐτοῦ, καὶ ἀπὸ Κυρίου

ἀποσταίη ἡ ψυχὴ αὐτοῦ» τοῦ λόγου διὰ μὲν τοῦ, «Ὃς τὴν ἐλπίδα ἔχει
ἐπ' ἄνθρωπον,» τῷ ἑτέρῳ ἐπελπίζειν·διὰ δὲ τοῦ, «Καὶ στηρίξει σάρκα
βραχίονος αὐτοῦ», τὸ ἐφ' ἑαυτῷ πεποιθέναι ἀπαγορεύοντος·
ἑκάτερον δὲ αὐτῶν **ἀποστασίαν** ἀπὸ Κυρίου ὀνομάζοντος ... ὅτι τὸ
ἑαυτῷ ἢ ἄλλῳ τινὶ ἐπελπίζειν ἀποστῆναί ἐστιν ἀπὸ Κυρίου.

— To the degree that a man places his trust in man, he is in danger of
falling under the curse which says, «Cursed is the man who puts his
trust in man and depends on the flesh of his arm, and his soul departs
from the Lord.» The first expression, «who has his hope in man» is
pinning his hope on someone else. The second expression, «He leans
on the flesh of his own arm,» is being confident in useless (worthless)
self. Each one is called **apostas**y from the Lord ... because hoping in
oneself or in another is departing from the Lord.

— Greek text — J.P. Migne. *Patrologiae cursus completus* (*series
Graeca 31*). Migne, 1857-1866. Retrieved from Thesaurus Linguae
Graecae (stephanus.tlg.uci.edu).

— English translation — The translation is my own.

— The context explains that putting your hope in yourself or in
another man is apostasy from the Lord.

— RELIGIOUS APOSTASY

(26) Basil of Caesaria, Ascetic Constitutions, Chapter 21, (Migne 31.1397)

— Σὺ δὲ προφασίζῃ τὰς τῶν ἀδελφῶν ὀλιγωρίας ἢ οὔσας, ἢ παρὰ σοῦ
πλαττομένας, **τὴν ἀποστασίαν** ἐννοῶν, καὶ τὴν ἀθέτησιν τοῦ ἁγίου
Πνεύματος μηχανώμενος, καὶ τῆς ἑαυτοῦ πονηρίας καὶ τῶν πόνων
τῶν ὑπὲρ ἀρετῆς ὀκνηρίας παραπέτασμα τὴν τῶν ἀδελφῶν ἐργάζῃ
διαβολήν.

— But you allege your brothers' neglect or (low spiritual) state, or
fabricated (failures) of your own (imagination), suspecting them of
apostasy, and (mentally) contriving their setting aside (resisting) of
the Holy Spirit, and regard their labors on behalf of virtue as a cloak
over their evil and laziness, you are framing slander against your
brother.

— Greek text — J.P. Migne. *Patrologiae cursus completus* (*series
Graeca 31*). Migne, 1857-1866. Retrieved from Thesaurus Linguae
Graecae (stephanus.tlg.uci.edu).

— English translation — The English translation is my own.
— The context is falsely accusing your brethren of serious departures from the faith.
— RELIGIOUS APOSTASY

(27) Basil of Caesaria, Ascetic Constitutions, Chapter 33, (Migne 31.1425)

— Εἰ γὰρ ἔνθα δύο ἢ τρεῖς συνηγμένοι εἰσὶν ἐπὶ τῷ ὀνόματι τοῦ Χριστοῦ, ἐν μέσῳ αὐτῶν ἐστι, πολλῷ μᾶλλον ἔνθα πολὺ πλέον καὶ πολυανθρωπότερον ἄθροισμα. Ἡ τοίνυν οὐδὲν ἐλλείψει τῶν ἀναγκαίων, Χριστοῦ παρόντος ἡμῖν, εἴπερ μηδὲ τοῖς Ἰσραηλίταις ἐν τῇ ἐρήμῳ τῶν χρησίμων ἔνδεια γέγονεν· ἢ εἰ καὶ λείψειε πρὸς δοκιμασίαν ἡμῶν, βέλτιον ἐνδεῶς ἔχειν καὶ εἶναι μετὰ Χριστοῦ, ἢ δίχα τῆς ἐκείνου κοινωνίας πᾶσι τοῖς κατὰ τὸν βίον πλουτεῖν. Οὐ μέχρι τούτου δὲ τὴν βλάβην ἡ τοιαύτη κτῆσις ἵστησιν, ἀλλὰ πορρωτέρω προάγει. Ὁ γὰρ ἴδιόν τι ἔχειν ἐσπουδακὼς οὐδὲν ἕτερον ἢ χωρισμὸν καὶ **ἀποστασίαν** μελετᾷ.

— For if where two or three are gathered in the name of Christ, he is in the midst, how much more so where there is an exceedingly great and numerous gathering? Therefore nothing shall lack of necessities when Christ is with us, since no lack of necessities happened with the Israelites in the wilderness. And even if something is lacking for our testing, it is better to have lack and to be with Christ than to be wealthy in all the things of life while separate from fellowship with him. The possession of such wealth brings pain, however, that does not stop with this (breach of fellowship) but goes much farther. For he that diligently pursues having his own great stuff, cares for nothing other than separation (from Christ) and **departure** (from the things of Christ).

— Greek text — J.P. Migne. *Patrologiae cursus completus* (*series Graeca 31*). Migne, 1857-1866. Retrieved from Thesaurus Linguae Graecae (stephanus.tlg.uci.edu).
— English translation — The English translation is my own.
— The context elaborates on the perils of pursuing this world's weath, which can lead to separation from Christ and apostasy.
— RELIGIOUS APOSTASY

(28) Basil of Caesaria, On Baptism, Question 10, (Migne 31.1617)

— Πρῶτον μὲν ἡγοῦμαι ἀναγκαῖον εἶναι γνῶναι, τί ἐστι σκάνδαλον· ἔπειτα δὲ καὶ τὴν διαφορὰν τῶν σκανδαλιζόντων, καὶ δι' ὧν σκανδαλίζουσι· καὶ οὕτω γνωρίσαι τό τε ἀκίνδυνον καὶ τὸ ἐπικίνδυνον. Σκάνδαλον μὲν οὖν ἐστιν, ὡς ἐγὼ λογίζομαι ἐκ τῶν γεγραμμένων ὁδηγούμενος, πᾶν τὸ ἤτοι εἰς **ἀποστασίαν** τινὰ τῆς κατ' εὐσέβειαν ἀληθείας ἄγον, ἢ πρόσκλησιν τῆς πλάνης ἐμποιοῦν, ἢ οἰκοδομοῦν εἰς ἀσέβειαν, ἢ καθόλου, πᾶν τὸ κωλύον τῇ ἐντολῇ τοῦ Θεοῦ ὑπακούειν μέχρι καὶ αὐτοῦ τοῦ θανάτου.

— First off, I regard it as necessary to know what a snare is. Then the different kinds of snares through which men are caught. And so to reveal the safe situation and the dangerous situation. For a snare is, as I reckon, being guided by what is written, everything which leads to **apostasy** from the truth as far as it concerns godliness (piety), or makes provision for deception, or encourages ungodliness, or — on the whole — everything which hinders obeying the command of God even to the point of death itself.

— Greek text — J.P. Migne. *Patrologiae cursus completus* (*series Graeca 31*). Migne, 1857-1866. Retrieved from Thesaurus Linguae Graecae (stephanus.tlg.uci.edu).

— English translation — The translation is my own as I could find none readily available.

— The context is a treatment of snares (stumbling blocks) which Basil defines as anything which leads to apostasy from the truth as far as it concerns godliness (piety).

— RELIGIOUS APOSTASY

(29) Basil of Caesaria, Exposition of the Prophet Isaiah, Chapter 1, Section 19

— Οὐκ ἄγει δὲ αὐτὸν ἡ πονηρὰ συνείδησις εἰς τὸν τόπον τῆς προσευχῆς, διότι ἐν τῇ τάξει τῶν πιστῶν οὐχ ἔστηκεν· ἐξέπεσε γάρ· ἐν δὲ τῇ τῶν ὑποκλαιόντων χώρᾳ οὐχ ἵσταται, αἰσχύνεται γάρ. Ἐντεῦθεν ὄκνος εἰς προσευχήν, προφάσεις πεπλασμένας ἐπινοῶν πρὸς τοὺς ἐπιζητοῦντας. ... Εἶτα ἐκ τῆς κατὰ μικρὸν συνηθείας μελέτη αὐτῷ πρὸς **ἀποστασίαν** ἐγγίνεται, καὶ εἰς παντελῆ ἀπώλειαν περιάγεται.

— The bad conscience does not lead him into the place of prayer because he does not stand in the ranks of the believers. For he has fallen away. He does not stand in the room of secret tears for he is ashamed. Whence he is lazy in prayer, thinking up fabricated excuses for those who seek (him) [to join them in prayer] … After a while, the exercise of this habit brings him to **apostasy** and leads him to utter destruction.

— Greek text — P. Trevisan, *San Basilio: Commento al profeta Isaia*, 2 vols. Società Editrice Internazionale, 1939. Retrieved from Thesaurus Linguae Graecae (stephanus.tlg.uci.edu).

— English translation — The translation is my own as I could find none readily available.

— The context regards withdrawal from fellow believers and prayer as an evil that leads to apostasy.

— RELIGIOUS APOSTASY

(30) Basil of Caesaria, Exposition of the Prophet Isaiah, Chapter 1, Section 42

— Ἐπειδὴ δὲ ὡς περὶ νύμφης ἑαυτοῦ τῆς τοῦ ἀνθρώπου ψυχῆς πολλαχοῦ τῆς Γραφῆς ὁ Θεὸς διαλέγεται, εἴη ἂν χήρα καὶ ἡ δι' **ἀποστασίαν** Χριστοῦ διὰ τῆς εἰδωλολατρείας νοητῶς ἐκπορνεύσασα, καὶ τῆς τοῦ νυμφίου Λόγου συναφείας ἐστερημένη, ἣν δεῖ δικαιοῦσθαι διὰ τὸ τῆς μετανοίας δικαίωμα παιδευομένην.

— Since God everywhere addresses the soul of a man itself in Scripture as a bride, so she also would be a widow who because of **apostasy** from Christ knowingly went whoring through idolatry and was deprived of connection with the bridegroom Logos, through which [connection] we ought to be justified, being disciplined through the righteous ordinance of repentance.

— Greek text — P. Trevisan, *San Basilio: Commento al profeta Isaia*, 2 vols. Società Editrice Internazionale, 1939. Retrieved from Thesaurus Linguae Graecae (stephanus.tlg.uci.edu).

— English translation — The translation is my own as I could find none readily available.

— The context associates apostasy with whoring from Christ through idolatry.

— RELIGIOUS APOSTASY

(31) Basil of Caesaria, Exposition of the Prophet Isaiah, Chapter 7, Section 192

— ὁ δὲ Ἰσραὴλ, Ἐφραῒμ ὀνομάζεται, διὰ τὸ ἐκ τῆς φυλῆς ἐκείνης ὡρμῆσθαι τὸν **τὴν ἀποστασίαν** ἐξ ἀρχῆς πεποιηκότα.

— Israel was called Ephraim because of that tribes' impetus from the beginning toward the **apostasy** which they committed.

— Greek text — P. Trevisan, *San Basilio: Commento al profeta Isaia*, 2 vols. Società Editrice Internazionale, 1939. Retrieved from Thesaurus Linguae Graecae (stephanus.tlg.uci.edu).

— English translation — The translation is my own as I could find none readily available.

— The context associates Israel's moniker of Ephraim with the fact that Israel had followed Ephraim in apostasy.

— RELIGIOUS APOSTASY

(32) Basil of Caesaria, Exposition of the Prophet Isaiah, Chapter 7, Section 204

— Ἀπέστη δὲ Ἐφραῒμ ἀπὸ τοῦ Ἰούδα ἐν ἡμέραις Ἱεροβοὰμ υἱοῦ Νάβατ, ὃς ἐξήμαρτε τὸν Ἰσραὴλ, ὃς πρῶτος κατῆρξε **τῆς ἀποστασίας**, εἰπών· Οὐκ ἔστιν ἡμῖν μερὶς ἐν Δαβὶδ, οὐδὲ κληρονομία ἐν υἱῷ Ἰεσσαί.

— Ephraim departed from Judah in the days of Jereboam the son of Nebat, who made Israel to sin, who was the architect of their **apostasy**, saying, there is no part for us with David, nor inheritance for us with the son of Jesse.

— Greek text — P. Trevisan, *San Basilio: Commento al profeta Isaia*, 2 vols. Società Editrice Internazionale, 1939. Retrieved from Thesaurus Linguae Graecae (stephanus.tlg.uci.edu).

— English translation — The translation is my own as I could find none readily available.

— The context is Ephraim's separation from Judah in the days of Jereboam when he led the northern tribes in sin and apostasy.

— RELIGIOUS APOSTASY

(33) Basil of Caesaria, Exposition of the Prophet Isaiah, Chapter 8, Section 211

— Ἐπειδὰν μέντοι παραδοθῶσι ταῖς ἂν τικειμέναις δυνάμεσι, περιπατήσουσιν ἐπὶ πᾶν τεῖχος τῶν ἀποστατούντων, τουτέστιν ἐπὶ πάντα τὰ ὀχυρὰ δόγματα καὶ ἐπὶ πάντα τὰ δοκοῦντα ἀσφαλίσματα αὐτῶν εἶναι. Διὰ δὲ **τὴν** ἀπὸ τοῦ Σιλωὰμ **ἀποστασίαν** καὶ τὴν πρὸς τοὺς ὀλεθρίους τῶν βασιλέων πρόσκλισιν, ἀπειλεῖ ὁ λόγος ἀφαιρεθήσεσθαι ἀπὸ τῆς Ἰουδαίας πάντα ἄνθρωπον,

— Every time, of course, they are delivered into the hands of hostile enemies, who shall walk upon every wall of the apostates, that is upon every defended dogma and upon everything thought by them to be secure. Because of **the apostasy** from Siloam and their headlong rush toward the destruction of the kings, the word threatens to take away all men from Judah.

— Greek text — P. Trevisan, *San Basilio: Commento al profeta Isaia*, 2 vols. Società Editrice Internazionale, 1939. Retrieved from Thesaurus Linguae Graecae (stephanus.tlg.uci.edu).

— English translation — The translation is my own as I could find none readily available.

— The context is Israel's apostasy from the quiet waters of Shiloh and her inclination down a path that led to the destruction of the kings.

— RELIGIOUS APOSTASY

(34) Basil of Caesaria, Exposition of the Prophet Isaiah, Chapter 8, Section 220

— Νεκροὺς δὲ λέγει, ἤτοι τὰ ἄψυχα εἴδωλα, λίθους καὶ ξύλα, καὶ χαλκὸν καὶ χρυσόν· ἢ νεκροὺς λέγει τοὺς τὴν ζωὴν τὴν ἀληθινὴν διὰ **τῆς ἀποστασίας** ἀποβεβληκότας.

— He calls dead the idols which are truly soulless, stone and wood and bronze and gold. Or he calls dead those who have cast away the true life through **apostasy**.

— Greek text — P. Trevisan, *San Basilio: Commento al profeta Isaia*, 2 vols. Società Editrice Internazionale, 1939. Retrieved from Thesaurus Linguae Graecae (stephanus.tlg.uci.edu).

— English translation — The translation is my own as I could find none readily available.

— The context is the awful spiritual state of those who cast aside the living truth through apostasy.
— RELIGIOUS APOSTASY

(35) Basil of Caesaria, Exposition of the Prophet Isaiah, Chapter 9, Section 227

— Πάντα γὰρ ὑποταγήσεται αὐτῷ, καὶ πάντα ἐπιγνώσεται τὴν αὐτοῦ δεσποτείαν· καὶ ἐπειδὰν γένηται ὁ Θεὸς τὰ πάντα ἐν πᾶσι, καθησυχασθέντων τῶν θορυβούντων **ταῖς ἀποστασίαις**, ἐν εἰρηνικῇ συμφωνίᾳ τὸν Θεὸν ὑμνήσουσιν.

— For all shall be subject to him and all shall recognize his ownership. And when God becomes the all in all, silencing the uproaring [rebels] in **their apostasies**, then [all men] shall sing in peaceful harmony.

— Greek text — P. Trevisan, *San Basilio: Commento al profeta Isaia*, 2 vols. Società Editrice Internazionale, 1939. Retrieved from Thesaurus Linguae Graecae (stephanus.tlg.uci.edu).

— English translation — The translation is my own as I could find none readily available.

— The context is the wonderful peace and harmony mankind shall enjoy when the rebels are silenced and their apostasies cease.
— RELIGIOUS APOSTASY

(36) Basil of Caesaria, Exposition of the Prophet Isaiah, Chapter 16, Section 307

— Ἐπὶ τὸν ἄρχοντα τοῦ κόσμου τούτου, τὸν πρῶτον **τὴν ἀποστασίαν** καινοτομήσαντα, τὸν ἐξυβρίσαντα εἰς τὸν Κτίστην, τὸν ἐνυβρίζοντα τοῖς ἀνθρώποις καὶ καταπατήσαντα αὐτοὺς ὕβρει καὶ ὑπερηφανίᾳ, εἴρηται ταῦτα. Οὗτος γάρ ἐστιν ὁ καθυβρίζων τοὺς ἐν τῇ Ἐκκλησίᾳ, τοὺς μὲν ὡς ἀνδραποδώδεις καὶ διὰ τὴν ἄγνοιαν οὐδὲν αὐτῶν διαφέροντας.

— These things are spoken of the prince of this world, who first introduced **apostasy**, who railed against the Creator, who railed against man and trampled him in hubris and high-mindedness. He is the one who rails against those in the church as slaves [to lies] and profitable for nothing because of their ignorance.

— Greek text — P. Trevisan, *San Basilio: Commento al profeta Isaia,* 2 vols. Società Editrice Internazionale, 1939. Retrieved from Thesaurus Linguae Graecae (stephanus.tlg.uci.edu).

— English translation — The translation is my own as I could find none readily available.

— The context is the character of the prince of the world, the evil being who first introduced apostasy.

— RELIGIOUS APOSTASY

(37) Basil of Caesaria, Letters, To the Alexandrians, 139

— ταῦτα ἡμᾶς ἐξέπληξε καὶ μικροῦ ἔξω ἐποίησε τῶν λογισμῶν. συνεισῆλθε δὲ τούτοις τοῖς διαλογισμοῖς κἀκείνη ἡ ἔννοια: ἆρα μὴ ἐγκατέλιπεν ἑαυτοῦ τὰς ἐκκλησίας παντελῶς ὁ Κύριος; ἆρα μὴ ἐσχάτη ὥρα ἐστί, καὶ **ἡ ἀποστασία** διὰ τούτων λαμβάνει τὴν εἴσοδον, ἵνα λοιπὸν «ἀποκαλυφθῇ ὁ ἄνομος, ὁ υἱὸς τῆς ἀπωλείας, ὁ ἀντικείμενος, καὶ ὑπεραιρόμενος ἐπὶ πάντα λεγόμενον Θεὸν ἢ σέβασμα;»

— These things have amazed (perplexed) us and almost made us lose our minds. Along with these reflections there comes to mind this thought also: Has the Lord abandoned His churches utterly? Is this the last hour, when **apostasy** uses these means to gain entrance, so that at length «the lawless one may be revealed, the son of perdition, who opposes and exalts himself above all that is called God or worshipped»?

— Greek text — Y. Courtonne, *Saint Basile: Lettres,* 3 vols. Les Belles Lettres, 1:1957; 2:1961; 3:1966. Retrieved from Thesaurus Linguae Graecae (stephanus.tlg.uci.edu).

— English translation — The translation is my own, compared with the B. Jackson translation in *Nicene and Post-Nicene Fathers, Second Series, Vol. 8,* Christian Literature Publishing, 1895, as revised and edited for New Advent by Kevin Knight (newadvent.org).

— The context is the apostasy in the last days that results in the revelation of the lawless one, the son of perdition, who opposes and exalts himself against all that is called God or worshipped.

— RELIGIOUS APOSTASY

(38) Basil of Caesaria, Letters, To Amphilochius, 233

— γνωρίζω τῶν ἀνθρώπων τὴν κατασκευήν. τί οὖν ἐροῦμεν πρὸς ταῦτα; ὅτι καλὸν μὲν ὁ νοῦς: καὶ ἐν τούτῳ ἔχομεν τὸ κατ᾿ εἰκόνα τοῦ κτίσαντος: καὶ καλὸν τοῦ νοῦ ἡ ἐνέργεια: καὶ ὅτι ἀεικίνητος ὢν οὗτος, πολλάκις μὲν φαντασιοῦται περὶ τῶν οὐκ ὄντων ὡς [p. 366] ὄντων, πολλάκις δὲ εὐθυβόλως ἐπὶ τὴν ἀλήθειαν φέρεται. ἀλλ᾿ ἐπειδὴ τούτῳ διτταὶ δυνάμεις παραπεφύκασι, κατὰ τὴν ἡμετέραν τῶν εἰς Θεὸν πεπιστευκότων ὑπόληψιν, ἡ μὲν πονηρά, ἡ τῶν δαιμόνων, πρὸς **τὴν** ἰδίαν **ἀποστασίαν** ἡμᾶς συνεφελκομένη, ἡ δὲ θειοτέρα καὶ ἀγαθὴ πρὸς τὴν τοῦ Θεοῦ ὁμοίωσιν ἡμᾶς ἀνάγουσα: ὅταν μὲν ἐφ᾿ ἑαυτοῦ μένῃ ὁ νοῦς, μικρὰ καθορᾷ καὶ τὰ ἑαυτῷ σύμμετρα, ὅταν δὲ τοῖς ἀπατῶσιν ἑαυτὸν ἐπιδῷ, ἀφανίσας τὸ οἰκεῖον κριτήριον φαντασίαις σύνεστιν ἀλλοκότοις. τότε καὶ τὸ ξύλον οὐχὶ ξύλον εἶναι νομίζει, ἀλλὰ Θεόν, καὶ χρυσὸν οὐχὶ χρήματα εἶναι κρίνει, ἀλλὰ σεβάσματα. ἐὰν δὲ πρὸς τὴν θειοτέραν ἀπονεύσῃ μερίδα, καὶ τὰς τοῦ Πνεύματος ὑποδέξηται χάριτας, τότε γίνεται τῶν θειοτέρων καταληπτικός, ὅσον αὐτοῦ τῇ φύσει σύμμετρον.

— I understand man's constitution. What then shall we say regarding this? Indeed, that the mind is wonderful; and in it we have what is according to the image of the Creator; and the activity of the mind is wonderful; and, ceaselessly active, many times it forms images of non-existent things as if existing, and many times it is carried straight to the truth. But since in this two faculties (powers) are present by nature, according to the view of us who believe in God, the one wicked, that of the demons, drawing us along to their own **apostasy**, the other more divine and good, leading us up to the likeness of God; whenever the mind relies upon itself, it contemplates small things and things commensurate with itself, but whenever it yields to those who deceive it, it obscures its own judgment and becomes involved in bizarre fancies. Then it even thinks that wood is not wood but God; and it considers that gold is not money but an object of worship. But if it inclines to its more divine part, and accepts the graces of the spirit, then it becomes more receptive of divine things, as far as is commensurate with its nature.

— Greek text — Y. Courtonne, *Saint Basile: Lettres*, 3 vols. Les Belles Lettres, 1:1957; 2:1961; 3:1966. Retrieved from Thesaurus Linguae Graecae (stephanus.tlg.uci.edu).

— English translation — The translation is my own, compared with the B. Jackson translation in *Nicene and Post-Nicene Fathers, Second Series, Vol. 8*, Christian Literature Publishing, 1895, as revised and edited for New Advent by Kevin Knight (newadvent.org).

— The context addresses the two faculties or powers that work in the mind, the evil or demonic power which draws us into apostasy and the divine power which leads us to be conformed to the image of God.

— RELIGIOUS APOSTASY

(39) Basil of Caesaria, Letters, To the Bishops of Italy and Gaul, 243

— νῦν δὲ φοβούμεθα, μήποτε αὐξανόμενον τὸ κακόν, ὥσπερ τις φλὸξ διὰ τῆς καιομένης ὕλης βαδίζουσα, ἐπειδὰν καταναλώσῃ τὰ πλησίον, ἅψηται καὶ τῶν πόρρω. ἐπινέμεται γὰρ τὸ κακὸν τῆς αἱρέσεως· καὶ δέος ἐστί, μὴ τὰς ἡμετέρας ἐκκλησίας καταφαγοῦσα, ἕρψῃ λοιπὸν καὶ ἐπὶ τὸ ὑγιαῖνον μέρος τῆς καθ᾽ ὑμᾶς παροικίας. τάχα μὲν οὖν διὰ τὸ παρ᾽ ἡμῖν πλεονάσαι τὴν ἁμαρτίαν, πρῶτοι παρεδόθημεν εἰς κατάβρωσιν τοῖς ὠμοφάγοις ὀδοῦσι τῶν ἐχθρῶν τοῦ Θεοῦ· τάχα δέ, ὃ καὶ μᾶλλόν ἐστιν εἰκάσαι, ὅτι ἐπειδὴ τὸ εὐαγγέλιον τῆς βασιλείας ἀπὸ τῶν ἡμετέρων τόπων ἀρξάμενον εἰς πᾶσαν ἐξῆλθε τὴν οἰκουμένην, διὰ τοῦτο ὁ κοινὸς τῶν ψυχῶν ἡμῶν ἐχθρός, τὰ **τῆς ἀποστασίας** σπέρματα, ἀπὸ τῶν αὐτῶν τόπων τὴν ἀρχὴν λαβόντα, εἰς πᾶσαν οἰκουμένην διαδοθῆναι φιλονεικεῖ. ἐφ᾽ οὓς γὰρ ἔλαμψεν ὁ φωτισμὸς τῆς γνώσεως τοῦ Χριστοῦ, ἐπὶ τούτους ἐλθεῖν καὶ τὸ τῆς ἀσεβείας σκότος ἐπινοεῖ.

— But as things are, we fear lest the evil as it increases, like a flame passing through the burning forest, after it has consumed what is nearby, may lay hold of what is afar. For the evil of heresy is spreading; and there is fear lest, after consuming our churches, it may creep presently upon the portion of your district that is sound. So perhaps, because iniquity has abounded with us, we have been the first to be given over to be devoured by the savage teeth of the enemies of God. But perhaps—and this is even more probable—since the gospel of the kingdom, having begun in our region, has gone forth to the whole world, on this account the common enemy of our souls strives that the seeds of **apostasy**, having taken their beginning in the same region, may be distributed to the whole world. For upon whom the

135

light of the knowledge of Christ has shone, upon these, the darkness of impiety also contrives to come.

— Greek text — Y. Courtonne, *Saint Basile: Lettres*, 3 vols. Les Belles Lettres, 1:1957; 2:1961; 3:1966. Retrieved from Thesaurus Linguae Graecae (stephanus.tlg.uci.edu).

— English translation — The translation is my own, compared with the B. Jackson translation in *Nicene and Post-Nicene Fathers, Second Series, Vol. 8*, Christian Literature Publishing, 1895, as revised and edited for New Advent by Kevin Knight (newadvent.org).

— The context is the enemy sowing the seeds of apostasy among those who are taking the light of Christ to the whole world. Notice that apostasia is associated with heresy.

— RELIGIOUS APOSTASY

(40) Basil of Caesaria, Letters, To Barses the Bishop of Edessa, 264

— ἀλλ' ὥσπερ τοῖς Ἰσραηλίταις τὴν ἑβδομηκονταετίαν ὥρισεν ὑπὲρ τῶν ἁμαρτημάτων εἰς τὴν τῆς αἰχμαλωσίας καταδίκην, οὕτω τάχα καὶ ἡμᾶς ὁ δυνατὸς χρόνῳ τινὶ ὡρισμένῳ παραδοὺς ἀνακαλέσεταί ποτε καὶ ἀποκαταστήσει εἰς τὴν ἐξ ἀρχῆς εἰρήνην: εἰ μὴ ἄρα ἐγγύς πού ἐστιν **ἡ ἀποστασία** καὶ τὰ νῦν γινόμενα προοίμιά ἐστι τῆς εἰσόδου τοῦ Ἀντιχρίστου. ὅπερ δὲ ἐὰν ᾖ, προσεύχου ἵνα ἢ τὰς θλίψεις παρενέγκῃ ἢ ἡμᾶς ἀπταίστους διὰ τῶν θλίψεων ὁ ἀγαθὸς διασώσηται.

— Nay, just as for the Israelites He appointed a term of seventy years of captivity as the punishment for their sins, so perhaps the Almighty, having given us also over to an appointed period, will someday call us back and restore us to the peace of old; unless indeed **the apostasy** is somewhere near, and what is now happening is a prelude to the entrance of the Antichrist. And if this thing should happen, pray that the good Lord may either take away our afflictions or preserve us unvanquished through our afflictions.

— Greek text — Y. Courtonne, *Saint Basile: Lettres*, 3 vols. Les Belles Lettres, 1:1957; 2:1961; 3:1966. Retrieved from Thesaurus Linguae Graecae (stephanus.tlg.uci.edu).

— English translation — The translation is my own, compared with the B. Jackson translation in *Nicene and Post-Nicene Fathers, Second*

Series, Vol. 8, Christian Literature Publishing, 1895, as revised and edited for New Advent by Kevin Knight (newadvent.org).
— The context is the apostasy in Basil's day which he figured would eventually pass unless it was the prelude to the entrance of the antichrist and the apostasy of the last days.
— RELIGIOUS APOSTASY

(41) Basil of Caesaria, Homily So-Called in Lacisis, (Migne 31.1452)

— Οὐ γὰρ εὐθὺς διάβολος ἐκτίσθη ὁ διάβολος, ἀλλ' ἀγγέλου ἐξουσίαν λαβὼν, κατεστράφη εἰς τὴν τοῦ δαίμονος φύσιν. Καὶ ἐγένετο πονηρὸς δαίμων ὁ ταύτῃ τῇ πονηρίᾳ χαρακτηρισθεὶς, καὶ ἀπαλλοτριωθεὶς τῆς πρὸς τὸν Θεὸν οἰκειότητος, ἀποστραφεὶς δὲ πρὸς τὸ μέρος **τῆς ἀποστασίας**, ἐπειδὴ εἶδε τὸν ἄνθρωπον μικρὸν μὲν ζῶον, παρὰ πᾶσαν δὲ τὴν κτίσιν τιμιώτερον.
— The devil was not outright created an accuser, but having the authority (province) of an angel, he was perverted into the demonic nature. And he became the evil demon characterized by this particular evil (accusing), and was alienated from kinship with God and turned to the part of **apostas**y when he saw man, who was a lower being [than the angels] being honored above all creation.
— Greek text — J.P. Migne. *Patrologiae cursus completus* (*series Graeca 31*). Migne, 1857-1866. Retrieved from Thesaurus Linguae Graecae (stephanus.tlg.uci.edu).
— English translation — The translation is my own as I could find none readily available.
— The context is the apostasy of Satan occasioned by man being elevated above all creation though being lower than the angels.
— RELIGIOUS APOSTASY

(42) Basil of Caesaria, Sermons on Manners: Collected by Symeon Metaphrastes, Message 12, (Migne 32.1280)

— ἆρα μὴ ἐσχάτη ὥρα ἐστὶ, καὶ **ἡ ἀποστασία** διὰ τούτων λαμβάνει τὴν εἴσοδον, ἵνα λοιπὸν ἀποκαλυφθῇ ὁ ἄνομος, ὁ υἱὸς τῆς ἀπωλείας, ὁ ἀντικείμενος, καὶ ὑπεραιρόμενος ἐπὶ πάντα λεγόμενον Θεὸν ἢ σέβασμα;

— Is it not the last hour, and **the apostasy** shall make its entrance through these things that the lawless one might be revealed thereafter, the son of perdition, who oppoess and exalts himself against all this is called god or worship.

— Greek text — J.P. Migne. *Patrologiae cursus completus* (*series Graeca 32*). Migne, 1857-1866. Retrieved from Thesaurus Linguae Graecae (stephanus.tlg.uci.edu).

— English translation — The translation is my own as I could find none readily available.

— The context addresses the apostasy which shall make its entrance in the last days and regards the revelation of the lawless one, the son of perdition as occasioned by the apostasy.

— RELIGIOUS APOSTASY

(43) Chrysostom, Concerning the Statues (Homilies to the People of Antioch), 19, Section 9, (Migne 49.193)

— «Ἰδοὺ ἔρχεται βασιλεὺς Βαβυλῶνος ἐπὶ Ἱερουσαλήμ.» Εἶτα εἰπὼν ἕτερά τινα μεταξὺ, λέγει τοὺς ὅρκους καὶ τὰς συμμαχίας· «Διαθήσεται γὰρ», φησὶ, «πρὸς αὐτὸν διαθήκην.» Εἶτα καὶ **τὴν ἀποστασίαν** δηλῶν, «Καὶ ἀποστήσεται, φησὶν, ἀπ᾽ αὐτοῦ τοῦ ἐξαποστέλλειν ἀγγέλους εἰς Αἴγυπτον τοῦ δοῦναι αὐτῷ ἵππους καὶ λαὸν πολύν.» Καὶ μετὰ ταῦτα ἐπάγει, δεικνὺς ὅτι διὰ τὸν ὅρκον ταῦτα πάντα γίνεται τὰ τῆς ἀπωλείας· «Εἰ μὴ ἐν τῷ τόπῳ τοῦ βασιλέως τοῦ βασιλεύσαντος αὐτὸν, ὃς ἠτίμωσε τὴν ἀράν μου, καὶ παρέβη τὴν διαθήκην μου, ἐν μέσῳ Βαβυλῶνος τελευτήσει, καὶ οὐκ ἐν δυνάμει μεγάλῃ, οὐδὲ ἐν ὄχλῳ πολλῷ, ὅτι ἠτίμωσε τὴν ὁρκωμοσίαν, τοῦ παραβῆναι τὴν διαθήκην μου, ἦ μὴν τὴν ὁρκωμοσίαν μου, ἣν ἠτίμωσε, καὶ τὴν διαθήκην μου, ἣν παρέβη, δώσω αὐτὴν εἰς κεφαλὴν αὐτοῦ, καὶ ἐκπετάσω ἐπ᾽ αὐτὸν τὸ δίκτυόν μου.»

— «Behold, the king of Babylon cometh against Jerusalem.» And then, after saying some other things between, he mentions the oaths and the treaties. «For» saith he, «he shall make a covenant with him;» and presently, speaking of the **departure** from it, he goes on to say, «And he will depart from him, by sending messengers into Egypt, that they might give him horses and much people.» And then he proceeds to shew that it is on account of the oath that all this destruction is to take place. «Surely in the place where the king dwelleth that made him king, he who hath despised My curse, and hath transgressed My covenant, in the midst of Babylon he shall die»; and not by great power nor by multitude, because he despised the oath in transgressing this My covenant; I will surely recompense upon his own head this My oath which he hath dishonoured, and My covenant which he hath broken; and I will spread My net upon him.»

— Greek text — J.P. Migne. *Patrologiae cursus completus* (*series Graeca 49*). Migne, 1857-1866. Retrieved from Thesaurus Linguae Graecae (stephanus.tlg.uci.edu).

— English translation — The Oxford translation revised by R.W. Stephens. *Nicene and Post-Nicene Fathers, First Series, Vol. 9.* Christian Literature Publishing, 1889, repr. Hendrickson 1999.

— The context is the king of Judah making a covenant with the king of Babylon, then later rebelling against him and sending messengers to Egypt asking for horses and soldiers.

— POLITICAL SEDITION OR REBELLION

(44) Chrysostom, On Repentance, Homily 1, Section 4, (Migne 49.283)

— ὅπερ οὖν καὶ πρὸς τοὺς Ἰουδαίους ἔλεγεν. Ἐπειδὴ γὰρ μυρίους ἀναλώσας διὰ τῶν προφητῶν λόγους, οὐκ ἔπεισεν οὐδὲ ἐπεσπάσατο, ἀφεὶς διὰ τῆς κολάσεως αὐτοὺς παιδευθῆναι, φησὶ πρὸς αὐτούς·«Παιδεύσει σε **ἡ ἀποστασία σου**, καὶ ἡ κακία σου ἐλέγξει σε.»

— Who therefore said to the Jews, when ten thousand were destroyed through the prophet's words, he neither persuaded nor drew [them], having given them up to be disciplined through judgment, and said to them, «Your **apostasy** shall discipline you, and your wickedness shall reprove you.»

— Greek text — J.P. Migne. *Patrologiae cursus completus* (*series Graeca 49*). Migne, 1857-1866. Retrieved from Thesaurus Linguae Graecae (stephanus.tlg.uci.edu).

— English translation — The translation is my own as I could find no translation available.

— The context is Israel's rebellion and their punishment at the hand of God. Notice the parallel statements, the one employing apostasy,

the other employing evil. This implies that these two terms are closely associated. Notice that apostasy will result in discipline.
— RELIGIOUS APOSTASY

(45) Chrysostom, The Obscurities of the Prophets, Section 4, (Migne 56.170)

— Διὰ τοῦτο καὶ Παῦλον ἐβούλοντο ἀνελεῖν, ὅτι ἔπειθεν αὐτοὺς μετατίθεσθαι ἀπὸ τῆς πολιτείας Πόθεν τοῦτο δῆλον; «Θεωρεῖς», φησὶν, «ἀδελφέ, πόσαι μυριάδες εἰσὶν Ἰουδαίων τῶν πεπιστευκότων, καὶ οὗτοι πάντες κατήχηνται περὶ σοῦ, ὅτι **ἀποστασίαν** τοῦ νόμου διδάσκεις». Οἱ πιστοὶ οὐκ ἠνείχοντο διδάσκεσθαι **ἀποστασίαν** τοῦ νόμου· καὶ οἱ οὐδέπω πιστεύσαντες πῶς ἂν ἠνέσχοντο ἀκοῦσαι, ὅτι παυθήσεται ὁ νόμος ποτέ;

— Therefore they determined to assassinate Paul, because he persuaded them to change from their religious polity. Whence is this clear? «You see brother», he says, «how many tens of thousands of Jews there are who have believed, and these have all been taught about you that you teach **apostasy** from the law». The faithful do not endure teaching **apostasy** from the law. And those who haven't yet believed, how could they bear to hear that the law shall pass away some time?

— Greek text — J.P. Migne. *Patrologiae cursus completus* (*series Graeca 56*). Migne, 1857-1866. Retrieved from Thesaurus Linguae Graecae (stephanus.tlg.uci.edu).

— English translation — The translation is my own as I could find none available.

— The context is Paul being falsely accused of teaching apostasy from the law.
— RELIGIOUS APOSTASY

(46) Chrysostom, Forty-Eight Excerpts from Diverse Homilies, Excerpt 9, (Migne 63.628)

— Καὶ καθάπερ ἀντεχομένου τοῦ Θεοῦ καὶ μεθ' ἡμῶν ὄντος, τὰ λυποῦντα ἐκποδὼν γίνεται· οὕτως ἀφισταμένου καὶ ἐπιλανθανομένου καὶ ψυχὴ διακόπτεται καὶ καρδία ὀδυνᾶται, καὶ οἱ λυποῦντες ἐπεμβαίνουσιν, ὥστε διὰ πάντων δακνομένους τοὺς ῥαθυμοτέρους, σπουδαιότερον ἐπανελθεῖν, ὅθεν ἐξέπεσον. Παιδεύσει γάρ σε **ἡ ἀποστασία** σου, φησὶ, καὶ ἡ κακία σου ἐλέγξει σε. Ὥστε καὶ ἡ ἐγκατάλειψις τοῦ Θεοῦ προνοίας εἶδός ἐστιν. Ὅταν γὰρ προνοῶν καὶ κηδόμενος καταφρονῆται, ἀφίησι μικρὸν καὶ ἐγκαταλιμπάνει, ἵνα τότε τῆς ῥαθυμίας ἐκβληθείσης, σπουδαιότεροι οἱ ὀλίγωροι γένωνται. — Just as when God defends and stands by us, the grieving circumstances are removed from us, so when God withdraws and forgets us, our soul is cut and our heart filled with sorrow, and grief-causing things fall upon us, so that the lazy, bitten through all [the trials], may more diligently return from when they fell. «Your **falling away** will instruct you,» Scripture says, «and your wickedness reprove you.» So we see that abandonment by God is a form of providence. When the one who providentially watches over us and cares for us is slighted, he withdraws and abandons in a minor degree so that spiritual laziness may be expelled and the negligent may become more diligent.

— Greek text — J.P. Migne. *Patrologiae cursus completus* (*series Graeca 63*). Migne, 1857-1866. Retrieved from Thesaurus Linguae Graecae (stephanus.tlg.uci.edu).

— English translation — The translation is my own as I could find none available.

— The context is God's partial withdrawal and abandonment that follows man's departure from him. This results in trials that drive men back to him.

— RELIGIOUS APOSTASY

(47) Chrysostom, Expositions on Psalms, 13.2-3 (LXX 12.3-4), Section 1, (Migne 55.150)

— «Ἕως πότε ὑψωθήσεται ὁ ἐχθρός μου ἐπ᾽ ἐμέ; Ἐπίβλεψον, εἰσάκουσόν μου, Κύριε ὁ Θεός μου. Φώτισον τοὺς ὀφθαλμούς μου, μή ποτε ὑπνώσω εἰς θάνατον.» Ὥσπερ γὰρ ἀντεχομένου τοῦ Θεοῦ, καὶ μεθ᾽ ἡμῶν ὄντος, τὰ λυποῦντα ἐκποδὼν ἅπαντα γίνεται· οὕτως ἀποστάντος καὶ ἐπιλαθομένου, καὶ ψυχὴ διακόπτεται, καὶ καρδία ὀδυνᾶται, καὶ οἱ λυποῦντες ἐπεμβαίνουσι, καὶ πάντα κρημνοὶ καὶ σκόπελοι. Συγχωρεῖται δὲ ταῦτα συμφερόντως, ὥστε διὰ πάντων δακνομένους τοὺς ῥαθυμοτέρους σπουδαιότερον ἐπανελθεῖν, ὅθεν ἐξέπεσον. «Παιδεύσει γάρ σε», φησὶν, «ἡ **ἀποστασία** σου, καὶ ἡ κακία σου ἐλέγξει σε». Ὥστε καὶ ἡ ἐγκατάλειψις τοῦ Θεοῦ προνοίας εἶδός ἐστιν. Ὅταν γὰρ προνοῶν καὶ κηδόμενος καταφρονῆται, ἀφίησι μικρὸν καὶ ἐγκαταλιμπάνει, ἵνα τότε τῆς ῥᾳθυμίας ἐκβληθείσης, σπουδαιότεροι οἱ ὀλίγωροι γένωνται.

— «How long will my enemy be exalted over me? Consider, hearken to me, O Lord my God. Give light to my eyes lest I should ever fall asleep in death.» You see, just as when God defends us and stands by us, everything damaging is removed from us, so when he keeps his distance and forgets us, our soul is cut in twain, our heart plunged in sorrow, those who do harm fall upon us, and life becomes craggy and precipitous [valleys and misfortunes]. Now, this is allowed to happen for our advantage, so that through the whole of it those more indifferent people may be goaded into becoming more zealous and return to the condition from which they fell. «Your **falling away** will instruct you, after all,» Scripture says, «and your wickedness censure you.» And so even abandonment by God is a form of providence. You see, when the one who exercises providence and care is slighted, he ignores and abandons us to some extent so that at that point indifference may be expelled and the negligent may turn more zealous [more diligent].

— Greek text — J.P. Migne. *Patrologiae cursus completus* (*series Graeca 55*). Migne, 1857-1866. Retrieved from Thesaurus Linguae Graecae (stephanus.tlg.uci.edu).

— English translation — Robert C. Hill. *St. John Chrysostom: Commentary on the Psalms, Vol. 1*. Holy Cross Orthodox Press, 1998. The comments in square brackets are my own clarifications.

— The context is God's discipline. When followers of God fall away or depart from him, he will withdraw from them, and they will face the consequences. These consequences are designed to restore men to faith. So even his withdrawal is a manifestation of loving providence.

— RELIGIOUS APOSTASY

(48) Chrysostom, Fragments in Jeremiah, (Migne 64.765)

— Ταῦτα δέ φησιν, ὡς πολλάκις μὲν Αἰγυπτίων ἐπικαλεσαμένων, καὶ Ἀσσυρίων τὴν βοήθειαν, καὶ νῦν δὲ ὡς τοῦ Ἰωακεὶμ μεγάλα ἐπὶ τῷ Αἰγυπτίῳ φρονοῦντος, καὶ ὡς οὐδὲν πείσεται ὑπὸ τοῦ Βαβυλωνίου τῇ ἐκείνου συμμαχίᾳ ... Ὅτε δὲ Ἀσσύριοι αὐτοῖς ἐπεστράτευσαν, πρὸς Αἰγυπτίους κατέφυγον. Γηῶν γὰρ τὸν Νεῖλον καλεῖ. «Παιδεύσει σε ἡ **ἀποστασία** σου.» Ἱκανὸν γὰρ εἰς παιδείαν τὸ ἔξω τοῦ Θεοῦ γενέσθαι.

— These things he addressed, how many times they had called upon Egypt, or sought the aid of Assyria, and how Jehoiakim was now expecting great things from Egypt, and how he shall not be subject to Babylon in the alliance with that nation … When the Assyrians made war on them, they fled to the Egyptians. Gihon called (summoned) the Nile. «Your **apostasy** shall discipline you.» That which happens apart from God is sufficient for discipline.

— Greek text — J.P. Migne. *Patrologiae cursus completus* (*series Graeca 64*). Migne, 1857-1866. Retrieved from Thesaurus Linguae Graecae (stephanus.tlg.uci.edu).

— English translation — The translation is my own as I could find none available.

— The context is Israel's departure from the Lord. She was looking to other nations for her help and stay rather than the Lord. These bad choices brought their own discipline with them. Notice the association of discipline with apostasy. Apostasy always exacts a price, often as a direct result of the bad choices themselves.

— RELIGIOUS APOSTASY

(49) Chrysostom, Homilies on John, 59, Section 3, (Migne 59.325)
— «Ἀλλοτρίῳ δὲ οὐ μὴ ἀκολουθήσουσιν, ὅτι οὐκ οἴδασι τῶν ἀλλοτρίων τὴν φωνήν.» Ἤτοι τοὺς περὶ Θευδᾶν λέγει ἐνταῦθα καὶ Ἰούδαν (καὶ γὰρ Ἅπαντες, ὅσοι ἐπίστευσαν αὐτοῖς, διεσκορπίσθησαν, φησίν)· ἢ τοὺς μετὰ ταῦτα μέλλοντας ἀπατᾶν ψευδοχρίστους. Ἵνα γὰρ μὴ λέγωσιν ἕνα ἐκείνων τοῦτον εἶναι, διὰ πολλῶν ἑαυτὸν ἀπ' ἐκείνων διαιρεῖ. Καὶ πρῶτον μὲν τίθησι διαφορὰν, τὴν ἀπὸ τῶν Γραφῶν διδασκαλίαν· αὐτὸς μὲν γὰρ διὰ τούτων αὐτοὺς προσήγετο, ἐκεῖνοι δὲ οὐκ ἐντεῦθεν αὐτοὺς ἐφείλκοντο. Δευτέραν τὴν τῶν προβάτων ὑπακοήν· αὐτῷ μὲν γὰρ οὐ ζῶντι μόνον, ἀλλὰ καὶ τελευτήσαντι πάντες ἐπίστευσαν· ἐκείνους δὲ εὐθέως εἴασαν. Καὶ τρίτην δὲ μετὰ τούτων ἔστιν εἰπεῖν οὐ μικράν. Ἐκεῖνοι μὲν γὰρ ὡς τύραννοι, καὶ ἐπὶ **ἀποστασίᾳ** πάντα ἐποίουν· αὐτὸς δὲ οὕτω πόρρω ἑαυτὸν τοιαύτης κατέστησεν ὑποψίας, ὡς καὶ θελόντων αὐτὸν ποιῆσαι βασιλέα φυγεῖν, καὶ ἐπερωτώντων, «εἰ ἔξεστι δοῦναι κῆνσον Καίσαρι», κελεῦσαι καταθεῖναι, καὶ αὐτὸν ἐπιδοῦναι τὸ δίδραχμα.

— «And a stranger will they not follow, for they know not the voice of strangers.» Certainly here He speaketh of Theudas and Judas, (for «all, as many as believed on them, were scattered» [Acts v. 36], It saith,) or of the false Christs who after that time should deceive. For lest any should say that He was one of these, He in many ways separateth Himself from them. And the first difference He setteth down is His teaching from the Scriptures; for He by means of these led men to Him, but the others did not from these draw men after them. The second is, the obedience of the sheep; for on Him they all believed, not only while He lived, but when He had died; the others they straightway left. With these we may mention a third difference, no trifling one. They did all as rebels, and to cause **revolts**, but He placed Himself so far from such suspicion, that when they would have made Him a king, He fled; and when they asked, «Is it lawful to give tribute unto Cæsar?» He bade them pay it, and Himself gave the two drachm piece.

— Greek text — J.P. Migne. *Patrologiae cursus completus* (*series Graeca 59*). Migne, 1857-1866. Retrieved from Thesaurus Linguae Graecae (stephanus.tlg.uci.edu).

— English translation — G.T. Stupart, edited by Philip Schaff. *Nicene and Post-Nicene Fathers, First Series, Vol. 14.* Christian Literature Publishing, 1889, repr. Hendrickson 1999.

— The context contrasts revolutionaries like Theudas and Judas with Jesus. They were tyrants who caused revolts. Jesus placed himself so far from such suspicion that when they tried to make him king, he fled.

— POLITICAL SEDITION OR REBELLION

(50) Chrysostom, Homilies on John, 64, Section 3, (Migne 59.359)

— «Ἐὰν ἀφῶμεν αὐτὸν οὕτως, ἔρχονται οἱ Ῥωμαῖοι, καὶ ἀροῦσιν ἡμῶν καὶ τὸ ἔθνος καὶ τὴν πόλιν.» Τί ἐστιν ὃ βουλεύονται ποιεῖν; Τὸν λαὸν ἐπισεῖσαι βούλονται λοιπόν, ὡς μέλλοντες κινδυνεύειν ἐπὶ ὑποψίᾳ τυραννίδος. «Ἐὰν γὰρ ὀχλαγωγοῦντα», φησὶ, «μάθωσιν αὐτὸν οἱ Ῥωμαῖοι, ὑποπτεύσουσιν ἡμᾶς, καὶ ἐλεύσονται, καὶ καθελοῦσιν ἡμῶν τὴν πόλιν.» Τίνος ἕνεκεν; εἰπέ μοι· μὴ γὰρ **ἀποστασίαν** ἐδίδασκεν; οὐκ ἐπέτρεψε φόρον δοῦναι Καίσαρι; οὐχὶ βασιλέα αὐτὸν ποιῆσαι ἠθελήσατε, καὶ ἔφυγεν; οὐχὶ τὸν εὐτελῆ καὶ ἀπέριττον ἐπεδείκνυτο βίον, μήτε οἰκίαν ἔχων, μήτε ἄλλο τῶν τοιούτων οὐδέν; Ταῦτα μὲν οὖν ἔλεγον, οὐ προσδοκῶντες, ἀλλὰ βασκαίνοντες. Ἐξέβη δὲ καὶ μὴ προσδοκώντων αὐτῶν, καὶ τὸ ἔθνος

144

καὶ τὴν πόλιν ἔλαβον, ἐπειδὴ ἀνεῖλον αὐτόν. Καὶ γὰρ πόρρω πάσης ὑποψίας ἦν τὰ γινόμενα. Ὁ γὰρ ἰώμενος νοσοῦντας, καὶ ἄριστον διδάσκων βίον, καὶ ἄρχουσι πείθεσθαι ἐπιτάττων, οὐχὶ τυραννίδα συνίστη, ἀλλὰ κατέλυεν. «Ἀλλ' ἀπὸ τῶν προτέρων στοχαζόμεθα», φησίν. Ἀλλ' ἐκεῖνοι **ἀποστασίαν** ἐδίδασκον· οὗτος δὲ τοὐναντίον. Ὁρᾷς ὅτι ὑπόκρισις ἦν τὰ λεγόμενα; Τί γὰρ ἐπεδείξατο τοιοῦτον; δορυφόρους σοβοῦντας ἐπήγετο; ὀχήματα ἐπεσύρετο;

— «If we let him thus alone, the Romans will come, and will take away both our nation and city.» What is it which they counsel to do? They wish to stir up the people, as though they themselves would be in danger on suspicion of establishing a kingdom. «For if», says one of them, «the Romans learn that this Man is leading the multitudes, they will suspect us, and will come and destroy our city.» Wherefore, tell me? Did He teach **revolt**? Did He not permit you to give tribute to Cæsar? Did not ye wish to make Him a king, and He fly from you? Did He not follow a mean and unpretending life, having neither house nor anything else of the kind? They therefore said this, not from any such expectation, but from malice. Yet it so fell out contrary to their expectation, and the Romans took their nation and city when they had slain Christ. For the things done by Him were beyond all suspicion. For He who healed the sick, and taught the most excellent way of life, and commanded men to obey their rulers, was not establishing but undoing a tyranny. «But», says some one, «we conjecture from former (impostors)». But they taught **revolt**, He the contrary. Seest thou that the words were but a pretense? For what action of the kind did He exhibit? Did He lead about with Him pompous guards? Had He a train of chariots?

— Greek text — J.P. Migne. *Patrologiae cursus completus* (*series Graeca 59*). Migne, 1857-1866. Retrieved from Thesaurus Linguae Graecae (stephanus.tlg.uci.edu).

— English translation — G.T. Stupart, edited by Philip Schaff. *Nicene and Post-Nicene Fathers, First Series, Vol. 14*. Christian Literature Publishing, 1889, repr. Hendrickson 1999.

— The context contrasts Jesus with the revolutionaries who taught revolt and rebellion. He taught the opposite. He commanded men to obey their rulers. He permitted men to pay taxes to Caesar.

— POLITICAL SEDITION OR REBELLION

(51) Chrysostom, Homilies on Matthew, 10, section 5, (Migne 57.190)

— Καὶ ὁ τοῦ κηρύγματος δὲ τρόπος ξένος καὶ παρηλλαγμένος. Οὐδὲν γὰρ τῶν συνήθων ἤκουον, οἷον, πολέμους καὶ μάχας καὶ νίκας τὰς κάτω, καὶ λιμοὺς καὶ λοιμοὺς, καὶ Βαβυλωνίους καὶ Πέρσας, καὶ πόλεως ἅλωσιν, καὶ τὰ ἄλλα τὰ συνήθη· ἀλλ’ οὐρανοὺς καὶ τὴν ἐκεῖ βασιλείαν, καὶ τὴν ἐν τῇ γεέννῃ κόλασιν. Διά τοι τοῦτο καὶ τῶν κατὰ τὴν ἔρημον ἀποστατῶν σφαγέντων ἁπάντων οὐ πρὸ πολλοῦ τοῦ χρόνου, τῶν μετὰ Ἰούδα καὶ Θευδᾶ, οὐκ ἐγένοντο ὀκνηρότεροι πρὸς τὴν ἔξοδον τὴν ἐκεῖσε. Οὐδὲ γὰρ ἐπὶ τοῖς αὐτοῖς αὐτοὺς ἐκάλει· οἷον, ἐπὶ τυραννίδι καὶ **ἀποστασίᾳ** καὶ νεωτεροποιίᾳ· ἀλλ’ ὥστε πρὸς τὴν ἄνω χειραγωγῆσαι βασιλείαν. Διόπερ οὐδὲ κατεῖχεν ἐν τῇ ἐρήμῳ μεθ’ ἑαυτοῦ περιφέρων, ἀλλὰ βαπτίζων, καὶ τοὺς περὶ φιλοσοφίας παιδεύων λόγους, ἀπέλυε· διὰ πάντων αὐτοὺς διδάσκων, τῶν μὲν ἐν τῇ γῇ πάντων ὑπερορᾶν, πρὸς δὲ τὰ μέλλοντα αἴρεσθαι, καὶ καθ’ ἑκάστην ἐπείγεσθαι τὴν ἡμέραν.

— And the nature of his preaching too was strange and unusual. For they heard of none of those things to which they were accustomed; such as wars and battles and victories below, and famine and pestilence, and Babylonians and Persians, and the taking of the city, and the other things with which they were familiar, but of Heaven and of the kingdom there, and of the punishment in hell. And it was for this cause, let me add, that although they that committed revolt in the wilderness, those in the company of Judas, and of Theudas, had been all of them slain no great while before, yet they were not the more backward to go out thither. For neither was it for the same objects that he summoned them, as for dominion, or **revolt**, or revolution; but in order to lead them by the hand to the kingdom on high. Wherefore neither did he keep them in the wilderness to take them about with him, but baptizing them, and teaching them the rules concerning self-denial, he dismissed them; by all means instructing them to scorn whatever things are on earth, and to raise themselves up to the things to come [to take up the coming things], and press on every day.

— Greek text — J.P. Migne. *Patrologiae cursus completus* (*series Graeca 58*). Migne, 1857-1866. Retrieved from Thesaurus Linguae Graecae (stephanus.tlg.uci.edu).

— English translation — G Prevost, revised by M. B. Riddle. *Nicene and Post-Nicene Fathers, First Series, Vol. 10.* Christian Literature Publishing, 1889, repr. Hendrickson 1999. I added material in square brackets for clarification.

— The context contrasts John the Baptist with Judas and Theudas. Both movements drew men into the wilderness. The former for the message of the kingdom of heaven and Gehenna (hell). The latter for the message of dominion, revolt, and revolution (ἐπὶ τυραννίδι καὶ ἀποστασίᾳ καὶ νεωτεροποιίᾳ). Note that ἀποστασία (apostasia) *revolt* is associated with νεωτεροποία (neōteropoia) *revolution.*

— POLTICAL SEDITION OR REBELLION

(52) Chrysostom, Homilies on Matthew, 70, (Migne 58.655)

— «Ἀποστέλλουσι» γὰρ «αὐτῷ τοὺς μαθητὰς αὐτῶν μετὰ τῶν Ἡρωδιανῶν, λέγοντες· Διδάσκαλε, οἴδαμεν ὅτι ἀληθὴς εἶ, καὶ τὴν ὁδὸν τοῦ Θεοῦ ἐν ἀληθείᾳ διδάσκεις, καὶ οὐ μέλει σοι περὶ οὐδενός· οὐ γὰρ βλέπεις εἰς πρόσωπον ἀνθρώπων. Εἰπὲ οὖν ἡμῖν, τί σοι δοκεῖ; ἔξεστι δοῦναι κῆνσον Καίσαρι, ἢ οὔ;» Καὶ γὰρ φόρου λοιπὸν ἦσαν ὑποτελεῖς, τῶν πραγμάτων αὐτοῖς εἰς τὴν Ῥωμαίων ἀρχὴν μεταπεσόντων. Ἐπειδὴ οὖν εἶδον, ὅτι οἱ πρὸ τούτου διὰ τοῦτο ἀπέθανον, οἱ περὶ Θευδᾶν καὶ Ἰούδαν, ὡς **ἀποστασίαν** μελετήσαντες, ἐβούλοντο καὶ αὐτὸν διὰ τῶν λόγων τούτων εἰς τοιαύτην ὑποψίαν ἐμβαλεῖν.

— For «they sent out unto Him their disciples with the Herodians saying, Master, we know that thou are true, and teachest the way of God in truth, neither carest thou for any man; for thou regardest not the person of men. Tell us therefore, What thinkest thou? Is it lawful to give tribute unto Caesar or not?» For they were now tributaries, their state having passed under the rule of the Romans. Forasmuch then as they saw that Theudas and Judas with their companies for this cause were put to death, as having prepared for a **revolt**, they were minded to bring Him too by these words into such a suspicion.

— Greek text — J.P. Migne. *Patrologiae cursus completus (series Graeca 58).* Migne, 1857-1866. Retrieved from Thesaurus Linguae Graecae (stephanus.tlg.uci.edu).

— English translation — G Prevost, revised by M. B. Riddle. *Nicene and Post-Nicene Fathers, First Series, Vol. 10.* Christian Literature Publishing, 1889, repr. Hendrickson 1999.

— The context portrays the Pharisees trying to trap Jesus with a subtle argument so he would fall under the same suspicion as Judas and Theudas, who had earlier died when they had pursued rebellion.

— POLITICAL SEDITION OR REBELLION

(53) Chrysostom, Homilies on Acts, 46, Section 1, (Migne 60.321)

— «Τῇ δὲ ἐπιούσῃ ἡμέρᾳ εἰσῄει ὁ Παῦλος σὺν ἡμῖν πρὸς Ἰάκωβον, πάντες τε παρεγένοντο οἱ πρεσβύτεροι. Καὶ ἀσπασάμενος αὐτοὺς, ἐξηγεῖτο καθ᾽ ἓν ἕκαστον ὧν ἐποίησεν ὁ Θεὸς ἐν τοῖς ἔθνεσι διὰ τῆς διακονίας αὐτοῦ» ... «Οἱ δὲ ἀκούσαντες ἐδόξαζον τὸν Θεὸν, εἰπόντες αὐτῷ· Θεωρεῖς, ἀδελφὲ, πόσαι μυριάδες εἰσὶν Ἰουδαίων τῶν πεπιστευκότων· καὶ πάντες ζηλωταὶ τοῦ νόμου ὑπάρχουσι. Κατηχήθησαν δὲ περὶ σοῦ, ὅτι **ἀποστασίαν** διδάσκεις ἀπὸ Μωϋσέως τοὺς κατὰ τὰ ἔθνη πάντας Ἰουδαίους, λέγων μὴ περιτέμνειν αὐτοὺς τὰ τέκνα, μηδὲ τοῖς ἔθεσι περιπατεῖν.»

— «The following day Paul went in with us to James, and all the elders were present. He greeted them and explained in detail the things that God had wrought among the Gentiles through his ministry» ... «When they heard it, they glorified God and said to him, Have you seen (noticed), brother, how many ten thousands of Jews there are who have believed? And they are all zealous for the law, And they all have been instructed about you, that you teach **apostasy** from Moses to all the Jews who are among the Gentiles, telling them to neither circumcise their children nor walk after the customs.»

— Greek text — J.P. Migne. *Patrologiae cursus completus* (*series Graeca 58*). Migne, 1857-1866. Retrieved from Thesaurus Linguae Graecae (stephanus.tlg.uci.edu).

— English translation — The translation is my own. The available translation in *Nicene and Post-Nicene Fathers, First Series* was unsuitable.

— The context addresses the fact that tens of thousands of Jews had been taught that Paul taught apostasy from Moses.

— RELIGIOUS APOSTASY

(54) Chrysostom, Homilies on Acts, 46, Section 1, (Migne 60.321)
— Καὶ αὐτοὶ πάντες κατηχήθησαν, φησὶ, περὶ σοῦ, ὅτι **ἀποστασίαν** διδάσκεις ἀπὸ Μωϋσέως τοὺς κατὰ τὰ ἔθνη πάντας Ἰουδαίους, λέγων μὴ περιτέμνειν αὐτοὺς τὰ τέκνα, μηδὲ τοῖς ἔθεσι περιπατεῖν.
— These have all been instructed, he said, about you, that you teach **apostasy** from Moses to the Jews among the Gentiles, telling them not to circumcise their children and not to walk in the [Mosaic] customs.
— Greek text — J.P. Migne. *Patrologiae cursus completus (series Graeca 58)*. Migne, 1857-1866. Retrieved from Thesaurus Linguae Graecae (stephanus.tlg.uci.edu).
— English translation — The translation is my own. The available translation in *Nicene and Post-Nicene Fathers, First Series* was unsuitable.
— The context addresses the fact that tens of thousands of Jews had been taught that Paul taught apostasy from Moses.
— RELIGIOUS APOSTASY

(55) Chrysostom, Homilies on Acts, 46, Section 1, (Migne 60.321)
— Οὐκ εἶπον, «Ἤκουσαν» ἀλλὰ, «Κατηχήθησαν», τουτέστιν, ἐδιδάχθησαν καὶ ἐπίστευσαν ὅτι **ἀποστασίαν** ἀπὸ Μωϋσέως διδάσκεις.
— They did not say «they heard» but «they were instructed», that is, they were taught and believed that you are teaching **apostasy** from Moses.
— Greek text — J.P. Migne. *Patrologiae cursus completus (series Graeca 58)*. Migne, 1857-1866. Retrieved from Thesaurus Linguae Graecae (stephanus.tlg.uci.edu).
— English translation — The translation is my own. The available translation in *Nicene and Post-Nicene Fathers, First Series* was unsuitable.
— The context addresses the fact that tens of thousands of Jews had been taught that Paul taught apostasy from Moses.
— RELIGIOUS APOSTASY

(56) Chrysostom, Commentary on Galations, 2.2, (Migne 61.634)

— Ἀλλὰ ἐπειδὴ γὰρ ἐν τοῖς Ἱεροσολύμοις πάντες ἐσκανδαλίζοντο, εἴ τις παραβαίη τὸν νόμον, εἴ τις κωλύοι χρήσασθαι τῇ περιτομῇ· διὸ καὶ ἔλεγε, «Θεωρεῖς, ἀδελφέ, πόσαι μυριάδες εἰσὶ τῶν πεπιστευκότων; καὶ οὗτοι πάντες εἰσὶ κατηχημένοι περὶ σοῦ, ὅτι **ἀποστασίαν** ἀπὸ τοῦ νόμου διδάσκεις».

— All at Jerusalem were offended, if the law was transgressed, or the use of circumcision forbidden; as James says, «Thou seest, brother, how many thousands [tens of thousands] there are among the Jews of them which have believed; and they are informed of thee, that thou teachest to **forsake** the law».

— Greek text — J.P. Migne. *Patrologiae cursus completus* (*series Graeca 58*). Migne, 1857-1866. Retrieved from Thesaurus Linguae Graecae (stephanus.tlg.uci.edu).

— English translation — The Oxford translation revised by G. Alexander. *Nicene and Post-Nicene Fathers, First Series, Vol. 13*. Christian Literature Publishing, 1889, repr. Hendrickson 1999.

— Context addresses the fact that tens of thousands of Jews had been taught that Paul taught apostasy from the law.

— RELIGIOUS APOSTASY

(57) Chrysostom, Homilies on Hebrews, Argument and Summary, Section 1, (Migne 63.10)

— Ἄκουσον γὰρ τί φησιν ὁ Ἰάκωβος πρὸς αὐτόν·«Θεωρεῖς, ἀδελφέ, πόσαι μυριάδες εἰσὶν Ἰουδαίων τῶν πεπιστευκότων; καὶ οὗτοι πάντες κατήχηνται περὶ σοῦ, ὅτι **ἀποστασίαν** ἀπὸ τοῦ νόμου διδάσκεις». καὶ πολλαὶ ζητήσεις αὐτῷ πολλάκις ἐγένοντο περὶ τούτου.

— For hear what James says to him, «Thou seest, brother, how many thousands [ten thousands] of Jews there are which believe ... and these all have been informed of thee that thou teachest men to **forsake** the law.» And oftentimes he had many disputings concerning this.

— Greek text — J.P. Migne. *Patrologiae cursus completus* (*series Graeca 63*). Migne, 1857-1866. Retrieved from Thesaurus Linguae Graecae (stephanus.tlg.uci.edu).

— English translation — The Oxford translation revised by F. Gardiner. *Nicene and Post-Nicene Fathers, First Series, Vol. 14*. Christian Literature Publishing, 1889, repr. Hendrickson 1999.

— The context is the trouble Paul faced because tens of thousands of Jews had been taught that he taught apostasy from the law.
— RELIGIOUS APOSTASY

(58) Chrysostom, Homilies on Hebrews, Argument and Summary, Section 1, (Migne 63.11)

— Πέτρος μὲν γὰρ καὶ οἱ περὶ αὐτὸν, ἅτε ἐν Ἱεροσολύμοις κηρύττοντες, ἔνθα πολὺς ἦν ὁ ζῆλος, ἀνάγκην εἶχον τὸν νόμον κελεύειν τηρεῖν· οὗτος δὲ ἐν ἐλευθερίᾳ πολλῇ ἦν. Καὶ πλείους ἦσαν οἱ ἐξ ἐθνῶν, ἢ οἱ Ἰουδαῖοι, ἅτε ἐκτὸς ὄντες· καὶ τούτῳ παρέλυε τὸν νόμον, καὶ οὐ τοσαύτην εἶχον περὶ αὐτὸν εὐλάβειαν, ὅτι πάντα καθαρῶς ἐκήρυττεν. Ἀμέλει ἐν τούτῳ αὐτὸν δοκοῦσι καταιδεῖν τῷ πλήθει, λέγοντες, «Θεωρεῖς, ἀδελφέ, πόσαι μυριάδες εἰσὶν Ἰουδαίων τῶν πεπιστευκότων;» Διὰ τοῦτο αὐτὸν ἐμίσουν καὶ ἀπεστρέφοντο, ὅτι κατηχήθησαν, φησὶ, περὶ σοῦ, ὅτι **ἀποστασίαν** ἀπὸ τοῦ νόμου διδάσκεις.

— For Peter and they that were with him, because they preached in Jerusalem, when there was great fierceness, of necessity enjoined the observance of the law; but this man was quite at liberty. The [converts] too from the Gentiles were more than the Jews because they were without. And this enfeebled the law, and they had no such great reverence for it, although he preached all things purely. Doubtless in this matter they think to shame him by numbers, saying, «Thou seest, brother, how many ten thousands of Jews there are which are come together.» On this account they hated him and turned away from him, because «They are informed of thee, he says, that thou teachest men to **forsake** the law.»

— Greek text — J.P. Migne. *Patrologiae cursus completus (series Graeca 63).* Migne, 1857-1866. Retrieved from Thesaurus Linguae Graecae (stephanus.tlg.uci.edu).

— English translation — The Oxford translation revised by F. Gardiner. *Nicene and Post-Nicene Fathers, First Series, Vol. 14.* Christian Literature Publishing, 1889, repr. Hendrickson 1999.

— The context is the trouble that Paul faced because tens of thousands of Jews had been taught that he taught apostasy from the law.
— RELIGIOUS APOSTASY

(59) Chrysostom, Homilies on Hebrews, 34, Section 4, (Migne 63.233)

— ἄκουε, Ἰακώβου λέγοντος·«Κατηχήθησαν γὰρ περὶ σοῦ, ὅτι **ἀποστασίαν** διδάσκεις.» Οὐχ ὡς ἐχθρός, φησὶν, οὐδὲ ὡς πολέμιος ταῦτα γράφω, ἀλλ᾽ ὡς φίλος. Καὶ τοῦτο καὶ ἐκ τοῦ ἑξῆς δηλοῖ·

— Hear what James says. «For they have been informed concerning thee» [it is said] «that thou teachest **apostasy**.» Not as an enemy, he means, nor as an adversary, I write these things, but as a friend. And this he shows also by what follows.

— Greek text — J.P. Migne. *Patrologiae cursus completus* (*series Graeca 63*). Migne, 1857-1866. Retrieved from Thesaurus Linguae Graecae (stephanus.tlg.uci.edu).

— English translation — The Oxford translation revised by F. Gardiner. *Nicene and Post-Nicene Fathers, First Series, Vol. 14.* Christian Literature Publishing, 1889, repr. Hendrickson 1999.

— The context concerns the trouble that arose for Paul because tens of thousands of Jews had been taught that he taught apostasy from the law.

— RELIGIOUS APOSTASY

(60) Chrysostom, Homilies on 2 Thessalonians, Homily 3, (Migne 62.482)

— Πανταχόθεν τοίνυν αὐτοὺς ἀσφαλισάμενος, οὕτω τὴν οἰκείαν γνώμην ἐκτίθεται, καὶ λέγει, «Μή τις ὑμᾶς ἐξαπατήσῃ κατὰ μηδένα τρόπον, ὅτι ἐὰν μὴ ἔλθῃ **ἡ ἀποστασία** πρῶτον, καὶ ἀποκαλυφθῇ ὁ ἄνθρωπος τῆς ἁμαρτίας, ὁ υἱὸς τῆς ἀπωλείας, ὁ ἀντικείμενος καὶ ὑπεραιρόμενος ἐπὶ πάντα λεγόμενον Θεὸν ἢ σέβασμα, ὥστε αὐτὸν εἰς τὸν ναὸν τοῦ Θεοῦ ὡς Θεὸν καθίσαι, ἀποδεικνύντα ἑαυτὸν ὅτι ἐστὶ Θεός.» Περὶ τοῦ ἀντιχρίστου ἐνταῦθα διαλέγεται, καὶ μεγάλα ἀποκαλύπτει μυστήρια. Τί ἐστιν **ἡ ἀποστασία**; Αὐτὸν καλεῖ τὸν ἀντίχριστον **ἀποστασίαν**, ὡς πολλοὺς μέλλοντα ἀπολλύναι καὶ ἀφιστᾶν· Ὥστε, φησί, σκανδαλισθῆναι, εἰ δυνατὸν, καὶ τοὺς ἐκλεκτούς.

— Having therefore secured them on every side, he thus sets forth his own doctrine, and says, «Let no man beguile you in any wise: for it will not be, except **the falling away** come first, and the man of sin be revealed, the son of perdition, he that opposes and exalts himself against all that is called God or that is worshipped; so that he sits in the temple of God, setting himself forth as God.» Here he discourses concerning the Antichrist, and reveals great mysteries. What is **the falling away**? He calls the antichrist himself **Apostasy**, as one who shall destroy many, and make them fall away [go away]. So that if it were possible, he says, the very elect should be stumbled.

— Greek text — J.P. Migne. *Patrologiae cursus completus* (*series Graeca 62*). Migne, 1857-1866. Retrieved from Thesaurus Linguae Graecae (stephanus.tlg.uci.edu).

— English translation — A revised version of John A. Broadus. *Nicene and Post-Nicene Fathers, First Series, Vol. 13.* Christian Literature Publishing, 1889. Revised and edited for New Advent by Kevin Knight. Accessed at New Advent (newadvent.org/fathers). Modified and amended by myself.

— The context is the final apostasy in the last days. Chrysostom identifies the antichrist himself as the apostasy pointing out that he shall destroy many and cause them to fall away (go away).

— RELIGIOUS APOSTASY

(61) Chrysostom, In illud: In faciem ei restiti ("I withstood him to his face"), Section 3, (Migne 51.375)

— Θεωρεῖς, ἀδελφέ, πόσαι μυριάδες εἰσὶν Ἰουδαίων τῶν συνεληλυθότων, καὶ οὗτοι πάντες ζηλωταὶ τοῦ νόμου εἰσὶ, καὶ κατήχηνται περὶ σοῦ, ὅτι **ἀποστασίαν** ἀπὸ τοῦ νόμου διδάσκεις.

— Have you noticed, brother, how many tens of thousands of Jews have come together, and they are all zealous of the law, and they have been instructed about you, that you teach **apostasy** from the law.

— Greek text — J.P. Migne. *Patrologiae cursus completus* (*series Graeca 51*). Migne, 1857-1866. Retrieved from Thesaurus Linguae Graecae (stephanus.tlg.uci.edu).

— English translation — The translation is my own as I could find none available.

— The context addresses the incident where Paul is informed that tens of thousands of Jews believe that he taught apostasy from the law.

— RELIGIOUS APOSTASY

(62) Chrysostom, In illud: In faciem ei restiti ("I withstood him to his face"), Section 11, (Migne 51.381)

— Θεωρεῖς, ἀδελφέ, πόσαι μυριάδες εἰσὶν Ἰουδαίων τῶν συνεληλυθότων, καὶ οὗτοι πάντες ζηλωταὶ τοῦ νόμου εἰσὶ, καὶ κατήχηνται περὶ σοῦ, ὅτι **ἀποστασίαν** ἀπὸ τοῦ νόμου διδάσκεις.

— Have you noticed, brother, how many tens of thousands of Jews have come together, and they are all zealous of the law, and they have been instructed about you, that you teach **apostasy** from the law.

— Greek text — J.P. Migne. *Patrologiae cursus completus* (*series Graeca 51*). Migne, 1857-1866. Retrieved from Thesaurus Linguae Graecae (stephanus.tlg.uci.edu).

— English translation — The translation is my own as I could find none available.

— The context is the incident where Paul is informed that tens of thousands of Jews believe that he taught apostasy from the law.

— RELIGIOUS APOSTASY

(63) Chrysostom, In illud: In faciem ei restiti ("I withstood him to his face"), Section 12, (Migne 51.382)

— Θεωρεῖς, ἀδελφέ, πόσαι μυριάδες εἰσὶν Ἰουδαίων τῶν συνεληλυθότων, καὶ οὗτοι πάντες ζηλωταὶ τοῦ νόμου εἰσὶ, καὶ κατήχηνται περὶ σοῦ, ὅτι **ἀποστασίαν** ἀπὸ τοῦ νόμου διδάσκεις.

— Have you noticed, brother, how many tens of thousands of Jews have come together, and they are all zealous of the law, and they have been instructed about you, that you teach **apostasy** from the law.

— Greek text — J.P. Migne. *Patrologiae cursus completus* (*series Graeca 51*). Migne, 1857-1866. Retrieved from Thesaurus Linguae Graecae (stephanus.tlg.uci.edu).

— English translation — The translation is my own as I could find none available

— The context addresses the incident where Paul is informed that tens of thousands of Jews believe that he taught apostasy from the law.

— RELIGIOUS APOSTASY

(64) Chrysostom, Introduction to Acts, Homily 3, (Migne 51.102)

— «Θεωρεῖς, ἀδελφὲ Παῦλε, πόσαι μυριάδες εἰσὶν Ἰουδαίων τῶν συνεληλυθότων, καὶ οὗτοι πάντες κατήχηνται περὶ σοῦ, ὅτι

ἀποστασίαν ἀπὸ τοῦ νόμου διδάσκεις. Τί οὖν; Ποίησον ὅ σοι λέγομεν. Εἰσὶ παρ' ἡμῖν ἄνδρες εὐχὴν ἔχοντες ἐν ἑαυτοῖς· τούτους λαβὼν ἁγνίσθητι σὺν αὐτοῖς, καὶ ξύρησαι τὴν κεφαλὴν μετ' αὐτῶν, ἵνα ἔργῳ πιστωθῶσιν, ὅτι ὧν κατήχηνται περὶ σοῦ οὐδέν ἐστιν, ἀλλὰ τηρεῖς καὶ αὐτὸς τὸν νόμον τοῦ Μωϋσέως.»

— «Do you see, brother Paul, how many tens of thousands of Jews have assembled, and these have all been instructed about you, that you teach **apostasy** from the law? What then? Do what we tell you. There are men in our midst who have made a vow amongst themselves. Take them and be purified with them, and shave your head with them, that they may be confident indeed that what they have been instructed concerning you is nothing, but you yourself keep the law of Moses.»

— Greek text — J.P. Migne. *Patrologiae cursus completus* (*series Graeca 51*). Migne, 1857-1866. Retrieved from Thesaurus Linguae Graecae (stephanus.tlg.uci.edu).

— English translation — The translation is mine, following the lead of the KJV and NKJV as far as possible in translating Chrysostom's Greek text, which is slightly paraphrastic.

— The context is the occasion where Paul was informed that tens of thousands of Jews had been taught that he was teaching apostasy from the law of Moses.

— RELIGIOUS APOSTASY

(65) Chrysostom, Synopsis Of Sacred Scripture, Synopsis of Joshua the son of Nun, (Migne 56.338)

— Ἐκπέμπεται Ἰησοῦς τὴν φυλὴν Ῥουβὶμ καὶ τὴν Γὰδ καὶ τὸ ἥμισυ φυλῆς Μανασσῆ εἰς τοὺς κλήρους αὐτῶν, οὓς ἔλαβον ἔτι ζῶντος Μωϋσέως. Οἱ δὲ ἀπελθόντες, παρὰ τὸν Ἰορδάνην ᾠκοδόμησαν βωμόν. Ἐτάραξε τοῦτο τὰς ἄλλας φυλάς. Ὤιοντο γὰρ **ἀποστασίας** ἕνεκεν τοῦτο πεποιηκέναι αὐτούς. Πέμπουσι πρὸς αὐτοὺς ἐγκαλοῦντες· οἱ δὲ ἀπελογοῦντο λέγοντες, οὐκ **ἀποστασίας** ἕνεκεν οἰκοδομῆσαι τὸν βωμόν· ἀλλ' ἵνα μὴ ἔχωσιν οἱ μεθ' ὑμᾶς γενόμενοι τοὺς ἡμετέρους υἱοὺς ὡς ἀλλοτρίους τῆς ἑαυτῶν συγγενείας, διὰ τὸ τὸν Ἰορδάνην μέσον ἑκατέρων ῥεῖν· ἀλλ' ἵνα ᾖ ὁ βωμὸς εἰς μαρτύριον, καὶ μὴ ἔχωσι λέγειν τὰ τέκνα ὑμῶν τοῖς ἐγγόνοις ἡμῶν, Οὐκ ἔστιν ὑμῖν μερὶς Κυρίου.

— Joshua sent the tribes of Reuben, Gad, and the half-tribe of Manasseh to their inheritances which they had received while Moses was still alive. When they departed, they built an altar on the other side of the Jordan. This stirred up the other tribes, for they supposed that they had done this as **an expression of apostasy**. They sent men to call them to account. But the three tribes defended themselves saying, we did not build the altar as **an expression of apostasy** but that those born of you might not hold our sons to be strangers from their own kindred because the Jordan flows between us. We built this altar that it might be a testimony that your children might not have grounds to say to our children, you do not have a portion with the Lord.

— Greek text — J.P. Migne. *Patrologiae cursus completus* (*series Graeca 56*). Migne, 1857-1866. Retrieved from Thesaurus Linguae Graecae (stephanus.tlg.uci.edu).

— The English translation is my own as I could find none available.

— The context is Manassah being accused of apostasy when they built an altar on the other side of the Jordan, but they insisted the effort was not an effort to pursue apostasy but one to pursue unity.

— RELIGIOUS APOSTASY

(66) Clement of Alexandria, Stromata (Miscellanies), 6.8.66

— Ναὶ μὴν οἱ λέγοντες τὴν φιλοσοφίαν ἐκ τοῦ διαβόλου ὁρμᾶσθαι κἀκεῖνο ἐπιστησάτωσαν, ὅτι φησὶν ἡ γραφὴ μετασχηματίζεσθαι τὸν διάβολον εἰς ἄγγελον φωτός. τί ποιήσοντα; εὔδηλον, ὅτι προφητεύσοντα. εἰ δὲ ὡς ἄγγελος φωτὸς προφητεύει, ἀληθῆ ἄρα ἐρεῖ. εἰ ἀγγελικὰ καὶ φωτεινά, προφητεύσει καὶ ὠφέλιμα τότε, ὅτε καὶ μετασχηματίζεται καθ᾽ ὁμοιότητα ἐνεργείας, κἂν ἄλλος ᾖ κατὰ τὸ ὑποκείμενον **τῆς ἀποστασίας**. ἐπεὶ πῶς ἂν ἀπατήσειέν τινα, μὴ διὰ τῶν ἀληθῶν ὑπαγόμενος τὸν φιλομαθῆ εἰς οἰκειότητα καὶ οὕτως ὕστερον εἰς ψεῦδος ὑποσύρων;

— Further, let those who say that philosophy took its rise from the devil know this, that the Scripture says that the devil is transformed into an angel of light. When about to do what? Plainly, when about to prophesy. But if he prophesies as an angel of light, he will speak what is true. And if he prophesies what is angelical, and of the light, then he prophesies what is beneficial when he is transformed according to the likeness of the operation, though he be different with respect to the matter of **apostasy**. For how could he deceive any one, without drawing the lover of knowledge into fellowship, and so drawing him afterwards into falsehood?

— Greek text — Clement of Alexandria. *Clemens Alexandrinus, Band 2: Stromata Buch 7-8, Excerpta ex Theodoto, Eclogae propheticae, Quis dives salvetur, Fragmente.* Stählin, [*Die Griechischen Christlichen Schriftsteller der Ersten Drei Jahrhunderte*], J.C. Hinrichs, 1909. Accessed at The Perseids Project (cts.perseids.org/read/greekLit).

— English translation — William Wilson. *Ante-Nicene Fathers, Vol. 2.* Christian Literature Publishing, 1885. Revised and edited for New Advent by Kevin Knight. Accessed at New Advent (newadvent.org/fathers).

— The context is Satan operating as an angel of light, first drawing men into truth to gain their confidence, then drawing them into falsehood. So apostasy is often found connected with beneficial teaching that is attached to heresy. Notice the association with ψεῦδος (pseudos) *lie, falsehood.*

— RELIGIOUS APOSTASY

(67) Clement of Alexandria, Stromata (Miscellanies), 7.14.87

— σῶμα δὲ ἀλληγορεῖται ἡ ἐκκλησία κυρίου. ὁ πνευματικὸς καὶ ἅγιος χορός. ἐξ ὧν οἱ τὸ ὄνομα ἐπικεκλημένοι μόνον. βιοῦντες δὲ οὐ κατὰ λόγον. σάρκες εἰσί. τὸ δὲ σῶμα τοῦτο τὸ πνευματικόν. τουτέστιν ἡ ἁγία ἐκκλησία. οὐ τῇ πορνείᾳ οὐδὲ τῇ ἀπὸ τοῦ εὐαγγελίου **ἀποστασία** πρὸς τὸν ἐθνικὸν βίον κατ᾽ οὐδένα τρόπον οὐδ᾽ ὁπωστιοῦν οἰκειωτέον. πορνεύει γὰρ εἰς τὴν ἐκκλησίαν καὶ τὸ αὐτοῦ σῶμα ὁ ἐθνικῶς ἐν ἐκκλησίᾳ πολιτευόμενος, εἴτ᾽ οὖν ἐν ἔργῳ, εἴτε καὶ ἐν λόγῳ, εἴτε καὶ ἐν αὐτῇ τῇ ἐννοίᾳ.

— As a body, the Church of the Lord, the spiritual and holy choir, is symbolized. Whence those, who are merely called, but do not live in accordance with the word, are the fleshy parts. Now this spiritual body, the holy Church, is not for fornication. Nor are those things which belong to heathen life to be adopted by **apostasy** from the Gospel. For he who conducts himself heathenishly in the Church, whether in deed, or word, or even in thought, commits fornication with reference to the Church and his own body.

— Greek text — Clement of Alexandria. *Clemens Alexandrinus, Band 2: Stromata Buch 7-8, Excerpta ex Theodoto, Eclogae propheticae, Quis dives salvetur, Fragmente.* Stählin, [*Die Griechischen Christlichen Schriftsteller der Ersten Drei Jahrhunderte*], J.C. Hinrichs, 1909. Accessed at The Perseids Project (cts.perseids.org/read/greekLit).

— English translation — William Wilson. *Ante-Nicene Fathers, Vol. 2.* Christian Literature Publishing, 1885. Revised and edited for New Advent by Kevin Knight. Accessed at New Advent (newadvent.org/fathers).

— The context is Christians who do not live in accordance with the word, but live heathenishly, and commit spiritual fornication. This is regarded as apostasy from the gospel.

— RELIGIOUS APOSTASY

(68) Constitutions of the Apostles, 1.6

— Σὺ οὖν, ἀναγνοὺς τὸν Νόμον σύμφωνον ὄντα τῷ Εὐαγγελίῳ καὶ τοῖς Προφήταις, ἀναγίνωσκε καὶ τὰς Βασιλείους, ὅπως εἰδέναι ἔχοις, ὁπόσοι δίκαιοι ἐγένοντο βασιλεῖς καὶ ηὐξήθησαν ὑπὸ θεοῦ, καὶ ἡ ἐπαγγελία τῆς αἰωνίου ζωῆς αὐτοῖς διέμεινεν παρ' αὐτῷ, ὅσοι δὲ βασιλεῖς ἐξεπόρνευσαν ἀπὸ Θεοῦ, ἐν **ἀποστασίᾳ** αὐτῶν συντόμως ἀπώλοντο τῇ τοῦ Θεοῦ δικαιοκρισίᾳ καὶ τῆς αὐτοῦ ζωῆς ἐστερήθησαν, ἀντὶ ἀναπαύσεως αἰωνίαν κόλασιν κληρωσάμενοι.

— When, therefore, you have read the Law, which is agreeable to the Gospel and to the Prophets, read also the books of the Kings, that you may thereby learn which of the kings were righteous, and how they were prospered by God, and how the promise of eternal life continued with them from Him; but those kings which went a-whoring from God did soon perish in their **apostasy** by the righteous judgment of God, and were deprived of His life, inheriting, instead of rest, eternal punishment.

— Greek text — B.M. Metzger. *Les constitutions apostoliques,* 3 vols. [*Sources chrétiennes 320, 329, 336*]. Éditions du Cerf, 1:1985; 2:1986; 3:1987. Retrieved from Thesaurus Linguae Graecae (stephanus.tlg.uci.edu).

— English translation — James Donaldson. *Ante-Nicene Fathers, Vol. 7*. Christian Literature Publishing, 1886; as revised and edited for New Advent by Kevin Knight. Accessed at New Advent (newadvent. org/fathers).

— The context shows there is no favor with God. Righteous kings will be saved. Unrighteous kings who indulge apostasy shall face eternal punishment. Notice the association of *apostasia* with whoring away from God.

— RELIGIOUS APOSTASY

(69) Cyril of Alexandria, Letter to Calosyrium, 83

— μὴ συγχώρει δὲ τοῖς ὀρθοδόξοις μετὰ τῶν καλουμένων Μελετιανῶν συνάγεσθαι, ἵνα μὴ γένωνται κοινωνοὶ **τῆς ἀποστασίας** αὐτῶν. ἀλλ᾽ εἰ μὲν ἐκεῖνοι μετανοοῦντες ἔρχονται πρὸς τοὺς ὀρθοδόξους, ἔστωσαν δεκτοί·

— It is not permissible for the orthodox to associate with those called Meletians that we don't fellowship with their **apostasy**. But if they come to the orthodox repentant, they shall be received.

— Greek text — P.E. Pusey, *Sancti patris nostri Cyrilli archiepiscopi Alexandrini in D. Joannis evangelium, vol. 3*. Clarendon Press, 1872. Retrieved from Thesaurus Linguae Graecae (stephanus.tlg.uci.edu).

— English translation — The translation is my own as I could find none readily available.

— The context is the apostate teachings of the Meletians.

— RELIGIOUS APOSTASY

(70) Cyril of Alexandria, Commentary on Isaiah the Prophet, 2:8 LXX, (Migne 70.84)

— «Καὶ ἐνεπλήσθη ἡ γῆ βδελυγμάτων τῶν ἔργων τῶν χειρῶν αὐτῶν, καὶ προσεκύνησαν οἷς ἐποίησαν οἱ δάκτυλοι αὐτῶν. Καὶ ἔκυψεν ἄνθρωπος, καὶ ἐταπεινώθη ἀνήρ, καὶ οὐ μὴ ἀνήσω αὐτούς.» Ἐγκαλεῖ πάλιν αὐτοῖς τὴν νοητὴν πορνείαν, καὶ τὸ πολλοῖς ἑλέσθαι προσκυνεῖν τῶν ψευδωνύμων θεῶν ... «Ἔκυψεν ἄνθρωπος, καὶ ἐταπεινώθη ἀνήρ, καὶ οὐ μὴ ἀνήσω αὐτούς.» Ἐμφαίνει δὲ διὰ τούτου τὸ ἀπαράτρεπτον τῆς ὀργῆς, εἰ καὶ δι᾽ ἄμφω, κατὰ τὸ εἰκός, σεσάλευται κατ᾽ αὐτῶν. Ὅτι καὶ τὴν θείαν λελυπήκασι δόξαν, ἀτιμοτάτην δὲ καὶ αὐτὴν τὴν ἰδίαν ἀπέφηναν φύσιν. Ἐμπεπλῆσθαι δὲ βδελυγμάτων τὴν γῆν αὐτῶν, οὐκ ὀλίγους ὄντας, οὔτε μὴν εὐαριθμήτους ἀποφαίνων τοὺς τοῖς **τῆς ἀποστασίας** ἐναλόντας ἐγκλήμασι, καὶ ὅτι τὸ σέβας αὐτοῖς οὐχ ἕν, προσκεκύνηται δὲ παρ' ἑκάστου τὸ αὐτῷ δοκοῦν, καὶ πολυειδὴς εἰδώλων ἑσμὸς ὅλην αὐτῶν ἐνέπλησε τὴν γῆν.

— «The land was full of abominations, the works of their hands, and they worshipped what their fingers had made. Everyone is bowed down and every man is humbled, and I shall not forgive them.» He goes on to accuse them of spiritual [intellectual] infidelity in choosing to adore [worship] many of the false [falsely-called] gods. ... «Everyone is bowed down and every man is humbled, and I shall not forgive them.» By this he highlights the immutability of his wrath, since it seems it is directed at them on both accounts; Because they impugned the divine glory, and presented their own nature in unflattering light. He says that «the land was full of their abominations», not just a few or a number easily counted, presenting them as caught up in the crime of **apostasy**; far from their worship [reverence] of them being single [unified], whatever appealed to each person was adored, and a multifarious swarm of their idols filled the whole earth.

— Greek text — J.P. Migne. *Patrologiae cursus completus* (*series Graeca 70*). Migne, 1857-1866. Retrieved from Thesaurus Linguae Graecae (stephanus.tlg.uci.edu).

— English translation — R.C. Hill. *Cyril of Alexandria: Commentary on Isaiah, Vol. 1: Chapters 1-14*. Holy Cross Orthodox Press, 2008. I added material in square brackets for clarification.

— The context is Israel's apostasy. The land was filled with abominations. The object of worship was not the one true God, but everyone worshipped whatever and however seemed right to him. Notice that *apostasia* is associated with idolatry, spiritual infidelity, and abominations.

— RELIGIOUS APOSTASY

(71) Cyril of Alexandria, Commentary on Isaiah the Prophet, 42:22 LXX, (Migne 70.876-877)

— «Καὶ εἶδον, καὶ ἐγένετο λαὸς πεπρονομευμένος. Ἡ γὰρ παγὶς ἐν τοῖς ταμείοις πανταχοῦ, καὶ ἐν οἴκοις ἅμα ὅπου ἔκρυψαν αὐτούς» ... Τίνας δὲ αὐτούς; Χωνευτοὺς δηλονότι θεούς. Ὑποπλαττόμενοι γὰρ

160

τὸ θεοσεβεῖν οἱ τῶν Ἰουδαίων καθηγηταὶ, καὶ τοῖς νομίμοις θεσπίσμασι τό γε ἧκον εἰς τοὐμφανὲς ὑποτιθέντες τὸν αὐχένα, **τῆς ἀποστασίας** τὴν νόσον εἰς νοῦν ἔκρυπτον καὶ καρδίαν, προσκυνοῦντες τοῖς οὐκ οὖσι θεοῖς· καὶ τούτους ἐν τοῖς ταμείοις τῶν ἰδίων οἴκων ἐγκατακλείοντες λαθραίας ἐποιοῦντο τὰς τῶν θυσιῶν προσαγωγάς. Γέγραπται γοῦν ἐν τῷ Ἰεζεχιήλ· «Υἱὲ ἀνθρώπου, ὄρυξον. Καὶ ὤρυξα δὴ ἐν τῷ τοίχῳ. Καὶ εἶδον, φησὶ, καὶ ἰδοὺ πᾶσα ὁμοίωσις ἑρπετοῦ καὶ κτήνους, καὶ πάντα τὰ εἴδωλα οἴκου Ἰσραὴλ διαγεγραμμένα ἐπ᾽ αὐτοῦ κύκλῳ. Καὶ εἶπε πρός με· Ἑώρακας, υἱὲ ἀνθρώπου, μὴ μικρὰ τῷ οἴκῳ Ἰσραὴλ ἃ ποιοῦσιν

— «I saw, and the people were pillaged and plundered. The trap, in fact, was laid everywhere in the dens and also in the houses wherever they hid them.» … Hid what? [lit. What is them?] Obviously graven images; the leaders of the Jews pretended to pay homage to God, and bend their neck to the oracles of the Law in externals, but they hid the malady of **apostasy** in mind and heart, adoring false gods. They deposited them in the recesses of their own homes and secretly performed sacrificial offerings. It is written in Ezekiel, for instance, «Son of man, make a hole, and I made a hole in the wall. I looked and, lo, there were images of all kinds of reptiles and animals, and all the idols of the house of Israel portrayed round about. He said to me, Have you seen, mortal man, that what each man is doing in secret in the house of Israel is no small thing?»

— Greek text — J.P. Migne. *Patrologiae cursus completus* (*series Graeca 70*). Migne, 1857-1866. Retrieved from Thesaurus Linguae Graecae (stephanus.tlg.uci.edu).

— English translation — R.C. Hill. *Cyril of Alexandria: Commentary on Isaiah, Vol. 3: Chapters 40-50.* Holy Cross Orthodox Press, 2008.

— The context addresses Israel's infection with the disease of apostasy that was buried deep in their minds and hearts, which had them worshipping gods who are not gods. Notice that apostasy is associated with crimes done in secret, with hypocrisy (pretending), with idolatry, and with moral sickness in the mind and heart.

— RELIGIOUS APOSTASY

(72) Cyril of Alexandria, Commentary on Isaiah the Prophet, 50:1 LXX, (Migne 70.1081-1084)

— «Οὕτως λέγει Κύριος· Ποῖον βιβλίον τοῦ ἀποστασίου τῆς μητρὸς ὑμῶν· ἐν ᾧ ἐξαπέστειλα αὐτήν; ἢ τίνι ὑπόχρεως πέπρακα ὑμᾶς; ἰδοὺ ταῖς ἁμαρτίαις ὑμῶν ἐξαπέστειλα τὴν μητέρα ὑμῶν.» ... Οὐκοῦν οὐκ ἐγώ, φησὶν, ἀποβέβληκα τὴν μητέρα ὑμῶν, καίτοι γεγονὼς αὐτῇ καθάπερ ἐν τάξει νυμφίου, καὶ τὰ τῆς ἐπιεικείας σπέρματα καταβαλὼν διά τε νόμου καὶ προφητῶν· ἀπεφοίτησε δὲ μᾶλλον αὐτὴ τῶν εἰς ἐμὲ δικαίων ὀλιγωρήσασα, καὶ μικροῦ παντελῶς ἀξιώσασα λόγου τὸ εἶναι μετὰ Θεοῦ. Ἐπεὶ ποῖον αὐτῇ δέδοται παρ' ἐμοῦ **τῆς ἀποστασίας** βιβλίον; Ἐκπέμπει μὲν γὰρ οὐδένα Θεὸς τῆς πρὸς αὐτὸν οἰκειότητος· ἀποσείεται δὲ τῶν ὀρθοποδεῖν εἰωθότων οὐδένα· ἀλλ' οἵπερ ἂν εἶεν γνήσιοί τε πρὸς πίστιν, καὶ ἀγαθουργίας ἁπάσης ἐπιστήμονες, τούτοις ἐφίησι τὸ ἐξεῖναι διὰ παντὸς τὴν πρὸς αὐτὸν οἰκειότητα καταπλουτεῖν ἀραρότως.

— «Thus says the Lord, What kind of bill of divorce is there with which I sent her away? Or to whom was I in debt and sold you? Lo, it was for your sins you were sold, and for your iniquities I sent your mother away.» ... Accordingly, he says, it was not that I cast your mother off, despite being like a bridegroom to her, and sowing the seeds of goodness through Law and Prophets. Rather, she took her leave, after ignoring what was due to me, and treating me as completely worthless being with God. What kind of bill of **divorce** has been given her by me? God, in fact, dismisses no one from relationship with him, or repeals anyone in the habit of right conduct; instead, anyone who is committed to faith and versed in all good works he wishes will always be able ardently to enrich himself with relationship to him.

— Greek text — J.P. Migne. *Patrologiae cursus completus* (*series Graeca 70*). Migne, 1857-1866. Retrieved from Thesaurus Linguae Graecae (stephanus.tlg.uci.edu).

— English translation — R.C. Hill. *Cyril of Alexandria: Commentary on Isaiah, Vol. 3: Chapters 40-50*. Holy Cross Orthodox Press, 2008.

— The context is Israel's apostasy. She took her leave of God's will and ways. She is the one who divorced God. God then ratified her decision. In the context *apostasia* is used for the letter of divorce, a rare use among the Fathers. Usually it is *apostasion*, almost always in the genitive form *apostasiou*, as we see earlier in the same passage. — DIVORCE

(73) Cyril of Alexandria, Commentary on John, (on John 7:9-10), (Migne 1.593)

— εἶτα λέγει πρὸς αὐτὸν ὁ Μωυσῆς «Εἰ μὴ αὐτὸς συμπορεύσῃ μετ᾽ ἐμοῦ, μή με ἀναγάγῃς ἐντεῦθεν· καὶ πῶς γνωστὸν ἔσται ἀληθῶς ὅτι εὕρηκα χάριν παρὰ σοί, ἐγὼ καὶ ὁ λαός σου, ἀλλ᾽ ἢ συμπορευομένου σου μεθ᾽ ἡμῶν; καὶ εἶπε Κύριος πρὸς Μωυσῆν Καὶ τοῦτόν σοι τὸν λόγον ὃν εἴρηκας ποιήσω· εὗρες γὰρ χάριν παρ᾽ ἐμοί.» ὁρᾷς ὅπως ἐπὶ μὲν τοῦ Ἰσραὴλ **ἀποστασίᾳ** λυπούμενος, οὐ συναναβήσεσθαι μὲν εἰς τὴν γῆν αὐτοῖς τῆς ἐπαγγελίας διισχυρίζετο, συναποστέλλειν δέ τινα ἄγγελον ἔφασκεν, αἰδοῖ δὲ τῇ πρὸς Μωυσέα, καὶ τῇ τῶν πατέρων μνήμῃ τὴν συγγνώμην ἐπιδιδούς, συμβαδιεῖσθαι πάλιν αὐτοῖς καθυπέσχετο. Ἀρνησάμενος τοιγαροῦν τὸ συνεορτάζειν Ἰουδαίοις, ὡς ἀλαζόσι καὶ ὑβρισταῖς, ὡς διὰ τῆς ἀρνήσεως ἀτιμάζουσι Θεόν, ὥσπερ οὖν ἐκεῖνοι διὰ τῆς μοσχοποιίας, οὐ σφόδρα φιλονεικήσας τοῖς τῶν λυπούντων πταίσμασιν, ἀποπληρῶν δὲ μᾶλλον τὴν εἰς τοὺς ἁγίους πατέρας ὑπόσχεσιν, ἄνεισι διδάξων, καὶ τὰ εἰς σωτηρίαν αὐτοῖς παραθήσων μαθήματα, οὐκ ἀγγέλῳ τὴν τοιαύτην ἐπιτρέψας διακονίαν, ὥσπερ οὖν οὐδὲ τότε, αὐτουργὸς δὲ μᾶλλον καὶ εἰς τὴν τῶν ἀχαρίστων σωτηρίαν γιγνόμενος

— Then Moses says to Him, «If Thyself go not with me, bring me not up hence, and how shall it be truly known that I have found grace in Thy Sight, I and Thy people, is it not in that Thou goest with us? And the Lord said unto Moses, I will do this thing also that thou hast spoken, for thou foundest grace in My Sight.» Seest thou how He, grieved at **the apostacy** of Israel, affirmed that He would not go up with them into the land of promise, but said that He would send an Angel, yet out of respect to Moses and the remembrance of their fathers, He granted them pardon and promised again to go with them. Having then said that He would not feast with the Jews as being haughty and violent, as dishonouring God by their denial of Him, as these did by making the calf, yet being very slow to anger towards the offences of those who grieve Him, and rather fulfilling His Promise to the holy fathers, He goes up to teach and to set before them the doctrines of salvation, not committing such a ministry to an Angel, just as He did not then, but rather being Himself the worker even for the salvation of the unthankful.

— Greek text — P.E. Pusey, *Sancti patris nostri Cyrilli archiepiscopi Alexandrini in D. Joannis evangelium*, 3 vols. Clarendon Press, 1872. Retrieved from Thesaurus Linguae Graecae (stephanus.tlg.uci.edu).

— English translation — P.E. Pusey. *Commentary on the Gospel According to S. John, by S. Cyril, Archbishop of Alexandria, Vol. 1* [*Library of Fathers 43*]. James Parker, Oxford, 1874. Online edition, transcribed by Roger Pearse. Accessed at The Tertullian Project (tertullian.org/fathers).

— The context is Israel offending (grieving) God with her apostasy.

— RELIGIOUS APOSTASY

(74) Cyril of Alexandria, Commentary on Luke, (on Luke 12:4-7), (Migne 72.725)

— «Λέγω δὲ ὑμῖν τοῖς φίλοις μου· μὴ φοβηθῆτε ἀπὸ τῶν ἀποκτεινόντων τὸ σῶμα.» Εἰς πνευματικὴν εὐανδρίαν ἀλείφει τοὺς ἀγαπῶντας αὐτόν. «Λέγω γὰρ ὑμῖν,» φησὶ, «τοῖς φίλοις μου.» Οὐχ ἅπασιν οὖν ἁπλῶς πρέποι ἂν, ὡς ἔοικεν, ὁ περὶ τούτων λόγος· ἐκείνοις δὲ μᾶλλον, οἷς ἂν ἐνυπάρχον ὁρῷτο τὸ ἐξ ὅλης καρδίας ἀγαπᾶν αὐτόν· οἷς καὶ ἁρμόζει λέγειν· «Τίς ἡμᾶς χωρίσει ἀπὸ τῆς ἀγάπης τοῦ Χριστοῦ; θλίψις, ἢ στενοχωρία, ἢ διωγμὸς, ἢ γυμνότης, ἢ μάχαιρα;» Οἱ γὰρ μὴ τοιοῦτοι, εὐπαρακόμιστοι λίαν εἰσὶν, καὶ πρὸς **ἀποστασίαν** ἑτοιμότεροι· οἱ δὲ τὰ αὐτὰ φρονοῦντες αὐτῷ, καὶ τοῖς ἴχνεσιν αὐτοῦ κατακολουθεῖν σπουδάζοντες, φαῖεν ἂν μετὰ τοῦ θεσπεσίου Πέτρου· «Χριστοῦ παθόντος ὑπὲρ ἡμῶν σαρκὶ, καὶ ὑμεῖς ὑπὲρ αὐτοῦ τὴν αὐτὴν ἔννοιαν ὁπλίσασθε.»

— «And I say unto you, My friends, Fear not them that kill the body.» He prepares those who love Him for spiritual fortitude, thus speaking; «I say unto you, My friends.» His present discourse, therefore, does not, as it seems, belong to everyone absolutely: but only to those who evidently love Him with all their heart, and can fitly say; «Who shall separate me from the love of Christ? shall tribulation, or distress, or persecution, or nakedness, or sword?» For those not of this stamp are very easily born away and ready-made for **apostasy**. But those minding these things with him, and diligently following in his footsteps, can say with the thespian Peter, Christ suffered in the flesh on our behalf, and you should arm yourself with the same mind to suffer on his behalf.

— Greek text — J.P. Migne. *Patrologiae cursus completus* (*series Graeca 72*). Migne, 1857-1866. Retrieved from Thesaurus Linguae Graecae (stephanus.tlg.uci.edu). The original Greek text has largely been lost. The remnants have been compiled from Byzantine catena commentaries. Thus the Greek version is much shorter than the Syriac version which has come down us.

— English translation — The translation is my own as I could not find a translation of the Greek version.

— The context addresses the heart. Those who love the Lord with all their heart cannot be separated from the Lord, but those that don't are ripe for apostasy.

— RELIGIOUS APOSTASY

(75) Cyril of Alexandria, Commentary on the Twelve Minor Prophets, Hosea 2:2 (2:4 LXX), (Pusey 1.46)

— «Κρίθητε πρὸς τὴν μητέρα ὑμῶν, κρίθητε, ὅτι αὕτη οὐ γυνή μου, καὶ ἐγὼ οὐκ ἀνὴρ αὐτῆς.» ... οὐ βραδὺς εἰς ἔλεον ὁ φύσει πατήρ, ὀκνεῖ δὲ εἶναι χρηστὸς ἐπὶ νόθῃ γονῇ. καὶ ταῦτα μὲν ἴσως φαίη τις ἂν ὡς ἐκ προσώπου τοῦ Θεοῦ· λογιεῖται δὲ αὖ, καὶ περινοήσει καλῶς, ὅτι τετραμμένης τῆς Συναγωγῆς εἰς **ἀποστασίαν** τὴν ἀπὸ Θεοῦ, καὶ τὴν τῶν δαιμόνων λατρείαν ἀνθῃρημένης, μόνον δὲ οὐχὶ πόρνης δίκην ἁπλούσης αὐτοῖς τὰ σκέλη, γεγόνασιν οἱ ἐξ αὐτῆς οὔτε φιλόθεοι καθαρῶς καὶ ἐρηρεισμένως, οὔτε μὴν ἐπιεικεῖς τοὺς τρόπους·

— «Pass sentence againt your mother, pass sentence, because she is not my wife and» therefore «I am not her husband» ... The natural father is not slow to have pity, but he is reluctant to be kind to illegitimate offspring. While you might equally claim that this is said in the person of God, you could likewise reason, and come to a correct understanding, that when the synagogue perversely **forsook** God and opted instead for the worship of demons, as it were, stretching out its limbs to them like a prostitute, its members proved neither neither purely and constantly godly nor genuine in their behavior.

— Greek text — P.E. Pusey. *Sancti patris nostri Cyrilli archiepiscopi Alexandrini in xii prophetas,* 2 vols. Clarendon Press, 1868. Retrieved from Thesaurus Linguae Graecae (stephanus.tlg.uci.edu).
— English translation — Robert C. Hill. *St. Cyril of Alexandria: Commentary on the Twelve Prophets, Vol. 1 [The Fathers of the Church, 115].* The Catholic University of America Press, 2007.
— The context is Israel's apostasy from God and embracing the service of demons.
— RELIGIOUS APOSTASY

(76) Cyril of Alexandria, Commentary on the Twelve Minor Prophets, Hosea 2:13-14 (2:15-16 LXX), (Pusey 1.63)
— «Καὶ ἐκδικήσω ἐπ' αὐτὴν τὰς ἡμέρας τῶν Βααλεὶμ, ἐν αἷς ἐπέθυεν ἐν αὐτοῖς, καὶ περιετίθετο τὰ ἐνώτια αὐτῆς καὶ τὰ καθόρμια αὐτῆς καὶ ἐπορεύετο ὀπίσω τῶν ἐραστῶν αὐτῆς, ἐμοῦ δὲ ἐπελάθετο, λέγει Κύριος.» ... «Διὰ τοῦτο ἰδοὺ ἐγὼ πλανῶ αὐτὴν καὶ τάξω αὐτὴν εἰς ἔρημον.» Ἐπειδὴ γάρ φησιν αὕτη μὲν ἐξώκειλε πολυτρόπως, ἐζήτησα δὲ καὶ λίαν ὀρθῶς **τῆς ἀποστασίας** τὰς δίκας·"ἐκδεδίκηκα γὰρ ἐπ' αὐτὴν τὰς ἡμέρας τῶν Βααλεὶμ," καὶ ἰσοπαλῆ τοῖς πταίσμασιν ἐπενήνοχα τὴν ὀργήν·
— «I shall take vengeance on her for the days of the Baals when she offered sacrifice to them, put on her nose rings and her jewelry, and went after her lovers and forgot me, says the Lord.» ... «For this reason, lo, I shall seduce her, and put her in the wilderness.» In other words, he is saying, since she offended in many ways, I very rightly sought satisfaction for her **abandonment**; I took vengeance on her for the days of the Baals, and vented my wrath in a way commensurate with her falls.
— Greek text — P.E. Pusey. *Sancti patris nostri Cyrilli archiepiscopi Alexandrini in xii prophetas,* 2 vols. Clarendon Press, 1868. Retrieved from Thesaurus Linguae Graecae (stephanus.tlg.uci.edu).
— English translation — Robert C. Hill. *St. Cyril of Alexandria: Commentary on the Twelve Prophets, Vol. 1 [The Fathers of the Church, 115].* The Catholic University of America Press, 2007.
— The context is judging Israel's apostasy with particular reference for the days when she served the Baalim.
— RELIGIOUS APOSTASY

(77) Cyril of Alexandria, Commentary on the Twelve Minor Prophets, Hosea 2:16-17 (2:18-19 LXX), (Pusey 1.70)

— «Καὶ ἔσται ἐν τῇ ἡμέρᾳ ἐκείνῃ λέγει Κύριος, καλέσει με Ὁ ἀνήρ μου, καὶ οὐ καλέσει με οὐκέτι Βααλείμ. καὶ ἐξαρῶ τὰ ὀνόματα τῶν Βααλείμ ἐκ τοῦ στόματος αὐτῆς, καὶ οὐ μὴ μνησθῶσιν οὐκ ἔτι τὰ ὀνόματα αὐτῶν.» ... λαμπραὶ δὲ ὥσπερ ἀνίσχουσιν αὐγαὶ κατὰ νοῦν τοῖς πεπιστευκόσι, καὶ ὁ τῆς δικαιοσύνης ἐπέλαμψεν ἥλιος, τῆς ἀληθοῦς θεογνωσίας τὸ φῶς ἑνιεὶς τοῖς ἀνευρύνειν εἰδόσι τῆς διανοίας τὸν ὀφθαλμόν. κατ᾿ ἐκεῖνο δὴ οὖν τοῦ καιροῦ, φησὶ, κεκλημένη πρὸς ἐπίγνωσιν τοῦ κατὰ ἀλήθειαν ὄντος Θεοῦ, καταλήξει μὲν τῆς ἀρχαίας ἐκείνης καὶ στυγητῆς ἐλαφρίας· εὐπαράφορος δὲ οὐκέτι πρὸς **ἀποστασίαν** ἔσται.

— «On that day, says the Lord, she will call me My husband, and will no longer call me Baal. I will remove the names of the Baals from her mouth, and they will no longer remember their names.» ... Bright beams, as it were, were shed on the mind of the believers, and the sun of righteousness shone forth, imparting the light of the true knowledge of God on those knowing how to open the eye of the mind. At that time, then, he is saying, when called to acknowledge the one who is truly God, she will abandon that hateful nonsense of former times, and will no longer be inclined to **infidelity** [apostasy].

— Greek text — P.E. Pusey. *Sancti patris nostri Cyrilli archiepiscopi Alexandrini in xii prophetas,* 2 vols. Clarendon Press, 1868. Retrieved from Thesaurus Linguae Graecae (stephanus.tlg.uci.edu).

— English translation — Robert C. Hill. *St. Cyril of Alexandria: Commentary on the Twelve Prophets, Vol. 1* [*The Fathers of the Church, 115*]. The Catholic University of America Press, 2007. I added the alternate translation in square brackets for clarification.

— The context is the restoration of the people of God. The light of the gospel will lead them to abandon their former ways and apostasy.

— RELIGIOUS APOSTASY

(78) Cyril of Alexandria, Commentary on the Twelve Minor Prophets, Hosea 4:16 LXX, (Pusey 1.115)

— «Ὅτι ὡς δάμαλις παροιστρῶσα, οὕτως παροίστρησεν Ἰσραήλ· καὶ νῦν νεμήσει αὐτοὺς Κύριος ὡς ἀμνὸν ἐν εὐρυχώρῳ.» ... Μὴ ζηλώσῃς τοιγαροῦν, ὦ Ἰούδα, φησίν· εἰ γὰρ καὶ ἐν ἴσῳ δαμάλεσι παροιστρήσας

167

ὁ Ἰσραὴλ ᾤχετο πρὸς ἀπόστασιν, ἀλλ' οὐκ ἀζήμιον ἔσται τὸ ἐγχείρημα αὐτῷ. ἀπελεύσεται γὰρ αἰχμάλωτος, καὶ τὴν ἐνεγκοῦσαν ἀφείς, τὴν Περσῶν καὶ Μήδων νεμηθήσεται οὐκέτι θρασὺς, καὶ οἰονείπως ἐξήνιος καὶ ἀτιμαγέλας· τοιαύτη γὰρ ἀεί πως ἐστὶν ἡ παροιστρῶσα δάμαλις. ἀλλ' ἐν ἴσῳ γεγονὼς τοῖς ἡπιωτάτοις ἀμνοῖς. ταπεινὸν γὰρ ἀεὶ καὶ περιδεὲς τῶν αἰχμαλώτων τὸ χρῆμα, καὶ τῆς τοῦ πάσχειν κακῶς ἐλπίδος οὐ μακράν, καὶ τῇ τῶν κρατούντων πλεονεξίᾳ κατηχθισμένον. ... Πάθοι δ' ἂν τοῦτο αὐτὸ καὶ ἀνθρώπου ψυχή, τῆς πρὸς Θεὸν ἀγάπης ὀλιγωρήσασα. περιενεχθήσεται γὰρ εἰς πᾶν ὁτιοῦν τῶν τοῖς δαιμονίοις ἠγαπημένων, αἰχμάλωτος καὶ δειλὴ καὶ ἄναλκις, καὶ δὴ καὶ δικαίως ἀκούσεται λέγοντος Θεοῦ "Παιδεύσει σε **ἡ ἀποστασία** σου, καὶ ἡ κακία σου ἐλέγξει σε."

— «Because Israel was in a frenzy like a frenzied heifer; the Lord will now graze them like a lamb in a broad pasture.» Accordingly, he says, do not imitate it, O Judah: even if Israel in its *frenzy* in the manner of heifers goes off into apostasy, its exploit will not go unpunished. It will in fact depart in captivity, leave its native land, and be allotted that of the Persians and Medes, no longer bold and, so to speak, hostile and rebellious (the constant manner of a *frenzied heifer*). Instead, it will become like the tamest of *lambs*; the situation of captives is lowly and fearful, with the expectation of maltreatment not remote, subject to the oppression of those in power. ... A person's soul could suffer the same experience after setting at naught the love for God: it will be carried in whatever direction pleases those who are beloved of demons, captive, miserable, and feeble. It will justly hear God's words, «Your **apostasy** will correct you, and your malice will reprove you.»

— Greek text — P.E. Pusey. *Sancti patris nostri Cyrilli archiepiscopi Alexandrini in xii prophetas,* 2 vols. Clarendon Press, 1868. Retrieved from Thesaurus Linguae Graecae (stephanus.tlg.uci.edu).

— English translation — Robert C. Hill. *St. Cyril of Alexandria: Commentary on the Twelve Prophets, Vol. 1 [The Fathers of the Church, 115].* The Catholic University of America Press, 2007.

— The context compares the believer's departure from God to Israel's departure from God. As Israel was taken captive to distant lands, so a soul can be carried off by demons. Where apostates end up because of

their apostasy shall discipline them, and their evil shall reprove them. Notice that *apostasia* is associated with demons.
— RELIGIOUS APOSTASY

(79) Cyril of Alexandria, Commentary on the Twelve Minor Prophets, Hosea 4:17-19 LXX, (Pusey 1.116)
— «Μέτοχος εἰδώλων Ἐφραῒμ ἔθηκεν ἑαυτῷ σκάνδαλα, ᾑρέτισε Χαναναίους· πορνεύοντες ἐξεπόρνευσαν, ἠγάπησαν ἀτιμίαν ἐκ φρυάγματος αὐτῶν. συστροφὴ πνεύματος σὺ εἶ ἐν ταῖς πτέρυξιν αὐτῆς, καὶ καταισχυνθήσονται ἐκ τῶν θυσιαστηρίων αὐτῶν.» ... καὶ ὥσπερ Ἰούδαν τὴν ἐν τοῖς Ἱεροσολύμοις ἀποκαλεῖ, τῇ βασιλευούσῃ φυλῇ τὴν κλῆσιν τετηρηκώς, οὕτω καὶ ἐπὶ τοῦ Ἰσραήλ, ὅταν ὀνομάζῃ τὸν Ἐφραῒμ, ἀπὸ τῆς βασιλευούσης φυλῆς ποιεῖται τὴν ὀνομασίαν. «μετέσχε δὴ οὖν ὁ Ἐφραῒμ εἰδώλων» φησί. προσκεκύνηκε γὰρ τῷ Αἰγυπτίων σεβάσματι· Ἄπις δὲ ἦν, ἤτοι δάμαλις τὸ ἐκείνων σέβας· μετέσχε δὲ οὐδὲν ἧττον καὶ τῆς τῶν Χαναναίων ἀνοσιότητος καὶ ἀμετρήτου φρενοβλαβείας, οἳ τὸ αἰσχρὸν οὕτως εἴδωλον περιέπειν τε καὶ προσκυνεῖν ἐγνώκασι, τὸν Βεελφεγώρ. ἀλλὰ καὶ τοῦτο δεδρακὼς ὁ Ἐφραῒμ ἔθηκεν ἑαυτῷ σκάνδαλα. προσκέκρουκε γὰρ τῷ καὶ ἐπαμύνοντι, καὶ διασώζειν εἰδότι Θεῷ. Ἡρέτισε Χαναναίους, ἀντὶ τοῦ, αἱρετὰ καὶ ἀξιόληπτα πεποίηται τὰ τῶν Χαναναίων ἔθη· ὅμοροι δὲ οὗτοι τῆς Ἰουδαίων χώρας, δυσσεβεῖς καὶ εἰδωλολάτραι. καὶ πρός γε δὴ τούτοις, πορνεύοντες ἐξεπόρνευσαν οἱ ἐξ Ἰσραήλ· δῆλον δὲ ὅτι διά τοι τὸ πέρα μέτρου καὶ τοῦ εἰκότος ἐπέκεινα τὴν νοητὴν ἐπιτηδεῦσαι πορνείαν, καὶ εἰς λῆξιν αἰσχρότητος **τῆς ἀποστασίας** αὐτοῖς ἔρχεσθαι τὰ ἐγκλήματα. ἠγαπήκασι δὲ καὶ τὴν ἀτιμίαν ἐκ φρυαγμάτων αὐτῶν, τουτέστιν, ἐξ ὑψηλῶν αὐχημάτων, ἅπερ εἶχον ἐπὶ Θεῷ καὶ δόξῃ τῇ παρ' αὐτοῦ.
— «Ephraim is involved with idols and has set stumbling blocks for themselves, opting for the Canaanites. They added promiscuity to promiscuity, they loved dishonor in their wantonness. You are a blast of wind in her wings, and they will be ashamed of their altars.» ... And just as by Judah he made reference to those in Jerusalem by restricting the reference to the ruling tribe, so, too, in the case of Israel when he cites Ephraim, he makes reference to the ruling tribe. He says, then, that «Ephraim is involved with idols,» adoring the Egyptian's divinity, namely, Apis, or the heifer that was their divinity. They were

involved no less also in the sacrilege and unbridled insanity of the *Canaanites,* who were in the habit of giving attention and adoration to the shameful idol Baal of Peor. In doing this, however, «Ephraim set stumbling blocks for themselves,» offending the God who assisted them and was accustomed to save them. «They opted for the Canaanites»; that is, they gave preference and priority to customs of the Canaanites, who as neighbors of the country of the Jews were impious worshipers of idols. In addition to this, the people of Israel «added promiscuity to promiscuity», obviously by pursuing spiritual infidelity beyond the bounds of restraint and propriety and through the extent of their crimes of shameful **apostasy** reaching the point of depravity. They also «loved dishonor in their wantonness», that is, with the loud boasting they uttered of God and the credit they gained from having him.

— Greek text — P.E. Pusey. *Sancti patris nostri Cyrilli archiepiscopi Alexandrini in xii prophetas,* 2 vols. Clarendon Press, 1868. Retrieved from Thesaurus Linguae Graecae (stephanus.tlg.uci.edu).

— English translation — Robert C. Hill. *St. Cyril of Alexandria: Commentary on the Twelve Prophets, Vol. 1 [The Fathers of the Church, 115].* The Catholic University of America Press, 2007.

— The context is Israel's apostasy, pursuing the Baalim of the Canaanites and the gods of Egyptians. Note that *apostasia* is associated with idolatry and spiritual infidelity.

—RELIGIOUS APOSTASY

(80) Cyril of Alexandria, Commentary on the Twelve Minor Prophets, Hosea 5:13 LXX, (Pusey 1.132)

— «Καὶ εἶδεν Ἐφραὶμ τὴν νόσον αὐτοῦ, καὶ Ἰούδας τὴν ὀδύνην αὐτοῦ· καὶ ἐπορεύθη Ἐφραὶμ πρὸς Ἀσσυρίους, καὶ ἀπέστειλε πρέσβεις πρὸς βασιλέα Ἰαρείμ, καὶ αὐτὸς οὐκ ἠδυνήθη ἰάσασθαι ὑμᾶς, καὶ οὐ μὴ διαπαύσῃ ἐξ ὑμῶν ὀδύνη.» ... ὁ δὲ τὴν Δαμασκὸν κατὰ κράτος ἑλών, ἐκ μέσου καὶ αὐτὸν ἐποίει τὸν Ῥαασών. ἀλλ᾽ εἰ καὶ πεπόρευταί φησι πρὸς Ἀσσυρίους ὁ Ἐφραΐμ, καὶ χρήμασιν ἐξεπρίατο καὶ λιταῖς τῆς ἐφόδου τὴν ἀνάβλησιν· κἂν εἰ ἀπέστειλε πρέσβεις Ἰούδας πρὸς βασιλέα Ἰαρεὶμ ... ἀλλ᾽ οὐ νενικήκασι τὴν θείαν ὀργήν, οὔτε μὴν περιέσονται Θεοῦ τῆς οὕτω δεινῆς **ἀποστασίας** ἐξαιτοῦντος δίκας.

— «Ephraim saw its ailment, and Judah its pangs. Ephraim went to [the] Assyrians. It sent ambassadors to King Jarib, but he was unable to heal you, and your pain will not leave you.» ... [Tiglath-Pileser] took Damascus by force, and from its midst he removed Rezin as king. But even if, as he says, «Ephraim went to [the] Assyrians» and bought them off and by petitions secured a delay in the attack, and even if Judah «sent ambassadors to King Jarib» ... they did not overcome the divine wrath or dissuade God from requiring an account of their dire **apostasy**.

— Greek text — P.E. Pusey. *Sancti patris nostri Cyrilli archiepiscopi Alexandrini in xii prophetas,* 2 vols. Clarendon Press, 1868. Retrieved from Thesaurus Linguae Graecae (stephanus.tlg.uci.edu).

— English translation — Robert C. Hill. *St. Cyril of Alexandria: Commentary on the Twelve Prophets, Vol. 1* [*The Fathers of the Church, 115*]. The Catholic University of America Press, 2007. I added the material in square brackets for clarification.

— The context is Israel's apostasy. One of the manifestations of this departure was looking to the Assyrians for help instead of God.

— RELIGIOUS APOSTASY

(81) Cyril of Alexandria, Commentary on the Twelve Minor Prophets, Hosea 6:7 LXX, (Pusey 1.143)

— «Αὐτοὶ δέ εἰσιν ὡς ἄνθρωπος παραβαίνων διαθήκην.» ... καταπεφρονήκασι καὶ αὐτοὶ τοῦ πάντων κρατοῦντος Θεοῦ, καίτοι λέγοντος ἐναργῶς διὰ τοῦ πανσόφου Μωυσέως, «Οὐ ποιήσεις σεαυτῷ εἴδωλον, οὐδὲ παντὸς ὁμοίωμα, ὅσα ἐν τῷ οὐρανῷ ἄνω καὶ ὅσα ἐν τῇ γῇ κάτω καὶ ὅσα ἐν τοῖς ὕδασιν ὑποκάτω τῆς γῆς.» καὶ πάλιν, «Οὐκ ἔσονταί σοι θεοὶ ἕτεροι πλὴν ἐμοῦ.» ἐπειδὴ δὲ ἐν ἴσῳ τῷ πρώτῳ, τουτέστι τῷ Ἀδάμ, παρώλισθον εἰς **ἀποστασίαν**, καὶ αὐτοὶ δὴ πάντως ἔξω πεσοῦνται τοῦ κατευφραίνειν εἰδότος· παραβεβήκασι γὰρ διαθήκην.

— «But they are like someone breaking a covenant.» ... they themselves scorned the God who controls all things. This was in spite of Moses in his great wisdom saying clearly, «You shall not make for yourself an idol or likeness of anything in heaven above or on earth below or in the water under the earth,» and again, «You shall have no other gods before me.» But since like the first man—Adam, that is—

they fell headlong [slipped] into **apostasy**, they, too, will be completely estranged [fallen] from the one who was in the habit of making them prosper [the one able to bless them], «having broken a covenant.»

— Greek text — P.E. Pusey. *Sancti patris nostri Cyrilli archiepiscopi Alexandrini in xii prophetas,* 2 vols. Clarendon Press, 1868. Retrieved from Thesaurus Linguae Graecae (stephanus.tlg.uci.edu).

— English translation — Robert C. Hill. *St. Cyril of Alexandria: Commentary on the Twelve Prophets, Vol. 1 [The Fathers of the Church, 115].* The Catholic University of America Press, 2007. I added the material in square brackets for clarification.

— Context is Israel's apostasy, which is compared to Adam's fall into apostasy. Notice that apostasy is paralleled with falling away.

— RELIGIOUS APOSTASY

(82) Cyril of Alexandria, Commentary on the Twelve Minor Prophets, Hosea 8:2-3 LXX, (Pusey 1.169)

— «Ἐμὲ κεκράξονται Ὁ Θεὸς ἐγνώκαμέν σε ὅτι Ἰσραὴλ ἀπεστρέψατο ἀγαθά, ἐχθρὸν κατεδίωξαν.» ... σύμβουλον δὲ ὥσπερ τὴν αὐτῶν τῶν δεινῶν δεξάμενοι πεῖραν, κατηγορήσουσι τότε τῆς ἑαυτῶν εὐηθείας, ἐκεῖνό που λέγοντες Ἰσραὴλ ἀπεστρέψατο ἀγαθά. ἐξὸν γὰρ ἔχειν αὐτά, καὶ τοῦτο πλουσίως, ἐρηρεισμένους μετὰ Θεοῦ, καὶ τὰ αὐτῷ δοκοῦντα διαπεραίνειν εὖ μάλα διεσπουδακότας, ἐχθρὸν κατεδίωξαν, τουτέστι, μονονουχὶ καὶ ἑκόντες αὐτοὶ δεδραμήκασι πρὸς ἐχθροὺς, καὶ ὑπὸ χεῖρα γεγόνασι τῶν μεμισηκότων, τὸν ἀεὶ σῴζοντα Θεὸν, καὶ ἀμείνους τιθέντα τῶν ἀνθεστηκότων, **ταῖς ἀποστασίαις** λελυπηκότες.

— «They will cry out to me, O God, we know you. Because Israel rejected good things, they pursued the enemy.» ... Accepting the experience of their actual calamities in order to learn from it, they will then allege their own guilelessness, saying as much: «Israel rejected good things.» Though it was possible, in fact, to have these things, even in rich measure, by depending on God, they eagerly devoted themselves to following their own will, and «they pursued the enemy,» that is, as it were, willingly they went after the enemy and became subject to those who hated the God who always saved them

and rendered them superior to their adversaries, thus grieving him by their **infidelities [apostasies]**.
— Greek text — P.E. Pusey. *Sancti patris nostri Cyrilli archiepiscopi Alexandrini in xii prophetas*, 2 vols. Clarendon Press, 1868. Retrieved from Thesaurus Linguae Graecae (stephanus.tlg.uci.edu).
— English translation — Robert C. Hill. *St. Cyril of Alexandria: Commentary on the Twelve Prophets, Vol. 1* [*The Fathers of the Church, 115*]. The Catholic University of America Press, 2007. I added the alternate translation in square brackets for clarification.
— The context is Israel's apostasy. Notice that apostasy is associated with rejecting God's good things and running after God's enemies.
— RELIGIOUS APOSTASY

(83) Cyril of Alexandria, Commentary on the Twelve Minor Prophets, Hosea 8:10 LXX, (Pusey 1.175)
— «Νῦν εἰσδέξομαι αὐτούς, καὶ κοπάσουσι μικρὸν τοῦ χρίειν βασιλέα καὶ ἄρχοντας.» Ἁπάσης, ὡς ἔπος εἰπεῖν, τῆς τοῦ Ἰσραὴλ φαυλότητος παραίτιοι γεγόνασιν οἱ ἐκ φυλῆς τοῦ Ἐφραῒμ ἐπ' αὐτοὺς βεβασιλευκότες. πρῶτος μὲν γὰρ ὁ ἐπάρατος Ἱεροβοὰμ **τῆς ἀποστασίας** γέγονεν εὑρετής, δαμάλεις αὐτοῖς ἀναστήσας χρυσᾶς, καὶ τῶν καλουμένων ὑψηλῶν, τουτέστι, τῶν ἐν ὄρεσι καὶ βουνοῖς τεμενῶν, καθιστὰς ἱερεῖς, τοὺς οὐκ ἐκ φυλῆς Λευΐ, ἀλλ' ὅσοι μᾶλλον «ἐπλήρουν τὴν χεῖρα αὐτῶν,» κατὰ τὸ γεγραμμένον. εἶτα μετ' ἐκεῖνον, τῶν Ἀσσυρίων προσδοκωμένων, ἐν καιρῷ τῆς βασιλείας Μαναεΐμ, πεπόμφασι χρήματα, πείθοντες ἀποσχέσθαι τῆς γῆς. Ταύτητοι δικαίως ἡ θεία γέγονεν ἀπειλὴ κατὰ τῆς βασιλείας τῆς ἐκ φυλῆς Ἐφραῒμ γεγενημένης ἐπὶ τὸν Ἰσραήλ.
— «Now I shall receive them, and they will shortly grow weary of anointing a king and rulers.» Those from the tribe of Ephraim that reigned over them were responsible for Israel's depravity in its entirety, so to speak. The accursed Jeroboam, in fact, was the first to instigate **the apostasy** by setting up for them the golden heifers, and by appointing for the «high places»—that is, the groves on mountains and hills—priests not from the tribe of Levi but rather any who «tried their hand,» as Scripture says. Later, when the Assyrians were expected during the reign of Menahem, they sent money to persuade them to leave the country. Consequently, the divine threat was

rightfully leveled at the monarchy of the tribe of Ephraim that ruled over Israel.

— Greek text — P.E. Pusey. *Sancti patris nostri Cyrilli archiepiscopi Alexandrini in xii prophetas,* 2 vols. Clarendon Press, 1868. Retrieved from Thesaurus Linguae Graecae (stephanus.tlg.uci.edu).

— English translation — Robert C. Hill. *St. Cyril of Alexandria: Commentary on the Twelve Prophets, Vol. 1 [The Fathers of the Church, 115].* The Catholic University of America Press, 2007.

— The context is Israel's depravity and apostasy, which was traced to Jeroboam. Note the association of *apostasia* with the golden heifers, the high places, priests not from the tribe of Levi, and buying the help of the Assyrians.

— RELIGIOUS APOSTASY

(84) Cyril of Alexandria, Commentary on the Twelve Minor Prophets, Hosea 8:10 LXX, (Pusey 1.176)

— ἀλλὰ «νῦν αὐτοὺς εἰσδέξομαί» φησιν, ἵνα τῇ τῶν δεινῶν πείρᾳ μανθάνωσι μόλις, ὅτι καὶ ὑπὸ Δεσπότην εἰσὶ, καὶ τῆς ἐμῆς οὐκ ἔξω χειρός. ὅτι δὲ οὐκ εἰς ἀνάβλησιν τὰ ἐξ ὀργῆς ἔτι, πεπληροφόρηκε λέγων τὸ νῦν. εἰσδεχθέντες δὴ οὖν ἵνα παιδεύωνται, πεπαύσονται λοιπὸν τοῦ χρίειν βασιλέα καὶ ἄρχοντας. δουλεύοντες γὰρ Ἀσσυρίοις καὶ Μήδοις, ποίαν ἂν ἔσχον σχολὴν τὰ **τῆς ἀποστασίας** ἔργα πληροῦν; οἵγε καὶ κατοιμώζοντες διετέλουν, καὶ τὴν ἀδόκητον κατεθρήνουν συμφοράν.

— But «now I shall receive them» in order that they may finally know by experience of the calamities that they are subject to the Lord and not beyond my power. The fact that the effects of his wrath would no longer be delayed he confirmed by saying «now.» So by being received for the purpose of correction they will then stop «anointing a king and rulers;» after all, when enslaved to Assyrians and Medes, what opportunity would they have to continue the process of **apostasy**, constantly bewailing and lamenting the unexpected misfortune?

— Greek text — P.E. Pusey. *Sancti patris nostri Cyrilli archiepiscopi Alexandrini in xii prophetas,* 2 vols. Clarendon Press, 1868. Retrieved from Thesaurus Linguae Graecae (stephanus.tlg.uci.edu).

— English translation — Robert C. Hill. *St. Cyril of Alexandria: Commentary on the Twelve Prophets, Vol. 1* [*The Fathers of the Church, 115*]. The Catholic University of America Press, 2007.
— The context is Israel's apostasy. God corrected the nation by sending them off to Assyria and Media, which seemed to break them from their apostatizing way.
— RELIGIOUS APOSTASY

(85) Cyril of Alexandria, Commentary on the Twelve Minor Prophets, Hosea 10:7-8 LXX, (Pusey 1.212)
— «Ἀπέρριψε Σαμάρεια βασιλέα αὐτῆς ὡς φρύγανον ἐπὶ προσώπου ὕδατος, καὶ ἐξαρθήσονται βωμοὶ ὦν, ἁμαρτήματα τοῦ Ἰσραὴλ, ἄκανθαι καὶ τρίβολοι ἀναβήσονται ἐπὶ τὰ θυσιαστήρια αὐτῶν.» Τὸ ἀνασφαλές τε ἅμα καὶ τὸ ἀνεπιεικὲς τοῦ τρόπου τῶν ἐξ Ἰσραὴλ, ἤτοι τῶν ἐν Σαμαρείᾳ, καὶ περὶ αὐτοὺς οὓς ᾤοντο θεοὺς, ἐπιδείξειεν ἂν εὐκόλως καὶ τόδε δὴ πάλιν. καὶ θαυμαστὸν οὐδέν. οἱ γὰρ τὸν ἕνα καὶ ἀληθῆ, καὶ φύσει Θεὸν **ταῖς ἀποστασίαις** καὶ ταῖς εἰς πᾶν ὁτιοῦν τῶν αἰσχίστων ἀποδρομαῖς ἀνοσίως περιυβρίσαντες, πῶς ἂν ἐγένοντο γνήσιοι περὶ πολλούς τε καὶ ψευδωνύμους καὶ λίθων πεποιημένους ἢ ξύλων θεούς; ἀπερρίφθαι δὴ οὖν φησὶ παρὰ τῶν ἐν Σαμαρείᾳ τὸν μόσχον, τὸν ἐν δόξῃ τῇ παρ' αὐτοῖς Θεοῦ τε καὶ βασιλέως· ἀπερρίφθαι δὲ οὕτως, ὡσανεὶ καὶ κάρφος ταῖς τῶν ὑδάτων δίναις ἐμπεπτωκὸς, ἀποφέροιτο λοιπὸν πρὸς τὸ τοῖς διωθοῦσι δοκοῦν.
— «Samaria cast off its king like a stick on the surface of the water. Altars of On will be carried off, sins of Israel; thorns and thistles will grow up on their altars.» This verse in turn would also highlight the dissolute and disedifying behavior of Israel, or Samaria, even in regard to what they thought to be gods. That is not surprising. After all, how could people be genuine in regard to a great number of falsely-named gods made of sticks and stones when they sacrilegiously insulted him who by nature is the one true God by their **infidelities [apostasies]** and their recourse to any base thing at all? So he says the calf was cast off by those in Samaria, though believed by them to be god and king, and was cast off like a stick falling on the eddies of water and then carried at the whim of what moved it.

— Greek text — P.E. Pusey. *Sancti patris nostri Cyrilli archiepiscopi Alexandrini in xii prophetas,* 2 vols. Clarendon Press, 1868. Retrieved from Thesaurus Linguae Graecae (stephanus.tlg.uci.edu).
— English translation — Robert C. Hill. *St. Cyril of Alexandria: Commentary on the Twelve Prophets, Vol. 1* [*The Fathers of the Church, 115*]. The Catholic University of America Press, 2007. I added the alternate translation in square brackets for clarification.
— The context is Israel's apostasy. Notice the association with idolatry, as that practiced on the high places of On, and with dissolute behavior.
— RELIGIOUS APOSTASY

(86) Cyril of Alexandria, Commentary on the Twelve Minor Prophets, Hosea 11:12 (12:1 LXX), (Pusey 1.241)

— «Νῦν ἔγνω αὐτοὺς ὁ Θεὸς καὶ λαὸς ἅγιος κεκλήσεται Θεοῦ.» Ἐκύκλωσε μὲν ἐν ψεύδει με καὶ ἀσεβείᾳ, φησὶν, οἶκος Ἐφραῒμ καὶ Ἰούδα· πλὴν καὶ οὕτως ἔσομαι χρηστὸς, σύμμετρον αὐτοῖς ἐπάγων τὴν κίνησιν. ἔγνων γὰρ αὐτοὺς, ὡς οὐκ ἂν ἑτέρως δύναιντο τὰ ἀμείνω μεταμαθεῖν, εἰ μή τι καὶ πάθοιεν τῶν ὅσα καταλυπεῖ καὶ καλεῖ πρὸς αἴσθησιν τῶν ἡμαρτημένων. ἔγνω τοίνυν αὐτοὺς ὁ Θεὸς, τουτέστιν, οὐκ ἠγνόηκε τῆς ὠφελούσης αὐτοὺς ἐπιστρεφείας τὴν ὁδόν. καὶ οὐκ ἀνόνητον ἔσται τὸ χρῆμα αὐτοῖς. ἐκβήσεται γὰρ ἐντεῦθεν τὸ καὶ ἐν λαοῖς ἁγίοις κατατάττεσθαι Θεοῦ. ἐκτακείσης γὰρ ἅπαξ τῆς ἐνούσης αὐτοῖς φαυλότητος διὰ πόνου καὶ θλίψεων, καθαροί τε ἔσονται καὶ ἡγιασμένοι, καὶ πείρᾳ μαθόντες, ὅτι τὸ μὲν γνήσιον τῆς εἰς Θεὸν ἀγάπης πρόξενον αὐτοῖς ἁπάσης ἔσται τρυφῆς καὶ εὐημερίας, καθάπερ ἀμέλει **τῆς ἀποστασίας** τὰ ἐγκλήματα τοῖς τῆς δουλείας καὶ θλίψεως ἐνήσι βόθροις.
— «Now God knows them, and a holy people will be called God's.» Whereas it «surrounded me with falsehood and impiety», he says—the house of Ephraim and Judah, that is—nevertheless I shall even be kind in making a measured response to them, knowing them as I do, that they would not otherwise succeed in changing for the better than by suffering for the sins that give offense and that require a recognition of their sins. «God knows them», therefore; that is, he is not ignorant of the way of conversion required of them. That event will not be without value for them: the result of it will be their being

ranked among «God's holy peoples». Once their inherent depravity is expunged with hardship and tribulation, they will be cleansed and sanctified, and will learn by experience that sincerity in love for God will be productive of complete enjoyment and prosperity for them, as of course, the crimes of **apostasy** cast them into the depths of servitude and distress.

— Greek text — P.E. Pusey. *Sancti patris nostri Cyrilli archiepiscopi Alexandrini in xii prophetas,* 2 vols. Clarendon Press, 1868. Retrieved from Thesaurus Linguae Graecae (stephanus.tlg.uci.edu).

— English translation — Robert C. Hill. *St. Cyril of Alexandria: Commentary on the Twelve Prophets, Vol. 1* [*The Fathers of the Church, 115*]. The Catholic University of America Press, 2007.

— The context is Ephraim's and Judah's departure from God. Note that apostasy is associated with lies and ungodliness, and wasting away in pain, servitude, and tribulation because of wickedness.

— RELIGIOUS APOSTASY

(87) Cyril of Alexandria, Commentary on the Twelve Minor Prophets, Hosea 12.4-5 (12:5-6 LXX), (Pusey 1.247)

—«Ἔκλαυσαν καὶ ἐδεήθησάν μου, ἐν τῷ οἴκῳ μου εὕροσάν με, καὶ ἐκεῖ ἐλαλήθη πρὸς αὐτόν. ὁ δὲ Κύριος ὁ Θεὸς ὁ Παντοκράτωρ ἔσται μνημόσυνον αὐτοῦ.» ... Οὐκοῦν ἦν μὲν ἐκ μήτρας πτερνιστὴς Ἰακώβ, ὑμεῖς δὲ ἀεὶ πτερνίζεσθε, καὶ οὐ πτερνίζετε μᾶλλον τὴν ἁμαρτίαν. καὶ φιλοπονώτατος μὲν ἐκεῖνος, καὶ ἐν ἱδρῶσιν εὐδόκιμος καὶ γνήσιος πρὸς Θεόν· ὑμεῖς δὲ τρυφῶντες **ταῖς ἀποστασίαις** ὑβρίζετε, τὸν ἁπάσης ὑμῖν εὐθυμίας οὐ τετιμήκατε χορηγόν. ἔκλαυσαν οἱ πατέρες ὑμῶν καὶ ἐδεήθησάν μου, φησίν. εἰ γάρ που γεγόνασιν ἐν ὑποψίαις τοῦ παθεῖν τὰ παρὰ τῆς τινῶν ἐπιβουλῆς, ἔκλαιον καὶ ἐδέοντό μου. δι' ἐμοῦ γὰρ καὶ μόνου σώζεσθαι προσεδόκων· ὑμεῖς δὲ πόλεις τειχίζετε, οἴεσθέ τε ὅτι, κἂν εἰ μὴ θέλοιμι, τάχα που σωθήσεσθε, καὶ κρατήσετε τῶν ἀνθεστηκότων. κἀκεῖνοι μὲν ἐν τῷ οἴκῳ μου εὕροσάν με. ἀνέβη γὰρ, ὡς ἔφην, εἰς Βαιθὴλ ὁ Ἰακὼβ, ἐπεφάνη τε Θεὸς αὐτῷ, καὶ ἐκεῖ ἐλαλήθη πρὸς αὐτὸν ἡ τῆς εὐλογίας ὑπόσχεσις, καθάπερ ἐδείξαμεν ἀρτίως· ὑμεῖς δὲ δὴ πάλιν οὐ ζητεῖτε Θεὸν ἐν τῷ οἴκῳ αὐτοῦ, εἰστρέχετε δὲ μᾶλλον, καὶ σφόδρα προθύμως ἐν τοῖς τεμένεσι τοῦ Βάαλ·ἐξαιτεῖτε λόγους οὐ παρὰ Θεοῦ, ἀλλὰ τὰ ἐκ τῶν δαιμόνων μαντεύματα.

— «They wept and implored me, in my house they found me, and there it was spoken to them. The Lord God Almighty will be his memorial.» Whereas Jacob was a supplanter from the womb, therefore, you for your part are always supplanted instead of supplanting sin. Whereas he loved toil, and by his sweat he was proven to be sincere towards God, you revel in **apostasy** and are insolent, not according honor to the source of all your satisfaction. Your ancestors «wept and implored me», he says; if they suspected that they would suffer the effects of some peoples' plotting, they wept and implored me, expecting to be saved by me and only me; you, on the other hand, fortify cities, thinking that, should I be unwilling, you would survive and get the better of your adversaries. «In my house they found me», for Jacob went up to Bethel, God appeared to him, and there the promise of blessing «was spoken to him» as we recently explained; you in turn, on the other hand, do not seek God in his house, but rather betake yourselves with great enthusiasm to the shrines of Baal. What you look for is not words from God but pronouncements from the demons.

— Greek text — P.E. Pusey. *Sancti patris nostri Cyrilli archiepiscopi Alexandrini in xii prophetas,* 2 vols. Clarendon Press, 1868. Retrieved from Thesaurus Linguae Graecae (stephanus.tlg.uci.edu).

— English translation — Robert C. Hill. *St. Cyril of Alexandria: Commentary on the Twelve Prophets, Vol. 1* [*The Fathers of the Church, 115*]. The Catholic University of America Press, 2007.

— The context is a comparison between Jacob and his descendants. He was sincere. They reveled in apostasy. He went up to Bethel. They go to the shrines of Baal. Notice that *apostasia* is associated with insincerity, insolence, idolatry, seeking the pronouncements of demons rather than the word of God, and not honoring God as the source of blessing and deliverance.

— RELIGIOUS APOSTASY

(88) Cyril of Alexandria, Commentary on the Twelve Minor Prophets, Hosea 12:13 (12:14 LXX), (Pusey 1.257)

— «Καὶ ἐν Προφήτῃ ἀνήγαγε Κύροις τὸν Ἰσραὴλ ἐξ Αἰγύπτου, καὶ ἐν Προφήτῃ διεφυλάχθη.» Τὴν αἰτίαν ἡμῖν ἐν τούτοις διατρανοῖ τοῦ μήτε φυλάξαι τὸν Ἰσραὴλ τὴν ὁρισθεῖσαν ἐντολὴν, καὶ καταφρονῆσαι

Θεοῦ λέγοντος «Οὐκ ἔσονταί σοι θεοὶ ἕτεροι πλὴν ἐμοῦ,» ... γεγόνασιν ὅλως οἱ ἐξ Ἰσραὴλ ὑπὸ τὴν ἀνθρώπων βασιλείαν, καίτοι βασιλεύοντος αὐτῶν τοῦ Θεοῦ διὰ Προφητῶν ἁγίων, καὶ ἐλλελοιπότος αὐτοῖς οὐδενός, εἰς τὸ εἶναι μακαρίους. ... ἐπειδὴ δὲ γεγόνασιν ὑπὸ βασιλέας, τῆς εἰς Θεὸν ἀγάπης ἐξώκειλαν. πρῶτος μὲν γὰρ ᾠκοδόμησε Σολομῶν καὶ βωμοὺς καὶ τεμένη τοῖς Βααλείμ· εἶτα μετ' αὐτὸν ὁ ἐπάρατος Ἰεροβοὰμ τὰς χρυσᾶς ἐποίει δαμάλεις. αἰτιᾶται τοίνυν ὡς παγκάλην οἰκονομίαν οὐ τετηρηκότας, τὸ παρὰ Θεοῦ, φημί, διὰ προφητῶν βασιλεύεσθαι, τὸ δὲ ὑπὸ χεῖρα πεσεῖν ἀνθρώπων ἀνθηρημένους, ὃ δὴ καὶ γέγονεν αὐτοῖς **τῆς ἀποστασίας** πρόξενον.

— «By a prophet the Lord brought Israel up out of Egypt, and by a prophet he was guarded.» In this he clarifies for us the reason for Israel's not observing the commandment imposed [the clearly defined commandment], for spurning God's words, «You shall have no other gods before me.» ... [they were] completely subject to human kingship, despite God being their king through holy prophets and there being nothing lacking for them to be blessed. ... But when they became subject to a king, they lost their love for God; Solomon was the first to build altars and shrines to the Baals, then after him the accursed Jeroboam made golden heifers. Accordingly, he blames them for not observing the excellent divine plan for them to be ruled by God, I mean, through prophets, and preferring to fall under the hand of human beings, which proved to be the source of **apostasy** for them.

— Greek text — P.E. Pusey. *Sancti patris nostri Cyrilli archiepiscopi Alexandrini in xii prophetas,* 2 vols. Clarendon Press, 1868. Retrieved from Thesaurus Linguae Graecae (stephanus.tlg.uci.edu).

— English translation — Robert C. Hill. *St. Cyril of Alexandria: Commentary on the Twelve Prophets, Vol. 1 [The Fathers of the Church, 115].* The Catholic University of America Press, 2007. I added some clarifying material in square brackets.

— The context points out that seeking human authority was the cause of Israel's apostasy. Solomon was the first to build high places and shrines for other gods. After him Jeroboam made the golden calves. Notice the association between apostasy and idolatry.

— RELIGIOUS APOSTASY

(89) Cyril of Alexandria, Commentary on the Twelve Minor Prophets, Hosea 13:7-8 LXX, (Pusey 1.267)

— «Καὶ ἔσομαι αὐτοῖς ὡς πάνθηρ καὶ ὡς πάρδαλις· κατὰ τὴν ὁδὸν Ἀσσυρίων ἀπαντήσομαι αὐτοῖς ὡς ἄρκτος ἀπορουμένη, καὶ διαρρήξω συγκλεισμὸν καρδίας αὐτῶν, καὶ φάγονται αὐτοὺς ἐκεῖ σκύμνοι δρυμοῦ, θηρία ἀγροῦ διασπάσει αὐτούς.» Ἐπειδὴ γὰρ τῆς εὐθυμίας τὸ πλάτος γέγονεν αὐτοῖς ὀλέθρου πρόξενον καὶ **ἀποστασίας** ἀφορμὴ, ταύτητοι λοιπὸν αἱ θλίψεις ἐπάγονται, καὶ ἀναλόγως τοῖς ἀρρωστήμασι. τὰ γάρ τοι πολὺ νενοσηκότα τῶν σωμάτων καὶ σεσηπότα λοιπόν, εἴξειεν οὐδαμῶς ἠπίοις μὲν ἔτι φαρμάκοις, δέοιτο δ' ἂν μᾶλλον καὶ σιδήρου καὶ πυρός.

— «I shall be to them like a panther and a leopard; in the path of the Assyrians, I shall encounter them like a bear that is at a loss, and shall tear open the covering of their heart. Whelps of the forest will devour them there, and wild beasts of the countryside will dismember them.» Since in fact the extent of their prosperity proved to be productive of ruin for them and an occasion for **apostasy**, consequently tribulation will now be applied as in the case of sick people; the severe ailments and infections of the body would in no way yield to mild medicines, requiring instead knife [iron] and fire.

— Greek text — P.E. Pusey. *Sancti patris nostri Cyrilli archiepiscopi Alexandrini in xii prophetas,* 2 vols. Clarendon Press, 1868. Retrieved from Thesaurus Linguae Graecae (stephanus.tlg.uci.edu).

— English translation — Robert C. Hill. *St. Cyril of Alexandria: Commentary on the Twelve Prophets, Vol. 1 [The Fathers of the Church, 115].* The Catholic University of America Press, 2007. I added clarifying material in square brackets.

— The context traces Israel's apostasy to her prosperity. The solution is not mild medicine but iron (the knife) and fire.

— RELIGIOUS APOSTASY

(90) Cyril of Alexandria, Commentary on the Twelve Minor Prophets, Hosea 14:1-3 (14:2-4 LXX), (Pusey 1.277)

— «Ἐπιστράφητι Ἰσραὴλ πρὸς Κύριον τὸν Θεόν σου, διότι ἠσθένησας ἐν ταῖς ἀδικίαις σου. λάβετε μεθ' ἑαυτῶν λόγους, καὶ ἐπιστράφητε πρὸς Κύριον τὸν Θεὸν ὑμῶν·εἴπατε αὐτῷ ὅπως μὴ λάβητε ἀδικίαν καὶ λάβητε ἀγαθά, καὶ ἀνταποδώσομεν καρπὸν χειλέων ἡμῶν. Ἀσσοὺρ οὐ μὴ σώσῃ ἡμᾶς, ἔφιπποι οὐκ ἀναβησόμεθα· οὐκ ἔτι μὴ εἴπωμεν Θεοὶ ἡμῶν, τοῖς ἔργοις τῶν χειρῶν ἡμῶν.» ... προκαταπτοήσας δὴ οὖν τοῖς δείμασιν, ἐπὶ καιροῦ λοιπὸν ταῖς τῶν νουθετουμένων καρδίαις τὸν καλοῦντα πρὸς μετάγνωσιν ἐνίησι λόγον, ὅτι χρὴ παλινδρομεῖν, καὶ πρὸς Θεὸν ἐπανήκειν εὖ μάλα παραφωνῶν. λέγων δὲ ὅτι ἠσθένησας ἐν ταῖς ἀδικίαις σοῦ, δίδωσι νοεῖν, ὅτι πάντη τε καὶ πάντως συγκαταλήξει ταῖς ἀδικίαις καὶ τὸ ἀσθενεῖν αὐτούς, καὶ τοῖς **τῆς ἀποστασίας** τρόποις, εἰ ἐκ μέσου γένοιντο, συνοιχήσεται καὶ τὰ δεινά.

— «Return, O Israel, to the Lord your God, because you have grown weak through your iniquities. Take words with you, and return to the Lord your God. Speak to him, so that instead of receiving iniquities, you may receive good things, and we shall repay with the fruit of our lips. Assyria will not save us, we shall not ride on horses, let us no longer say 'our gods' to the works of our hands.» ... Having stunned them in advance with these terrors, therefore, he then chooses the moment to impart to the hearts of those being counseled an instruction summoning them to repentance, announcing clearly the need to change course and return to God. By saying «because you have grown weak through your iniquities», he gives them to understand that their weaknesses will cease altogether along with their iniquities; and if the forms of **apostasy** are removed, the calamities will also disappear.

— Greek text — P.E. Pusey. *Sancti patris nostri Cyrilli archiepiscopi Alexandrini in xii prophetas,* 2 vols. Clarendon Press, 1868. Retrieved from Thesaurus Linguae Graecae (stephanus.tlg.uci.edu).

— English translation — Robert C. Hill. *St. Cyril of Alexandria: Commentary on the Twelve Prophets, Vol. 1 [The Fathers of the Church, 115].* The Catholic University of America Press, 2007.

— Context is God's handling of Israel. If she will entirely lay aside her unrighteousness and apostasies, and they are removed from her midst, the terrible judgments will also go away. Notice the association between apostasy and iniquity.

— RELIGIOUS APOSTASY

(91) Cyril of Alexandria, Commentary on the Twelve Minor Prophets, Hosea 14:1-3 (14:2-4 LXX), (Pusey 1.278)

— «λάβετε γὰρ μεθ' ἑαυτῶν λόγους, εἴπατε τῷ Θεῷ, ὅπως μὴ λάβητε ἀδικίαν καὶ λάβητε ἀγαθὰ,» τουτέστιν ἵνα μὴ ταῖς ἀδικίαις ἰσομέτρως κολάζησθε, καταπλουτῆτε δὲ μᾶλλον ταῖς τῶν ἀγαθῶν χορηγίαις, ἐπαγγείλασθε δὲ προσκομίζειν αὐτῷ τὰ ἀπὸ χειλέων, χαριστηρίους ᾠδὰς καὶ ἐξομολόγησιν. γλώσσης γὰρ τὰ τοιάδε καρποί. πλὴν ἐκεῖνο βοᾶτέ φησι, καὶ ἀραρότως ἐπαγγέλλεσθε, ὡς «οὔτε Ἀσοὺρ σώσει ἡμᾶς, οὔτε μὴν ἔφιπποι ἀναβησόμεθα» ἀλλ' οὐδὲ ἐροῦμεν ἔτι «Θεοὶ ἡμῶν, τοῖς ἔργοις τῶν χειρῶν ἡμῶν». ἦσαν γὰρ οὗτοι **τῆς ἀποστασίας** οἱ τρόποι. διὰ ταῦτα προσκεκρούκασιν, ὅτι καὶ λελατρεύκασιν εἰδώλοις, καὶ τὸν ἀεὶ σώζοντα Θεὸν ἀτιμάσαντες, ταῖς ἐξ ἀνθρώπων ἐπικουρίαις προσνενεμήκασι τὴν ἐλπίδα.

— «Take words with you» he is saying, «speak to God, so that instead of receiving iniquity, you receive good things.» In other words, lest you be punished with your iniquities instead of abounding in the supply of good things, promise to offer to him what comes from your lips, thanksgiving hymns and confession, such things being the fruits of your tongue. But shout it out, he says, and make a firm promise that «Assyria will not save us, we shall not ride on horses»; nor shall we say «our Gods to the works of our hands», which is [are] a form [forms] of **apostasy**. It was on account of this that they offended, because they served the idols, and, while dishonoring the God who had always saved them, they placed their hope in human assistance.

— Greek text — P.E. Pusey. *Sancti patris nostri Cyrilli archiepiscopi Alexandrini in xii prophetas,* 2 vols. Clarendon Press, 1868. Retrieved from Thesaurus Linguae Graecae (stephanus.tlg.uci.edu).

— English translation — Robert C. Hill. *St. Cyril of Alexandria: Commentary on the Twelve Prophets, Vol. 1* [*The Fathers of the Church, 115*]. The Catholic University of America Press, 2007. I added clarifying material in square brackets.

— The context is Israel's apostasy. She is exhorted to talk things out with God and make things right so she can receive good things instead of judgment for her iniquity. Notice that apostasy is associated with serving idols, dishonoring the God who was continually saving her, and setting her hope on the aid of men.

— RELIGIOUS APOSTASY

182

(92) Cyril of Alexandria, Commentary on the Twelve Minor Prophets, Joel 3:16-17 (4:16-17 LXX), (Pusey 1.359)

— «Ὁ δὲ Κύριος φείσεται τοῦ λαοῦ αὐτοῦ, καὶ ἐνισχύσει Κύριος τοὺς υἱοὺς Ἰσραήλ. καὶ ἐπιγνώσεσθε ὅτι ἐγὼ Κύριος ὁ Θεὸς ὑμῶν ὁ κατασκηνῶν ἐν Σιὼν ἐν ὄρει ἁγίῳ μου· καὶ ἔσται Ἰερουσαλὴμ ἁγία, καὶ ἀλλογενεῖς οὐ διελεύσονται δι' αὐτῆς οὐκέτι.» Ὅτε τὰ ἐγκλήματα **τῆς ἀποστασίας** τοῖς ἐξ Ἰσραὴλ ἐπεγράφοντο, καὶ δαμάλεσι μὲν προσεκύνουν ταῖς χρυσαῖς, ἔφασκον δὲ ἀνοσίως «Οὗτοι οἱ θεοί σου Ἰσραήλ, οἵ τινες ἀνήγαγόν σε ἐκ γῆς Αἰγύπτου,» τότε καὶ ἀσθενεῖς καὶ εὐάλωτοι, καὶ τοῖς πολεμίοις ἑτοιμοτάτη προὔκειντο θήρα· ταύτῃτοι καὶ εἰς αἰχμαλωσίαν ἐπέμποντο.

— «The Lord will spare his people, and the Lord will empower the children of Israel. You will know that I am the Lord your God, who dwells in Zion on my holy mountain. Jerusalem will be holy, and aliens will nevermore pass through it.» When the crimes of **apostasy** were registered against the people of Israel because they adored golden heifers and said sacrilegiously, «The, Israel, are your gods who led you out of the land of Egypt», at that time they were weak and vulnerable, ready prey for the enemy, and consequently were dispatched into captivity.

— Greek text — P.E. Pusey. *Sancti patris nostri Cyrilli archiepiscopi Alexandrini in xii prophetas,* 2 vols. Clarendon Press, 1868. Retrieved from Thesaurus Linguae Graecae (stephanus.tlg.uci.edu).

— English translation — Robert C. Hill. *St. Cyril of Alexandria: Commentary on the Twelve Prophets, Vol. 1* [*The Fathers of the Church, 115*]. The Catholic University of America Press, 2007.

— The context is Israel's apostasy. Notice that *apostasia* is associated with worshiping the golden calves and embracing the foolish notion that they were the gods of Israel which brought them up from the land of Egypt.

— RELIGIOUS APOSTASY

(93) Cyril of Alexandria, Commentary on the Twelve Minor Prophets, Amos 5:4-6 LXX, (Pusey 1.456)

— «Διότι τάδε λέγει Κύριος πρὸς τὸν οἶκον Ἰσραὴλ Ἐκζητήσατέ με καὶ ζήσεσθε· καὶ μὴ ἐκζητεῖτε Βαιθὴλ καὶ εἰς Γάλγαλα μὴ εἰσπορεύεσθε, καὶ ἐπὶ τὸ φρέαρ τοῦ ὅρκου μὴ ἀναβαίνετε, ὅτι

Γάλγαλα αἰχμαλωτευομένη αἰχμαλωθευθήσεται, καὶ Βαιθὴλ ἔσται ὡς οὐχ ὑπάρχουσα. ἐκζητήσατε τὸν Κύριον καὶ ζήσατε, ὅπως μὴ ἀναλάμψῃ ὡς πῦρ ὁ οἶκος Ἰωσὴφ καὶ καταφάγεται αὐτόν, καὶ οὐκ ἔσται ὁ σβέσων τῷ οἴκῳ Ἰσραήλ.» ... φύσει γὰρ ἀγαθὸς ὁ Δημιουργός, «Μακρόθυμος καὶ πολυέλεος καὶ "μετανοῶν ἐπὶ ταῖς κακίαις,» καθὰ γέγραπται, καὶ ᾗ φησιν αὐτὸς διὰ φωνῆς Ἰεζεκιήλ «Οὐ θέλει τὸν θάνατον τοῦ ἀποθνήσκοντος, ὡς τὸ ἀποστρέψαι αὐτὸν ἀπὸ τῆς ὁδοῦ αὐτοῦ τῆς πονηρᾶς καὶ ζῆν αὐτόν.» εἴπερ οὖν περὶ πολλοῦ ποιεῖσθε τὸ ζῆν, καὶ ἀξιόληπτον ὑμῖν τὸ χρῆμα φαίνεται, καταλήγετε τῆς ἀπάτης, καὶ τῆς οὕτω μακρᾶς ἀμαθίας ἀποπηδήσαντες, ἐκζητήσατέ με φησὶ, τουτέστιν, ἐμοὶ λατρεύσατε τῷ φύσει Θεῷ, τῷ ζωοποιῷ, τῷ σώζειν ἰσχύοντι, ἔξω τε παντὸς τιθέντι κακοῦ τοὺς σεβομένους αὐτόν. δεῖ δὲ δὴ, φησὶ, προαπονίπτειν ἑαυτούς, τῆς ἑαυτῶν ψυχῆς ἐξωθοῦντας **τῆς ἀποστασίας** τὸν ῥύπον, καὶ προεκτήκειν εὖ μάλα τὴν ἐκ τοῦ πεπλανῆσθαι κηλῖδα, κολλᾶσθαί τε οὕτω λοιπὸν τῷ παναγάθῳ Θεῷ.

— «Hence the Lord says this to the house of Israel: Seek me out, and you will live. Do not seek out Bethel, do not go off to Gilgal, and do not go up to the well of the oath, because Gilgal will surely be captured, and Bethel will be nonexistent. Seek the Lord, and live, lest the house of Joseph light up like a fire, and it will devour it, and there will be no one to extinguish it for the house of Israel.» ... The Creator, after all, is kind, «longsuffering and rich in mercy, and repenting of the troubles», as it is written, and as he himself says in Ezekiel, «He does not wish the death of the dying so much as to convert him from his wicked path, and have him live». If, therefore, you set great store by being alive, which seems desirable for you to be, desist from the deception, abandon such longstanding ignorance, and seek me out, he is saying—that is, serve me, the one who is by nature God, the Life-giver, the one able to save, rescuing from every trouble those who reverence me. It is necessary, however, he says, to cleanse yourselves in advance, removing the stain of **apostasy** from your soul, utterly canceling the stain of being deceived, and then cleaving to God in his goodness.

— Greek text — P.E. Pusey. *Sancti patris nostri Cyrilli archiepiscopi Alexandrini in xii prophetas,* 2 vols. Clarendon Press, 1868. Retrieved from Thesaurus Linguae Graecae (stephanus.tlg.uci.edu).

— English translation — Robert C. Hill. *St. Cyril of Alexandria: Commentary on the Twelve Prophets, Vol. 1 [The Fathers of the Church, 115].* The Catholic University of America Press, 2007.

— The context reminds readers of the goodness of God and of the necessity of removing apostasy (our departures) from our souls if we want to experience the goodness of God. Notice the association of apostasy with wicked paths, deception, intentional ignorance, and not seeking God.

— RELIGIOUS APOSTASY

(94) Cyril of Alexandria, Commentary on the Twelve Minor Prophets, Amos 9:7 LXX, (Pusey 1.537)

— «Οὐχ ὡς υἱοὶ Αἰθιόπων ὑμεῖς ἐστὲ ἐμοὶ υἱοὶ Ἰσραήλ; λέγει Κύριος· οὐ τὸν Ἰσραὴλ ἀνήγαγον ἐκ γῆς Αἰγύπτου, καὶ τοὺς ἀλλοφύλους ἐκ Καππαδοκίας, καὶ τοὺς Σύρους ἐκ βόθρου; ἰδοὺ οἱ ὀφθαλμοὶ Κυρίου τοῦ Θεοῦ ἐπὶ τὴν βασιλείαν τῶν ἁμαρτωλῶν, καὶ ἐξαρῶ αὐτὴν ἀπὸ προσώπου τῆς γῆς.» ... «Οὐ γὰρ πάντες οἱ ἐξ Ἰσραὴλ, οὗτοι Ἰσραὴλ, οὐδ' ὅτι εἰσὶ σπέρμα Ἀβραὰμ, πάντες τέκνα.» ἀλλ' ἡ τῶν ἔργων ὁμοιότης καὶ τὸ ἐπαυχεῖν δύνασθαι λαμπρῶς ταῖς τῶν πατέρων εὐκλείαις ἀπονέμει δικαίως. κατεσοβαρεύοντο δὲ τῶν ἄλλων ἁπάντων ἐθνῶν κἀκεῖνο λέγοντες, ὡς ἐξ ἁπάντων αὐτοὺς τῶν ἐθνῶν ἀπολέκτους ἐποιήσατο ὁ Θεὸς, καὶ ἐξείλατο μὲν ἐκ τῆς Αἰγυπτίων γῆς, μετεκόμισε δὲ εἰς τὴν γῆν τῆς ἐπαγγελίας. καὶ ἀληθὴς μὲν ὁ λόγος. οἱ δὲ δὴ μάλιστα ταῖς καθηκούσαις ἀμοιβαῖς κατευφραίνειν ὀφείλοντες τὸν τετιμηκότα, **ταῖς** ὁλοτρόποις **ἀποστασίαις** καὶ ταῖς εἰς φαυλότητα παρατροπαῖς ἐκτόπως ὑβρίζοντες κατὰ πολλοὺς ἡλίσκοντο τρόπους. ἤκουσι δὲ ἤδη φρενοβλαβείας εἰς τοῦτο λοιπὸν οἱ τάλανες, ὡς οἴεσθαί σφισιν αὐτοῖς πρὸς τὸ εὖ εἶναί τε καὶ τὸ εἰς δόξαν ἀρκέσειν τὸ ἐκ ῥίζης γενέσθαι τῆς Ἀβραὰμ, καὶ ὅτι μετεκομίσθησαν ἐκ γῆς Αἰγυπτίων εἰς τὴν τῆς ἐπαγγελίας γῆν.

— «Are you not to me like the people of Ethiopia, people of Israel? says the Lord. Did I not bring Israel up from the land of Egypt, the Philistines from Cappadocia, and the Syrians from Bothros? Lo, the eyes of the Lord God are upon the kingdom of sinners, and I shall remove it from the face of the earth.» ... In fact, «not all Israelites truly belong to Israel, and not all Abraham's children are his true descendants.» It is rather the similarity of works that rightly confers the ability to make open boasts of ancestors' nobility. By contrast, they disparaged all the other nations by claiming that of all the nations God treated them as special, rescuing them from the land of Egypt and bringing them into the land of promise. While the claim was true, and they in particular should with due recompense have brought joy to the one who showed them esteem, they wrongfully insulted him with complete **apostasy** and sank into all sorts of depravity. The wretches then reached such a degree of derangement as to think that for them, descent from Abraham was sufficient grounds for prosperity and good reputation, and from their being brought from Egypt to the land of promise.

— Greek text — P.E. Pusey. *Sancti patris nostri Cyrilli archiepiscopi Alexandrini in xii prophetas,* 2 vols. Clarendon Press, 1868. Retrieved from Thesaurus Linguae Graecae (stephanus.tlg.uci.edu).

— English translation — Robert C. Hill. *St. Cyril of Alexandria: Commentary on the Twelve Prophets, Vol. 1 [The Fathers of the Church, 115].* The Catholic University of America Press, 2007.

— The context is Israel's apostasy. Despite the manifested goodness of God in bringing her out of the bondage of Egypt into the promised land, she fell into apostasy, depravity, and deranged thinking which associated blessing with mere descent from Abraham.

— RELIGIOUS APOSTASY

(95) Cyril of Alexandria, Commentary on the Twelve Minor Prophets, Micah 1:13 LXX, (Pusey 1.620)

— «Κατοικοῦσα Λάχις ἀρχηγὸς ἁμαρτίας αὕτη ἐστὶ τῇ θυγατρὶ Σιὼν, ὅτι ἐν σοὶ εὑρέθησαν ἀσέβειαι τοῦ Ἰσραήλ.» ... Τί οὖν ὁ λόγος βούλεται δηλοῦν; ἀπολογεῖται τρόπον τινὰ τοῖς τῶν ἀλλοφύλων δήμοις, καὶ ἀναπείθειν πειρᾶται διακεῖσθαι λοιπὸν, ὡς οὐκ ἂν ἠσθένησεν ὁ σώζων Θεός. ἐπειδὴ δὲ δεδυσσεβήκασιν εἰς αὐτὸν αἱ τοῦ Ἰούδα πόλεις, παραδέδονται τοῖς ἐχθροῖς. «ἀρχηγὸς» γάρ φησιν ἡ Λάχις «ἁμαρτίας τῇ Σιὼν γινομένη», καὶ **ἀποστασίας** πρόφασις πρώτη δέδοται τῷ Σεναχηρείμ. ἀπόλωλε δὴ οὖν ὁ Ἰσραὴλ, ὡς ἀπό γε τῆς Λάχεως ἔξεστιν ἰδεῖν, οὐκ ἠρρωστηκότος Θεοῦ τὸ ἄναλκι· πολλοῦ γε καὶ δεῖ· τὸ πλανᾶσθαι δὲ μᾶλλον ἠρρωστηκὼς, καὶ ταῖς τῶν εἰδώλων λατρείαις ἀσυνέτως προσκείμενος.

— «Inhabiting Lachish, she is the leader in sin for daughter Zion, because in you were found the offenses of Israel.» ... So what does the verse mean? In some way he mounts a defense to the Philistine population and endeavors to persuade them to adopt the attitude in the future that the saving God has not lost his strength. Since the cities of Judah offended him, however, they were surrendered to the foe; Lachish was «leader in sin for daughter Zion», and as the principal base of **apostasy** was given over to Sennacherib. So Israel perished, as it is possible to see from Lachish, not that God was lacking strength—far from it—but because it suffered from being deceived and foolishly attached to the worship of idols.

— Greek text — P.E. Pusey. *Sancti patris nostri Cyrilli archiepiscopi Alexandrini in xii prophetas,* 2 vols. Clarendon Press, 1868. Retrieved from Thesaurus Linguae Graecae (stephanus.tlg.uci.edu).

— English translation — Robert C. Hill. *St. Cyril of Alexandria: Commentary on the Twelve Prophets, Vol. 1 [The Fathers of the Church, 115]*. The Catholic University of America Press, 2007.

— The context is Israel's apostasy which had spread to Judah and Jerusalem through Lachish. Apostasy is associated with deception and idolatry.

— RELIGIOUS APOSTASY

(96) Cyril of Alexandria, Commentary on the Twelve Minor Prophets, Micah 6:3-4 LXX, (Pusey 1.694)

— «Λαός μου, τί ἐποίησά σοι, ἢ τί ἐλύπησά σε, ἢ τί παρηνώχλησά σοι; ἀποκρίθητί μοι. διότι ἀνήγαγόν σε ἐκ γῆς Αἰγύπτου, καὶ ἐξ οἴκου δουλείας ἐλυτρωσάμην σε, καὶ ἐξαπέστειλα πρὸ προσώπου σου τὸν Μωυσῆν καὶ Ἀαρὼν καὶ Μαριάμ.» Δικάζεται Θεὸς ἀπὸ προσώπου φωνῆς τοῦ Προφήτου, ἀπροφάσιστον ἀποφαίνων τῶν εἰς αὐτὸν δεδυσσεβηκότων **τῆς ἀποστασίας** τὸν τρόπον, καὶ πέρα λόγου τοῦ πρέποντος, μᾶλλον δὲ καὶ ἀποπληξίας ἀπάσης, τὰ τολμήματα, καὶ τὸ τῆς ἀναισθησίας μέγεθος ἀσύνηθές τε καὶ ξένον καὶ αὐτοῖς που τάχα τοῖς λίαν ἀγνώμοσι. ποία γὰρ εἰπέ μοι, φησὶ, τῶν εἰς ἐμὲ δεδυσσεβημένων ἡ πρόφασις;

— «My people, what have I done to you, what grief have I caused you, what trouble have I brought you? Answer me. Because I brought you from the land of Egypt, I ransomed you from the hose of slavery and sent before you Moses, Aaron, and Miriam.» God delivers judgment in the person of the prophet, showing the form of **apostasy** on the part of those offending him to be inexcusable and unreasonable. Rather, the crime was the result of complete folly, and its unusual and unprecedented enormity even in people so very ungrateful was due to insensitivity. After all, what excuse could there be, tell me, he asks, for those who offended against me?

— Greek text — P.E. Pusey. *Sancti patris nostri Cyrilli archiepiscopi Alexandrini in xii prophetas,* 2 vols. Clarendon Press, 1868. Retrieved from Thesaurus Linguae Graecae (stephanus.tlg.uci.edu).

— English translation — Robert C. Hill. *St. Cyril of Alexandria: Commentary on the Twelve Prophets, Vol. 1 [The Fathers of the Church, 115].* The Catholic University of America Press, 2007.

— The context is Israel's apostasy. Notice the association with ungratefulness, insensitivity, and unreasonableness, and folly.

— RELIGIOUS APOSTASY

(97) Cyril of Alexandria, Commentary on the Twelve Minor Prophets, Nahum LXX, Introduction, (Pusey 2.2)

— Ἐπειδὴ γὰρ ἥλω τῶν Ἰουδαίων ἡ χώρα, καὶ εἰς τὴν Περσῶν τε καὶ Μήδων ἐξεκομίσθησαν δορίληπτοι γεγονότες οἱ **ταῖς** ἐκτόποις **ἀποστασίαις** καταλυπήσαντες τὸν ἀεὶ προεστηκότα καὶ ὑπεραθλοῦντα Θεὸν καὶ ἀμείνους ἀποφαίνοντα τῶν ἀνθεστηκότων αὐτούς, οἱ μὲν ἤδη τοῦτο πεπονθότες, τοῖς τῆς αἰχμαλωσίας ἐνισχημένοι κακοῖς καὶ δύσοιστον ἔχοντες ἀθλιότητα διετέλου.·

— When the country of the Jews was taken, remember, and the people were enslaved and deported to the land of the Persians and Medes after offending by their wrongful **apostasy** [apostasies or departures] the one who had ever been their protector and champion and rendered them superior to their adversaries, some who suffered that fate passed an intolerable life of misery caught up in the hardship of captivity.

— Greek text — P.E. Pusey. *Sancti patris nostri Cyrilli archiepiscopi Alexandrini in xii prophetas,* 2 vols. Clarendon Press, 1868. Retrieved from Thesaurus Linguae Graecae (stephanus.tlg.uci.edu).

— English translation — Robert C. Hill. *St. Cyril of Alexandria: Commentary on the Twelve Prophets, Vol. 1 [The Fathers of the*

Church, 115]. The Catholic University of America Press, 2007. I added material in square brackets for clarification.
— The context is Israel's apostasy (indeed her numerous departures) which led to her being taken to Persia and Medea as captives.
— RELIGIOUS APOSTASY

(98) Cyril of Alexandria, Commentary on the Twelve Minor Prophets, Zephaniah 1:13 LXX, (Pusey 2.186)

— «Καὶ ἔσται ἡ δύναμις αὐτῶν εἰς διαρπαγὴν, καὶ οἱ οἶκοι αὐτῶν εἰς ἀφανισμόν· καὶ οἰκοδομήσουσιν οἰκίας καὶ οὐ μὴ κατοικήσουσιν ἐν αὐταῖς, καὶ καταφυτεύσουσιν ἀμπελῶνας καὶ οὐ μὴ πίωσι τὸν οἶνον αὐτῶν.» Ἐπὶ καιροῦ τάχα που καὶ νῦν πρὸς ἡμῶν εἰρήσεται «Οὐκ ὠφελήσουσι θησαυροὶ ἀνόμους.» δραπέτης μὲν γὰρ ὁ πλοῦτος ἀεί, καὶ τὸ βεβηκὸς οὐκ ἔχει· μεθύει δὲ μᾶλλον καὶ διανένευκεν εἰς **ἀποστασίαν**, καὶ πόδας ἔχει σαθρούς. τὸ δὲ δὴ καὶ ἐπ' αὐτῷ μέγα φρονεῖν ἐθέλειν, ἠλίθιον κομιδῇ. ἐξελεῖται γὰρ ἥκιστά γε τοὺς ὑπὸ θείαν ὀργὴν, οὐδ' ἂν ἀπαλλάξειεν αἰτιαμάτων τινάς, Θεοῦ ποινὴν καθορίζοντος, καὶ τὴν τοῖς πλημμελοῦσι πρέπουσαν ἐπάγοντος δίκην.
— «Their power [wealth] will become booty, and their houses disappear. They will build houses and not live in them; they will plant vineyards and not drink their wine.» It will be timely for us even now to say, «Treasures will be of no use to the lawless.» Wealth is ever fleeting [a runaway servant] and has no permanence [fixed place or stability], in fact; rather it totters [is inebriated] and is inclined to depart [has nodded to **revolt**], having itchy feet [has cracked feet]. Wanting also to take pride in it is very precarious; it hardly rescues those under God's wrath, nor would it rid anyone of blame if God assigns punishment and inflicts retribution befitting the crime.
— Greek text — P.E. Pusey. *Sancti patris nostri Cyrilli archiepiscopi Alexandrini in xii prophetas,* 2 vols. Clarendon Press, 1868. Retrieved from Thesaurus Linguae Graecae (stephanus.tlg.uci.edu).
— English translation — Robert C. Hill. *St. Cyril of Alexandria: Commentary on the Twelve Prophets, Vol. 1* [*The Fathers of the Church, 115*]. The Catholic University of America Press, 2007. I added material in square brackets for clarification.
— Robert Hill appears to have translated δραπέτης and the stretch of descriptions which follow (τὸ βεβηκὸς, μεθύει, διανένευκεν εἰς

ἀποστασίαν, and πόδας σαθρούς) as if the entire stretch was somehow expanding on the concept of *vanishing*, which led to several translations which are questionable. I think that the stretch introduces δραπέτης (drapetēs) *runaway slave or servant* as a metaphor for the *uselessness* of wealth and that the descriptions which follow continue this illustration. The runaway servant has no stability, is inebriated, is committed to revolt (rebellion), and has cracked feet. He is worthless for his master. That the concept Cyril was pursuing with this metaphor isn't *vanishing* but *worthless* can be seen by his preceding statement "treasures will be *useless* to the lawless" and his following statement "wealth *can't rescue* those under God's wrath." The wealth the Jews had—homes and vineyards and the like—didn't keep them from being taken captive. Their wealth was as useless to them as a runaway slave.

— The context is a sober view of wealth. It is like a δραπέτης (drapetēs) runaway slave or servant, committed to revolt, that isn't profitable to its master and should not be depended upon. Men should depend upon God instead.

— POLITICAL SEDITION OR REBELLION

(99) Cyril of Alexandria, Against Julian the Emperor, Prologue, Section 4, (Section 3-4 on Tertullian.org)

— Τίς οὖν ἄρα ἐστὶν ὁ τῇ τοῦ Χριστοῦ δόξῃ μεμαχημένος; Πλεῖστοι μὲν οὖν ὅσοι κατὰ καιροὺς οἱ πρός γε τοῦτο διὰ τῆς τοῦ διαβόλου σκαιότητος κατενηνεγμένοι, μάλιστα δὲ πάντων ὁ τῆς βασιλείας αὐχήμασιν ἐμπρέψας ποτὲ Ἰουλιανός, ἀγνοήσας δὲ τὸν τῆς βασιλείας καὶ τοῦ δύνασθαι κρατεῖν δοτῆρα Χριστόν. Ἦν μὲν γὰρ πρὸ τῶν τῆς βασιλείας καιρῶν τοῖς πιστεύσασιν ἐναρίθμιος, ἠξιώθη δὲ καὶ αὐτοῦ τοῦ ἁγίου βαπτίσματος, ἐνήσκητο δὲ καὶ βίβλοις ταῖς ἱεραῖς. Ἀλλ' οὐκ οἶδ' ὅπως ἄνδρες αὐτῷ μιαροί τε καὶ δεισιδαίμονες γεγονότες γνώριμοι τοὺς ὑπέρ γε **τῆς ἀποστασία** καθῆκαν λόγους, εἶτα σύνοπλον εἰς τοῦτο λαβόντες τὸν Σατανᾶν παρεκόμισαν εἰς τὰ Ἑλλήνων ἔθη καὶ λάτριν ἀπέφηναν δαιμονίων ἀκαθάρτων τὸν ἐν ἁγίαις ἐκκλησίαις καὶ μοναστηρίοις ἐντεθραμμένον· «φθείρουσι γὰρ ἤθη χρηστὰ ὁμιλίαι κακαί», καθά φησιν ὁ πάνσοφος Παῦλος.

— However who is it that has entered into war against the glory of Christ? They are legion, those who at various periods have let themselves go at this foolishness, driven by the perversity of the devil;

but none as went far as Julian, who damaged the prestige of the Empire by refusing to recognize Christ, dispenser of royalty and power. Before his accession to the throne, he was counted among the believers: he had even been admitted to Holy Baptism and had studied the Holy Scriptures. But some sinister characters, followers of superstition, entered—I do not know how—into connections with him and sowed in him the maxims of **apostasy**; then, allied with Satan in this design, they led him towards the practices of the Greeks and transformed into a servant of impure demons one who had been raised in holy churches and monasteries: «bad company corrupts good upbringing», as the very wise Paul says.

— Greek text — Th. Brüggemann, W. Kinzig, and C. Riedweg. *Kyrill von Alexandrien: Gegen Julian, Buch 1-10 und Fragmente, Teil 1-2* [*Die Griechischen Christlichen Schriftsteller der ersten Jahrhunderte Neue Folge 20-21*. De Gruyter, 2016-17. Retrieved from Thesaurus Linguae Graecae (stephanus.tlg.uci.edu).

— English translation — The translation is a public domain translation provided for Tertullian.org by Roger Pearse.

— The context addresses the emperor's apostasy from the Christian faith. Notice that apostasy is here associated with sinister men, superstition, Satan, and impure demons.

— RELIGIOUS APOSTASY

(100) Cyril of Alexandria, Against Julian the Emperor, 5.2

— Κράτιστον μὲν γὰρ ἁπάντων εἶναί φημι τὴν εἰς Θεὸν εὐσέβειαν, ἀποπεραίνεται δὲ πρὸς ἡμῶν διὰ τοῦ προσερηρεῖσθαι φιλεῖν αὐτῷ, καὶ τοὺς **τῆς ἀποστασίας** παραιτεῖσθαι τρόπους καὶ διὰ τοῦ μὴ ἑτέροις τισὶ διανέμειν τὰς αὐτῷ καὶ μόνῳ πρεπούσας τε καὶ ὀφειλομένας τιμάς. «Ἐγὼ» γάρ «εἰμι», φησί, «κύριος ὁ θεός σου», καί·«Οὐκ ἔσονταί σοι θεοὶ ἕτεροι πλὴν ἐμοῦ.»

— For the most excellent of all is, in my estimation, devotion to God, and it shall be performed [satisified] with us through pressing hard to love him, rejecting the ways of **apostasy**, and through not giving to any others the honor that to him alone is both proper and due [obligatory]. For «I am» he said «the Lord your God» and «There shall not be to you any other gods beside me.»

— Greek text — Th. Brüggemann, W. Kinzig, and C. Riedweg. *Kyrill von Alexandrien: Gegen Julian, Buch 1-10 und Fragmente, Teil 1-2* [*Die Griechischen Christlichen Schriftsteller der ersten Jahrhunderte Neue Folge 20-21. De Gruyter, 2016-17.* Retrieved from Thesaurus Linguae Graecae (stephanus.tlg.uci.edu).

— English translation — The translation is my own as I could find none available.

— The context contrasts the excellent way of honoring God as God with the ways of apostasy. Apostasy is associated with giving honor to gods that belongs to God alone.

— RELIGIOUS APOSTASY

(101) Cyril of Alexandria, Against Julian the Emperor, 6.2

— Αἰτιᾶται μὲν οὖν, ὥς γε οἶμαι, πάλιν τὸ πραχθῆναι δίκας τοὺς ἀπό γε τῶν Μωαβιτῶν, ὡς ὑφέντας τοῖς ἐξ Ἰσραὴλ τὰ τῶν γυναίων ἑταιριζόμενα, ἃ ταῖς τῶν σωμάτων ὥραις σεσαγηνεύκασιν εἰς ἀσέλγειαν οὐκ εὐαριθμήτους τῶν ὑπὸ θεῷ καὶ τοῖς **τῆς ἀποστασίας** ἐγκλήμασιν ἐνιεῖσαι τοὺς ἀπατωμένους 'τελεσθῆναι' παρεσκεύασαν 'τῷ Βεελφεγώρ'.

— Now these are the reasons, as I suppose, the Israelites again experienced judgments, this time from the Moabites, when they slipped the courtesans of the women into the men of Israel, who in the season of their bodies (the prime of their face and figure) snared into lasciviousness a multitude of those under God, and inciting them in the crimes of **apostasy**, the prepared the deceived to be initiated (consecrated) to Baal-Peor.

— Greek text — Th. Brüggemann, W. Kinzig, and C. Riedweg. *Kyrill von Alexandrien: Gegen Julian, Buch 1-10 und Fragmente, Teil 1-2* [*Die Griechischen Christlichen Schriftsteller der ersten Jahrhunderte Neue Folge 20-21. De Gruyter, 2016-17*]. Retrieved from Thesaurus Linguae Graecae (stephanus.tlg.uci.edu).

— English translation — The translation is my own as I could find none available.

— The context is the Israelites being led into fornication and apostasy by the Moabite women.

— RELIGIOUS APOSTASY

(102) Cyril of Alexandria, Against Julian the Emperor, 7.24

— Ἐμὲ γοῦν ἰάσατο πολλάκις Ἀσκληπιὸς κάμνοντα, ὑπαγορεύσας φάρμακα. Καὶ τούτων μάρτυς ἐστὶν ὁ Ζεύς. Εἰ τοίνυν οἱ προσνείμαντες ἑαυτοὺς τῷ **τῆς ἀποστασίας** πνεύματι, τὰ περὶ ψυχὴν ἄμεινον ἔχομεν, καὶ περὶ σῶμα, καὶ τὰ ἐκτός, τίνος ἔνεκεν ἀφέντες ταῦτα, ἐπ’ ἐκεῖνα βαδίζετε;

— Now I have been healed my times by Asclepios when I was sick, he having suggested the remedy. Zeus is a witness of these things. If, therefore, some have dedicated themselves to the spirit of **apostasy**, we have better things concerning the soul, and the body, and the externals. For the sake of what have you left these (better) things and gone after those things (the things of apostasy).

— Greek text — Th. Brüggemann, W. Kinzig, and C. Riedweg. *Kyrill von Alexandrien: Gegen Julian, Buch 1-10 und Fragmente, Teil 1-2 [Die Griechischen Christlichen Schriftsteller der ersten Jahrhunderte Neue Folge 20-21]*. De Gruyter, 2016-17. Retrieved from Thesaurus Linguae Graecae (stephanus.tlg.uci.edu).

— English translation — The translation is my own as I could find none available.

— The context mentions apostasy from paganism in the midst of a diatribe in which Julian advocates the temporal benefits of paganism, of which he mentions in particular many healings received from Asclepius. Why leave paganism when it gives you a better life down here? What gain do you get from leaving paganism? This tension is still true in our day. The answer is, we don’t serve Christ for earthly or temporal gain but for heavenly and eternal gain.

— RELIGIOUS APOSTASY

(103) Cyril of Alexandria, Against Julian the Emperor, 7.27

— Οὐκοῦν ὁ Ποιητὴς ἁπάντων ἡμῖν αἴτιος καὶ δοτὴρ τῶν καλῶν ὁμολογοῖτ’ ἂν εἰκότως. Ἀποφέροι δὲ τἀληθοῦς αὐτός, Ἄρει καὶ Ἡφαίστῳ, Μούσαις τε καὶ Ἑρμῇ λογίῳ, καὶ Ἀσκληπιῷ, προσνενεμηκὼς ἀνὰ μέρος ἕκαστα, καὶ οἷόν τινα κλῆρον τὴν ἐμπειρίαν διαμοιρήσασθαι λέγων αὐτούς. Ὡς δὲ ἀποχρόντως ἐλέγξας, ὅτι τῶν παρ’ ἡμῖν εἶεν ἂν τὰ Ἑλλήνων κρείττονα διά τοι τὸ εἰδέναι ζωγραφεῖν αὐτούς, καὶ μέντοι τὸ λιθουργεῖν ἠσκῆσθαι καλῶς, «Εἰ οὖν», φησίν, «οἱ προσνείμαντες ἑαυτοὺς τῷ **τῆς ἀποστασίας** πνεύματι, τὰ περὶ ψυχὴν ἄμεινον ἔχομεν καὶ περὶ σῶμα, καὶ τὰ ἐκτός, τίνος ἕνεκεν ἀφέντες ταῦτα, ἐπ' ἐκεῖνα βαδίζετε;»

— Should not the Maker of all things be reasonably confesssed by us [to be] the cause and giver of good things? But he (Julian) would turn away from the truth to Ares and Hephaestus, to the Muses and Hermes the Oracle, and to Asclepios, dedicating to each one in turn, and whatever lot the experiment determined, choosing them. But when he was sufficiently reproved—because the better things of the Greeks actually were well beyond us, because they truly know how to paint their gods and truly are very skilled to carve them in stone—he said, «If, therefore, some have dedicated themselves to the spirit of **apostasy**, we have better things concerning the soul, and the body, and the externals. For the sake of what have you left these (better) things and gone after those things (the things of apostasy).»

— Greek text — Th. Brüggemann, W. Kinzig, and C. Riedweg. *Kyrill von Alexandrien: Gegen Julian, Buch 1-10 und Fragmente, Teil 1-2 [Die Griechischen Christlichen Schriftsteller der ersten Jahrhunderte Neue Folge 20-21*. De Gruyter, 2016-17. Retrieved from Thesaurus Linguae Graecae (stephanus.tlg.uci.edu).

— English translation — The translation is my own as I could find none available.

— The context is the debate between Cyril defending the true God in heaven and Julian defending the Greek pantheon. Cyril contrasted the true God in heaven to Julian's plurality of gods, and he ridiculed the superiority of the Greek gods that could be represented with paint or stone. Julian replied with his defense of paganism, that those who apostatized from paganism were turning their backs on the temporal benefits of paganism. Even paganized Christianity offers temporal benefits that are lost when men turn to the Christ of the Bible and the Bible of Christ.

— RELIGIOUS APOSTASY

(104) Cyril of Alexandria, Dialogue on the Holy Trinity, 532

— Καὶ γοῦν ὁ μακάριος Ἰωάννης μεμαρτύρηκεν ὅτι «Καὶ ἐν τῷ κόσμῳ ἦν, καὶ ὁ κόσμος δι' αὐτοῦ ἐγένετο, καὶ ὁ κόσμος αὐτὸν οὐκ ἔγνω.» Ἆρα οὖν, ὦ Ἑρμεία, φρονοῦντες ὀρθῶς, **τῆς ἀποστασίας** τὸν τρόπον καὶ τῆς μεταξὺ πεσούσης διακοπῆς οὐχ ἕτερόν τινα παρὰ

194

τοῦτον εἶναι δώσομεν, τὸ μὴ ἐγνωκέναι φημὶ τὸν κόσμον τὸν ἀεὶ συνόντα Δημιουργόν;

— At any rate, the blessed John testified that «He was in the world, and the world was made through Him, and the world knew him not.» How then, O Hermeia, if we are thinking rightly, shall we give this to be the character of **apostasy** and the attendant cleft, not something else, when I say the world does not know the always existant Creator?

— Greek text — G.-M. de Durand. *Cyrille d'Alexandrie. Dialogues sur la Trinité,* 3 vols. [*Sources chrétiennes 231, 237, 246*]. Éditions du Cerf, 1:1976; 2:1977; 3:1978. Retrieved from Thesaurus Linguae Graecae (stephanus.tlg.uci.edu).

— English translation — The translation is my own as I as I could find none available.

— The context is theological apostasy in regard to the doctrine of Christ.

— RELIGIOUS APOSTASY

(105) Cyril of Alexandria, Easter Homilies (Festal Letters), Message 11, Section 2, (Migne 77.637)

— Καὶ εἴρηται μέν που πρὸς Ἰουδαίους «Εἰ ἀλλάξεται Αἰθίοψ τὸ δέρμα αὐτοῦ, καὶ πάρδαλις τὰ ποικίλματα αὐτῆς, καὶ ὑμεῖς δυνήσεσθε εὖ ποιῆσαι, μεμαθηκότες τὰ κακά.» Ἀλλὰ τὸ οὕτως ἔχον ὀρθῶς τε καὶ καλῶς καὶ ταῖς πονηραῖς καὶ ἀντικειμέναις δυνάμεσιν ἐπαυδήσαι τις ἂν, καὶ μάλα εἰκότως, αἳ τόνδε περινοστοῦσι τὸν κόσμον, ἑκάστου τῶν ἐν αὐτῷ πολυπραγμονοῦσαι βίον, δεινοῖς τε καὶ ἀγρίοις ὄμμασι τοὺς ἁγίους κατασκεπτόμεναι, καὶ τοὺς μὲν ἤδη νενευκότας εἰς πονηρίαν παραθήγουσαι πρὸς **ἀποστασίαν** τὴν ἔτι μειζόνως χείρονα, καὶ φαυλότητος ἁπάσης ἐπ' αὐτὸ λοιπὸν ἰοῦσαν τὸ ἀκρότατον·

— It was said somewhere to the Jews, «If the Ethiopian will change his skin, and the leopardess her spots, you also will be able to do good, having learned evil». But this saying, which is so fair and right, one might repeat, and quite understandably, to the wicked, hostile powers that go about this world, prying into the life of each person in it, staring at [reconnoitering] the saints with their fearsome, savage eyes, and inciting those already inclined to evil to that **apostasy** which is still worse, and which now tends toward the very last measure of all wickedness.

— Greek text — J.P. Migne. *Patrologiae cursus completus* (*series Graeca 77*). Migne, 1857-1866. Retrieved from Thesaurus Linguae Graecae (stephanus.tlg.uci.edu).

— English translation — Philip R. Amidon. *St. Cyril of Alexandria: Festal Letters 1-12* [*The Fathers of the Church, 118*]. The Catholic University of America Press, 2009.

— The context addresses the immutable wickedness of the demons and their wicked efforts to turn mankind to apostasy. Notice the association of *apostasia* with the fallen angels, with evil, and extreme wickedness.

— RELIGIOUS APOSTASY

(106) Cyril of Alexandria, Easter Letters or Easter Homilies, Message 26, Section 2, (Migne 77.917)

— Παροτρύνει δὲ μάλιστα πρὸς ὀργὰς τῶν ἄλλων τὸν ἐπὶ πάντας Θεὸν τὸ ἐφ' ἃ μὴ θέμις εὐπαρακόμιστον καὶ διεστραμμένον ἐννοιῶν ἀναπίμπλασθαι φιλεῖν, ἀποφέρεσθαι δὲ καὶ εἰς ἀδόκιμον νοῦν, καὶ πνεύμασι πλάνοις ἀκολουθεῖν ἑλέσθαι τινὰς, τὴν ἀκριβῆ τε καὶ ἀκαπήλευτον πίστιν οὐ προσιεμένους. Εἰσὶ γὰρ, εἰσὶν οἱ τῆς ἀληθείας τὴν δύναμιν παρευθύνοντες ἐπὶ τὸ αὐτοῖς ἰδίᾳ δοκοῦν, καὶ δοκησισόφων ἐννοιῶν κατασωρεύοντες ὄχλον τῆς τῶν ἀγελαίων πληθύος. Οἷς ἀναγκαῖον εἰπεῖν·«Ἕως πότε ἐπιτίθεσθε ἐπ' ἄνθρωπον, φονεύετε πάντες;» Προσεποίσω δὲ οἷς ἔφην κἀκεῖνο· Τὸ Χριστιανῶν ὄνομα λαχόντες τινὲς, οὔπω μὲν εἰσὶν, ὅπερ εἶναι λέγονται δυνάμει καὶ ἀληθείᾳ, τοὺς δὲ **τῆς ἀποστασίας** ἀγαπῶσι τρόπους, καὶ ταῖς τῶν δαιμονίων ἀπάταις προσνενεύκασιν·

— But what most provokes the God of all to anger is the habit of filling one's thoughts with what is unlawful in being easily swayed and perverse, and of diverting the mind to what is discreditable, and the decision some people make to follow spirits of error while giving no admission to the accurate, genuine faith. For there are those, there are indeed, who twist the meaning of truth to their own private views, and accumulate a heap of specious ideas derived from the common herd. To them we must say, «How long will you attack a man, and all of you kill?» And I will add to what I have said that some who have received the name of Christian are no longer [not yet, or not at all] in

essence and truth what they are said to be, but love the ways of **apostasy** and have gone over to the deceptions of demons.
— Greek text — J.P. Migne. *Patrologiae cursus completus* (*series Graeca 77*). Migne, 1857-1866. Retrieved from Thesaurus Linguae Graecae (stephanus.tlg.uci.edu).
— English translation — Philip R. Amidon. *St. Cyril of Alexandria: Festal Letters 13-30* [*The Fathers of the Church, 127*]. The Catholic University of America Press, 2009. I added material in square brackets for clarification. The citation is from Psalm 62:3 in the LXX.
— The context concerns men who bear the name of Christian but are not so in spirit and truth but love the ways of apostasy. Notice the association of apostasy with filling one's mind with unlawful thoughts, having an undiscerning mind, following spirits of error, not heeding the true faith, and embracing spiritual deception.
— RELIGIOUS APOSTASY

(107) Cyril of Jerusalem, Catechetical Lectures, 15.9
— Περὶ τούτου γράφων ὁ ἀπόστολος Παῦλος φανερὸν ἔδωκε σημεῖον λέγων· ὅτι «ἐὰν μὴ ἔλθη **ἡ ἀποστασία** πρῶτον καὶ ἀποκαλυφθῇ ὁ ἄνθρωπος τῆς ἀνομίας, ὁ υἱὸς τῆς ἀπωλείας, ὁ ἀντικείμενος καὶ ὑπεραιρόμενος ἐπὶ πάντα λεγόμενον θεὸν ἢ σέβασμα, ὥστε αὐτὸν εἰς τὸν ναὸν τοῦ θεοῦ καθίσαι ἀποδεικνύοντα ἑαυτὸν ὅτι ἐστὶ θεός. οὐ μνημονεύετε, ὅτι ἔτι ὢν πρὸς ὑμᾶς ταῦτα ἔλεγον ὑμῖν; καὶ νῦν τὸ κατέχον οἴδατε, εἰς τὸ ἀποκαλυφθῆναι αὐτὸν ἐν τῷ ἑαυτοῦ καιρῷ. τὸ γὰρ μυστήριον ἤδη ἐνεργεῖται τῆς ἀνομίας, μόνον ὁ κατέχων ἄρτι ἕως ἐκ μέσου γένηται. καὶ τότε ἀποκαλυφθήσεται ὁ ἄνομος, ὃν ὁ κύριος ἀνελεῖ τῷ πνεύματι τοῦ στόματος αὐτοῦ καὶ καταργήσει τῇ ἐπιφανείᾳ τῆς παρουσίας αὐτοῦ. οὗ ἐστιν ἡ παρουσία κατ' ἐνέργειαν τοῦ σατανᾶ ἐν πάσῃ δυνάμει καὶ σημείοις καὶ τέρασι ψεύδους, ἐν πάσῃ ἀπάτῃ ἀδικίας τοῖς ἀπολλυμένοις.» Ταῦτα μὲν ὁ Παῦλος. νῦν δὲ ἔστιν **ἡ ἀποστασία**. ἀπέστησαν γὰρ οἱ ἄνθρωποι τῆς ὀρθῆς πίστεως. καὶ οἱ μὲν υἱοπατορίαν καταγγέλλουσιν, οἱ δὲ τὸν Χριστὸν ἐξ οὐκ ὄντων εἰς τὸ εἶναι παρενεχθέντα λέγειν τολμῶσιν. καὶ πρότερον μὲν ἦσαν φανεροὶ οἱ αἱρετικοί, νῦν δὲ πεπλήρωται ἡ ἐκκλησία κεκρυμμένων αἱρετικῶν. ἀπέστησαν γὰρ οἱ ἄνθρωποι ἀπὸ τῆς ἀληθείας καὶ κνήθονται τὴν ἀκοήν. λόγος πιθανός, καὶ πάντες ἀκούουσιν ἡδέως. λόγος ἐπιστροφῆς, καὶ πάντες ἀποστρέφονται. ἀπέστησαν οἱ πλεῖστοι

τῶν ὀρθῶν λόγων, καὶ μᾶλλον τὸ κακὸν αἱροῦνται ἢ τὸ ἀγαθὸν προαιροῦνται. αὕτη τοίνυν ἐστὶν **ἡ ἀποστασία**, καὶ μέλλει προσδοκᾶσθαι ὁ ἐχθρός. καὶ τέως κατὰ μέρος ἤρξατο ἀποστέλλειν τοὺς ἑαυτοῦ προδρόμους, ἵνα ἕτοιμος ἔλθῃ λοιπὸν ἐπὶ τὴν θήραν.

— Writing concerning this matter, the Apostle Paul gave manifest sign, saying, «For that day shall not come, except there came first **the falling away**, and the man of sin be revealed, the son of perdition, who opposeth and exalteth himself against all that is called God, or that is worshipped; so that he sitteth in the temple of God, shewing himself that he is God. Remember ye not that when I was yet with you, I told you these things? And now ye know that which restraineth, to the end that he may be revealed in his own season. For the mystery of iniquity doth already work, only there is one that restraineth now, until he be taken out of the way. And then shall the lawless one be revealed, whom the Lord Jesus shall slay with the breath of His mouth, and shall destroy with the brightness of His coming. Even him, whose coming is after the working of Satan, with all power and signs and lying wonders, and with all deceit of unrighteousness for them that are perishing». Thus wrote Paul, and now is **the falling away**. For men have fallen away from the right faith; and some preach the identity of the Son with the Father, and others dare to say that Christ was brought into being out of nothing. And formerly the heretics were manifest; but now the Church is filled with heretics in disguise. For men have fallen away from the truth, and have itching ears. Is it a plausible discourse? all listen to it gladly. Is it a word of correction? all turn away from it. Most have departed from right words, and rather choose the evil, than desire the good. This therefore is **the falling away**, and the enemy is soon to be looked for: and meanwhile he has in part begun to send forth his own forerunners, that he may then come prepared upon the prey.

— Greek text — W.C. Reischl and J. Rupp. *Cyrilli Hierosolymorum archiepiscopi opera quae supersunt omnia,* 2 vols. Lentner, 1:1848; 2:1860 (repr. Hildesheim: Olms, 1967). Retrieved from Thesaurus Linguae Graecae (stephanus.tlg.uci.edu).

— English translation — Revision of the Oxford translation by E. H. Gifford. *Nicene and Post-Nicene Fathers, Second Series, Vol. 7.* Christian Literature Publishing, 1887. Accessed in *The Catechetical*

Lectures of St. Cyril of Jerusalem. Veritatis Splendor Publications, Kindle Edition, 2014.

— The context is the prophesied apostasy of the last days, which Cyril clearly associates with the man of sin. The apostasies we see now are forerunners, preparing the way for the antichrist, so everything will be prepared for him to seize upon his prey—the world.

— RELIGIOUS APOSTASY

(108) Cyril of Jerusalem, Lectures on the Mysteries, 1.4

— Ἀλλ᾽ ὅμως ἀκούεις τεταμένη τῇ χειρὶ ὡς πρὸς παρόντα εἰπεῖν· «Ἀποτάσσομαί σοι, Σατανᾶ.» ... ἀποτάσσεσθε τῷ σκοτεινῷ ἐκείνῳ καὶ ζοφερῷ ἄρχοντι ... τῷ πονηρῷ καὶ ὠμοτάτῳ τυράννῳ· οὐκέτι σου δέδοικα, λέγων, τὴν ἰσχύν. Κατέλυσε γὰρ ταύτην ὁ Χριστός, αἵματός μοι καὶ σαρκὸς κοινωνήσας, ἵνα διὰ τούτων τῶν παθημάτων καταργήσῃ θανάτῳ τὸν θάνατον, ὅπως μὴ διὰ παντὸς ἔνοχος γένωμαι δουλείας. «Ἀποτάσσομαί σοι» τῷ δολερῷ καὶ πανουργοτάτῳ ὄφει. «Ἀποτάσσομαί σοι» ἐπιβούλῳ ὄντι, καὶ προσποιήσει φιλίας πράξαντι πᾶσαν ἀνομίαν, καὶ ἐμποιήσαντι τοῖς ἡμετέροις προγόνοις **ἀποστασίαν**. «Ἀποτάσσομαί σοι, Σατανᾶ», τῷ πάσης κακίας δημιουργῷ καὶ συνεργῷ.

— But nevertheless, thou art bidden to say, with arm outstretched towards him as though he were present, «I renounce thee, Satan.»... renounce that dark and gloomy potentate ... thou wicked and most cruel tyrant! I fear thy might no longer; for that Christ hath overthrown, having partaken with me of flesh and blood, that through these He might by death destroy death, that I might not be made subject to bondage for ever. «I renounce thee», thou crafty and most subtle serpent. «I renounce thee», plotter as thou art, who under the guise of friendship didst contrive all disobedience, and work **apostasy** in our first parents. «I renounce thee, Satan», the artificer and abettor of all wickedness.

— Greek text — P. Paris and A. Piedagnel. *Cyrille de Jérusalem. Catéchèses mystagogiques; [Sources chrétiennes 126].* Éditions du Cerf, 1966. Retrieved from Thesaurus Linguae Graecae (stephanus. tlg.uci.edu).

— English translation — Revision of the Oxford translation by E. H. Gifford. *Nicene and Post-Nicene Fathers, Second Series, Vol. 7.*

Christian Literature Publishing, 1887. Accessed in *The Catechetical Lectures of St. Cyril of Jerusalem.* Veritatis Splendor Publications, Kindle Edition, 2014.

— The context is renouncing Satan, the deceitful and cunning serpent, who introduced apostasy to our forefathers. Notice the association of apostasy with wickedness, the serpent, darkness, and disobedience.

— RELIGIOUS APOSTASY

(109) Didymus the Blind, Commentary on Zechariah, 7:11, (2.170 in Doutreleau)

— Περὶ τῶν τοιούτων ὁ σοφώτατος Ἰωάννης, ὁ ἀγαπώμενος ὑπὸ τοῦ Ἰησοῦ μαθητής, ἐν ᾗ ἐχάραξεν ἁγίᾳ ἐπιστολῇ φησιν·«Ἐξ ἡμῶν ἐξῆλθον, ἀλλ' οὐκ ἦσαν ἐξ ἡμῶν· εἰ γὰρ ἦσαν ἐξ ἡμῶν, μεμενήκεισαν ἂν μεθ' ἡμῶν.» Ἐκ τῶν γὰρ ἀποστόλων καὶ Χριστοῦ μαθητῶν δοκοῦντες εἶναι, καὶ τὸ αὐτὸ εὐαγγέλιον προσηκάμενοι, καὶ «διὰ λουτροῦ παλιγγενεσίας» γεννηθέντες, ἔξω γέγοναν τῆς τεκούσης ἁγίας μητρὸς καὶ τῶν γεννηθέντων ἐξ αὐτῆς παραμεινάντων ἐν τῷ ἔχειν «τὸ τῆς υἱοθεσίας πνεῦμα». Τί δ' ἠκολούθησεν **τῇ ἀποστασίᾳ** αὐτῶν, ἢ τὸ βῦσαι τὰ ὦτα καὶ βαρῦναι αὐτὰ κατὰ τὴν παλαμναίαν ἀσπίδα, μηδαμῶς ἀκούουσαν τῶν ἐπᾳδόντων τοὺς ἱεροὺς τοῦ Θεοῦ λόγους.

— Regarding such people the most wise John, Jesus' beloved disciple, says in the holy epistle he wrote, «They went out from us, but they did not belong to us; for if they had belonged to us, they would have remained with us.» In other words, they appeared to come from the apostles and disciples of Christ, attached to the same Gospel and born of «the bath of rebirth»; but they left the holy mother who bore them and those born of her who continued to have «the spirit of adoption». What followed their **apostasy** was their stopping their ears and blocking them, like the murderous asp that never heeds those who chant the sacred words of God.

— Greek text — L. Doutreleau. *Didyme l'Aveugle sur Zacharie,* 3 vols. [*Sources chrétiennes 83, 84, 85*]. Éditions du Cerf, 1962. Retrieved from Thesaurus Linguae Graecae (stephanus.tlg.uci.edu).

— English translation — Robert Hill. *Didymus the Blind: Commentary on Zechariah;* [*The Fathers of the Church, Vol. 111*]. The Catholic University of America Press, 2006.

— The context addresses those who go out from us because they were never of us. This departure is regarded as apostasy.
— RELIGIOUS APOSTASY

(110) Didymus the Blind, Fragments in Psalms, (fragment 726 in Mühlenberg)
— τὴν γὰρ ψυχήν μου εἰς τὴν αὐτὴν αὐτοῖς κακίαν ἀγαγεῖν ἐζήτησαν, ἢ ἀποκτεῖναί με, ἐπεὶ μὴ συντρέχω αὐτοῖς εἰς **τὴν ἀποστασίαν** καθ' ἣν ἐκτὸς θεοῦ εἰσιν.

— They seek to bring my soul into the same evil with them or kill me since I do not run with them into **the apostasy** in which they are separated from God.

— Greek text — E. Mühlenberg. *Psalmenkommentare aus der Katenenüberlieferung,* 2 vols. [*Patristische Texte und Studien 15 & 16*]. De Gruyter, 1:1975; 2:1977. Retrieved from Thesaurus Linguae Graecae. (stephanus.tlg.uci.edu).

— English translation — The translation is my own as I could find none readily available.

— The context is departure from God. Note that apostasy is associated with evil and with being away from or outside of God.
— RELIGIOUS APOSTASY

(111) Diadochus, The Vision, Question 23,
— Ἐρ. Οἱ ἄγγελοι ἐν αἰσθήσει εἰσὶν ἢ οὔ;
Ἀπ. Κατὰ μὲν τὸν τῆς γνώσεως, ἔφη, λόγον ἐν αἱρετῇ τινι ἐτύγχανον αἰσθήσει κατὰ τὸν αὐτεξούσιον λόγον· διὸ καί τινες ἐξ αὐτῶν πάθει δουλεύσαντες ἔπεσον. Ἐπειδὴ δὲ ὑπὸ τῆς τοῦ θείου καὶ ἐνδόξου πνεύματος δοξολογίας οἱ μὴ συναπαχθέντες **τῇ ἀποστασίᾳ** ἀσινεῖς διεφυλάχθησαν εἰς ἀπάθειαν, κρείττονές εἰσι καὶ αἰσθήσεων, ἐν ἡδονῇ δέ τινι ἀτρέπτου δόξης ὑπάρχουσιν· ὅθεν καὶ ὅμοια αὐτοῖς ἐστι διὰ παντὸς τὰ νοήματα· οὐ γὰρ μόνον ὁμοίως γινώσκουσι τὰ καλά, ἀλλὰ καὶ ὁμοίως ἀγνοοῦσι τὰ τούτοις ἐναντία· ὅπερ καὶ ἐπὶ τῶν δικαίων ἐν τῇ ἀναστάσει· γενήσεσθαι ἐλπίζεται, ὅταν ὁ καρπὸς τῶν αὐτεξουσίων ἐν ὑποταγῇ τελείᾳ παρ' αὐτῶν προσενεχθῇ τῷ Θεῷ.

— **Q.** Do angels have sense or not?
— **R.** According to the discourse on knowledge it was theirs to choose their "sense" by virtue of their freedom. Thus some of them submitted

to passion and fell. On the other hand, since those who did not permit themselves to be seduced by **apostasy** kept themselves innocent and impassable by professing the glorious and divine Spirit, they are also above all senses, enjoying immutable glory. Hence they also always have like thoughts. For not only do they know beauty in a similar way, they are similarly unaware of all that is contrary to it. And this is what the just can expect upon reaching the resurrection, when the fruit of their free acts is presented to God in perfect submission.

— Greek text — É. des Places. *Diadoque de Photicé. Oeuvres spirituelles, 3rd ed. [Sources chrétiennes 5 ter.]* Éditions du Cerf, 1966. Retrieved from Thesaurus Linguae Graecae (stephanus. tlg.uci.edu).

— English translation — Cliff Ermatinger. *Following the Footsteps of the Invisible: The Complete Works of Diadochus of Photikē, [Cistercian Studies Series Number Two Hundred Thirty-Nine].* Cistercian Publications/ Liturgical Press, 2010.

— The context addresses the freedom (free will) of the angels and how some were enslaved by their own passions and fell, being led away into apostasy.

— RELIGIOUS APOSTASY

(112) Dionysius the Areopagite, Ecclesiastical Hierarchy, 2.3.3

— Πρὸς ταύτην ὁ θεῖος ἱεράρχης ἀποτυποῦται τὴν μίμησιν τὰς φωτοειδεῖς αὐτοῦ τῆς ἐνθέου διδασκαλίας αὐγὰς ἀφθόνως ἐπὶ πάντας ἁπλῶν καὶ τὸν προσιόντα φωτίσαι θεομιμήτως ἑτοιμότατος ὢν οὐ φθόνῳ οὐδὲ ἀνιέρῳ **τῆς** προτέρας **ἀποστασίας** ἢ ἀμετρίας μήνιδι χρώμενος, ἀλλ' ἐνθέως ἀεὶ τοῖς προσιοῦσι ταῖς αὐτοῦ φωταγωγίαις ἱεραρχικῶς ἐλλάμπων ἐν εὐκοσμίᾳ καὶ τάξει καὶ ἀναλογίᾳ τῆς ἑκάστου πρὸς τὰ ἱερὰ συμμετρίας.

— To this imitation, the divine Hierarch is fashioned, unfolding to all, without grudging, the luminous rays of his inspired teaching, and, after the Divine example, being most ready to enlighten the proselyte, neither using a grudging nor an unholy wrath for former **back-slidings** or excess, but, after the example of God, always enlightening by his conducting light those who approach him, as becomes a Hierarch, in fitness, and order, and in proportion to the aptitude of each for holy things.

— Greek text — G. Heil and A.M. Ritter. *Corpus Dionysiacum ii: Pseudo-Dionysius Areopagita. De coelesti hierarchia, de ecclesiastica hierarchia, de mystica theologia, epistulae* [*Patristische Texte und Studien 36*]. De Gruyter, 1991. Retrieved from Thesaurus Linguae Graecae (stephanus.tlg.uci.edu).

— English translation — John Parker. *The Works of Dionysius the Areopagite, Vol. 2*. James Parker, 1899. Transcribed for the Tertullian Project by Roger Pearse, 2004. Accessed at tertullian.org/fathers.

— The context states that teachers should not hold grudges or unholy anger for their students' former excesses and departures from the truth.

— RELIGIOUS APOSTASY

(113) Dionysius the Areopagite, Ecclesiastical Hierarchy, 3.3.11

— Τὴν ἀνθρωπείαν φύσιν ἀρχῆθεν ἀπὸ τῶν θείων ἀγαθῶν ἀνοήτως ἐξολισθήσασαν ἡ πολυπαθεστάτη ζωὴ διαδέχεται καὶ τὸ τοῦ φθοροποιοῦ θανάτου πέρας. Ἀκολούθως γὰρ ἡ τῆς ὄντως ἀγαθότητος ὀλέθριος **ἀποστασία** καὶ τῆς ἱερᾶς ἐν παραδείσῳ θεσμοθεσίας ὑπερβασία τὸν ἐξοιστρήσαντα τοῦ ζωοποιοῦ ζυγοῦ ταῖς θελκτικαῖς τοῦ ἐναντίου καὶ δυσμενέσιν ἀπάταις, τοῖς ἐναντίοις τῶν θείων ἀγαθῶν, οἰκείαις ὀπαῖς παραδέδωκεν.

— When, in the beginning, our human nature had thoughtlessly fallen from the good things of God, it received, by inheritance, the life subject to many passions, and the goal of the destructive death. For, as a natural consequence, the pernicious **falling away** from genuine goodness and the transgression of the sacred Law in Paradise delivered the man fretted with the life-giving yoke, to his own downward inclinations and the enticing and hostile wiles of the adversary—the contraries of the divine goods.

— Greek text — G. Heil and A.M. Ritter. *Corpus Dionysiacum ii: Pseudo-Dionysius Areopagita. De coelesti hierarchia, de ecclesiastica hierarchia, de mystica theologia, epistulae* [*Patristische Texte und Studien 36*]. De Gruyter, 1991. Retrieved from Thesaurus Linguae Graecae (stephanus.tlg.uci.edu).

— English translation — John Parker. *The Works of Dionysius the Areopagite, Vol. 2*. James Parker, 1899. Transcribed for the Tertullian Project by Roger Pearse, 2004. Accessed at tertullian.org/fathers.

— The context is man's falling away (apostasy) in the garden, when he turned from the good things of God and transgressed God's law.
— RELIGIOUS APOSTASY

(114) Ephraim of Syria, Design of the Spiritual Life (Consiliium de vita spiritaliu), Phrantzoles 2, starts page 209; section 30

— Ἐὰν οὖν τῆς χαρᾶς ἐκείνης κατατυχεῖν ἀγωνίζῃ, μὴ πάρεχε δίοδον σκολιοῖς λογισμοῖς, **ἀποστασίαν** ἀπὸ Θεοῦ ποιοῦσιν· ἀψευδὴς γὰρ ὁ εἰπών· ὁ εὑρὼν τὴν ψυχὴν αὐτοῦ, ἀπολέσει αὐτήν· ὁ δὲ ἀπολέσας τὴν ψυχὴν αὐτοῦ ἕνεκεν ἐμοῦ, εὑρήσει αὐτήν. Διὸ καὶ ὁ Ἀπόστολος λέγει· ἀπεθάνετε γάρ, καὶ ἡ ζωὴ ὑμῶν κέκρυπται σὺν τῷ Χριστῷ· ὅταν ὁ Χριστὸς φανερωθῇ ἡ ζωὴ ὑμῶν, τότε καὶ ὑμεῖς σὺν αὐτῷ φανερωθήσεσθε ἐν δόξῃ.

— If therefore you are fighting to obtain that joy, do not give safe passage to perverted reasonings promoting **apostasy** from God. For he is not a liar who said, He that finds his soul shall lose it. But he that loses his soul for my sake shall find it. Therefore the apostle said, For you have died, and your life is hid with Christ. When Christ your life shall be revealed, then you also shall be revealed with him in glory.

— Greek text — K.G. Phrantzoles. *Ὁσίου Ἐφραίμ τοῦ Σύρου ἔργα,* vol. 2. To Perivoli tis Panagias, 1989. Retrieved from Thesaurus Linguae Graecae (stephanus.tlg.uci.edu).

— English translation — The translation is my own as I could find none available.

— The context is trusting the promises of God and lot listening to perverted reasonings which promote apostasy from God.
— RELIGIOUS APOSTASY

(115) Ephraim of Syria, An Apology to His Brother Concerning Eli the Priest, Phrantzoles 6.82

— Τοιγαροῦν ἐκ τῶν τοῦ πατρὸς μαρτυριῶν δεῖ σχολάσασθαι τὴν ὑπερβάλλουσαν τῶν ἀνθρώπων ἐκείνων παρανομίαν· οὐ γὰρ εἰς μονώτατος κατεβόα αὐτῶν, ἀλλὰ πάντες ἀπὸ μικροῦ ἕως μεγάλου, καθὼς αὐτὸς ὁ Ἠλὶ μαρτυρεῖ λέγων· «ἵνα τί ποιεῖτε κατὰ τὰ ῥήματα ταῦτα, ἃ ἐγὼ ἀκούω λαλούμενα καθ᾽ ὑμῶν ἐκ στόματος τοῦ λαοῦ Κυρίου;» Πάντας ἠδίκουν καὶ ἐσκανδάλιζον, βεβηλοῦντες τὰς ἱερὰς θυσίας· οὐ μόνον γὰρ τοῦ θύειν τὸν λαὸν διεσκέδαζον, ἀλλὰ λοιπὸν καὶ ὁ λαὸς πρὸς **ἀποστασίαν** ἐμελέτα, ἐκπληττόμενος ὑπ' αὐτῶν ἐκ τῶν ἀθεμίτων ἔργων, ὧν κατεσκεύαζον οἱ τοῦ Ἡλὶ υἱοί. Ἄκουε γὰρ τοῦ Ἡλὶ λέγοντος·«οὐκ ἀγαθὴ ἡ ἀκοή, ἣν ἀκούω περὶ ὑμῶν, τοῦ ποιεῖν τὸν λαὸν μὴ λατρεύειν τῷ Κυρίῳ».

— Wherefore from the testimonies of the father the exceeding transgression of those men ought to be learned. For not one solitary man cried against them, but all from the least to the greatest [were strayed], as Eli himself testifies saying, «why are you doing according to the rumors which I hear spoken against you from the mouth of the people of the Lord?» They go wrong and stumble across the board, profaning the holy sacrifices. For not only have they diverted the people from sacrificing, but furthermore, the people have a mind for **apostasy**, being dismayed by their unlawful deeds which the sons of Eli established. Hear what Eli says. «The report is not good which I hear about you, making the people to not serve the Lord.»

— Greek text — K.G. Phrantzoles. Ὁσίου Ἐφραίμ τοῦ Σύρου ἔργα, vol. 2. To Perivoli tis Panagias, 1989. Retrieved from Thesaurus Linguae Graecae (stephanus.tlg.uci.edu).

— English translation — The translation is my own as I could find none available.

— The context is Israel's apostasy. It points out that the people of Israel, offended and scandalized with Eli's sons defiling the holy offerings, were themselves taken up with apostasy.

— RELIGIOUS APOSTASY

(116) Ephraim of Syria, Testament of Blessed Ephraim, Phrantzoles 7.423-424

— πόσῳ μᾶλλον κατακρίτου τιμωρίας καταξιωθήσονται, ἀδελφοί, οἱ μερισμὸν **ἀποστασίας** δόξαντες διασπεῖραι ἐν καρδίᾳ βροτῶν, κατὰ τοῦ Θεοῦ καὶ Πατρός, καὶ τοῦ Υἱοῦ, καὶ τοῦ Ἁγίου Πνεύματος;

— How much more, brothers, shall they be counted worthy of eternal punishment, who have thought to sow the division of **apostasy** in the hearts of mortal man, against God the Father, against the Son, and against the Holy Spirit?

— Greek text — K.G. Phrantzoles. Ὁσίου Ἐφραίμ τοῦ Σύρου ἔργα, vol. 2. To Perivoli tis Panagias, 1989. Retrieved from Thesaurus Linguae Graecae (stephanus.tlg.uci.edu).

— English translation — The translation is my own as I could find none available.

— The context addresses apostasy from God. Notice that apostasy is associated with division and is committed against God.

— RELIGIOUS APOSTASY

(117) Ephraim of Syria, Testament of Blessed Ephraim, Phrantzoles 7.424-425

— Ὅστις καταλείψῃ τῆς συνέσεως τὴν ὀρθὴν πίστιν, συσχεθείη τῷ τῆς ἀνομίας σχοινίσματι τοῦ προδότου Ἰούδα. Ἣν γὰρ ἐγὼ πίστιν παρέλαβον, ἐξ Ἀποστόλων ἁγίων ταύτην ἔμαθον· αὐτοί τε αὐτὴν λαβόντες παρὰ Θεοῦ, πάσῃ τῇ κτίσει διεκήρυξαν. Ἀνυπόστατος δὲ καὶ ἀδιάφευκτος ἀνομία ἡ εἰς τὸν Θεὸν βλασφημία· ἧς δὲ τὸ δέλεαρ φεύγετε ἐναργῶς, ὦ μαθηταί μου εἰς γὰρ τὸν τῶν ὅλων Θεὸν **τὴν ἀποστασίαν** κηρύσσει ὁ δυσφήμως ἐπαιρόμενος καὶ τὸν θεμέλιον τοῦ λόγου παρασαλεύει τῆς πίστεως·

— Whoever abandons the orthodox understanding of the faith, he could be kept with (classified with) the lawless lot of the traitor Judas. For the faith which I received, I learned it from the holy apostles. And they received it from God and preached it in all creation. Blasphemy against God is irresistable and inescapable lawlessness. Manifestly (visibly) flee the bait of lawlessness, O my disciples. For the arrogant slanderer preaches **apostasy** against the God of the universe and he shakes men loose from the foundation of the word of faith.

— Greek text — K.G. Phrantzoles. Ὁσίου Ἐφραίμ τοῦ Σύρου ἔργα, vol. 2. To Perivoli tis Panagias, 1989. Retrieved from Thesaurus Linguae Graecae (stephanus.tlg.uci.edu).

— English translation — The translation is my own as I could find none available.

— The context is apostasy against God. Notice the association with arrogance, slander, abandoning the word of God, and being identified with Judas the traitor.

— RELIGIOUS APOSTASY

(118) Ephraim of Syria, Testament of Blessed Ephraim, Phrantzoles 7.428

— Οἱ μὲν γὰρ δαίμονες εἶπον, ὁμολογοῦντες τὸν Υἱὸν τοῦ Θεοῦ, «σὺ εἶ ὁ Χριστὸς ὁ Υἱὸς τοῦ Θεοῦ». οἱ δὲ **τῆς ἀποστασίας** κήρυκες Ἰουδαῖοι ἐμφιλονείκως ἔχουσι μὴ εἶναι αὐτὸν Υἱὸν τοῦ Θεοῦ. Καὶ ὅρα τὸ δυσκάθεκτον αὐτῶν ἦθος τὸ πικρόν. Ὁ ἀρχηγὸς **τῆς ἀποστασίας** αὐτῶν ἐκβοᾷ καὶ λέγει· «τί ἡμῖν καὶ σοί, Υἱὲ τοῦ Θεοῦ;» Καὶ αὐτοὶ ἀρνοῦνται διηνεκῶς.

— For the demons spoke, confessing the son of God, «You are the Christ, the Son of God.» But the Jewish preachers of **apostasy** contemptuously hold him to not be the Son of God. Do you see their bitter and hard-to-maintain custom? The founder of their **apostasy** cries out and says, «what between me and you, Son of God?» And they continuously deny him.

— Greek text — K.G. Phrantzoles. *Ὁσίου Ἐφραίμ τοῦ Σύρου ἔργα, vol. 2.* To Perivoli tis Panagias, 1989. Retrieved from Thesaurus Linguae Graecae (stephanus.tlg.uci.edu).

— English translation — The translation is my own as I could find none available.

— The context concerns Israel's apostasy which has gone even farther than that of the demons. For the demons own that Christ is the Son of God, but the Jews deny that he is.

— RELIGIOUS APOSTASY

(119) Epiphanius, Panarion (Against Heresies), (No. 31) Against Valentinians 14.9, (Holl 1.407)

— Τὸ δὲ περὶ τὸν δωδέκατον Αἰῶνα γεγονὸς πάθος ὑποσημαίνεσθαι λέγουσι διὰ τῆς **ἀποστασίας** Ἰούδα, ὅς δωδέκατος ἦν τῶν ἀποστόλων, καὶ ὅτι τῷ δωδεκάτῳ μηνὶ ἔπαθεν· ἐνιαυτῷ γὰρ ἑνὶ βούλονται αὐτὸν μετὰ τὸ βάπτισμα αὐτοῦ κεκηρυχέναι.

— The passion encountered by the twelfth Aeon is suggested, they say, by the **defection** of Judas who was the twelfth of the apostles, and because (the Savior) suffered in the twelfth month, they hold that he preached for one year after his baptism.

— Greek text — K. Holl. *Epiphanius, Bände 1-3: Ancoratus und Panarion [Die griechischen christlichen Schriftsteller 25, 31, 37.]*

Hinrichs; 1:1915; 2:1922; 3:1933. Retrieved from Thesaurus Linguae Graecae (stephanus.tlg.uci.edu).
— English translation — Frank Williams. *The Panarion of Epiphanius of Salamis, Book 1 (Sects 1-46).* [*Nag Hammadi & Manichaean Studies 63*]. Brill, 2009. Accessed at Internet Archive (archive.org).
— The context is the bizarre analogy the Valentinians drew between the passion of the twelfth Aeon and the apostasy of Judas.
— RELIGIOUS APOSTASY

(120) Epiphanius, Panarion (Against Heresies), (No. 31) Against Valentinians 30.6-8, (Holl 1.432)
— ἵνα Χριστῷ Ἰησοῦ τῷ κυρίῳ ἡμῶν καὶ θεῷ καὶ σωτῆρι καὶ βασιλεῖ κατὰ τὴν εὐδοκίαν τοῦ πατρὸς τοῦ ἀοράτου πᾶι γόνυ κάμψῃ ἐπουρανίων καὶ ἐπιγείων καὶ καταχθονίων καὶ πᾶσα γλῶσσα ἐξομολογήσηται αὐτῷ καὶ κρίσιν δικαίαν ἐν τοῖς πᾶσι ποιήσηται, τὰ μὲν πνευματικὰ τῆς πονηρίας καὶ ἀγγέλους τοὺς παραβεβηκότας καὶ ἐν **ἀποστασίᾳ** γεγονότας καὶ τοὺς ἀσεβεῖς καὶ ἀδίκους καὶ ἀνόμους καὶ βλασφήμους τῶν ἀνθρώπων εἰς τὸ αἰώνιον πῦρ πέμψῃ, τοῖς δὲ δικαίοις καὶ ὁσίοις καὶ τὰς ἐντολὰς αὐτοῦ τετηρηκόσι καὶ ἐν τῇ ἀγάπῃ αὐτοῦ διαμεμενηκόσι (τοῖς μὲν ἀπ' ἀρχῆς, τοῖς δὲ ἐκ μετανοίας) ζωὴν χαρισάμενος ἀφθαρσίαν δωρήσηται καὶ δόξαν αἰωνίαν περιποιήσῃ.
— That, by the invisible Father's good pleasure, every knee in heaven, on earth, and under the earth may bow to Christ Jesus, our Lord, God, Savior, and King, and every tongue confess Him. And that he may pronounce a righteous judgment on all, and consign the spirits of wickedness, the angels who have transgressed and **rebelled**, and wicked, unrighteous, lawless and blasphemous men, to the eternal fire; but grant life, bestow immortality, and secure eternal glory for the righteous and holy, who have kept his commandments and abode in his love, some from the first, others after repentance.
— Greek text — K. Holl, *Epiphanius, Bände 1-3: Ancoratus und Panarion* [*Die griechischen christlichen Schriftsteller* 25, 31, 37.] Hinrichs; 1:1915; 2:1922; 3:1933. Retrieved from Thesaurus Linguae Graecae (stephanus.tlg.uci.edu).
— English translation — Frank Williams. *The Panarion of Epiphanius of Salamis, Book 1 (Sects 1-46).* [*Nag Hammadi &*

Manichaean Studies 63]. Brill, 2009. Accessed at Internet Archive (archive.org).
— The context addresses the angels who trespassed and went into rebellion
— RELIGIOUS APOSTASY

(121) Epiphanius, Panarion (Against Heresies), (No. 31) Against Valentinians 31.5-6, (Holl 1.433)

— Τὸ δὲ πλεῖον ἢ ἔλαττον κατὰ σύνεσιν εἰδέναι τινὰς οὐκ ἐν τῷ τὴν ὑπόθεσιν αὐτὴν ἀλλάσειν γίνεται καὶ ἄλλον θεὸν παρεπινοεῖν παρὰ τὸν δημιουργὸν καὶ ποιητὴν καὶ τροφέα τοῦδε τοῦ παντός, ὡς μὴ ἀρκουμένους τούτῳ, ἢ ἄλλον Χριστὸν ἢ ἄλλον Μονογενῆ, ἀλλὰ ἐν τῷ τὰ ὅσα ἕν παραβολαῖς εἴρηται προσεπεξεργάζεσθαι καὶ συνοικειοῦν τῇ τῆς πίστεως ὑποθέσει καὶ ἐν τῷ τήν τε πραγματείαν καὶ τὴν οἰκονομίαν τοῦ θεοῦ τὴν ἐπὶ τῇ ἀνθρωπότητι γενομένην ἐκδιηγεῖσθαι καὶ ὅτι ἐμακροθύμησεν ὁ θεὸς ἐπί τε τῇ τῶν παραβεβηκότων ἀγγέλων **ἀποστασίᾳ** καὶ ἐπὶ τῇ παρακοῇ τῶι ἀνθρώπων σαφηνίζειν·

— For one to know more or less with understanding means, not changing the actual subject (of our knowledge) and—as though not satisfied with him—inventing a new God other than the creator, maker and sustainer of all, or another Christ or Only-Begotten. It means giving further explanation of what has been said in parables, and suiting it to the subject of the faith. It means expounding God's dealings with mankind and his provision for them, and making it plain that God bore with the **rebellion** of the angels who transgressed, and the disobedience of men.

— Greek text — K. Holl, *Epiphanius, Bände 1-3: Ancoratus und Panarion* [*Die griechischen christlichen Schriftsteller* 25, 31, 37.] Hinrichs; 1:1915; 2:1922; 3:1933. Retrieved from Thesaurus Linguae Graecae (stephanus.tlg.uci.edu).

— English translation — Frank Williams. *The Panarion of Epiphanius of Salamis, Book 1 (Sects 1-46)*. [*Nag Hammadi & Manichaean Studies 63*]. Brill, 2009. Accessed at Internet Archive (archive.org).

— The context points out that one of God's amazing traits is his longsuffering over the apostasy of the angels in their transgression and the associated disobedience of man.

— RELIGIOUS APOSTASY

(122) Epiphanius, Panarion (Against Heresies), (No. 32) Against Secundians 2.5-9, (Holl 1.441)

— ποῦ τοίνυν ὁ ἀπατεὼν ἐφηῦρεν ἑαυτῷ τὴν κατὰ θεὸν γεωμετρίαν; καὶ ὦ τῆς τοιαύτης πολλῆς ληρολογίας τῆς τὰ πάντα συγχεούσης. φάσκει δὲ τὸ Ὑστέρημα μετὰ τοὺς τριάκοντα αἰῶνας γεγενῆσθαι. πόθεν ἄρα τὴν τοῦ Ὑστερήματος φύσιν κατείληφας, ὦ οὗτος, ἢ τὴν ἀποστᾶσαν δύναμιν, λέγε; εἰ μὲν γὰρ εὗρες ταύτην ἀπὸ βλαστήματος τῶν ἄνω, οὐ κτιστὴν ἀλλὰ γεννητήν, (ἐπειδὴ σοί τε καὶ τῷ σου ἐπιστάτῃ οὐκ ἐκτισμένα τὰ κτιστὰ ὁρίζεται, ἀλλὰ γεννητὰ καὶ ἀπὸ μετουσίας, ἑκάστης φύσεως παρ' ἑκάστης λαβούσης, τὰ αὖθις γεννώμενα ἀναφῦναι), ἄρα γε κατὰ τὸν ἑαυτοῦ λόγον κατὰ σαυτοῦ ὁπλίζῃ. εἰ γὰρ ἀπὸ τῶν ἄνω καὶ ἡ ὑστέρα δύναμις καὶ **ἡ ἀποστασία** γεγένηται, ἔφυ δὲ ὡς εἰπεῖν καὶ ἐβλάστησεν, μετέχει ἄρα τῶν ἄνω χαρισμάτων, ἐπειδὴ ἐπικοινωνεῖ τῷ Πληρώματι ἡ ὑστέρα καὶ τὸ Πλήρωμα τῇ ὑστέρᾳ, καὶ οὐδὲν διενεχθήσεται τοῦτο πρὸς ἐκεῖνο οὔτε ἐκεῖνο πρὸς τοῦτο, ἑκατέρων κατὰ τὰ τέρματα ἀλλήλοις ἐπικοινωνούντων. καὶ ἐκ παντὸς λόγου διελεγχθήσῃ ἐξ ἐπισπορᾶς δαίμονος ἔχων τὴν τῆς πλάνης σου βόσκησιν, πάντων ἐλεεινῶν ἐλεεινότατε.

— Very well, where did the fraud find his divinely ordained geometry? What a lot of nonsense there is of this kind, which mixes everything up! But he claims that the Deficiency came into being after the thirty Aeons. All right, Mister, tell me, where did you get the origin of the Deficiency, or the power that fell away! If you found it grown from a shoot of the things on high, not a created thing but something generated (created things are not defined as created by you and your master, but the products of successive generations [are supposed] to have grown up, generated and by participation, with each nature receiving from each). If this is what you mean, on your own terms you are taking up arms against yourself. For if both the later power and **the defection** have been generated by the things on high, and if it sprouted, let us say, and grew from them, then it partakes of the benefits on high. For the later power communicates with the Pleroma and the Pleroma with the later power, and there can be no difference between the one and the other, or between the other and the one, since they are both in contact at their ends. And on every account, you most wretched of all wretches, you will be caught getting the fodder for your imposture from a devil's second sowing.

— Greek text — K. Holl, *Epiphanius, Bände 1-3: Ancoratus und Panarion* [*Die griechischen christlichen Schriftsteller* 25, 31, 37.] Hinrichs; 1:1915; 2:1922; 3:1933. Retrieved from Thesaurus Linguae Graecae (stephanus.tlg.uci.edu).

— English translation — Frank Williams. *The Panarion of Epiphanius of Salamis, Book 1* (*Sects 1-46*). [*Nag Hammadi & Manichaean Studies 79*]. Brill, 2009. Accessed at Internet Archive (archive.org).

— The context is Epiphanius' exposure of the Gnosticism of Secundus, a disciple of Valentinus, whose conception of the origin of the devil and darkness make God the author of Satan and apostasy.

— RELIGIOUS APOSTASY

(123) Epiphanius, Panarion (Against Heresies), (No. 69) Against the Arian Nuts 59.3, (Holl 3.207)

— οἱ ἀπόστολοι Ἰουδαίοις προσδιελέγοντο, διὰ τὸ νομίζειν **ἀποστασίαν** κηρύσσειν τοὺς ἀποστόλους ἀπὸ τοῦ θεοῦ τοῦ νόμου καὶ διὰ τὸ πρὸς τὸ γνωστὸν τοῦ ἁγίου πνεύματος, τοῦ γινώσκοντος ὅτι ἤμελλον αἱρέσεις ἀφηνιάζειν τὸν Χριστὸν ἀπὸ τοῦ πατρῴου θελήματος.

— The apostles were in a dispute with Jews who thought they were preaching **apostasy** from the God of the Law, and because they had received from the Holy Spirit the knowledge that sects would set Christ in opposition to the will of the Father.

— Greek text — K. Holl, *Epiphanius, Bände 1-3: Ancoratus und Panarion* [*Die griechischen christlichen Schriftsteller* 25, 31, 37.] Hinrichs; 1:1915; 2:1922; 3:1933. Retrieved from Thesaurus Linguae Graecae (stephanus.tlg.uci.edu).

— English translation — Frank Williams. *The Panarion of Epiphanius of Salamis, Books II and III.* [*Nag Hammadi &*

Manichaean Studies 79]. Brill, 2013. Accessed at Internet Archive (archive.org)
— The context related that the Jews thought the apostles were preaching apostasy from the law of God.
— RELIGIOUS APOSTASY

(124) Epiphanius, Panarion (Against Heresies), (No. 73) Against Semi-Arians, 2.4-5, (Holl 3.269)
— ἐπειδὴ δὲ ὡς ἔοικεν οὐ παύεται ὁ διάβολος διὰ τῶν οἰκείων σκευῶν σπουδάζων καθ᾽ ἑαυτόν, ἵνα δὴ πάντως κατὰ τά τε παρὰ τοῦ κυρίου προρρηθέντα καὶ διὰ τοῦ ἁγίου ἀποστόλου συμφώνως ἐπὶ προφυλακῇ τῶν πιστῶν κηρυχθέντα [εἰς] **ἀποστασίαν** ἐργάσηται, ἐπινοῶν καινισμοὺς κατὰ τῆς ἐκκλησιαστικῆς πίστεως, καὶ νῦν ἐν «μορφώσει τινὰς εὐσεβείας» οἰκειώσασθαι καὶ «βεβήλους καινοφωνίας» δι᾽ αὐτῶν ἐπινοήσας κατὰ τῆς εὐσεβοῦς γνησιότητος τοῦ μονογενοῦς υἱοῦ τοῦ θεοῦ.
— Since, as I take it, the devil does not cease diligently working through his own vessels on his behalf, that he might entirely transform the things being preached, being spoken by the Lord and correspondingly through his apostles, into **apostasy**, thinking up new things against the church's faith, even now to settle in some likeness of godliness, and new expressions of profaneness are contrived by them against the godly genuineness of the only begotten son of God.
— Greek text — K. Holl, *Epiphanius, Bände 1-3: Ancoratus und Panarion* [*Die griechischen christlichen Schriftsteller* 25, 31, 37.] Hinrichs; 1:1915; 2:1922; 3:1933. Retrieved from Thesaurus Linguae Graecae (stephanus.tlg.uci.edu).
— English translation — The translation is my own as I felt it was superior to that offered by Frank Williams.
— The context indicates that twisting the things taught by the Lord and his apostles is apostasy
— RELIGIOUS APOSTASY

(125) Epiphanius, Panarion (Against Heresies), (No. 73) Against Semi-Arians, 2.11-12, (Holl 3.271)
— καὶ παρακαλοῦμεν ὑμᾶς, κύριοι τιμιώτατοι συλλειτουργοί, ἐντυχόντας, ὅτι ἡδράσθητε τῇ ἐκ πατέρων παραδοθείσῃ πίστει καὶ ὡς

σύμφωνα ὑμῖν φρονοῦμεν, ὡς πεπιστεύκαμεν, ὑποσημήνασθαι, ἵνα πληροφορηθέντες οἱ τὴν αὐτὴν ἀσέβειαν ἐπεισάγειν τολμῶντες, ὅτι καθάπερ κλῆρόν τινα τὴν ἐκ τῶν ἀποστολικῶν χρόνων διὰ τῶν ἐν τῷ μέσῳ ἄχρι καὶ ἡμῶν παραδοθεῖσαν ἀπὸ τῶν πατέρων ὑποδεξάμενοι πίστιν φυλάσσομεν, ἢ αἰσχυνθέντες διορθωθήσονται ἢ ἐπιμένοντες ἀποκηρυχθῶσι τῆς ἐκκλησίας, ὡς **τὴν ἀποστασίαν** τῷ υἱῷ τῆς ἀνομίας, ὃς τολμᾶν ἀπειλεῖ καὶ «εἰς τὸν ναὸν τοῦ θεοῦ καθίσαι».

— And because you, most honored sirs and colleagues, have stood firm in the faith which has been handed down to us from our fathers, and because our faith, as we believe, is in accord with yours, we urge you, on reading this, to append your signatures. Thus those who dare to introduce this impiety will be assured that we have accepted and guard as our inheritance, the faith of the fathers transmitted from the time of the apostles, through the intervening generations, even to us. Hence they will either be ashamed and submit to correction, or persist in error and be expelled from the church, for preparing, by their own efforts, **the falling away** for the son of iniquity who threatens to venture «to sit even in the temple of God.»

— Greek text — K. Holl, *Epiphanius, Bände 1-3: Ancoratus und Panarion* [*Die griechischen christlichen Schriftsteller* 25, 31, 37.] Hinrichs; 1:1915; 2:1922; 3:1933. Retrieved from Thesaurus Linguae Graecae (stephanus.tlg.uci.edu).

— English translation — Frank Williams. *The Panarion of Epiphanius of Salamis, Books II and III.* [*Nag Hammadi & Manichaean Studies 79*]. Brill, 2013. Accessed at Internet Archive (archive.org)

— The context regards the serious errors of the semi-Arians as preparing the apostasy of the last days for the son of perdition, who dares to threaten and to sit in the temple of God. Notice that Epiphanius intimately associates the apostasy and the son of perdition. He seems to believe that the son of perdition rides into power on the wings of the apostasy.

— RELIGIOUS APOSTASY

(126) Eusebius of Caesarea, Commentary on Isaiah, 9:11-13, (Book 1, section 55)

— καὶ πάντας δὲ τοὺς ἐκ τῶν λοιπῶν ἐθνῶν ἐπανισταμένους τῷ ὄρει Σιὼν καὶ τῷ θεῷ τῷ ἐνταῦθα τιμωμένῳ διασκεδάσειν ἐπαγγέλλεται, ὧν οἱ μὲν ἦσαν ἀνατολικοί τινες, οἱ δὲ ἀφ' ἡλίου δυσμῶν, μέσοι δὲ τούτων οἱ Ἕλληνες πάντες γὰρ οὗτοι τὸν προλεχθέντα Ἰσραὴλ ὅλῳ τῷ στόματι κατεσθίοντες καὶ καταβάλλοντες ἐπὶ τὴν τῆς εἰδωλολατρίας αὐτῶν πλάνην, βοηθεῖν καὶ συμμαχεῖν ἐπηγγέλλοντο τοῖς ἐπανισταμένοις κατὰ τοῦ ὄρους Σιών. οὐκ ἂν δὲ ἁμάρτοις ὅλῳ τῷ στόματι τῶν Ἑλλήνων καὶ τῶν ἀλλοφύλων κατεσθίεσθαι λέγων τοὺς διὰ «τῆς σοφίας τοῦ αἰῶνος τούτου» τῆς Ἑλληνικῆς ἀπάτης εἰς **ἀποστασίαν** χωροῦντας, οἷος ἦν ὁ διὰ τῶν μετὰ χεῖρας κατηγορούμενος Ἰσραήλ, διόπερ ὁ θυμὸς τοῦ θεοῦ κατ' αὐτῶν ἠγείρετο καὶ ἡ χεὶρ ἡ ὑψηλὴ παρεσκευάζετο πρὸς τὴν κατ' αὐτῶν ὀργήν. οἱ δὲ οὐδὲ οὕτως ἐπέστρεφον οὐδὲ τὸν κύριον τῶν δυνάμεων ἐπεζήτουν, «κατὰ δὲ τὴν σκληρότητα αὐτῶν καὶ τὴν ἀμετανόητον καρδίαν ἐθησαύριζον ἑαυτοῖς ὀργὴν ἐν ἡμέρᾳ ὀργῆς».

— And he announces that he will dash down from the other nations all those who rise up against Mount Zion and against God in that revered place, those who were from the rising of the sun and those who were from the setting of the sun, and the Greeks in between these peoples. For all of these devour the aforementioned Israel with open mouths, and, reinforcing the error of their idolatry, they promised to come to their aid and to be allied with those who rise up against Mount Zion. May you never sin by devouring with the open mouth of the Greeks and of the other tribes, that is to say, those who advance into **apostasy** through the deception of «the wisdom of this age» of the Greeks. For Israel, who is at present accused by the prophet, was of this sort. Therefore the anger of God was raised against them and his hand uplifted and poised in wrath against them. And thus neither did they turn back nor did they seek the Lord of powers. «But by their hard and impenitent heart they were storing up wrath for themselves on the day of wrath.»

— Greek text — J. Ziegler, *Eusebius Werke, Band 9: Der Jesajakommentar;* [*Die griechischen christlichen Schriftsteller*]. Akademie Verlag, 1975. Retrieved from *Thesaurus Linguae Graecae* (stephanus.tlg.uci.edu).

— English translation — Jonathan J. Armstrong. *Eusebius of Caesarea: Commentary on Isaiah*; [*Ancient Christian Texts*]. Inter-Varsity Press Academic, 2013. Kindle Edition.

— The context is apostasy. Men advance into apostasy by giving heed to the wisdom of this age as exemplified in the wisdom of the Greek. Notice the association of apostasy with rising up against Mt. Zion and God, devouring Israel, idolatry, turning one's back on God and not seeking him, and having hard and impenitent hearts.

— RELIGIOUS APOSTASY

(127) Eusebius of Caesarea, Commentary on Isaiah, 33:14-15, (Book 2, section 5)

— «ἀπέστησάν μου οἱ ἐν Σιὼν ἄνομοι». οὗ χάριν διὰ **τὴν ἀποστασίαν** αὐτῶν λήψεται αὐτοὺς τρόμος. εἶτα ὡς πρὸς αὐτοὺς τοὺς ἀπιστήσαντας τοῦ ἐκ περιτομῆς λαοῦ ἑξῆς ἐπιλέγει,·«τίς ἀναγγελεῖ ὑμῖν ὅτι πῦρ καίεται;» περὶ οὗ μικρῷ πρόσθεν ἔλεγεν· «πῦρ κατέδεται ὑμᾶς», καὶ πάλιν·«τίς ἀναγγελεῖ ὑμῖν τὸν τόπον τὸν αἰώνιον;» «τὸν ἡτοιμασμένον» δηλονότι «τῷ διαβόλῳ καὶ τοῖς ἀγγέλοις αὐτοῦ». τίς οὖν ἔσται ὁ ταῦτα εἰδὼς καὶ τοῖς μὴ εἰδόσι προμαρτυρόμενος ἢ πᾶς ὁ πορευόμενος ἐν δικαιοσύνῃ καὶ λαλῶν εὐθεῖαν ὁδὸν καὶ πᾶς μισῶν ἀσέβειαν καὶ ἀδικίαν.

— «The lawless ones in Zion have departed from me». Because of their **departure**, trembling will seize them. Then, as to those from the people of the circumcision who did not believe, he continues on to say: «Who will declare to you that a fire is burning?» Concerning them he said a little earlier: «Fire will consume you,» and again: «Who will declare to you the everlasting place,» clearly referring to the place "prepared for the devil and his angels." Who therefore will be the one who has seen these things and bears witness for those who have not seen if not everyone walking in righteousness, speaking straight talk, and everyone hating ungodliness and unrighteousness.

— Greek text — J. Ziegler, *Eusebius Werke, Band 9: Der Jesajakommentar*; [*Die griechischen christlichen Schriftsteller*]. Akademie Verlag, 1975. Retrieved from Thesaurus Linguae Graecae (stephanus.tlg.uci.edu).

— English translation — Jonathan J. Armstrong. *Eusebius of Caesarea: Commentary on Isaiah*; [*Ancient Christian Texts*]. Inter-

Varsity Press Academic, 2013. Kindle Edition. The first sentence in square brackets is my own emendation of Armstrong's translation.
— The context is Israel's departure from God. Notice the association of *apostasia* with lawlessness and unbelief.
— RELIGIOUS APOSTASY

(128) Eusebius of Caesarea, Commentary on Psalms, 18:17ff (LXX 17:18), (PG Migne 23.176)
— «Καὶ ἐγένετο Κύριος ἀντιστήριγμά μου. Καὶ ἐξήγαγέ με εἰς πλατυσμὸν, ῥύσεταί με, ὅτι ἠθέλησέ με. Καὶ ἀνταποδώσει μοι Κύριος κατὰ τὴν δικαιοσύνην μου.» Ἤδη μὲν, φησὶ, τῆς ἐξομολογήσεώς μου καὶ τῶν προσευχῶν καὶ τῶν ἱκετηρίων ἐπακούσας ὁ Κύριος, γέγονέ μοι ἀντιστήριγμα. Μέλλοντα γάρ με περιτρέπεσθαι, καὶ μέγα πτῶμα ὑπομένειν, εἰ μετὰ τὴν ἁμαρτίαν εἰς παντελῆ ἐξέπιπτον **ἀποστασίαν**, αὐτὸς παραστὰς ἔρεισμά μοι καὶ ἀντιστήριγμα γέγονεν, ὁπηνίκα, τὸν αὐτοῦ προφήτην Ναθὰν πέμψας, ἔλεγχόν μοι ἐπήγαγε τῆς ἁμαρτίας, καὶ ἀνώρθωσεν.
— «But the LORD was my stay. He brought me forth also into a large place; he delivered me because he delighted in me. The LORD rewarded me according to my righteousness.» Now, he says, the Lord has heard my confession, my prayer, and my supplication, and has become my stay. When I was certainly corrupted and enduring a great fall, lest after my sin I fall away into absolute **apostasy**, he offered support to me and became my stay. At that time he sent his prophet Nathan, who produced a rebuke of my sin and restored me.
— Greek text — J.P. Migne. *Patrologiae cursus completus* (*series Graeca 23*). Migne, 1857-1866. Retrieved from Thesaurus Linguae Graecae (stephanus.tlg.uci.edu).
— English translation —The translation is my own as I could find none available.
— The context is David's fall and restoration. David figured that he was on the verge of apostasy knowing that he had continued in a great fall for a long time. Notice that this passage says David fell away into apostasy. This implies that falling away and apostasy are synonyms.
— RELIGIOUS APOSTASY

(129) Eusebius of Caesarea, Commentary on Psalms, Psalm 25 (LXX 24), (Migne 23.224-225)

— Ἀντὶ δὲ «τοῦ ἀνομοῦντες», οἱ λοιποὶ καὶ ἡ πέμπτη ἔκδοσις «οἱ ἀποστατοῦντες» ἡρμηνεύκασιν· σαφῶς τοὺς παραβάτας, καὶ μὴ τῷ προτέρῳ ἑαυτῶν σκοπῷ ἐμμένοντας καταισχυνθήσεσθαι ἀποφηνάμενοι. Τῆς γὰρ **ἀποστασίας** ἑαυτῶν καρπὸν ὑπόκενον εὑρόντες, ὡς ἂν διακενῆς ἀποστατήσαντες τοῦ Θεοῦ, καταισχυνθήσονται.

— Instead of "the lawless," the rest and the fifth edition have translated "the apostates." Clearly being set forth as transgressors, who have not remained in their former view, to be shamed. For finding the empty fruits of their own **apostasy**—however they have emptily apostatized from God—they shall be ashamed.

— Greek text — J.P. Migne. *Patrologiae cursus completus* (*series Graeca 23*). Migne, 1857-1866. Retrieved from Thesaurus Linguae Graecae (stephanus.tlg.uci.edu).

— English translation — The translation is my own as I could find none available.

— The context is departure from God. Note the association of *apostasia* with παραβάτας (parabatas) *transgressors* and ἀνομοῦντες (anamountes) *ones living lawlessly*.

— RELIGIOUS APOSTASY

(130) Eusebius of Caesarea, Commentary on Psalms, Psalm 33 (LXX 32), (Migne 23.288)

— Ἔχοντες δὲ μέγα φυλακτήριον τοὺς τῆς προνοίας αὐτοῦ ὀφθαλμοὺς, ἐπ' αὐτὸν ἐλπίζετε μόνον καὶ ἐπὶ τὸ ἔλεος αὐτοῦ, εἰς τὸ ῥύσασθαι ἐκ θανάτου τὰς ψυχὰς αὐτῶν. Θάνατος δ' ἂν εἴη ψυχῆς ἡ ἄρνησις τοῦ Θεοῦ καὶ **ἡ παντελὴς ἀποστασία**, καὶ αἱ πρὸς θάνατον ἁμαρτίαι·

— Having for a great phylactery, the eyes of his foresight. Hope on him only and his mercy, for their souls to be delivered from death. The denial of God, and utter **apostasy**, and sin unto death would be the death of the soul.

— Greek text — J.P. Migne. *Patrologiae cursus completus* (*series Graeca 23*). Migne, 1857-1866. Retrieved from Thesaurus Linguae Graecae (stephanus.tlg.uci.edu).

— English translation — The translation is my own as I could find none available.

— The context is the contrast between death and deliverance from death. Notice that *apostasia* is associated with the death of the soul. Notice further that *apostasia* is associated with ἡ ἄρνησις τοῦ Θεοῦ (denial of God) and αἱ πρὸς θάνατον ἁμαρτίαι (sin unto death).

— RELIGIOUS APOSTASY

(131) Eusebius of Caesarea, Commentary on Psalms, Psalm 70 (LXX 69), (Migne 23.785)

— Συμβαίνει γὰρ πολλάκις ἐκλείπειν κατὰ τοὺς καιροὺς τῶν διωγμῶν, ἐπειδὰν οἱ πολλοὶ τοῦ σώματος τῆς Ἐκκλησίας δι' ἀσθένειαν πίστεως ἐξομνύονται τὴν πίστιν. Καὶ μήποτε ταῦτα ἀναπέμπεται ἐπὶ τὸν καιρὸν **τῆς ἀποστασίας**, περὶ οὗ καιροῦ ὁ Ἀπόστολος ἐδίδασκε λέγων· «Ἐὰν μὴ ἔλθῃ ἡ **ἀποστασία** πρῶτον, καὶ ἀποκαλυφθῇ ἄνθρωπος τῆς ἁμαρτίας, ὁ Υἱὸς τῆς ἀπωλείας.» Τοῦτον δὲ τὸν καιρὸν ὁ Σωτὴρ ἐδήλου λέγων· «Ἆρα ἐλθὼν ὁ Υἱὸς τοῦ ἀνθρώπου εὑρήσει τὴν πίστιν ἐπὶ τῆς γῆς;» Καὶ πάλιν· «Διὰ δὲ τὸ πληθυνθῆναι τὴν ἀνομίαν, ψυγήσεται ἡ ἀγάπη τῶν πολλῶν.» Τότε γὰρ ἔσται γηραλέον καὶ ἀσθενὲς τὸ σῶμα τῆς Ἐκκλησίας.

— Many times [men] happen to fail in times of persecution, when many of the body of the [professing] church deny the faith because of weakness of faith. And lest these things return at the time of **apostasy**, concerning that time the apostle taught, saying, «that day shall not come, except there come a **falling away** first, and the man of sin be revealed, the son of perdition;» The Saviour was clearly speaking of this time when he said, «Therefore, shall the Son of man find faith on the earth when he comes?» And again, «because of the increase of iniquity, the love of the most shall grow cold.» Then shall the body of the church be old and weak.

— Greek text — J.P. Migne. *Patrologiae cursus completus* (*series Graeca 23*). Migne, 1857-1866. Retrieved from Thesaurus Linguae Graecae (stephanus.tlg.uci.edu).

— English translation — The translation is my own as I could find none available.

218

— The context is the apostasy in the last days. Notice that Eusebius associates *apostasia* with a lack of faith on the earth and the love of the most grown cold.
— RELIGIOUS APOSTASY

(132) Eusebius of Caesarea, Proof of the Gospel, 7.1.118

— ὁ δὲ Ῥαασὶμ βασιλεὺς ἦν πάλιν τῶν ἐν Δαμασκῷ εἰδωλολατρῶν ἐθνῶν, ὡς καὶ ὁ υἱὸς Ῥομελίου τῶν ἐν Σαμαρείᾳ τοῦ Ἰουδαίων ἔθνους ἀποστάντων τῆς πατρίου θρησκείας. ἀπειλεῖ τοιγαροῦν ὁ θεὸς τοῖς μὴ τὸν Σιλωάμ, τοῦτ' ἔστιν τὸν ἀπεσταλμένον Ἐμμανουήλ, καὶ τὸν ἐκ τῆς προφήτιδος γεγεννημένον υἱὸν τόν τε πότιμον καὶ γόνιμον αὐτοῦ λόγον παραδεξαμένοις, ἀλλὰ τοῦτον μὲν καίτοι πράως καὶ ἡσυχῇ φερόμενον παραιτουμένοις, καθ' ἑαυτῶν δὲ ἤτοι τὸν τῶν εἰδωλολατρῶν ἐθνῶν ἄρχοντα ἢ τὸν **τῆς ἀποστασίας** τοῦ λαοῦ τοῦ θεοῦ ἑλομένοις, ἐπάξειν «τὸ ὕδωρ τοῦ ποταμοῦ τὸ ἰσχυρὸν καὶ τὸ πολύ», ὅπερ ὕδωρ αὐτὸς ὁ τῆς προφητείας λόγος ἑρμηνεύει, λέγων αὐτὸν εἶναι «τὸν βασιλέα τῶν Ἀσσυρίων», οὕτω πάλιν ἤτοι κατὰ διάνοιαν σημαίνων τὸν ἄρχοντα τοῦ αἰῶνος τούτου, ἢ τὴν νῦν ἐπικρατοῦσαν Ῥωμαίων ἀρχήν, ᾗ καὶ παρεδόθησαν οἱ τὸ μὲν δηλωθὲν τοῦ Σιλωὰμ ὕδωρ τὸ πορευόμενον ἡσυχῇ παραιτησάμενοι τοῖς δὲ ἐναντίοις καὶ πολεμίοις τοῦ ὀρθοῦ λόγου δόγμασιν ἑαυτοὺς ὑποβεβληκότες.

— And Raashim again was king of the idolatrous Gentiles in Damascus, as was also the son of Romelias of the Jews in Samaria who deserted the Jewish worship of their ancestors. And so God threatens that on those who will not accept Siloam, that is to say, Emmanuel, who is sent to them, and the Son born of the prophetess, and His pleasant and fruitful Word, but reject it, though it flows softly and gently, and choose for their own selves the prince of idolatrous Gentiles or the leaders of **the apostasy** of God's people, He will bring the strong and full flood of the river, which the word of the prophecy interprets for us to be the king of the Assyrians: meaning here again either figuratively the Prince of this world, or the power of Rome actually dominant, to which they were delivered who rejected the said water of Siloam that went softly, and embraced beliefs utterly hostile to good teaching.

— Greek text — I.A. Heikel, *Eusebius Werke, Band 6: Die Demonstratio evangelica;* [*Die griechischen christlichen Schriftsteller 23*]. Hinrichs, 1913. Retrieved from Thesaurus Linguae Graecae (stephanus.tlg.uci.edu).

— English translation — W.J. Ferrar. *Eusebius Pamphilii of Caesarea: Demonstratio Evangelica;* [*Translations of Christian Literature, Series I, Greek Texts*]. Society for Promoting Christian Knowledge, 1920. Transcribed for the Tertullian Project by Roger Pearse, 2003. Accessed at The Tertullian Project (tertullian.org/fathers).

— The context is Israel's apostasy. They chose the idolatry of the Gentiles and the excitement of apostasy over the quiet waters of Siloam. Notice the association of *apostasia* with beliefs contrary to good teaching, with idolatry, with departure from the worship which the Jews had received from God.

— RELIGIOUS APOSTASY

(133) Eusebius of Caesarea, Proof of the Gospel, Fragments from Book 15, fragment 5

— ἐντεῦθεν οἶμαι τὸν ἱερὸν ἀπόστολον Παῦλον ὁρμᾶσθαι, περὶ τῆς δευτέρας ἀφίξεως τοῦ Χριστοῦ γράφων τὰ τοιάδε· «ὅτι αὐτὸς ὁ κύριος ἐν κελεύσματι, ἐν φωνῇ ἀρχαγγέλου καὶ ἐν σάλπιγγι θεοῦ καταβήσεται ἀπ' οὐρανοῦ», καὶ τὰ ἑξῆς. ὁ δ' αὐτὸς ἀπόστολος καὶ τὴν ὑστάτην τοῦ ἀντιχρίστου ἄφιξίν τε καὶ ἀπώλειαν καὶ ἐπὶ ταύτῃ τὴν τοῦ σωτῆρος ἡμῶν ἔνδοξον παρουσίαν ἀκολούθως τῇ προφητείᾳ παρίστησι λέγων· «μήτις ὑμᾶς ἐξαπατήσει κατὰ μηδένα τρόπον, ὅτι ἐὰν μὴ ἔλθῃ **ἡ ἀποστασία** πρῶτον καὶ ἀποκαλυφθῇ ὁ ἄνθρωπος τῆς ἁμαρτίας, ὁ υἱὸς τῆς ἀπωλείας, ὁ ἀντικείμενος καὶ ὑπεραιρόμενος ἐπὶ πάντα λεγόμενα θεὸν ἢ σέβασμα ὥστε αὐτὸν εἰς τὸν ναὸν τοῦ θεοῦ καθίσαι, ἀποδεικνύντα ἑαυτὸν ὅτι ἐστὶ θεός. οὐ μνημονεύετε, ὅτι ἔτι ὢν πρὸς ὑμᾶς ταῦτα ἔλεγον ὑμῖν».

— Hence I think that the holy apostle Paul was impelled to write the following about the second coming of Christ, «Because the Lord himself shall descend from heaven with a command, with the call of the archangel, and with the trumpet of God» and so forth. For the apostle himself presented in order the last coming of the antichrist and his destruction, and after this the glorious coming of our Saviour saying, «Let no man deceive you by any means: for that day shall not come, except there come **a falling away** first, and the man of sin be revealed, the son of perdition; Who opposes and exalts himself above all that is called God, or that is worshipped; so that he as God sits in the temple of God, presenting himself as God. Remember that, when I was yet with you, I told you these things?»

— Greek text — I.A. Heikel, *Eusebius Werke, Band 6: Die Demonstratio evangelica;* [*Die griechischen christlichen Schrift-steller 23*]. Hinrichs, 1913. Retrieved from Thesaurus Linguae Graecae (stephanus.tlg.uci.edu).

— English translation — The translation is my own as I could find none available.

— The context is the apostasy associated with the man of sin. The antichrist's exalting of himself over all that is called god or worshiped and his threatening death to all who won't submit is the cause of the final phase of the apostasy of the last days.

— RELIGIOUS APOSTASY

(134) Eusebius of Caesarea, Fragments on Daniel, 24.528

— Ἐντεῦθεν οἶμαι τὸν ἀπόστολον Παῦλον ὁρμᾶσθαι περὶ τῆς δευτέρας ἀφίξεως τοῦ Χριστοῦ γράφοντα τοιάδε· «Ὅτι αὐτὸς ὁ Κύριος ἐν κελεύσματι, ἐν φωνῇ ἀρχαγγέλου καὶ ἐν σάλπιγγι Θεοῦ καταβήσεται ἀπ' οὐρανοῦ,» καὶ τὰ ἑξῆς. Ὁ δ' αὐτὸς ἀπόστολος καὶ τὴν ὑστάτην τοῦ Ἀντιχρίστου ἄφιξιν τὴν καὶ ἀπώλειαν, καὶ ἐπὶ ταύτῃ τὴν τοῦ Σωτῆρος ἡμῶν ἔνδοξον παρουσίαν ἀκολούθως τῇ προφητείᾳ παρίστησι λέγων· «Μήτις ὑμᾶς ἐξαπατήσῃ κατὰ μηδένα τρόπον· ὅτι ἐὰν μὴ ἔλθῃ **ἡ ἀποστασία** πρῶτον, καὶ ἀποκαλυφθῇ ὁ ἄνθρωπος τῆς ἁμαρτίας, ὁ υἱὸς τῆς ἀπωλείας, ὁ ἀντικείμενος καὶ ὑπεραιρόμενος ἐπὶ πάντα λεγόμενα Θεὸν ἢ σέβασμα, ὥστε αὐτὸν εἰς τὸν ναὸν τοῦ Θεοῦ καθίσαι, ἀποδεικνύντα ἑαυτὸν ὅτι ἔστι Θεός· οὐ μνημονεύετε ὅτι ἔτι ὢν πρὸς ὑμᾶς ταῦτα ἔλεγον ὑμῖν;» καὶ τὰ ἑξῆς. Τοσαῦτα ὁ θαυμάσιος Ἀπόστολος ἐν τοῖς περὶ συντελείας τοῦ βίου διεξῆλθε λόγοις, τὰ διὰ τοῦ προφήτου Δανιὴλ περὶ τοῦ Ἀντιχρίστου, καὶ τῆς τοῦ Σωτῆρος ἡμῶν ἐνδόξου βασιλείας τεθεσπισμένα πιστούμενος.

— Hence I think that the apostle Paul was impelled to write the following about the second coming of Christ, «Because the Lord himself shall descend from heaven with a command, with the call of the archangel, and with the trumpet of God» and so forth. For the apostle himself presented in order the last coming of the antichrist and his destruction, and after this the glorious coming of our Saviour saying, «Let no man deceive you by any means: for that day shall not come, except there come **a falling away** first, and the man of sin be revealed, the son of perdition; Who opposes and exalts himself above all that is called God, or that is worshipped; so that he as God sits in the temple of God, presenting himself as God. Remember that, when I was yet with you, I told you these things?» So the amazing apostle, with messages written near the end of his life, detailed things prophesied by the prophet Daniel about the antichrist and about the glorious kingdom of our Saviour, things which he believed.

— Greek text — J.P. Migne. *Patrologiae cursus completus* (*series Graeca 24*). Migne, 1857-1866. Retrieved from Thesaurus Linguae Graecae (stephanus.tlg.uci.edu).

— English translation — The translation is my own as I could find none available.

— The context is the falling away in the last days. Eusebius associates these passages with Daniel's prophecy of the antichrist, which implies that he associates the falling away with the antichrist.

— RELIGIOUS APOSTASY

(135) Eusebius of Caesarea, Fragments in Luke, 17:23-25, (Migne 24.584)

— «Καὶ ἐροῦσιν ὑμῖν· Ἰδοὺ ὧδε, ἢ ἰδοὺ ἐκεῖ.» Ταῦτα κατὰ μὲν τὸν Ματθαῖον ἐλέγετο περὶ τῆς ἐρημώσεως Ἱερουσαλήμ· διὸ καὶ προσέκειτο·«Τότε οἱ ἐν τῇ Ἰουδαίᾳ φευγέτωσαν εἰς τὰ ὄρη»· ἐνταῦθα δὲ περὶ τῶν καιρῶν τοῦ Ἀντιχρίστου προλέγει· διὸ οὐ πρόσκειται τοῦτο. «Πρῶτον δεῖ αὐτὸν πολλὰ παθεῖν.» Αἰνίττεται δὲ καὶ ἐν τούτοις **τήν** ποτε γενησομένην **ἀποστασίαν** εἰπών·«Πρῶτον δὲ δεῖ αὐτὸν πολλὰ παθεῖν καὶ ἀποδοκιμασθῆναι ἀπὸ τῆς γενεᾶς ταύτης», δηλονότι τῆς τῶν ἀνθρώπων· ἀποβληθῆναι γὰρ καὶ ἀποδοκιμασθῆναι τὸν περὶ αὐτοῦ λόγον, πολλά τε παθεῖν τὸν αὐτοῦ λαόν, ἐθέσπισεν· εἴτε ἐν τοῖς μετὰ ταῦτα διωγμοῖς, καθ᾽ οὓς μυρία πέπονθεν αὐτός τε βλασφημούμενος ὁ Σωτὴρ παρὰ τοῖς ἀνθρώποις, ἥ τε Ἐκκλησία αὐτοῦ καὶ ὁ λόγος ἐλαυνόμενος καὶ πολεμούμενος· εἴτε πρὸς τῷ πάντων τέλει, καθ' ὃ ἀποδοκιμασθήσεται πάμπαν ἀποβληθεὶς ἀπὸ τῆς τῶν ἀνθρώπων γενεᾶς.

— «And they will say to you, 'Look, he is here' or 'Look he is there'» In Matthew this is said about the desolation of Jerusalem, which is why it continues, «at that time let those in Judaea flee to the hills.» But here he is speaking in advance about the times of the antichrist. As such, the passage does not continue that way. «It is necessary first that he suffer many things.» He speaks obscurely in this passage about **the apostasy** that will then take place when he says, «first he must suffer many things and be rejected by this generation,» that is, by this generation of men. For he prophesied that the message about him would be cast out and rejected, and that his people would suffer many things. This may refer to the persecutions that took place soon after, in which the Savior suffered countless things and was reviled among men; or it may refer to his church and its message being driven out and fought against; or it may refer to the end of all things, when the message will be entirely rejected and cast out by the race of men.

— Greek text — J.P. Migne. *Patrologiae cursus completus* (*series Graeca 24*). Migne, 1857-1866. Retrieved from Thesaurus Linguae Graecae (stephanus.tlg.uci.edu).

— English translation — Alex Poulos, 2017. The translation was commissioned and edited by Roger Pearse and released publically on roger-pearse.com/weblog.

— The context is the apostasy (the rejection of Christ) which occurred in the years following the cross, continued in the church age, and will explode at the end of the age in the days of the antichrist when the message will be entirely rejected by mankind.

— RELIGIOUS APOSTASY

(136) Eusebius of Caesarea, Fragments in Luke, 17:26 ff, (Migne 24.584)

— «Καὶ καθὼς ἐγένετο ἐν ταῖς ἡμέραις τοῦ Νῶε, κ. τ. λ.» Οὕτω τοίνυν, ὡς εἴρηται, ἐκβληθέντος διὰ **τὴν ἀποστασίαν** τοῦ λόγου τοῦ εὐαγγελικοῦ, κατὰ τὴν ὁμοίωσιν τῶν ἐπὶ τοῦ κατακλυσμοῦ συμβεβηκότων, ὁ κατὰ τῶν ἀσεβῶν ὄλεθρος ἐπιστήσεται, φησί. Ἀλλ' ὡς τότε πάντας μὲν ἀπώλεσεν, οὐ μὴν καὶ τοὺς συνηγμένους ἅμα τῷ Νῶε ἐν τῇ κιβωτῷ, οὕτω καὶ ἐπὶ τῆς αὐτοῦ παρουσίας οἱ μὲν ἀσεβεῖς κατὰ τὸν καιρὸν **τῆς ἀποστασίας** τρυφαῖς καὶ μέθαις καὶ γάμοις καὶ ταῖς τοῦ βίου ἡδοναῖς κατατριβόμενοι ὁμοίως τοῖς ἐπὶ τοῦ Νῶε κατακλυσθέντες ἀπολοῦνται.

— «And just as happened in the days of Noah…» As was stated, he says that the destruction of the wicked will take place like it did for those who lived at the time of the flood, since the message of the gospel had been driven out due to their **apostasy**. Indeed, just as he destroyed all people then, except those who had gone with Noah into the ark, so too at his coming he will shut out and destroy as in the days of Noah the ungodly and unfaithful, who [in the time of **apostasy**] waste their time on luxury, sex, drink, and the pleasures of this life.

— Greek text — J.P. Migne. *Patrologiae cursus completus* (*series Graeca 24*). Migne, 1857-1866. Retrieved from *Thesaurus Linguae Graecae* (stephanus.tlg.uci.edu).

— English translation — Alex Poulos, 2017. The translation was commissioned and edited by Roger Pearse and released publically on roger-pearse.com/weblog. The material in square brackets is my translation of material left out of Alex's translation.

— The context compares the judgment in the day of Noah because of mankind's apostasy with the judgment at Christ's second coming because of mankind's debauchery.

— RELIGIOUS APOSTASY

(137) Eusebius of Caesarea, Fragments in Luke, 17:26 ff, (Migne 24.585)

— «Βάδιζε, λαός μου, εἴσελθε εἰς τὸ ταμεῖόν σου … ἕως οὗ παρέλθοι ἡ ὀργὴ Κυρίου»· ὥσπερ καὶ ἐπὶ τοῦ Λὼτ ἐποίησεν, ἵνα μὴ οἱ δίκαιοι συναπόλωνται τοῖς ἀσεβέσιν· οὕτως καὶ ἐπὶ τῆς συντελείας τοῦ αἰῶνος οὐ πρότερον αὕτη ἔσται, ἢ πάντας τοὺς ἐπὶ γῆς δικαίους καὶ θεοσεβεῖς ἀφορισθῆναι τῶν ἀσεβῶν, καὶ συναχθῆναι εἰς τὴν ἐπουράνιον τοῦ Θεοῦ κιβωτόν· οὕτω γὰρ μηκέτι μηδενὸς δικαίου ἐν ἀνθρώποις εὑρισκομένου, πάντων δὲ ἀθέων ἀσεβῶν τῶν ὑπὸ τοῦ Ἀντιχρίστου γεγονότων, **τῆς** τε **ἀποστασίας** καθ' ὅλης τῆς οἰκουμένης κρατησάσης, ἡ τοῦ Θεοῦ ὀργὴ τοὺς ἀσεβεῖς μετελεύσεται.

— «Go, my people, enter into your inner room … until the wrath of the Lord passes by». Now just as in the time of Lot, he acted so that the righteous did not perish along with the wicked, so at the end of age this destruction will not take place until all the righteous and God-fearing men on the earth are separated from the wicked and gathered into God's heavenly ark. So when no righteous man can any longer be found among men, but all are godless, impious, and born from the antichrist [but all have been made ungodly atheists by the antichrist] and **apostasy** rules throughout the whole world, then the wrath of God will come upon the wicked.

— Greek text — J.P. Migne. *Patrologiae cursus completus* (*series Graeca 24*). Migne, 1857-1866. Retrieved from Thesaurus Linguae Graecae (stephanus.tlg.uci.edu).

— English translation — Alex Poulos, 2017. The translation was commissioned and edited by Roger Pearse and released publically on roger-pearse.com/weblog. The comment in square brackets is my translation of the preceding phrase.

— The context is the apostasy that engulfs the entire world under the influence of the antichrist and makes every man an ungodly atheist.

— RELIGIOUS APOSTASY

(138) Eusebius of Caesarea, Fragments in Luke, 17:31, (Migne 24.585)

— «Ἐν ἐκείνῃ τῇ ἡμέρᾳ ὃς ἂν ἔσται ἐπὶ τοῦ δώματος, κ. τ. λ.» Σημαίνει δὲ διὰ τούτων τὸν κατὰ τῶν θεοσεβῶν ἐπενεχθησόμενον διωγμὸν ὑπὸ τοῦ υἱοῦ τῆς ἀπωλείας. Ἡμέραν δὲ ἐκείνην ὀνομάζει τὸν χρόνον τὸν πρὸ τῆς συντελείας, ἐν ᾧ φησιν· «Ὁ φεύγων μὴ ἐπιστρεφέτω, μηδὲ μιμητὴς γινέσθω τῆς γυναικὸς Λὼτ, ἥτις μετὰ τὸ φυγεῖν καὶ ἔξω γενέσθαι τῆς Σοδομιτῶν χώρας, στραφεῖσα εἰς τὰ ὀπίσω, ἀπενεκρώθη, στήλη ἁλὸς γενομένη.» Ἀφειδεῖν γὰρ τότε προσήκει οὐχ ὑπαρχόντων μόνον, ἀλλὰ καὶ τῆς ἑαυτῶν ζωῆς τε καὶ ψυχῆς τοὺς ἐν μέσῳ **τῆς ἀποστασίας** καταληφθησομένους, μήποτε, βουληθέντες τῆς ἑαυτῶν περιποιήσασθαι προσκαίρου ζωῆς, σὺν ταύτῃ καὶ τὴν αἰώνιον ζωὴν ἀπολέσειαν, **τῇ ἀποστασίᾳ** ἑαυτοὺς παραδόντες.

— «And on that day whoever shall be on the roof...» He is referring through this to the persecution that will be carried out against the godly by the son of destruction. He calls the time before the end of the age «that day», when he says, «Let the one who flees not turn back, nor become an imitator of Lot's wife, who after fleeing the region of Sodom turned around and was put to death by being turned into a column of salt.» For those then caught in the midst of **apostasy** should not only look away from their possessions, but also from their own life and soul, so that they do not lose eternal life by surrendering themselves to **apostasy** by deciding to put too great a value on this temporary life.

— Greek text — J.P. Migne. *Patrologiae cursus completus* (*series Graeca 24*). Migne, 1857-1866. Retrieved from Thesaurus Linguae Graecae (stephanus.tlg.uci.edu).

— English translation — Alex Poulos, 2017. The translation was commissioned and edited by Roger Pearse and released publically on roger-pearse.com/weblog.

— The context is apostasy, which overtakes men when they put too great an emphasis on this temporal and temporary life. Notice that Lot's wife is an example of *apostasia*, for she turned around and looked back at the doomed city and her doomed possessions.

— RELIGIOUS APOSTASY

(139) Eusebius of Caesarea, Fragments in Luke, 17:34, (Migne 24.585)

— Ταύτη τῇ νυκτὶ ἔσονται δύο ἐπὶ κλίνης μιᾶς, κ. τ. λ. Σφόδρα δὲ θαυμαστῶς τὸν **τῆς ἀποστασίας** καιρὸν καὶ τὴν στέρησιν τοῦ νοεροῦ λογικοῦ φωτὸς νύκτα ὠνόμασε· νυκτὸς γὰρ καὶ σκότους χείρων ἡ τότε τῶν ἀνθρώπων ἔσται κατάστασις διὰ τὴν ἐπικρατήσασαν αὐτῶν ἄνοιάν τε καὶ πλάνην. Διὸ φησι· «Λέγω ὑμῖν· Δύο ἔσονται ἐπὶ κλίνης καὶ δύο ἐπὶ μυλῶνος, εἷς παραλαμβανόμενος» ὡς ἀλλότριος τῆς ὀργῆς, καὶ «εἷς ἀφιέμενος», ὥστε τῇ ὀργῇ παραδοθησόμενος, ὁ θησαυρίσας ἑαυτῷ ὀργὴν ἐν ἡμέρᾳ ὀργῆς·δι' ὧν παρίστησι τὸν χωρισμὸν τῶν ἁγίων καὶ θεοφιλῶν ψυχῶν τὸν ἀπὸ τῶν ἀσεβῶν.

— «On that night there will be two on a single bed...» It is truly noteworthy how he calls the time of **the apostasy** and the deprivation of spiritual and rational light "night." For the condition of men in that day will be worse than darkness and night, since senselessness and deceit will overtake them completely. Therefore he says, «I said to you, there shall be two on one bed and two around the millstone and one shall be taken» as to be kept apart from the wrath «and the other,»

who had stored up wrath for himself for that day, «shall be passed over» so as to be delivered to the wrath. Through this he shows the division of the holy and God-loving souls from the ungodly ones.
— Greek text — J.P. Migne. *Patrologiae cursus completus (series Graeca 24)*. Migne, 1857-1866. Retrieved from Thesaurus Linguae Graecae (stephanus.tlg.uci.edu).
— English translation — Alex Poulos, 2017. The translation was commissioned and edited by Roger Pearse and released publically on roger-pearse.com/weblog.
— The context is the season of apostasy at the end of the age, which time is called night. Notice the association between apostasy and the deprivation of the light of the rational mind.
— RELIGIOUS APOSTASY

(140) Eusebius of Caesarea, Fragments in Luke, 18.2, (Migne 24.588)
— Κριτής τις ἦν τὸν Θεὸν μὴ φοβούμενος. Ἐπισυνάπτει γοῦν καὶ παραβολὴν τὴν περὶ τοῦ κριτοῦ τῆς ἀδικίας, πρὸς τὸ δεῖν πάντοτε προσεύχεσθαι καὶ μὴ ἐκκακεῖν. Τὸ δὲ εἰπεῖν· Ἆρα ἐλθὼν ὁ Υἱὸς τοῦ ἀνθρώπου εὑρήσει τὴν πίστιν ἐπὶ τῆς γῆς; ἔκλειψιν δηλοῖ τῆς πίστεως, ὡς μηδένα πιστὸν εὑρεθήσεσθαι, ἢ εἴ που ἄρα σπάνιόν τινα κατὰ τὸν τῆς δευτέρας αὐτοῦ θεοφανείας χρόνον. Ὅπερ μέγα τεκμήριον τυγχάνει τοῦ καιροῦ **τῆς ἀποστασίας**, ἐν ᾧ σπάνιος ἔσται ὁ εὑρεθησόμενος πιστός· τάχα δὲ οὐδὲ εἷς ἔσται, διὰ τὸ τοὺς μὲν παραληφθήσεσθαι, τοὺς δὲ καταλειφθήσεσθαι τοῖς ἀετοῖς παραδοθησομένους·
— «There was a judge who did not fear God». Therefore, he connects the parable about the unjust judge to this one to show that we must always pray and not lose heart. There is also the statement, «will the son of man find faith on the earth?» This indicates such a lack of faith, that few or no faithful people will be found at the time of his second divine appearance. This is an important sign of the time of **the apostasy**, when a faithful person will be found only very rarely. Perhaps there will not be even one, since some will be taken, and some left to be handed over to the vultures.

— Greek text — J.P. Migne. *Patrologiae cursus completus* (*series Graeca 24*). Migne, 1857-1866. Retrieved from Thesaurus Linguae Graecae (stephanus.tlg.uci.edu).

— English translation — Alex Poulos, 2017. The translation was commissioned and edited by Roger Pearse and released publically on roger-pearse.com/weblog.

— The context is apostasy at the end of the age when few or no faithful people will be found.

— RELIGIOUS APOSTASY

(141) Eusebius of Caesarea, Fragments in Luke, 21:28, (Migne 24.600-601)

— Ταῦτα δὲ ἐπὶ τέλει τῶν χρόνων ἔσται, **τῆς ἀποστασίας** ἐνεργουμένης. Μελλούσης γὰρ τὰ τῆς θεομαχίας τέρατα καταργεῖν τῆς ἐπιφανείας τοῦ Σωτῆρος, τὰ τῆς ὀργῆς προοίμια ἐκ τῶνδε ἄρξεται, ἐξ αὐχμῶν δηλαδὴ καὶ ἀπορίας ἤχου θαλάσσης·οὗ γενομένου ἐπακολουθήσει συνοχὴ τῶν ἐπὶ γῆς ἐθνῶν, ἀποψυχόντων ἀνθρώπων ἀπὸ φόβου καὶ προσδοκίας τῶν ἐπερχομένων τῇ οἰκουμένῃ. Τίνα δὲ τὰ ἐπερχόμενα, ἑρμηνεύει συνάπτων ἑξῆς καὶ λέγων·«Αἱ γὰρ δυνάμεις τῶν οὐρανῶν σαλευθήσονται.»·

— This will occur at the end of the age, when the **apostasy** is in full effect. For when the Savior is about to come and abolish the false miracles of those fighting against God, certain preludes to his wrath will begin to occur through droughts and the deprivation of sound from the sea. [When this happens, there shall come distress among the nations on the earth, for men's hearts shall fail from fear and from the expectation of what is coming to the world.] He explains what comes after by saying the following, [He explains the coming things by appending the following and saying] "for the powers of the heavens will be shaken."

— Greek text — J.P. Migne. *Patrologiae cursus completus* (*series Graeca 24*). Migne, 1857-1866. Retrieved from Thesaurus Linguae Graecae (stephanus.tlg.uci.edu).

— English translation — Alex Poulos, 2017. The translation was commissioned and edited by Roger Pearse and released publically on roger-pearse.com/weblog. The first set of square brackets is a sentence that was inexplicably left out, either in Alex Poulos'

translation or in Roger Pearse's transcription. So this material is my own translation. The second set of square brackets is a clarification that I added where I felt that the translation was ambiguous.
— The context is the apostasy at the end of the age. It is associated with fighting against God and false miracles. Notice also that the apostasy comes to an end when the full wrath of God is poured out.
— RELIGIOUS APOSTASY

(142) Eusebius of Caesarea, Fragments in Luke, 21:29, (Migne 24.601)
— «Καὶ εἶπε παραβολὴν αὐτοῖς Ἴδετε τὴν συκῆν, κ. τ. λ. Οὕτω καὶ ὑμεῖς ὅταν ἴδητε ταῦτα γινόμενα, κ. τ. λ.» Ποῖα «ταῦτα» γινόμενα ἀλλ᾽ ἢ τὰ προλεγόμενα; Ἰερουσαλὴμ πατουμένην ὑπὸ ἐθνῶν, τὴν συμπλήρωσιν «τῶν καιρῶν τῶν ἐθνῶν,» τοὺς **τῆς ἀποστασίας** χρόνους, τὰ ἐν τοῖς φωστῆρσι καὶ τοῖς ἄστροις σημεῖα, τὴν ἐπὶ γῆς συνοχὴν τῶν ἐθνῶν.
— «And he spoke to them a parable, Look at the fig tree... likewise when you see these things happening...» What could «these things» mean other than what had just been said? The signs are the trampling of Jerusalem by the nations, the fulfillment of the «times of the nations,» the times of **apostasy**, the signs among the heavenly lights and stars, the assembling of the nations on the earth.
— Greek text — J.P. Migne. *Patrologiae cursus completus* (*series Graeca 24*). Migne, 1857-1866. Retrieved from Thesaurus Linguae Graecae (stephanus.tlg.uci.edu).
— English translation — Alex Poulos, 2017. The translation was commissioned and edited by Roger Pearse and released publically on roger-pearse.com/weblog.
— The context is the time of apostasy in the last days. Notice that everything the apostasy is associated with occurs during the seventieth week: the trampling of Jerusalem by the nations, the fulfilling of the times of the Gentiles, the signs in the lights and stars in the heavens, and the distress of the nations. Notice the phrase "the times of the apostasy" which suggests a definite event at a definite time.
— RELIGIOUS APOSTASY

(143) Eusebius of Caesarea, Ecclesiastical History, 1.5.6

— καὶ ἐν τῇ δευτέρᾳ δὲ τῶν ἱστοριῶν τοῦ Ἰουδαϊκοῦ πολέμου περὶ τοῦ αὐτοῦ ταῦτα γράφει· "ἐπὶ τούτου τις ἀνὴρ Γαλιλαῖος Ἰούδας ὄνομα εἰς **ἀποστασίαν** ἐνῆγε τοὺς ἐπιχωρίους, κακίζων εἰ φόρον τε Ῥωμαίοις τελεῖν ὑπομενοῦσιν καὶ μετὰ τὸν θεὸν οἴσουσι θνητοὺς δεσπότας." ταῦτα ὁ Ἰώσηπος.

— And in the second book of the History of the Jewish War he writes concerning the same man, "At this time a Galilean called Judas incited the inhabitants to **revolt**, calling them cowards to suffer the payment of tribute to the Romans, and after serving God to endure mortal masters." So far Josephus.

— Greek text and English translation — *Eusebius of Caesarea: Historia ecclesiastica*, with English translation by Kirsopp Lake, *The Loeb Classical Library 153*. Harvard University Press; William Heinemann; 1926. Accessed at Perseus Digital Library (perseus. tufts.edu) and Internet Archive Wayback Machine (web.archive.org).

— The context is the rebellion when Judas incited the Jews to revolt against the Romans.

— POLITICAL SEDITION OR REBELLION

(144) Eusebius of Caesarea, Ecclesiastical History, 4.6.1, [citation from Ariston of Pella]

— Καὶ δῆτα τῆς Ἰουδαίων **ἀποστασίας** αὖθις εἰς μέγα καὶ πολὺ προελθούσης, Ῥοῦφος ἐπάρχων τῆς Ἰουδαίας, στρατιωτικῆς αὐτῷ συμμαχίας ὑπὸ βασιλέως πεμφθείσης, ταῖς ἀπονοίαις αὐτῶν ἀφειδῶς χρώμενος ἐπεξῄει, μυριάδας ἀθρόως ἀνδρῶν ὁμοῦ καὶ παίδων καὶ γυναικῶν διαφθείρων πολέμου τε νόμῳ τὰς χώρας αὐτῶν ἐξανδραποδιζόμενος.

— The **rebellion** of the Jews once more progressed in character and extent, and Rufus, the governor of Judaea, when military aid had been sent him by the Emperor, moved out against them, treating their madness without mercy. He destroyed in heaps thousands of men, women, and children, and under the law of war, enslaved their land.

— Greek text and English translation — *Eusebius of Caesarea: Historia ecclesiastica*, with English translation by Kirsopp Lake, *The Loeb Classical Library 153*. Harvard University Press; William

Heinemann; 1926. Accessed at Perseus Digital Library (perseus. tufts.edu) and Internet Archive Wayback Machine (web.archive.org).
— The context is the Jewish rebellion against the Romans.
— POLITICAL SEDITION OR REBELLION

(145) Eusebius of Caesarea, Ecclesiastical History, 5.28.6
— πῶς οὖν ἐκ τοσούτων ἐτῶν καταγγελλομένου τοῦ ἐκκλησιαστικοῦ φρονήματος, ἐνδέχεται τοὺς μέχρι Βίκτορος οὕτως ὡς οὗτοι λέγουσιν κεκηρυχέναι; πῶς δὲ οὐκ αἰδοῦνται ταῦτα Βίκτορος καταψεύδεσθαι, ἀκριβῶς εἰδότες ὅτι Βίκτωρ Θεόδοτον τὸν σκυτέα, τὸν ἀρχηγὸν καὶ πατέρα ταύτης **τῆς** ἀρνησιθέου **ἀποστασίας**, ἀπεκήρυξεν τῆς κοινωνίας, πρῶτον εἰπόντα ψιλὸν ἄνθρωπον τὸν Χριστόν; εἰ γὰρ Βίκτωρ κατ᾽ αὐτοὺς οὕτως ἐφρόνει ὡς ἡ τούτων διδάσκει βλασφημία, πῶς ἂν ἀπέβαλεν Θεόδοτον τὸν τῆς αἱρέσεως ταύτης εὑρετήν.
— How then is it possible that after the mind of the church had been announced for so many years that the generation before Victor can have preached as they say? Why are they not ashamed of so calumniating Victor when they know quite well that Victor excommunicated Theodotus the cobbler, the founder and father of this **insurrection [apostasy]** which denies God, when he first said that Christ was a mere man? For if Victor was so minded towards them as their blasphemy teaches, how could he have thrown out Theodotus who invented this heresy?
— Greek text and English translation — *Eusebius of Caesarea: Historia ecclesiastica*, with English translation by Kirsopp Lake, *The Loeb Classical Library 153*. Harvard University Press; William Heinemann; 1926. Accessed at Perseus Digital Library (perseus. tufts.edu) and Internet Archive Wayback Machine (web.archive.org).
— In the context, Victor was regarded by Eusebius as the father of the God-denying apostasy, the first to teach that Christ was a spotted (tainted) human being (εἰπόντα ψιλὸν ἄνθρωπον τὸν Χριστόν).
— RELIGIOUS APOSTASY

(146) Eusebius of Caesarea, Ecclesiastical History, 6.45.1
— Ταῦτα ὁ Διονύσιος. ἴδωμεν δ᾽ ὁ αὐτὸς ὁποῖα καὶ τῷ Νοουάτῳ διεχάραξεν, ταράττοντι τηνικάδε τὴν Ῥωμαίων ἀδελφότητα· ἐπειδὴ οὖν **τῆς ἀποστασίας** καὶ τοῦ σχίσματος πρόφασιν ἐποιεῖτο τῶν

ἀδελφῶν τινας, ὡς δὴ πρὸς αὐτῶν ἐπὶ τοῦτ᾽ ἐλθεῖν ἐκβεβιασμένος, ὅρα τίνα τρόπον αὐτῷ γράφει· ‘Διονύσιος Νοουατιανῷ ἀδελφῷ χαίρειν. εἰ ἄκων, ὡς φής, ἤχθης, δείξεις ἀναχωρήσας ἑκών. ἔδει μὲν γὰρ καὶ πᾶν ὅτι οὖν παθεῖν ὑπὲρ τοῦ μὴ διακόψαι τὴν ἐκκλησίαν τοῦ θεοῦ, καὶ ἦν οὐκ ἀδοξοτέρα τῆς ἕνεκεν τοῦ μὴ εἰδωλολατρῆσαι γινομένης ἡ ἕνεκεν τοῦ μὴ σχίσαι μαρτυρία, κατ᾽ ἐμὲ δὲ καὶ μείζων. ἐκεῖ μὲν γὰρ ὑπὲρ μιᾶς τις τῆς ἑαυτοῦ ψυχῆς, ἐνταῦθα δὲ ὑπὲρ ὅλης τῆς ἐκκλησίας μαρτυρεῖ. καὶ νῦν δὲ εἰ πείσαις ἢ βιάσαιο τοὺς ἀδελφοὺς εἰς ὁμόνοιαν ἐλθεῖν, μεῖζον ἔσται σοι τοῦ σφάλματος τὸ κατόρθωμα, καὶ τὸ μὲν οὐ λογισθήσεται, τὸ δὲ ἐπαινεθήσεται. εἰ δὲ ἀπειθούντων ἀδυνατοίης, σῴζων σῷζε τὴν σεαυτοῦ ψυχήν. ἐρρῶσθαί σε, ἐχόμενον τῆς εἰρήνης ἐν κυρίῳ, εὔχομαι.

— Such is the account of Dionysius. But let us see the kind of letter that the same person wrote also to Novatus, who was then disturbing the Roman brotherhood. Since, then, he put forward some of the brethren as an excuse for his **defection** and schism, as having been compelled by them to proceed to this length, see how Dionysius writes to him: "Dionysius to Novatianus a brother, greeting. If thou wast led on unwillingly, as thou sayest, thou wilt prove it by retiring willingly. For a man ought to suffer anything and everything rather than divide the Church of God, and it were not less glorious to incur martyrdom to avoid schism than to avoid idolatry, nay, in my opinion it were more so. For in the one case a man is a martyr for the sake of his own single soul, but in the other for the sake of the whole Church. And if thou wert even now to persuade or compel the brethren to come by one mind, thy recovery will be greater than thy fall, and the one will not be reckoned, while the other will be praised. But if they obey thee not, and thou hast no power, by all means save thine own soul. I pray that thou mayest fare well and cleave to peace in the Lord."

— Greek text and English translation — *Eusebius of Caesarea*: *Historia ecclesiastica*, with English translation by Kirsopp Lake, *The Loeb Classical Library 265*. Harvard University Press; William Heinemann; 1926. Accessed at Perseus Digital Library (perseus. tufts.edu) and Internet Archive Wayback Machine (web.archive.org).

— The context is the schism of Novation from the Rome-dominated church over whether the church had the authority and power to absolve the sins of those who had lapsed, the recent occasion being

the Decian persecution. Cyprian and the Catholic church said yes. Novatian said while the church could readmit the penitent to penitence-for-life, only God could grant forgiveness. This is often misunderstood as the Catholic church simply being willing to readmit those who had lapsed and Novation being unwilling to readmit them.
— RELIGIOUS APOSTASY

(147) Eusebius of Caesarea, Ecclesiastical History, 7.24.6
— Τούτοις μεθ' ἕτερα ἐπιφέρει λέγων: 'ἐν μὲν οὖν τῷ Ἀρσενοΐτῃ γενόμενος, ἔνθα, ὡς οἶδας, πρὸ πολλοῦ τοῦτο ἐπεπόλαζεν τὸ δόγμα, ὡς καὶ σχίσματα καὶ **ἀποστασίας** ὅλων ἐκκλησιῶν γεγονέναι, συγκαλέσας τοὺς πρεσβυτέρους καὶ διδασκάλους τῶν ἐν ταῖς κώμαις ἀδελφῶν, παρόντων καὶ τῶν βουλομένων ἀδελφῶν, δημοσίᾳ τὴν ἐξέτασιν ποιήσασθαι τοῦ λόγου προετρεψάμην.
— After other remarks he adds as follows: "Now when I came to the nome of Arsinoe, where, as thou knowest, this doctrine had long been prevalent, so that schisms and **defections** of whole churches had taken place, I called together the presbyters and teachers of the brethren in the villages (there were present also such of the brethren as wished), and I urged them to hold the examination of the question publically."
— Greek text and English translation — *Eusebius of Caesarea: Historia ecclesiastica*, with English translation by Kirsopp Lake, *The Loeb Classical Library 265*. Harvard University Press; William Heinemann; 1926. Accessed at Perseus Digital Library (perseus. tufts.edu) and Internet Archive Wayback Machine (web.archive.org).
— The context is the defections of churches from the fellowship and doctrinal platform of the Catholic church.
— RELIGIOUS APOSTASY

(148) Eusebius of Caesarea, Preparation for the Gospel, 2.4.3-4
— καὶ τί χρὴ μηκύνειν εὐαγγελιζομένους πάντα βάρβαρον ὁμοῦ καὶ Ἕλληνα τὴν ἀπὸ τῶν εἰρημένων κακῶν ἐλευθερίαν **τῆς** τε τῶν ψευδωνύμων θεῶν **ἀποστασίας** τὸ εὔλογον εἰς φῶς ἀγαγόντας, ὁπότε καὶ αὐτῶν ἤδη τῶν σφόδρα δεισιδαιμόνων οἱ πλείους, ὥσπερ ἐκ βαθέος κάρου ἀνανήψαντες καὶ τῆς παλαιᾶς ἀχλύος τὸ τῆς ψυχῆς ὄμμα διανοίξαντες τὸν βαθὺν λῆρον συνεῖδον τῆς πατρικῆς πλάνης

καὶ στάντες ἐπὶ λογισμοῦ τὴν ἑτέραν ὁδὸν εἵλοντο, τῆς παλαιᾶς ἀναχωρήσαντες;

— But why need we spend time in proclaiming to every man, barbarian and Greek alike, his deliverance from the evils described, and in bringing to light the reasonableness of our **revolt** from gods falsely so called, when already the greater number even of the most superstitious, having woke up as it were from a deep slumber, and cleared the eye of the soul of its ancient film, became conscious of the deep folly of the error of their fathers, and took their stand upon reasoning, and withdrew from the old path, and chose the other way?

— Greek text — K. Mras. *Eusebius Werke, Band 8: Die Praeparatio evangelica;* [*Die griechischen christlichen Schriftsteller 43.1 & 43.2*]. Akademie Verlag, 1954, 1956. Retrieved from Thesaurus Linguae Graecae (stephanus.tlg.uci.edu).

— English translation — E. H. Gifford. *Eusebii Pamphili Evangelicae Praeparationis.* Oxford Univ. Press, 1903. Transcribed for the Tertullian Project by Peter Kirby, 2003. Accessed at The Tertullian Project (tertullian.org/fathers).

— The context is the believers' departure from those falsely called gods. Notice that *apostasia* is used here in connection with departure from evil, from false gods, from superstition, from spiritual slumber, from deep folly, and choosing to stand upon reason.

— RELIGIOUS APOSTASY

(149) Eusebius of Caesarea, Preparation for the Gospel, 7.16.2-4

— τὴν δὲ ἐκ τούτων παρατετραμμένην καὶ τῆς τῶν κρειττόνων χορείας δι' οἰκείαν φαυλότητα στερομένην σκότος τε ἀντὶ φωτὸς ἀλλαξαμένην ἔμπαλιν ἢ τὰ πρῶτα ταῖς ἁρμοττούσαις τῇ τοῦ τρόπου μοχθηρίᾳ προσηγορίαις ὀνομάζει. τὸν γοῦν κατάρξαντα τῆς πτώσεως, αὐτῷ τε καὶ ἑτέροις **τῆς** τῶν κρειττόνων **ἀποστασίας** γενόμενον αἴτιον, ὡς ἂν διόλου χαμαὶ τῆς τῶν θειοτέρων εὐσεβείας ἐκπεπτωκότα καὶ κακίας μὲν ἰοῦ καὶ δυσσεβείας αὐτὸν αὐτῷ δημιουργὸν ὑποστάντα, σκότους δὲ καὶ ἀλογίας ποιητὴν ἐκ τῆς τοῦ φωτὸς αὐθεκουσίου ἀναχωρήσεως γεγονότα, δράκοντα καὶ ὄφιν μέλανά τε καὶ ἑρπυστικόν, ἰοῦ θανατηφόρου γεννητικὸν θῆρά τε ἄγριον καὶ ἀνθρωποβόρον λέοντα καὶ πάλιν τὸν ἐν ἑρπετοῖς βασιλίσκον ἀποκαλεῖν εἴωθεν.

234

— But the nature which is turned away from these, and for its own wickedness is deprived of the company of the better spirits, and contrary to the former has exchanged light for darkness, Scripture calls by the names which befit the badness of their disposition. The leader for instance of their fall, who had been the cause both for himself and for others of their **apostasy** from, the better angels, as having fallen down utterly beneath the piety of the more godlike, and wrought for himself the venom of malice and impiety, and become the author of darkness and folly in consequence of his willful departure from the light—-him the Scripture is wont to call dragon and serpent, and black and creeping, an engenderer of deadly poison, a wild beast, and a lion devouring mankind, and the adder among reptiles.

— Greek text — K. Mras. *Eusebius Werke, Band 8: Die Praeparatio evangelica;* [*Die griechischen christlichen Schriftsteller 43.1 & 43.2*]. Akademie Verlag, 1954, 1956. Retrieved from Thesaurus Linguae Graecae (stephanus.tlg.uci.edu).

— English translation — E. H. Gifford. *Eusebii Pamphili Evangelicae Praeparationis.* Oxford Univ. Press, 1903. Transcribed for the Tertullian Project by Roger Pearse, 2003. Accessed at The Tertullian Project (tertullian.org/fathers).

— The context is the apostasy of the evil angels from the good angels, which departure was led by the author of darkness, which the Scriptures call the dragon and the serpent. Notice the association of *apostasia* with wickedness, darkness, badness, falling away from piety, and the venom of malice and impiety. Notice too that ἀποστασία (apostasia) *apostasy* and ἐκπεπτωκότα (ekpeptōkota) *falling away* are employed as synonyms.

— RELIGIOUS APOSTASY

(150) Eusebius of Caesarea, Preparation for the Gospel, 10.10.15-18

— Ἀπὸ Ὠγύγου τοίνυν ἐπὶ Κῦρον, ὁπόσα ἀπὸ Μωσέως ἐπὶ τὸν αὐτὸν χρόνον, ἔτη ασλζ΄. καὶ Ἑλλήνων δέ τινες ἱστοροῦσι κατὰ τοὺς αὐτοὺς χρόνους γενέσθαι Μωσέα· Πολέμων μὲν ἐν τῇ πρώτῃ τῶν Ἑλληνικῶν ἱστοριῶν λέγων· «Ἐπὶ Ἄπιδος τοῦ Φορωνέως μοῖρα τοῦ Αἰγυπτίων στρατοῦ ἐξέπεσεν Αἰγύπτου, οἳ ἐν τῇ Παλαιστίνῃ καλουμένῃ Συρίᾳ οὐ πόρρω Ἀραβίας ᾤκησαν», αὐτοὶ δηλονότι οἱ μετὰ Μωσέως· Ἀπίων δὲ ὁ Ποσειδωνίου, περιεργότατος γραμματικῶν, ἐν τῇ κατὰ Ἰουδαίων βίβλῳ καὶ ἐν τῇ τετάρτῃ τῶν ἱστοριῶν φησι κατὰ Ἴναχον Ἄργους βασιλέα, Ἀμώσιος Αἰγυπτίων βασιλεύοντος, ἀποστῆναι Ἰουδαίους, ὧν ἡγεῖσθαι Μωσέα. μέμνηται δὲ καὶ Ἡρόδοτος **τῆς ἀποστασίας** ταύτης καὶ Ἀμώσιος ἐν τῇ δευτέρᾳ.

— From Ogyges therefore to Cyrus there were as many years as from Moses to the same date, namely one thousand two hundred and thirty-seven. And some of the Greeks also relate that Moses lived about those same times; as Polemon in the first book of his Hellenic histories says, that «in the time of Apis son of Phoroneus a part of the Egyptian army was expelled from Egypt, who took up their abode not far from Arabia in the part of Syria called Palestine,» being evidently those who went with Moses. And Apion the son of Poseidonius, the most inquisitive of grammarians, in his book *Against the Jews*, and in the fourth book of his *Histories*, says that in the time of Inachus king of Argos, when Amosis was reigning in Egypt, the Jews **revolted**, with Moses as their leader. Herodotus also has made mention of this revolt and of Amosis in his second Book.

— Greek text — K. Mras. *Eusebius Werke, Band 8: Die Praeparatio evangelica; [Die griechischen christlichen Schriftsteller 43.1 & 43.2]*. Akademie Verlag, 1954, 1956. Retrieved from Thesaurus Linguae Graecae (stephanus.tlg.uci.edu).

— English translation — E. H. Gifford. *Eusebii Pamphili Evangelicae Praeparationis*. Oxford Univ. Press, 1903. Transcribed for the Tertullian Project by Roger Pearse, 2003. Accessed at The Tertullian Project (tertullian.org/fathers).

— The context is the revolt of the Jews against their enslavement by the Egyptians. This revolt, while essentially peaceful on their part, was backed up with judgments from the hand of God, and it led to Israel's departure from Egypt.

— POLITICAL SEDITION OR REBELLION

(151) Eustathias of Antioch, De engastrimytho contra Originem, 2.5

— τί δὲ μετὰ ταῦτα πράττει, τῆς ἀνωτάτω γυμνωθεὶς ἐπικουρίας; ἀντὶ τοῦ μᾶλλον ἐξιλεώσασθαι συχνοτέρᾳ δεήσει καὶ καρτερᾷ ψυχολατρείᾳ, τοὐναντίον ἀποπηδήσας αὔξει μὲν τὰ **τῆς ἀποστασίας** ἐπιτηδεύματα, τοῖς δὲ παισὶν αὐτοῦ προσέταττεν γυναῖκα ζητήσειν ἐγγαστρίμυθον, ἵνα ἀφίκοιτο πρὸς αὐτὴν πευσόμενος ὡς ἐν μαντείῳ.

— Somewhat after these things it so happened [that Saul], stripped of heavenly aid, instead of making much propitiation in prayer and soul worship, on the contrary, he departed [these things] and advanced in the business of **apostasy**, and commanded his disciples (spiritual children) to seek a female oracle, that he might inquire of her as with an oracle.

— Greek text — M. Simonetti. *Origene, Eustazio, Gregorio di Nissa: La maga di Endor.* Centro Internazionale del Libro, 1989. Retrieved from Thesaurus Linguae Graecae (stephanus.tlg.uci.edu).

— English translation — The translation is my own as I could find none readily available.

— The context is Saul's apostasy which led to him seeking help from the witch of Endor.

— RELIGIOUS APOSTASY

(152) Evagrius of Pontus, On the Vices Opposed to the Virtues, chapter 4, (Migne 79.1144)

—Κενοδοξία, συντυχίας φαντασία, σχημάτισμα φιλοπονίας, ἀληθείας ἐναντία, αἱρέσεων ἀρχηγέτις, ὄρεξις προεδρίας, ἐσχάτη προσηγορίας, ἐπαίνων δουλεία, πολυσχημάτιστον πνεῦμα, μυριόδοντον θηρίον, κενοδοξίας μέση ὑπερηφανίᾳ πέπλεκται καὶ φθόνῳ, ἐν ἀλλήλοις ὄντα, καὶ δι' ἀλλήλων πολεμοῦντα, ἡ τρίσυρος ἄλυσις τῶν κακῶν, τὸ τριφάρμακον κέρασμα τῶν παθῶν, ἡ τριττὴ γλῶττα τῶν αἱρετικῶν. Ἀκενοδοξία, ταπεινοφροσύνης ἐργασία, ἀρεσκείας **ἀποστασία**, ἐπαίνων ἀβλεψία, γνώσεως θεωρία, κόσμου ἐναντία, ψυχῆς εὐαισθησία, εὐτελείας δόγμα, πόνων κρυπτηρία, εὐφημίας πολεμία, ἐν φθαρτῷ σώματι ἀπόκρυφος θησαυρός

— Vain glory involves fantasizing about social encounters, a pretence of industriousness, the contrary of the truth, author of heresies, desire for privilege, the ultimate title, slavery to praises, a spirit with many forms, a beast with many teeth, the mean of vainglory is entwined with pride and jealousy, which are found within one another and which make war through one another, the three-strand chain of vices, the threefold poisonous mixture of passions, the threefold tongue of heretics. Freedom from vainglory is the working of humility, a

defection from obsequiousness, blindness to praises, contemplation of knowledge, a counter to the world, keep perception of the soul, a teaching of lowliness, a hiding place for ascetic works, hostility to fame, a hidden treasure in a corruptible body.

— Greek text — J.P. Migne. *Patrologiae cursus completus* (*series Graeca 79*). Migne, 1857-1866. Retrieved from Thesaurus Linguae Graecae (stephanus.tlg.uci.edu).

— English translation — Robert Sinkewicz. *Evagrius of Pontus: The Greek Ascetic Corpus* [*Oxford Early Christian Studies*], Oxford University Press, 2003, repr. 2010.

— The context contrasts the vice of vainglory with the virtue of freedom from vainglory.

— REPENTANCE

— Three observations. First of all, this is the first known appearance of *apostasia* in the sense of *departure from sin/repentance*. This sense still falls within the pale of the realm of spiritual departure or heart departure. Secondly, this is the first known appearance of *apostasia* with a positive connotation. Thirdly, this sense has no bearing on the question of whether *apostasia* can bear the meaning of human beings physically or spatially *departing* from one location to another.

— I found a similar usage in Basil, also in the mid-to-late fourth century, which is an articular infinitive — πρὸς τὸ ἀποστῆσαι τῆς ἁμαρτίας καὶ ἐπαναγαγεῖν πρὸς Θεόν· "with departure from sin and returning to God", Basil, Asceticon magnum 1, Question 245 (Migne 31.1245).

(153) Gaius of Rome, Fragments, 130 (cited under Eusebius, Ecclesiastical History, 5.28)

— πῶς οὖν ἐκ τοσούτων ἐτῶν καταγγελλομένου τοῦ ἐκκλησιαστικοῦ φρονήματος, ἐνδέχεται τοὺς μέχρι Βίκτορος οὕτως ὡς οὗτοι λέγουσι κεκηρυχέναι; πῶς δὲ οὐκ αἰδοῦνται ταῦτα Βίκτορος καταψεύδεσθαι· ἀκριβῶς εἰδότες, ὅτι Βίκτωρ τὸν σκυτέα Θεόδοτον τὸν ἀρχηγὸν καὶ πατέρα ταύτης **τῆς** ἀρνησιθέου **ἀποστασίας**, ἀπεκήρυξε τῆς κοινωνίας, πρῶτον εἰπόντα ψιλὸν ἄνθρωπον τὸν Χριστόν. εἰ γὰρ Βίκτωρ κατ᾽ αὐτοὺς οὕτως ἐφρόνει ὡς ἡ τούτων διδάσκει βλασφημία, πῶς ἂν ἀπέβαλλε Θεόδοτον τὸν τῆς αἱρέσεως ταύτης εὑρετήν;

— How then is it possible that after the mind of the church had been announced for so many years that the generation before Victor can have preached as they say? Why are they not ashamed of so calumniating Victor when they know quite well that Victor excommunicated Theodotus the cobbler, the founder and father of this **insurrection** [apostasy] which denies God, when he first said that Christ was a mere man? For if Victor was so minded towards them as their blasphemy teaches, how could he have thrown out Theodotus who invented this heresy?

— Greek text and English translation — Eusebius of Caesarea, *Historia ecclesiastica*, with English translation by Kirsopp Lake, *The Loeb Classical Library 153*. Harvard University Press; William Heinemann; 1926. Accessed at Perseus Digital Library (perseus. tufts.edu) and Internet Archive Wayback Machine (web.archive.org).

— In the context, Victor was regarded by Eusebius as the father of the God-denying apostasy, being the first to teach that Christ was a spotted human being (εἰπόντα ψιλὸν ἄνθρωπον τὸν Χριστόν).

— RELIGIOUS APOSTASY

(154) Gelasius Cyzicenus, Ecclesiastical History, 2.3.3

— ἐν τῇ ἡμετέρᾳ τοίνυν παροικίᾳ ἐξῆλθον νῦν ἄνδρες παράνομοι καὶ χριστομάχοι, διδάσκοντες **ἀποστασίαν**, ἣν εἰκότως ἄν τις πρόδρομον τοῦ ἀντιχρίστου ὑπονοήσειε καὶ καλέσειε.

— Moreover, in our own community, lawless, Christ-fighting men have departed, teaching **apostasy**, which one could reasonably regard and call as forerunners of the antichrist.

— Greek text — M. Heinemann and G. Loeschcke. *Gelasius. Kirchengeschichte* [*Die griechischen christlichen Schriftsteller der ersten drei Jahrhunderte 28*]. Hinrichs, 1918. Retrieved from Thesaurus Linguae Graecae (stephanus.tlg.uci.edu).

— The English translation is my own as I could find none available.

— The context concerns apostasy witnessed in Gelasius' time in circles which he regarded as forerunners of the antichrist.

— RELIGIOUS APOSTASY

(155) Gregory of Nazianzus, Oration 4: First Invective Against Julian the Emperor, 21, (Migne 35.549)

— Ἐκεῖνος ἓν μὲν καὶ πρῶτον, ὑπὸ τοῦ μεγάλου Κωνσταντίου σωθείς, ἄρτι παρὰ τοῦ πατρὸς διαδεξαμένου τὸ κράτος (ἡνίκα τὸ στρατιωτικὸν ἐξωπλίσθη κατὰ τῶν ἐν τέλει, καινοτομοῦν φόβῳ καινοτομίας, καὶ διὰ νέων προστατῶν καθίστατο τὰ βασίλεια)·καὶ σωθείς γε σὺν τῷ ἀδελφῷ σωτηρίαν ἄπιστον καὶ παράδοξον, οὔτε τῷ Θεῷ χάριν ἔσχε τῆς σωτηρίας, οὔτε τῷ βασιλεῖ, δι' οὗ σέσωστο· ἀλλ' ἀμφοτέροις ὤφθη κακός, τῷ μὲν **ἀποστασίαν** ὠδίνων, τῷ δὲ ἐπανάστασιν.

— First and foremost then, this man having been saved by the great Constantius, immediately on his succession to his father, at what time the army rose against those in power (making a revolution through their apprehension of revolution), and settled the government under new sovereigns; being saved together with his brother (a preservation beyond belief and all expectation), he neither felt gratitude to God for his escape nor to the emperor through whose means he had been preserved, but showed himself wicked towards both, by conceiving **apostacy** from the one and rebellion against the other.

— Greek text — J.P. Migne. *Patrologiae cursus completus* (*series Graeca 35*). Migne, 1857-1866. Retrieved from Thesaurus Linguae Graecae (stephanus.tlg.uci.edu).

— English translation — C.W. King. *Julian the Emperor*. George Bell and Sons, 1888. Transcribed by Roger Pearse, 2003. Accessed at The Tertullian Project (tertullian.org/fathers)

— The context addresses the wickedness of Julian who apostatized from God and rebelled against Constantius. Notice the association of *apostasia* with ἐπανάστασις (epanastasis) *insurrection* and καινοτομία (kainotomia) *revolution*.

— RELIGIOUS APOSTASY

(156) Gregory of Nazianzus, Oration 5: Second Invective Against Julian the Emperor, 3, (Migne 35.668)

— Ἐμαίνετο καθ' ἡμῶν ἀεί τι πλέον, ὥσπερ κύμασιν ἐπεγείρων κύματα, ὁ καθ' ἑαυτοῦ πρῶτον μανεὶς καὶ πατήσας τὰ ἅγια, καὶ τὸ Πνεῦμα τῆς χάριτος ἐνυβρίσας. Ἱεροβοὰμ εἰπεῖν οἰκειότερον, ἢ Ἀχαὰβ τὸν Ἰσραηλίτην, τοὺς παρανομωτάτους, ἢ Φαραὼ τὸν

240

Αἰγύπτιον, ἢ Ναβουχοδονόσορ τὸν Ἀσσύριον, ἢ ταῦτα πάντα συνελόντες, ἕνα καὶ τὸν αὐτὸν ὀνομάσομεν· ἐπεὶ καὶ τὰς πάντων κακίας εἰς ἑαυτὸν συλλεξάμενος φαίνεται, Ἱεροβοὰμ **τὴν ἀποστασίαν**, Ἀχαὰβ τὴν μιαιφονίαν, Φαραὼ τὴν σκληρότητα, Ναβουχοδονόσορ τὴν ἱεροσυλίαν, πάντων ὁμοῦ τὴν ἀσέβειαν.

— He [Julian] was daily growing more infuriated against us, as though raising up waves by other waves, he that went mad first against himself, that trampled upon things holy, and that did despite unto the Spirit of Grace: is it more proper to call him Jeroboam or Ahab, those most wicked of the Israelites; or Pharaoh the Egyptian, or Nebuchadnezzar the Assyrian; or combining all together shall we name him one and the same since he shows himself to have united in himself the vices of them all—-the **apostasy** of Jeroboam, the bloodthirstiness of Ahab, the hardness of heart of Pharaoh, the sacrilegious acts of Nebuchadnezzar, the impiety of all put together!

— Greek text — J.P. Migne. *Patrologiae cursus completus (series Graeca 35)*. Migne, 1857-1866. Retrieved from Thesaurus Linguae Graecae (stephanus.tlg.uci.edu).

— English translation — C.W. King. *Julian the Emperor*. George Bell and Sons, 1888. Transcribed by Roger Pearse, 2003. Accessed at The Tertullian Project (tertullian.org/fathers)

— The context addresses the wickedness of Julian, comparing it to the apostasy of Jeroboam, the resistance of Pharaoh, and the sacrilege of Nebuchadnezzar. Notice the association of *apostasia* with trampling upon things holy, doing despite to the Spirit of grace, and engaging in impiety.

— RELIGIOUS APOSTASY

(157) Gregory of Nyssa, Against Eunomius, (Book 1, 1.87-88), (English, 1.9)

— ὁ κατ᾽ ἀλήθειαν τοῦ Φινεὲς ζηλωτής, ὁ ἐξολοθρεύων ἐν τῇ ῥομφαίᾳ τοῦ λόγου πάντα τὸν ἀπὸ τοῦ κυρίου πορνεύσαντα, τὴν ἰατικὴν μὲν τῆς ψυχῆς, ἀναιρετικὴν δὲ τῆς ἀσεβείας ἐπήγαγε μάχαιραν, τὴν ἀντίρρησιν λέγω τῆς βλασφημίας. εἰ δὲ ἀντιτύπως οὗτος ἔχει καὶ τὴν θεραπείαν οὐ δέχεται ὁ τὴν ψυχὴν ἑαυτοῦ διὰ **τῆς ἀποστασίας** νεκρώσας, τοῦ ἑλομένου τὸ κακὸν ἡ αἰτία·

— That genuine emulator of Phineas' zeal, destroying as he does with the sword of the Word every spiritual fornicator, dealt in the "Answer to his blasphemy" a sword-thrust that was calculated at once to heal a soul and to destroy a heresy. If he resists that stroke, and with a soul deadened by **apostacy** will not admit the cure, the blame rests with him who chooses the evil.

— Greek text — W. Jaeger. *Gregorii Nysseni opera, vol. 1.1*. Brill, 1960. Retrieved from Thesaurus Linguae Graecae (stephanus. tlg.uci.edu).

— English translation — W. Moore and H.A. Wilson. *Nicene and Post-Nicene Fathers, Second Series, Vol.5*. Christian Literature Publishing, 1893, revised and edited by Kevin Knight for New Advent. Accessed at New Advent (newadvent.org/fathers).

— The context is the apostasy in the days of Phinehas. Notice the association of *apostasia* with spiritual fornication, ungodliness, and blasphemy.

— RELIGIOUS APOSTASY

(158) Gregory of Nyssa, Against Eunomius, (Jaeger, 163) (English, 2.12)

— καὶ μὴν αὐτὸ τοῦτο διερμηνεύων φησὶν ὁ Παῦλος, ὅτι χαρακτήρ ἐστιν οὐ τῆς ἐνεργείας, ἀλλὰ τῆς ὑποστάσεως. ἢ τὸ τῆς δόξης ἀπαύγασμα σφραγίς ἐστιν ἐνεργείας θεοῦ; ὢ τῆς ἀσεβοῦς ἀμαθίας. τί μέσον ἐστὶ τοῦ θεοῦ καὶ τῆς ἰδίας μορφῆς; τίνι δὲ μεσιτεύεται πρὸς τὸν χαρακτῆρα ἑαυτῆς ἡ ὑπόστασις; τί δὲ μεταξὺ νοεῖται τῆς δόξης καὶ τοῦ ἀπαυγάσματος; ἀλλὰ τοιούτων καὶ τοσούτων ὄντων δι' ὧν τὸ μεγαλεῖον ἀνακηρύσσεται τοῦ δεσπότου τῆς κτίσεως παρὰ τῶν πεπιστευμένων τὸ κήρυγμα, οἷα περὶ αὐτοῦ διεξέρχεται ὁ **τῆς ἀποστασίας** πρόδρομος;

— Surely Paul when expounding this very truth says He is the express image, not of His energy, but of His Person. Is the Brightness of His glory a seal of the energy of God? Alas for his impious ignorance! What is there intermediate between God and His own form? And Whom does the Person employ as mediator with His own express image? And what can be conceived as coming between the glory and its brightness? But while there are such weighty and numerous testimonies wherein the greatness of the Lord of the creation is proclaimed by those who were entrusted with the proclamation of the Gospel, what sort of language does this forerunner of **the final apostasy** hold concerning Him?

— Greek text — W. Jaeger, *Gregorii Nysseni opera, vol. 2.2.* Brill, 1960. Retrieved from Thesaurus Linguae Graecae (stephanus. tlg.uci.edu).

— English translation — H.C. Ogle and H.A. Wilson. *Nicene and Post-Nicene Fathers, Second Series, Vol. 5.* Christian Literature Publishing, 1893. Revised and edited by Kevin Knight for New Advent. Accessed at New Advent (newadvent.org/fathers).

— The context concerns the Christological errors of Eunomius, whom Gregory regarded as the forerunner of the apostasy in the last days.

— RELIGIOUS APOSTASY

(159) Gregory of Nyssa, Against Eunomius, (Book 3, 10.14-15), (English, 12.1)

— Ἰδοὺ γάρ, φησίν, ἐγὼ καὶ τὰ παιδία ἅ μοι ἔδωκεν ὁ θεός· ὅθεν ὑμεῖς ἀπεφοιτήσατε σάρκες καὶ αἷμα διὰ τὴν ἁμαρτίαν γενόμενοι, ἐκεῖ πάλιν ὑμᾶς ἀναλαβὼν ἐπανήγαγεν ὁ δι' ἡμᾶς κεκοινωνηκὼς σαρκός τε καὶ αἵματος. καὶ οὕτω γέγονε καὶ ἡμέτερος πατὴρ καὶ θεός, οὗ πρότερον διὰ **τῆς ἀποστασίας** ἠλλοτριώθημεν. οὐκοῦν εὐαγγελίζεται τὴν ἀγαθὴν ταύτην εὐεργεσίαν διὰ τῶν εἰρημένων ὁ κύριος, καὶ ἔστι τὰ ῥήματα οὐ τῆς τοῦ υἱοῦ ταπεινότητος ἔλεγχος, ἀλλὰ τῆς ἡμετέρας πρὸς τὸν θεὸν καταλλαγῆς εὐαγγέλια. τὸ γὰρ περὶ τὸν κατὰ Χριστὸν ἄνθρωπον γεγενημένον κοινὴ τῆς φύσεως τῶν ἀνθρώπων χάρις ἐστίν.

— For behold, He says, I and the children whom God has given Me. He Who for our sakes was partaker of flesh and blood has recovered you, and brought you back to the place whence ye strayed away, becoming mere flesh and blood by sin. And so He from whom we were formerly alienated by our **revolt** has become our Father and our God. Accordingly in the passage cited above the Lord brings the glad tidings of this benefit. And the words are not a proof of the degradation of the Son, but the glad tidings of our reconciliation to God. For that which has taken place in Christ's Humanity is a common boon bestowed on mankind generally.

— Greek text — W. Jaeger. *Gregorii Nysseni opera*, vols. 1.1 & 2.2. Brill, 1960. Retrieved from *Thesaurus Linguae Graecae* (stephanus. tlg.uci.edu).

— English translation — H.C. Ogle and H.A. Wilson. *Nicene and Post-Nicene Fathers, Second Series, Vol.5*. Christian Literature Publishing, 1893. Revised and edited by Kevin Knight for New Advent. Accessed at New Advent (newadvent.org/fathers).

— The context is man's revolt from God, which revolt is resolved in Christ.

— RELIGIOUS APOSTASY

(160) Gregory of Nyssa, Commentary on Ecclesiastes, 3.20
— Ὡρισμένος οὖν ἦν ὁ καιρὸς καὶ τῆς θείας ἐνανθρωπήσεως, δι᾽ ἧς τὸν ἀσεβῆ καὶ μεγάλαυχον κατέκρινε Σατανᾶν, τὸν διὰ **τῆς ἀποστασίας** ἀσεβῆ πρῶτον φανέντα καὶ διὰ τοῦτο γεγονότα σκότος ἀντὶ φωτός, ἐν κρίσει καὶ δικαιοσύνῃ τὴν κατ᾽ αὐτοῦ κατάκρισιν ποιησάμενος διὰ σταυροῦ καὶ θανάτου καὶ ταφῆς καὶ τῆς ζωαρχικῆς ἀναστάσεως.

— Now was the appointed season, even the divine incarnation, through which he condemned the ungodly and boastful Satan—who through his **apostasy** ungodliness first appeared, and because of this darkness was manifested (in the world) instead of light—in judgment and in righteousness, executing condemnation against him through the cross and death and burial and the resurrection of the prince of life.

— Greek text — G.H. Ettlinger and J. Noret. *Pseudo-Gregorii Agrigentini seu Pseudo-Gregorii Nysseni commentarius in Ecclesiasten [Corpus Christianorum. Series Graeca 56]*. Brepols, 2007. Retrieved from Thesaurus Linguae Graecae (stephanus. tlg.uci.edu).

— English translation — The translation is my own as I could find none available.

— Context is the condemnation of Satan who first introduced ungodliness through his apostasy.

— RELIGIOUS APOSTASY

(161) Gregory of Nyssa, Addresses on the Psalms, 5.128

— Οἵτινες, φησίν, ἰδόντες, οὕτως ἐθαύμασαν· καὶ τὴν αἰτίαν διηγεῖται τοῦ θαύματος, ἐπειδὴ οἱ πρότερον κατοικοῦντες ἀναξίως τὴν πόλιν ταύτην, ὅτε ἦν πλευρὰ τοῦ βορρᾶ, ἐταράχθησαν καὶ ἐσαλεύθησαν καὶ τρόμος ἐπελάβετο αὐτῶν καὶ οὐ μόνον τρόμος, ἀλλὰ καὶ πόνοι μιμούμενοι ὠδῖνας τικτούσης. ἅπερ πάντα φησὶ κατ' αὐτῶν γεγενῆσθαι ὑπὸ τοῦ βιαίου πνεύματος τοῦ τὰ πλοῖα **τῆς ἀποστασίας** συντρίβοντος τὰ κακῶς τῇ θαλάσσῃ τοῦ βίου ἐπιπολάζοντα·

— Now some, he says, when they saw this were so amazed. And the reason for the amazement he explains. Since the former unworthy residents of this city [Jerusalem], when it was the sides of the north, were terrified and shaken and the trembles took them, and not only the trembles, but also pains mimicking labor pains. All of which, he says, happened against them by the strong wind which drives the ships of **apostasy**, which are common on the sea of life.

— Greek Text — J. McDonough. *Gregorii Nysseni opera, vol. 5.* Brill, 1962. Retrieved from Thesaurus Linguae Graecae (stephanus. tlg.uci.edu).

— English translation — The translation is my own as I could find none available.

— The context is Israel's apostasy. Gregory points out that the unworthy residents of Jerusalem brought their problems upon themselves, which left them terrified because they heeded the winds of apostasy which drives the vessels of apostasy upon the sea of life.

— — RELIGIOUS APOSTASY

(162) Hermias the Philosopher, Derision of Gentile Philosophers, first paragraph

— Παῦλος ὁ μακάριος ἀπόστολος τοῖς τὴν Ἑλλάδα τὴν Λακωνικὴν παροικοῦσι Κορινθίοις γράφων, 'ὦ ἀγαπητοί,' ἀπεφήνατο λέγων· «ἡ σοφία τοῦ κόσμου τούτου μωρία παρὰ τῷ θεῷ», οὐκ ἀσκόπως εἰπών· δοκεῖ γάρ μοι τὴν ἀρχὴν εἰληφέναι ἀπὸ **τῆς** τῶν ἀγγέλων **ἀποστασίας.** δι' ἣν αἰτίαν οὔτε σύμφωνα οὔτε ὁμόλογα οἱ φιλόσοφοι πρὸς ἀλλήλους λέγοντες ἐκτίθενται τὰ δόγματα.

— Paul, the blessed apostle—O beloved brethren—writing to the Laconian Greeks who inhabited Corinthia declared, «the wisdom of this world is foolishness with God». He did not say this unadvisedly,

for it seems to me to have had its origin with the **rebellion** of the angels, for which cause the philosophers have neither harmony nor agreement with each other when they set forth their dogmas.
— Greek text — H. Diels. *Doxographi Graeci*. Reimer, 1879, (repr. De Gruyter, 1965). Retrieved from Thesaurus Linguae Graecae (stephanus.tlg.uci.edu).
— English translation — The translation is my own, compared with that found in J.A. Giles, *The Writings of the Early Christians of the Second Century*, John Russell Smith, 1857, as transcribed by Roger Pearse for the Tertullian Project and available at tertullian.org/fathers.
— The context is the discordant wisdom of the world, which was introduced by the rebellion of the angels.
— RELIGIOUS APOSTASY

(163) Hippolytus, Commentary on Daniel, Book 4, Chapter 15, Section 1-2

— 1) Δεῖ οὖν πάντα ἄνθρωπον τὸν ἐντυγχάνοντα ταῖς θείαις γραφαῖς μιμεῖσθαι τὸν προφήτην Δανιὴλ καὶ μὴ εἶναι εἰκαῖόν τε καὶ προαλῆ, πρὸ καιροῦ καιρὸν ἐπιζητοῦντα καὶ τοὺς ὀλύνθους τῆς συκῆς ἰδεῖν ἐπιθυμοῦντα, ἀλλὰ κατέχειν μετὰ φόβου τὸ μυστήριον τοῦ θεοῦ ἐν καρδίᾳ, ἵνα μὴ αὐτὸς ὑφ' ἑαυτοῦ τοῖς ἰδίοις χείλεσιν παγιδευθεὶς ἔνοχος γένηται τῆς ἰδίας ψυχῆς. 2) ἥξει γὰρ ὁ καιρός, ὅτε ἀνθήσει τὸ ἀμύγδαλον καὶ τραχυνθῇ ἡ κάππαρις καὶ πληθυνθῇ ἡ ἀκρὶς καὶ βλαστήσει ἡ συκῆ καὶ προκόψουσιν οἱ **τῆς ἀποστασίας** καρποί. τότε κλεισθήσεται ἡ θύρα τῆς ζωῆς καὶ συντριβήσεται ἡ ὑδρία ἐπὶ τὴν πηγὴν καὶ συντροχάσει ὁ τροχὸς ἐπὶ τὸν λάκκον καὶ ἀργήσουσιν αἱ ἀλήθουσαι, ὅτι ὠλιγώθησαν καὶ ἐξεγερθήσονται πάντες ἀπὸ φωνῆς τοῦ στρουθίου καὶ ταραχθήσονται πᾶσαι αἱ θυγατέρες τοῦ ᾄσματος καὶ συναχθήσονται ἐν ἀγορᾷ οἱ κοπτόμενοι καὶ ἀπελεύσεται ἄνθρωπος εἰς οἶκον αἰῶνος αὐτοῦ.

— 1) It is necessary, therefore, for every man who reads the divine writings to imitate the prophet Daniel and not be rash and hasty, seeking the season before the season and desiring to see the early figs of the fig tree, but to hold with fear the mystery of God in his heart, that he may no be snared by his own lips and become liable for his own soul. 2) For the season shall come when the almond shall blossom, the caper shall be roughened, and the grasshopper

multiplied. And the fig shall bud, and the fruit of **apostasy** shall prosper. Then the door of life shall be shut, and the water pots at the spring shall be shattered, and the wheel shall get stuck at the pit, and the millers (grain grinders) shall be idle because their business is diminished, and all will be aroused by the song of the sparrow, and the daughters of song shall be troubled, and the mourners shall be gathered in the market, and man shall depart to his eternal home.
— Greek text — G.N. Bonwetsch and M. Richard. *Hippolyt Werke, Erster Band, Erster Teil: Kommentar zu Daniel; [Die griechischen christlichen Schriftsteller der ersten Jahrhunderte 7]*. Akademie Verlag, 2000. Retrieved from Thesaurus Linguae Graecae (stephanus. tlg.uci.edu).
— English translation — The English translation is based on that of T. C. Schmidt, available at chronicon.net. I made many emendations, some for accuracy and some for style.
— The context is the budding of the fig tree in the last days and the advancement of the fruits of apostasy. This is obviously a reference to the budding of the fig tree in Matthew 24, which is the budding of the circumstances and events of the tribulation time, though Hippolytus has the apostasy aspects in particular view: false Christs, tribulation, betrayal, hate, false prophets, lawlessness, love for God growing cold.
— RELIGIOUS APOSTASY

(164) Hippolytus, Commentary on Daniel, Book 4, Chapter 21, Sections 1-3
— 1) Ἐπεὶ οὖν τὰ τοῦ κυρίου ῥήματά ἐστιν ἀληθῆ, «πᾶς δὲ ἄνθρωπος ψεύστης», καθὼς γέγραπται, ἴδωμεν εἰ καὶ ὁ ἀπόστολος Παῦλος σύμφωνός ἐστιν τοῖς τοῦ κυρίου ῥήμασιν. (2) Γράφων γὰρ πρὸς Θεσσαλονικεῖς καὶ παραινῶν τούτοις ἀεὶ μὲν γρηγορεῖν καὶ προσκαρτερεῖν ταῖς εὐχαῖς, μηδέπω δὲ τὴν ἡμέραν τῆς κρίσεως προσδοκᾶν διὰ τὸ τὸν καιρὸν μήπω πεπληρῶσθαι, οὕτως ἔφη [πρὸς αὐτούς] «Ἐρωτῶμεν δὲ ὑμᾶς, ἀδελφοί, ὑπὲρ τῆς παρουσίας τοῦ κυρίου, ἵνα μὴ θορυβῆσθε μήτε διὰ λόγου μήτε δι' ἐπιστολῆς ὡς ἐξ ἡμῶν, ὡς ὅτι ἐνέστηκεν ἡ ἡμέρα κυρίου. Μηδεὶς ὑμᾶς ἐξαπατήσῃ κατὰ μηδένα τρόπον· ὅτι ἐὰν μὴ πρῶτον ἔλθῃ ἡ **ἀποστασία** καὶ ἀποκαλυφθῇ ὁ ἄνθρωπος τῆς ἁμαρτίας, ὁ υἱὸς τῆς ἀπωλείας, ὁ ἀντικείμενος καὶ ὑπεραιρόμενος ὑπὲρ πάντα θεὸν λεγόμενον, ἢ

σέβασμα, ὥστε αὐτὸν εἰς τὸν ναὸν τοῦ θεοῦ καθίσαι, ἀποδεικνύντα ἑαυτὸν ὅτι ἐστὶν θεός. Οὐ μνημονεύετε, ὅτι ἔτι ὢν πρὸς ὑμᾶς ταῦτα ἔλεγον ὑμῖν; καὶ νῦν τὸ κατέχον οἴδατε εἰς τὸ ἀποκαλυφθῆναι αὐτὸν ἐν τῷ ἑαυτοῦ καιρῷ. Τὸ γὰρ μυστήριον ἤδη ἐνεργεῖται τῆς ἀνομίας, μόνον ὁ κατέχων ἄρτι ἕως ἐκ μέσου γένηται· καὶ τότε ἀποκαλυφθήσεται ὁ ἄνομος. ὃν ὁ κύριος Ἰησοῦς ἀνελεῖ τῷ πνεύματι τοῦ στόματος αὐτοῦ καὶ καταργήσει τῇ ἐπιφανείᾳ τῆς παρουσίας αὐτοῦ, οὗ ἐστιν ἡ παρουσία κατ' ἐνέργειαν τοῦ σατανᾶ.» (3) Τίς οὖν ἐστιν «ὁ κατέχων ἕως ἄρτι», ἀλλ' ἢ τὸ τέταρτον θηρίον, οὗ μετατεθέντος καὶ ἐκ μέσου γεναμένου ἐλεύσεται ὁ πλάνος;

— 1) Since, therefore, the words of the Lord are true, and «every man is a liar», as it is written, let us see if the apostle Paul also is in agreement with the words of the Lord. 2) For writing to the Thessalonians and advising them to always watch and to continue in prayers, but not yet expect the day of judgment, because the time is not yet fulfilled, he spoke to them in this manner, «We beseech you brethren, by the coming of the Lord, that you not be troubled, neither by word, nor by letter as from us, as that the day of the Lord has come. Let no man deceive you by any means, because that day will not come except there come a **falling away** first, and the man of sin be revealed, the son of perdition, who opposes and exalts himelf over all this is called god or that is worshipped, so that he sits in the temple of God, proclaiming himself to be God. Do you not remember, when I was yet with you that I told you these things? And now know what restrains him so that he may be revealed in his time. For the mystery of lawlessness is already working, except he who restrains now until he comes out from the midst. And then shall the lawless one be revealed whom the Lord Jesus will destroy with the spirit of his mouth and will bring to nothing by the brightness of his coming, whose coming is after the working of Satan.» 3) And so who is «He who restrains until now,» except the fourth beast? and when he is set aside, the deceiver shall come forth, arising from the midst.

— Greek text — G.N. Bonwetsch and M. Richard. *Hippolyt Werke, Erster Band, Erster Teil: Kommentar zu Daniel; [Die griechischen christlichen Schriftsteller der ersten Jahrhunderte 7.* Akademie Verlag, 2000]. Retrieved from Thesaurus Linguae Graecae (stephanus.tlg.uci.edu).

— English translation — The English translation is based on that of T. C. Schmidt, available at chronicon.net. I made many emendations, some for accuracy and some for style, and I transformed the 2 Thessalonians citation into a hybrid of the KJV and my own translation from the Greek.

— The passage is largely an abbreviated citation of the first eight and a half verses of 2 Thessalonians 2. None of the following commentary gives us any clue to the sense which Hippolytus understood *apostasia* to convey. His view we must gather from his other comments on the subject. And in those comments, it is apparent that he understands ἀποστασία (apostasia) to be a reference to apostasy.

— RELIGIOUS APOSTASY

(165) Hippolytus, On the Antichrist, sections 62-63

— Δανιὴλ δὲ λέγει· «καὶ δώσουσι βδέλυγμα ἐρημώσεως ἡμέρας χιλίας διακοσίας ἐνενήκοντα. μακάριος ὁ ὑπομείνας καὶ φθάσας εἰς ἡμέρας χιλίας τριακοσίας τριάκοντα πέντε.» (63) ὁ δὲ μακάριος Παῦλος ὁ ἀπόστολος γράφων πρὸς Θεσσαλονικεῖς φησιν· «ἐρωτῶμεν δὲ ὑμᾶς, ἀδελφοί, ὑπὲρ τῆς παρουσίας τοῦ κυρίου ἡμῶν Ἰησοῦ Χριστοῦ καὶ ἡμῶν ἐπισυναγωγῆς ἐπ' αὐτόν, εἰς τὸ μὴ ταχέως σαλευθῆναι ὑμᾶς ἀπὸ τοῦ νοὸς μηδὲ θροεῖσθαι, μήτε διὰ πνεύματος μήτε διὰ λόγου μήτε δι' ἐπιστολῆς ὡς δι' ἡμῶν, ὡς ὅτι ἐνέστηκεν ἡ ἡμέρα τοῦ κυρίου. μήτις ὑμᾶς ἐξαπατήσῃ κατὰ μηδένα τρόπον, ὅτι ἐὰν μὴ ἔλθῃ **ἡ ἀποστασία** πρῶτον καὶ ἀποκαλυφθῇ ὁ ἄνθρωπος τῆς ἁμαρτίας, ὁ υἱὸς τῆς ἀπωλείας, ὁ ἀντικείμενος καὶ ὑπεραιρόμενος ἐπὶ πάντα λεγόμενον θεὸν ἢ σέβασμα, ὥστε αὐτὸν εἰς τὸν ναὸν τοῦ θεοῦ καθίσαι, ἀποδεικνύντα ἑαυτὸν ὡς ὅτι ἐστὶ θεός. οὐ μνημονεύετε ὅτι ἔτι ἐμοῦ ὄντος πρὸς ὑμᾶς ταῦτα ἔλεγον ὑμῖν. καὶ νῦν τὸ κατέχον οἴδατε, εἰς τὸ ἀποκαλυφθῆναι αὐτὸν τῷ ἑαυτοῦ καιρῷ. τὸ γὰρ μυστήριον ἤδη ἐνεργεῖται τῆς ἀνομίας, μόνον ὁ κατέχων ἄρτι ἕως ἐκ μέσου γένηται. καὶ τότε ἀποκαλυφθήσεται ὁ ἄνομος, ὃν ὁ κύριος Ἰησοῦς ἀνελεῖ τῷ πνεύματι τοῦ στόματος αὐτοῦ καὶ καταργήσει τῇ ἐπιφανείᾳ τῆς παρουσίας αὐτοῦ, οὗ ἐστιν ἡ παρουσία κατ' ἐνέργειαν τοῦ σατανᾶ ἐν πάσῃ δυνάμει καὶ σημείοις καὶ τέρασι ψεύδους καὶ ἐν πάσῃ ἀπάτῃ ἀδικίας τοῖς ἀπολλυμένοις, ἀνθ' ὧν τὴν ἀγάπην τῆς ἀληθείας οὐκ ἐδέξαντο εἰς τὸ σωθῆναι αὐτούς. καὶ διὰ τοῦτο πέμπει αὐτοῖς ὁ θεὸς ἐνέργειαν πλάνης εἰς τὸ πιστεῦσαι αὐτοὺς τῷ ψεύδει, ἵνα κριθῶσι πάντες οἱ μὴ πιστεύσαντες τῇ ἀληθείᾳ, ἀλλ᾽ εὐδοκήσαντες τῇ ἀδικίᾳ.»

— And Daniel says, «And they shall place the abomination of desolation a thousand two hundred and ninety days. Blessed is he that waits, and comes to the thousand two hundred and ninety-five days.» And the blessed Apostle Paul, writing to the Thessalonians, says: «Now we beseech you, brethren, concerning the coming of our Lord Jesus Christ, and our gathering together at it, that you be not soon shaken in mind, or be troubled, neither by spirit, nor by word, nor by letters as from us, as that the day of the Lord is at hand. Let no man deceive you by any means; for (that day shall not come) except there come **the falling away** first, and that man of sin be revealed, the son of perdition, who opposes and exalts himself above all that is called God, or that is worshipped: so that he sits in the temple of God, showing himself that he is God. Do you not remember that when I was yet with you, I told you these things? And now you know what withholds, that he might be revealed in his time. For the mystery of iniquity does already work; only he who now lets (will let), until he be taken out of the way. And then shall that wicked be revealed, whom the Lord Jesus shall consume with the Spirit of His mouth, and shall destroy with the brightness of His coming: (even him) whose coming is after the working of Satan, with all power, and signs, and lying wonders, and with all deceivableness of unrighteousness in them that perish; because they received not the love of the truth. And for this cause, God shall send them strong delusion, that they should believe a lie: that they all might be damned who believed not the truth, but had pleasure in unrighteousness.»

— Greek text — H. Achelis. *Hippolyt's kleinere exegetische und homiletische Schriften* [*Die griechischen christlichen Schriftsteller 1.2*]. Hinrichs, 1897. Retrieved from Thesaurus Linguae Graecae (stephanus.tlg.uci.edu).

— English translation — J.H. MacMahon. *Ante-Nicene Fathers, Vol. 5*. Christian Literature Publishing, 1886. Revised and edited for New Advent by Kevin Knight. Accessed at New Advent (newadvent. org/fathers).

— The context is the passage in 2 Thessalonians on the apostasy and the man of sin, preceded by a snippet from Daniel on the abomination

of 1290 days and the blessing of those who endure and attain unto the 1335 days. Hippolytus apparently believed that some would endure the time of tribulation and others would not endure but apostatize.
— RELIGIOUS APOSTASY

(166) Hippolytus, Refutation of All Heresies, book 4, chapter 2
— Τούτοις χρησάμενοι Εὐφράτης ὁ Περατ(ικὸς) καὶ Ἀκεμβὴς ὁ Καρύστιος καὶ ὁ λοιπὸς τούτων χορός, τῷ λόγῳ τῷ τῆς ἀληθείας ἐπονομάσαντες, αἰώνων στάσιν καὶ **ἀποστασίας** ἀγαθ(ῶν) δυνάμεων εἰς κακὰ καὶ συμφωνίας ἀγαθῶν μετὰ πονηρῶν προσαγορεύουσι, καλοῦντες τοπάρχας καὶ προαστείους καὶ ἄλλα πλεῖστα ὀνόματα· ὧν πᾶσαν τὴν ἐπικεχειρημένην αἵρεσιν ἐκθήσομαι καὶ διελέγξω, ἐπὰν εἰς τὸν περὶ τούτων λόγον φθάσωμεν.

— Employing these (as analogies), Euphrates the Peratic, and Acembes the Carystian, and the rest of the crowd of these (speculators), imposing names different from the doctrine of the truth, speak of a sedition of Aeons, and of a **revolt** of good powers over to evil (ones), and of the concord of good with wicked (Aeons), calling them Toparchai and Proastioi, and very many other names. But the entire of this heresy, as attempted by them, I shall explain and refute when we come to treat of the subject of these (Aeons).

— Greek text — M. Marcovich. *Hippolytus. Refutatio omnium haeresium [Patristische Texte und Studien 25]*. De Gruyter, 1986. Retrieved from Thesaurus Linguae Graecae (stephanus.tlg.uci.edu).

— English translation — J.H. MacMahon. *Ante-Nicene Fathers, Vol. 5*. Christian Literature Publishing, 1886. Revised and edited for New Advent by Kevin Knight. Accessed at New Advent (newadvent. org/fathers).

— The context is the errors of Euphrates and Acembes, who hold to a sedition of Aeons, a revolt of good powers over to evil, and the harmony of good and evil Aeons.
— RELIGIOUS APOSTASY

(167) Hippolytus, Refutation of All Heresies, book 5, chapter 13 (chapter 8 in English)
— Ταύτην τὴν σύστασιν καὶ τὴν διαφορὰν τῶν ἄστρων, Χαλδαϊκὴν ὑπάρχουσαν, πρὸς ἑαυτοὺς ἐπισπασάμενοι οἱ Περάται οὓς

προείπομεν, ἐπιψευσάμενοι τῷ τῆς ἀληθείας ὀνόματι ὡς Χριστοῦ λόγον κατήγγειλαν. αἰώνων οὖν στάσιν καὶ **ἀποστασίας** ἀγαθῶν δυνάμεων εἰς κακὰ καὶ συμφωνίας ἀγαθῶν μετὰ πονηρῶν προσαγορεύουσι, καλοῦντες τοπάρχας καὶ προαστείους καὶ ἄλλα πλεῖστα ὀνόματα ἀναπλάσσοντες, ἑαυτοῖς οὐχ ὑποκείμενα. ἀλλὰ μὴν τὴν τῶν ἀστρολόγων περὶ τοὺς ἀστέρας πᾶσαν φαντασίαν ἀτέχνως τεχνολογοῦντες, μεγάλης πλάνης ὑπόθεσιν ἐπεισάγοντες, ἐξελεγχθήσονται σὺν τῇ ἡμετέρᾳ ἐμμελείᾳ. ἀντιπαραθήσω γὰρ τῇ προλελεγμένῃ τῶν ἀστρολόγων Χαλδαϊκῇ τέχνῃ ἔνια τῶν Περατικῶν συνταγμάτων, ἀφ' ὧν ὑπάρξει συγκρίναντας κατανοῆσαι ὡς οἱ Περατικοὶ λόγοι τῶν ἀστρολόγων ὁμολογουμένως εἰσίν, οὐ Χριστοῦ.

— This combination and divergence of the stars, which is a Chaldean (tenet), has been arrogated to themselves by those of whom we have previously spoken. Now these, falsifying the name of truth, proclaim as a doctrine of Christ an insurrection of Aeons and **revolts** of good into (the ranks of) evil powers; and they speak of the confederations of good powers with wicked ones. Denominating them, therefore, Toparchai and Proastioi, and (though thus) framing for themselves very many other names not suggested (to them from other sources), they have yet unskilfully systematized the entire imaginary doctrine of the astrologers concerning the stars. And since they have introduced a supposition pregnant with immense error, they shall be refuted through the instrumentality of our admirable arrangement. For I shall set down, in contrast with the previously mentioned Chaldaic art of the astrologers, some of the Peratic treatises, from which, by means of comparison, there will be an opportunity of perceiving how the Peratic doctrines are those confessedly of the astrologers, not of Christ.

— Greek text — M. Marcovich. *Hippolytus. Refutatio omnium haeresium [Patristische Texte und Studien 25]*. De Gruyter, 1986. Retrieved from Thesaurus Linguae Graecae (stephanus.tlg.uci.edu).
— English translation — J.H. MacMahon. *Ante-Nicene Fathers, Vol. 5*. Christian Literature Publishing, 1886. Revised and edited for New Advent by Kevin Knight. Accessed at New Advent (newadvent. org/fathers).

— The context is the doctrines of the Chaldaeans which the Peratics had embraced, inlcuding the insurrection of the Aeons and the revolts of good powers unto the camp of evil.
— RELIGIOUS APOSTASY

(168) Hippolytus, Refutation of All Heresies, book 6, chapter 52
— ἀλλὰ Πυθαγόρου καὶ τῶν περὶ τὰ μετέωρα [τῶν] ἀστρολόγων ἀπ(ηο)λημένων, ὅσα ἐν ἐπιτομῇ δυνατόν ἐστιν ἐκθήσομαι. λέγουσι γὰρ ταῦτα· Ἐκ μονάδος καὶ δυάδος τὰ ὅλα συνεστάναι· καὶ ἀπὸ μὲν μονάδος ἕως τῶν τεσσάρων ἀριθμοῦντες οὕτως γεννῶσι τὴν δεκάδα. πάλιν δ᾽ αὖ ἡ δυὰς ἀφ᾽ αὐτῆς προελθοῦσα ἕως τοῦ ἐπισήμου, οἷον δύο καὶ τέσσαρες καὶ ἕξ, τὴν δωδεκάδα ἐπέδειξε. καὶ πάλιν ἀπὸ τῆς δυάδος ὁμοίως ἀριθμούντων ἡμῶν ἕως τῶν δέκα ἡ τριακοντὰς ἀνεδείχθη, ἐν ᾗ ὀγδοὰς καὶ δεκὰς καὶ δωδεκάς. τὴν οὖν δωδεκάδα, διὰ τὸ ἐπίσημον ἐσχηκέναι συνεπακολουθῆσαν αὐτῇ, τὸ ἐπίσημον πάθος λέγουσι. καὶ διὰ τοῦτο, περὶ τὸν δωδέκατον ἀριθμὸν τοῦ σφάλματος γενομένου, τὸ πρόβατον ἀποσκιρτῆσαν πεπλανῆσθαι, ἐπειδὴ **τὴν ἀποστασίαν** ἀπὸ δωδεκάδος φάσκουσι γεγενῆσθαι. ὁμοίως δὲ καὶ ἐπὶ τῆς δεκάδος·καὶ ἐπὶ τούτων τὴν δραχμὴν λέγουσιν, ἣν ἀπολέσασα γυνή, ἅψασα λύχνον ἐζήτει. τὴν δὲ ἐπὶ ἑνὶ προβάτῳ ἀπώλειαν καὶ τὴν ἐπὶ μιᾶς δραχμῆς συντιθέντες, τὸν τῶν ἐνενήκοντα ἐννέα ἑαυτοῖς ἀριθμὸν μυθεύουσιν, ὡς τῶν ἕνδεκα ἐπισυμπλεκομένων τοῖς ἐννέα ποιεῖν τὸν τῶν ἐνενήκοντα ἐννέα ἀριθμόν· καὶ τούτου χάριν λέγεσθαι τὸ ἀμήν, περιέχον ἀριθμὸν ἐνενήκοντα ἐννέα.
— Now the Pythagoreans make the following statements: that the universe consists of a Monad and Duad, and that by reckoning from a monad as far as four they thus generate a decade. And again, a duad coming forth as far as the remarkable (letter) — for instance, two and four and six — exhibited the (number) twelve. And again, if we reckon from the duad to the decade, thirty is produced; and in this are comprised the ogdoad, and decade, and dodecade. And therefore, on account of its having the remarkable (letter), the dodecade has concomitant with it a remarkable passion. And for this reason (they maintain) that when an error had arisen respecting the twelfth number, the sheep skipped from the flock and wandered away; for that **the apostasy** took place, they say, in like manner from the decade. And with a similar reference to the dodecade, they speak of the piece of

money which, on losing, a woman, having lit a candle, searched for diligently. (And they make a similar application) of the loss (sustained) in the case of the one sheep out of the ninety and nine; and adding these one into the other, they give a fabulous account of numbers. And in this way, they affirm, when the eleven is multiplied by nine, that it produces the number ninety and nine; and on this account that it is said that the word Amen embraces the number ninety-nine.

— Greek text — M. Marcovich. *Hippolytus. Refutatio omnium haeresium [Patristische Texte und Studien 25]*. De Gruyter, 1986. Retrieved from Thesaurus Linguae Graecae (stephanus.tlg.uci.edu).

— English translation — J.H. MacMahon. *Ante-Nicene Fathers, Vol. 5.* Christian Literature Publishing, 1886. Revised and edited for New Advent by Kevin Knight. Accessed at New Advent (newadvent. org/fathers). Minor corrections by myself.

— The context addresses the errors of the Pythagoreans, among which is a bizarre teaching about an apostasy from the number twelve.

— RELIGIOUS APOSTASY

(169) Irenaeus, Against Heresies, Book 1, chapter 1, section 5

— Τὸ δὲ περὶ τὸν δωδέκατον Αἰῶνα γεγονὸς πάθος [ὑποσημαίνεσθαι λέγουσι] **τῆς ἀποστασίας** διὰ Ἰούδαν, ὃς δωδέκατος ἦν τῶν Ἀποστόλων, γενομένης προδοσίας δείκνυσθαι λέγουσι, καὶ ὅτι τῷ δωδεκάτῳ μηνὶ ἔπαθεν.

— But concerning the twelfth Aeon, they allege it signifies the passion [of Jesus] which happened through the **apostasy** of Judas—who was the twelfth of the apostles—when he traitorously revealed [Jesus]. They also allege that he [Jesus] died in the twelfth month.

— Greek text —W.W. Harvey, *Sancti Irenaei episcopi Lugdunensis libri quinque adversus haereses, vol. 1.* Cambridge University Press, 1857. Retrieved from Thesaurus Linguae Graecae (stephanus. tlg.uci.edu).

— English translation — The translation is my own as I could find none available.

— NOTE — The commonly published English editions of Irenaeus' *Against Heresies* only include the first three sections of Chapter 1. The fuller editions, as that collated and edited by W. Wigan Harvey, contain a significant body of material that isn't included in the common editions.

— The context is the erroneous teaching of Valentinus, a gnostic who interpreted the Bible through his artificial grid of Aeons. His writings, like all gnostic writings, are filled with far-fetched typologies and chronological errors. Here he makes a connection between his twelfth Aeon, Judas being the twelfth apostle, and Jesus dying in the twelfth month. Note that Judas' apostasy is associated with προδοσία (prodosia) *betrayal, treason.*

— RELIGIOUS APOSTASY

(170) Irenaeus, Against Heresies, Book 1, Chapter 2, Section 1

— τὰ μὲν πνευματικὰ τῆς πονηρίας, καὶ ἀγγέλους [τοὺς] παραβεβηκότας, καὶ ἐν **ἀποστασίᾳ** γεγονότας, καὶ τοὺς ἀσεβεῖς, καὶ ἀδίκους, καὶ ἀνόμους, καὶ βλασφήμους τῶν ἀνθρώπων εἰς τὸ αἰώνιον πῦρ πέμψῃ·.

— The evil spirits, even the angels who transgressed and fell into **apostasy**, and the ungodly, the unrighteous, the lawless, and the blasphemers among mankind are sent into eternal fire.

— W.W. Harvey, *Sancti Irenaei episcopi Lugdunensis libri quinque adversus haereses, vol. 1.* Cambridge University Press, 1857. Retrieved from Thesaurus Linguae Graecae (stephanus.tlg.uci.edu).

— English translation — The translation is my own as I could find none available.

— The context is the ungodly angels who fell into apostasy and ungodly mankind being cast into the eternal fire.

— RELIGIOUS APOSTASY

(171) Irenaeus, Against Heresies, Book 1, Chapter 4, Section 1

— καὶ ὅτι ἐμακροθύμησεν ὁ Θεὸς ἐπί τε **τῇ** τῶν παραβεβηκότων ἀγγέλων **ἀποστασίᾳ**, καὶ ἐπὶ τῇ παρακοῇ τῶν ἀνθρώπων, σαφηνίζειν.

— And to explain that God long suffered over **the apostasy** of the angels who transgressed and over the disobedience of man.

— W.W. Harvey, *Sancti Irenaei episcopi Lugdunensis libri quinque adversus haereses, vol. 1.* Cambridge University Press, 1857. Retrieved from Thesaurus Linguae Graecae (stephanus.tlg.uci.edu).

— English translation — The translation is my own as I could find none available.

— The context is God's longsuffering over the apostasy of the angels and the disobedience of man.

— RELIGIOUS APOSTASY

(172) Irenaeus, Against Heresies, Book 4, Fragment 27

— Εἷς καὶ ὁ αὐτὸς Πατήρ, ὁ τοῖς μὲν γλιχομένοις αὐτοῦ τῆς κοινωνίας καὶ προσμένουσιν αὐτοῦ τῇ ὑποταγῇ τὰ παρ' αὐτῷ ἡτοιμακὼς ἀγαθά, τῷ δὲ ἀρχηγῷ **τῆς ἀποστασίας** διαβόλῳ καὶ τοῖς συναποστᾶσιν αὐτῷ τὸ αἰώνιον πῦρ ἡτοιμακώ.

— The one and only Father, who has prepared good things for those who cling to his fellowship and abide in his command, but to the devil, the orchestrator of **the rebellion**, and to those who sympathized with him he has prepared eternal fire.

— L. Doutreleau, B. Hemmerdinger, B.C. Mercier, and A. Rousseau. *Irénée de Lyon. Contre les hérésies, vol. 2*; [*Sources chrétiennes 100*]. Éditions du Cerf, 1965. Retrieved from Thesaurus Linguae Graecae (stephanus.tlg.uci.edu)

— English translation — The translation is my own as I could find none available.

— The context fingers Satan as the author of the rebellion against God.

— RELIGIOUS APOSTASY

(173) Irenaeus, Against Heresies, Book 5, Fragment 18

— Καὶ καλῶς ὁ Ἰουστῖνος εἶπεν ὅτι πρὸ μὲν τῆς τοῦ Κυρίου παρουσίας οὐδέποτε ἐτόλμησεν ὁ Σατανᾶς βλασφημῆσαι τὸν Θεόν, ἅτε μηδέπω εἰδὼς τὴν ἑαυτοῦ κατάκρισιν, διὰ τὸ ἐν παραβολαῖς καὶ ἀλληγορίαις κεῖσθαι, μετὰ δὲ τὴν παρουσίαν τοῦ Κυρίου ἐκ τῶν λόγων αὐτοῦ καὶ τῶν ἀποστόλων μαθὼν ἀναφανδὸν ὅτι πῦρ αἰώνιον αὐτῷ ἡτοίμασται κατ' ἰδίαν γνώμην ἀποστάντι τοῦ Θεοῦ καὶ πᾶσι τοῖς ἀμετανοήτως παραμείνασιν ἐν **τῇ ἀποστασίᾳ**, διὰ τῶν τοιούτων ἀνθρώπων βλασφημεῖ τὸν τὴν κρίσιν ἐπάγοντα Κύριον, ὡς ἤδη κατακεκριμένος, καὶ τὴν ἁμαρτίαν **τῆς** ἰδίας **ἀποστασίας** τῷ ἐκτικότι αὐτὸν ἀποκαλεῖ, ἀλλ' οὐ τῇ ἰδίᾳ αὐθαιρέτῳ γνώμῃ, ὡς καὶ οἱ παραβαίνοντες τοὺς νόμους, ἔπειτα δίκας διδόντες, αἰτιῶνται τοὺς νομοθέτας, ἀλλ' οὐχ ἑαυτούς.

— And well Justin said that before the coming of the Lord Satan never dared to blaspheme God since he didn't yet know his own condemnation, it being couched in parables and allegories, but after the coming of the Lord from his words and the apostles he learned clearly that, in God's own determination, eternal fire had been prepared for those who departed from God and to all who remained impenitent in **apostasy**, through men he blasphemed the Lord who had brought the judgment against him as already condemned, and blamed his own sin of **apostasy** on the one who had created him.

— L. Doutreleau, B.C. Mercier, and A. Rousseau. *Irénée de Lyon. Contre les hérésies, vol. 2*; [*Sources chrétiennes 153*]. Éditions du Cerf, 1969. Retrieved from Thesaurus Linguae Graecae (stephanus. tlg.uci.edu).

— English translation — The translation is my own as I could find none available.

— The context is eternal punishment for all who remain impenitent in apostasy, and Satan blaming God for his own apostasy.

— RELIGIOUS APOSTASY

(174) Irenaeus, Against Heresies, Book 5, Fragment 20

— Ὅσα ἀφίστανται κατὰ τὴν γνώμην αὐτῶν τοῦ Θεοῦ, τούτοις τὸν ἀπ' αὐτοῦ χωρισμὸν ἐπάγει· χωρισμὸς δὲ Θεοῦ θάνατος, καὶ χωρισμὸς φωτὸς σκότος, καὶ χωρισμὸς Θεοῦ ἀποβολὴ πάντων τῶν παρ' αὐτοῦ ἀγαθῶν. Οἱ οὖν διὰ **τῆς ἀποστασίας** ἀποβαλόντες τὰ προειρημένα, ἅτε ἐστερημένοι πάντων τῶν ἀγαθῶν, ἐν πάσῃ κολάσει καταγίνονται, τοῦ Θεοῦ μὲν προηγητικῶς μὴ κολάζοντος, ἐπακολουθούσης δὲ ἐκείνοις τῆς κολάσεως διὰ τὸ ἐστερῆσθαι πάντων τῶν ἀγαθῶν.

— Whosoever departs in the heart (purpose) from God, they procure for themselves separation from Him. Separation from God is death, and separation from light is darkness, and separation from God is casting away all good things from Him. Those who through **apostasy** have cast away these foresaid things, in that they are deprived of all good things, shall abide in full punishment, not being punished from

257

the initial purpose of God, but punishment coming upon them because of their deprivation of all good things.

— L. Doutreleau, B.C. Mercier, and A. Rousseau. *Irénée de Lyon. Contre les hérésies, vol. 2*; [*Sources chrétiennes 153*]. Éditions du Cerf, 1969. Retrieved from Thesaurus Linguae Graecae (stephanus. tlg.uci.edu).

— English translation — The translation is my own as I could find none available.

— The context is man's apostasy from God which results in separation from Him and separation from light and the loss of all the good things that come from Him.

— RELIGIOUS APOSTASY

(175) Irenaeus, Against Heresies, Book 5, Fragment 22

— Καὶ «τὸν ἀριθμὸν δὲ τοῦ ὀνόματος αὐτοῦ» φησιν καὶ ἄλλα τινὰ «καὶ εἶναι τὸν ἀριθμὸν χξϛ΄», ὅ ἐστιν ἑκατοντάδες ἓξ καὶ δεκάδες ἓξ καὶ μονάδες ἓξ εἰς ἀνακεφαλαίωσιν πάσης τῆς ἐν τοῖς ἑξακισχιλίοις ἔτεσιν γεγονυίας **ἀποστασίας**.

— And «the number of his name,» he said, among other things, «is the number 666,» which is six hundreds, six tens, and six ones which summarize all the six thousand years which have passed since the **apostasy** happened.

— L. Doutreleau, B.C. Mercier, and A. Rousseau. *Irénée de Lyon. Contre les hérésies, vol. 2*; [*Sources chrétiennes 153*]. Éditions du Cerf, 1969. Retrieved from Thesaurus Linguae Graecae (stephanus. tlg.uci.edu).

— English translation — The translation is my own as I could find none available.

— The context is the original apostasy of Satan and man.

— RELIGIOUS APOSTASY

(176) Irenaeus, Against Heresies, Book 5, Fragment 22

— Καὶ διὰ τοῦτο ἐν παντὶ τούτῳ τῷ χρόνῳ πλασθεὶς ἐν ἀρχῇ ὁ ἄνθρωπος διὰ τῶν χειρῶν τοῦ Θεοῦ, τουτέστιν Υἱοῦ καὶ Πνεύματος, γίνεται κατ᾽ εἰκόνα καὶ ὁμοίωσιν Θεοῦ, τοῦ μὲν ἀχύρου ἀποσκευαζομένου, ὅπερ ἐστὶν **ἡ ἀποστασία**, τοῦ δὲ σίτου εἰς ἀποθήκην ἀναλαμβανομένου, ὅπερ ἐστὶν οἱ τὴν πρὸς Θεὸν πίστιν καρποφοροῦντες.

— And therefore in the fulness of that time man was formed through the hand of God, that is the Son and the Spirit, he became in the image and likeness of God, some being prepared for chaff, which is **the apostasy**, some being wheat layed up in the barn, which are those who bear fruit to God.

— L. Doutreleau, B.C. Mercier, and A. Rousseau. *Irénée de Lyon. Contre les hérésies, vol. 2*; [*Sources chrétiennes 153*]. Éditions du Cerf, 1969. Retrieved from Thesaurus Linguae Graecae (stephanus. tlg.uci.edu).

— English translation — The translation is my own as I could find none available.

— The context is the departure of wicked mankind from God.

— RELIGIOUS APOSTASY

(177) Irenaeus, Against Heresies, Book 5, Fragment 24

— Καὶ διὰ τοῦτο εἰς τὸ θηρίον τὸ ἐρχόμενον ἀνακεφαλαίωσις γίνεται πάσης ἀδικίας καὶ παντὸς δόλου, ἵνα ἐν αὐτῷ συρρεύσασα καὶ συγκλυδωνισθεῖσα πᾶσα δύναμις ἀποστατικὴ εἰς τὴν κάμινον βληθῇ τοῦ πυρός. Καταλλήλως οὖν καὶ τὸ ὄνομα αὐτοῦ ἕξει τὸν ἀριθμὸν χξϛ΄, ἀνακεφαλαιούμενον ἐν ἑαυτῷ τὴν πρὸ τοῦ κατακλυσμοῦ πᾶσαν τῆς κακίας ἐπίδειξιν ἐξ ἀγγελικῆς **ἀποστασίας** γεγενημένης — Νῶε γὰρ ἦν ἐτῶν ἑξακοσίων καὶ ὁ κατακλυσμὸς ἐπῆλθε τῇ γῇ, ἐξαλείφων τὸ ἀνάστημα τῆς γῆς διὰ τὴν ἐπὶ τοῦ Ἀδὰμ κίβδηλον γενεάν — ἀνακεφαλαιούμενος δὲ καὶ τὴν ἀπὸ τοῦ κατακλυσμοῦ πᾶσαν εἰδωλολατρείαν, μέχρις οὗ ἡ τοῦ Ναβουχοδονόσορ ἀνασταθεῖσα εἰκών, ἥτις ὕψος μὲν εἶχε πηχῶν ἑξήκοντα, εὖρος δὲ πηχῶν ἕξ· ὅλη γὰρ ἡ εἰκὼν ἐκείνη προτύπωσις ἦν τῆς τοῦ ἀντιχρίστου παρουσίας. Τὰ οὖν χ΄ ἔτη τοῦ Νῶε ἐφ᾽ οὗ ἐγένετο ὁ κατακλυσμὸς διὰ **τὴν ἀποστασίαν** καὶ ὁ πηχισμὸς τῆς εἰκόνος τὸν ἀριθμόν, ὡς εἴρηται, σημαίνουσι τοῦ ὀνόματος, εἰς ὃν συγκεφαλαιοῦται τῶν ἑξακισχιλίων ἐτῶν πᾶσα **ἀποστασία** καὶ ἀδικία καὶ πονηρία.

— And therefore, as for the beast who is coming, he shall be a summing up of all unrighteousness and all deceit, that the entire apostate force, having flowed to him and found confluence in him, shall be cast into the furnace of fire. Fittingly, therefore, his hame has the number 666, summing up in himself the whole commixture of wickedness prior to the cataclysm which happened because of the **apostasy** of the angels. For Noah was six hundred years old and the cataclysm came upon the earth, wiping away the heights of the earth because of the debased generation of Adam. And summing up all the idolatry from the flood until Nebuchadnezzar raised his image which had a height of sixty cubits and a breadth of six cubits. The whole image was a foreshadow of the coming of the antichrist. For the years of Noah, upon whom the cataclysm came because of **apostasy**, and the number of the cubits of the image, as was mentioned, signify the number in which is summed up all the **apostasy**, injustice, and evil of the six thousand years.

— L. Doutreleau, B.C. Mercier, and A. Rousseau. *Irénée de Lyon. Contre les hérésies, vol. 2*; [*Sources chrétiennes 153*]. Éditions du Cerf, 1969. Retrieved from Thesaurus Linguae Graecae (stephanus. tlg.uci.edu).

— English translation — The translation is my own as I could find none available.

— The context is the apostasy of the angels leading to the flood in Noah's day, and the apostasy of man for the whole six thousand years of his history.

— RELIGIOUS APOSTASY

(178) John of Antioch, Fragments, 196

— Πλακιδία εἶχε δύο στρατηγοὺς, ὧν τῷ μὲν ἑνὶ Βονιφατίῳ τὴν Λιβύην ἐπέτρεψεν, Ἀέτιον δὲ παρακατέσχεν. Ἐφθόνησεν Ἀέτιος καὶ ἔγραψε Βονιφατίῳ, ὅτι «ἡ βασίλισσα ἔχει κατὰ σοῦ, καὶ τούτου σημεῖον, ὅτι μετακαλέσεταί σε ὑπ᾽ οὐδεμιᾶς αἰτίας. Ἐὰν οὖν γράψῃ σοι ἐλθεῖν, μὴ ὑπακούσῃς· ἀναιρήσει γάρ σε.» Εἶτα κατῆλθε τὴν βασίλισσαν λέγων, ὡς «**ἀποστασίαν** μελετᾷ ὁ Βονιφάτιος. Καὶ τοῦτο γνώσῃ σαφῶς· ἐὰν γὰρ μετακαλέσῃ, φησὶν, αὐτὸν, οὐκ ἐλεύσεται.»

— Placidia had two generals. She entrusted Libya to Boniface and retained Aetius. Aetius was incensed with envy and wrote to Boniface that "he queen has something against you, and the sign (evidence) of this is that she will recall you without a single reason. If she writes to you to come, do not obey for she will slay you." Then he went back to the queen informing her that "Boniface is planning **sedition**. And

this you can clearly know. For if you summon him, he will say he shall not come."
— Greek text — K. Müller. *Fragmenta historicorum Graecorum 4*. Didot, 1841-1870. Retrieved from Thesaurus Linguae Graecae (stephanus.tlg.uci.edu).
— English translation — The translation is my own as I could find none available.
— The context is the interaction between Queen Placidia, General Boniface, and General Aetius. The latter falsely accused Boniface of sedition to the queen.
— POLITICAL SEDITION OR REBELLION

(179) John of Antioch, Fragments, 214
— Ὁ δὲ Ἰλλοῦς ἐς φανερὰν **ἀποστασίαν** ἐλθών, τότε Μαρκιανὸν ἀναζώννυσι, καὶ πρὸς τὸν Ὀδόακρον ἔστελλε, τὸν τῆς ἑσπερίας Ῥώμης τύραννον, καὶ πρὸς τοὺς τῶν Περσῶν καὶ Ἀρμενίων ἄρχοντας· παρεσκεύαζεν δὲ καὶ πλοῖα.
— When Illus came into open **rebellion**, then Marcian girded himself and sent [messengers] to Odoacer the tyrant of western Rome and to the rulers of the Persians and Armenians. He also prepared ships.
— Greek text — K. Müller. *Fragmenta historicorum Graecorum 4*. Didot, 1841-1870. Retrieved from Thesaurus Linguae Graecae (stephanus.tlg.uci.edu).
— English translation — The translation is my own as I could find none available.
— The context is the sedition of Illus, a Roman general who first supported the revolt of Basilicus against Zeno, then changed sides and threw his weight behind Zeno's return to the throne.
— POLITICAL SEDITION OR REBELLION

(180) Julian of Eclanum, Commentary on Job, 40:20, (Hagedorn, p. 285)
— διὸ εἴρηται· προστάγματι ἐθανάτωσε δράκοντα ἀποστάτην καὶ δράκων οὗτος, ὃν ἔπλασας ἐμπαίζειν αὐτῷ, ὅτι ἀποστὰς θεοῦ τοῦ πάντων αἰτίου καὶ σωτῆρος ἀσεβείᾳ προστεθεὶς ἀρχὴ δαιμόνων τῶν συναρεσθέντων αὐτοῦ τῇ κακονοίᾳ ἐγένετο. ὡς γὰρ ὁ δράκων κατὰ τῶν ὄφεων, οὕτως καὶ ὁ διάβολος κατὰ τῶν δαιμόνων. ἀρχὴ δὲ τούτων

οὐχ ὡς αἴτιος αἰτιατῶν, ἀλλ᾽ ὡς ἀρέσκων καὶ ἀρεσκόμενος ἐπὶ **τῇ** κοινῇ **ἀποστασίᾳ**· παρήλλακται δὲ τῇ φύσει πρὸς αὐτούς, ἐπειδὴ ὁ μὲν ἀρχάγγελος, οἱ δὲ ἄγγελοι ὑπῆρχον. ᾑρήσαντο δὲ οἱ μὲν δαίμονες καλεῖσθαι καὶ χαίρουσιν ἐπὶ τῇ προσηγορίᾳ ταύτῃ, ὁ δὲ διάβολος ὀνομάζεσθαι καὶ Βελίαρ καὶ Σατάν.

— Therefore it is said, by command he slew the apostate dragon. And this dragon, whom [God] had formed, [choose] to mock him, for he departed from the God who is the cause (Creator) of all things, submitted to [being] the savior for ungodliness, and became the prince of the demons who were pleased to join him in perversity. For as the dragon is over the serpents, so also the devil is over the demons. But their prince is not the cause of the caused (not the cause of their actions), but rather as ones who were pleased and one who was pleased [the joined] in **the** common **apostasy**. They were altered in their nature — they had existed as an archangel and angels — and the latter chose to be called demons and rejoiced upon this term, while the devil was named Beliar and Satan.

— Greek text — D. Hagedorn. *Der Hiobkommentar des Arianers Julian [Patristische Texte und Studien 14]*. De Gruyter, 1973. Retrieved from Thesaurus Linguae Graecae (stephanus.tlg.uci.edu).

— English translation — The English translation is my own. I ordered the recent translation — Thomas Scheck; *Julian of Eclanum: Exposition on the Book of Job*; [*Ancient Christian Texts*]; InterVarsity Press, 2021. But I was unable to find any clear correlation between the Greek text in Hagedorn and the English text in Scheck. The length of the comments under the verses, the material under the verses, and the verse numberings were so disparate that they appeared to be two distinct works.

— The context is the apostate dragon and his fellow fallen angels happily joining together in a common apostasy.

— RELIGIOUS APOSTASY

(181) Justin Martyr, Dialogue with Trypho, 110

— ἀλόγιστοι, μὴ συνιέντες, ὅπερ διὰ πάντων τῶν λόγων ἀποδέδεικται, ὅτι δύο παρουσίαι αὐτοῦ κατηγγελμέναι εἰσί· μία μέν, ἐν ᾗ παθητὸς καὶ ἄδοξος καὶ ἄτιμος καὶ σταυρούμενος κεκήρυκται, ἡ δὲ δευτέρα, ἐν ᾗ μετὰ δόξης ἀπὸ τῶν οὐρανῶν παρέσται, ὅταν καὶ ὁ τῆς **ἀποστασίας** ἄνθρωπος, ὁ καὶ εἰς τὸν ὕψιστον ἔξαλλα λαλῶν, ἐπὶ τῆς γῆς ἄνομα τολμήσῃ εἰς ἡμᾶς τοὺς Χριστιανούς, οἵτινες, ἀπὸ τοῦ νόμου καὶ τοῦ λόγου τοῦ ἐξελθόντος ἀπὸ Ἰερουσαλὴμ διὰ τῶν τοῦ Ἰησοῦ ἀποστόλων τὴν θεοσέβειαν ἐπιγνόντες, ἐπὶ τὸν θεὸν Ἰακὼβ καὶ θεὸν Ἰσραὴλ κατεφύγομεν.

— O unreasoning men! understanding not what has been proved by all these passages, that two advents of Christ have been announced: the one, in which He is set forth as suffering, inglorious, dishonoured, and crucified; but the other, in which He shall come from heaven with glory, when the man of **apostasy**, who speaks strange things against the Most High, shall venture to do unlawful deeds on the earth against us the Christians, who, having learned the true worship of God from the law, and the word which went forth from Jerusalem by means of the apostles of Jesus, have fled for safety to the God of Jacob and God of Israel.

— Greek text — E.J. Goodspeed. *Die ältesten Apologeten*. Vandenhoeck & Ruprecht, 1915. Retrieved from Thesaurus Linguae Graecae (stephanus.tlg.uci.edu).

— English translation — Marcus Dods and George Reith. *Ante-Nicene Fathers, Vol. 1*. Christian Literature Publishing, 1885. Revised and edited for New Advent by Kevin Knight. Accessed at New Advent (newadvent.org/fathers).

— The context is the antichrist, speaking strange things against the Most High and committing unlawful deeds against the Christians. Notice that Justin Martyr expressly calls him "the man of apostasy."

— RELIGIOUS APOSTASY

(182) Justin Martyr, Fragments of Lost Works, fragment 2

— Πρὸ μὲν τῆς τοῦ κυρίου παρουσίας οὐδέποτε ἐτόλμησεν ὁ σατανᾶς βλασφημῆσαι τὸν θεόν, ἅτε μηδέπω εἰδὼς αὐτοῦ τὴν κατάκρισιν, διὰ τὸ ἐν παραβολαῖς καὶ ἀλληγορίαις κεῖσθαι. Μετὰ δὲ τὴν παρουσίαν τοῦ κυρίου, ἐκ τῶν λόγων αὐτοῦ καὶ τῶν ἀποστόλων μαθὼν ἀναφανδὸν ὅτι πῦρ αἰώνιον αὐτῷ ἡτοίμασται, κατ' ἰδίαν γνώμην ἀποστάντι τοῦ θεοῦ, καὶ πᾶσι τοῖς ἀμετανοήτως παραμείνασιν ἐν **τῇ ἀποστασίᾳ**, διὰ τῶν τοιούτων ἀνθρώπων βλασφημεῖ τὸν τὴν κρίσιν ἐπάγοντα κύριον, ὡς ἤδη κατακεκριμένος, καὶ τὴν ἁμαρτίαν **τῆς** ἰδίας

ἀποστασίας τῷ ἐκτικότι αὐτὸν ἀποκαλεῖ, ἀλλ' οὐ τῇ ἰδίᾳ αὐθαιρέτῳ γνώμῃ.·

— Before the coming of the Lord, Satan never dared to blaspheme God, seeing that he didn't yet know his condemnation because it had been couched in parables and allegories. But after the coming of the Lord, from the Lord's own words and the teaching of the apostles, it was made apparent that eternal fire had been prepared for him against his purpose in apostatizing from God, and for all those who joined him in **the apostasy**. And through these men he blasphemes the Lord who brought this judgment against him—as one already condemned— and he pins his own **apostasy** on the one who created him, but not on his own self-willed purpose.

— Greek text — J.C.T. Otto. *Corpus apologetarum Christianorum saeculi secundi, vol. 3, 3rd ed.* Mauke, 1879. Retrieved from Thesaurus Linguae Graecae (stephanus.tlg.uci.edu).

— English translation — The translation is my own as I could find none available.

— The context addresses Satan's apostasy from God.

— RELIGIOUS APOSTASY

(183) Macarius, Apocriticus, Book 3, Chapter 11

— Ἐπεὶ δ' ἐρωτᾶν ὡς ἀγνοοῦντα τὸν Χριστὸν ὁ Μάρκος ἱστόρησε λέγοντα τί ὄνομα τῷ δαίμονι, οὐκ ἀγνοῶν ὁ Χριστὸς τίς ὁ δαίμων λέγεται ἐξετάζει τὸν βδελυρόν·ἀλλ' ἵν' αὐτὸν ἐκ τῶν οἰκείων ἐλέγξῃ ῥημάτων, ὡς ἀποστάτης γέγονε τῆς ἄνω βασιλείας, λέγει·«Τί σοι ἦν ὄνομα;» ὁ δ' ἀπεκρίθη «Λεγεών». Οὐ γὰρ ὑπῆρχε τότε, ἀλλ' ἦν ποτε λεγεών, δορυφοροῦσα τῆς ἄνω βασιλείας τὸ κράτος, κατὰ τὸ γεγραμμένον «Ἢ οὐ δύναμαι ἄρτι παρακαλέσαι τὸν πατέρα μου, καὶ παραστήσει μοι δώδεκα λεγεῶνας ἀγγέλων;» Ἐδραπέτευσε δ' ἡ λεγεὼν ἐκείνη καὶ τῷ **τῆς ἀποστασίας** ἐνεκυλίσθη κακῷ, κρυπτηρίαν ἐξ εὐχερείας εὐροῦσα τὸν ἄνθρωπον. Ῥίψασπις ὄντως καὶ δύστηνος λεγεών, οὐ λεγεών, ἀλλὰ λῃστής, τὸν περίγειον ἐκδύων τόπον καὶ λῃϊζόμενος καὶ τοὺς ἁλόντας ἀνηκέστοις ὑποβάλλων ταῖς συμφοραῖς.

— As for Mark's record that Christ asked what the demon's name was, as though He were ignorant of it, it was not in ignorance of the loathsome creature that He inquires what he is called, but in order that He might convict him from his own words, as a deserter from the heavenly kingdom. So He asks «What is thy name ?» and he answers «Legion». He did not exist as such then, but he once was a legion, wielding the might of the kingdom above, even as it is written, «Can I not now pray to my Father, and he will give me twelve legions of angels?» But that legion ran away, and was involved in the evil of **desertion**, finding the man a ready hiding-place; a sorry legion, indeed, which threw away its shield; not really a legion, but a bandit, stripping the earthly sphere and plundering it, and casting into incurable sorrows those who are taken captive.

— Greek text — R. Goulet. *Macarios de Magnésie: Le monogénès (Tome II)*. Librairie Philosophique J. Vrin, 2003. Retrieved from Thesaurus Linguae Graecae (stephanus.tlg.uci.edu).

— English translation — T.W. Crafer. *The Apocritus of Macarius Magnes*. Society For Promoting Christian Knowledge, Macmillan, 1919. Transcribed for the Tertullian Project by Roger Pearse, 2002. Accessed at tertullian.org/fathers.

— The context is the legion of demons that possessed the man blind and dumb, which legion had participated in the evil of apostasy when the wicked angels apostatized from God. The spirits of this desertion seek to take men captive.

— RELIGIOUS APOSTASY

(184) Martyrdom of Pionius, chapter 14, section 9

— παντὶ τῷ ἀποστάτῃ γενομένῳ θεοῦ οἱ **τῆς ἀποστασίας** παρέπονται ἄγγελοι, καὶ παντὶ φαρμακῷ καὶ μάγῳ καὶ γόητι καὶ μάντει διαβολικοὶ ὑπουργοῦσι λειτουργοί.

— All who become an apostate from God, the **apostate** angels help them along. And every witch, magi, howler (sorcerer), and diviner, diabolical servants (ministers) render them assistance.

— Greek text — H. Musurillo. *The Acts of the Christian Martyrs*. Clarendon Press, 1972. Retrieved from Thesaurus Linguae Graecae (stephanus.tlg.uci.edu).

— English translation — The translation is my own as I could find none available.

— The context is departure from God into errors encouraged by the fallen angels.

— RELIGIOUS APOSTASY

(185) Methodius, Apocalypse, 11.17, (redaction 1)

— ἡ γὰρ ὑπὸ τοῦ ἀποστόλου λεχθεῖσα παιδεία, ἤτοι **ἀποστασία**, αὕτη ἐστίν· φησὶ γὰρ «ὅτι ἐὰν μὴ ἔλθῃ **ἡ ἀποστασία** πρῶτον, καὶ ἀποκαλυφθῇ ὁ ἄνθρωπος τῆς ἀνομίας, ὁ υἱὸς τῆς ἀπωλείας». **ἡ γὰρ ἀποστασία** παιδεία ἐστί· καὶ παιδευθήσονται πάντες οἱ κατοικοῦντες τὴν γῆν.

— For the chastisement mentioned by the apostle, which is **the apostasy**, is this. For he says, «that unless **the apostasy** come first, and the man of lawlessness be revealed, the son of perdition». For **the apostasy** is chastisement. And all the inhabitants of the earth shall be chastised.

— Greek text — A.C. Lolos. *Die Apokalypse des Ps.-Methodios* [*Beiträge zur klassischen Philologie 83*]. Hain, 1976. Retrieved from Thesaurus Linguae Graecae (stephanus.tlg.uci.edu).

— English translation — The translation is my own as I could find none available.

— The context is the apostasy of the last days which Methodius specifically states is a punishment for the inhabitants of the earth. The Bible says as much, "because they received not the love of the truth that they might be saved ... God will send them a strong delusion."

— RELIGIOUS APOSTASY

(186) Methodius, Apocalypse, 12.1-2 (redaction 1)

— Φησὶ γὰρ ὁ ἱερὸς ἀπόστολος·«οὐχὶ πάντες οἱ ἐξ Ἰερουσαλὴμ οὗτοι υἱοὶ Ἰσραήλ»· οὐκοῦν οὐ πάντες ὅσοι χριστιανοὶ λέγονται, οὗτοι χριστιανοὶ τυγχάνουσιν. «ἑπτὰ γάρ», καθώς φησιν ἡ γραφή, «χιλιάδες ἐσώθησαν τῶν υἱῶν Ἰσραήλ, οἵτινες οὐκ ἔκαμψαν γόνυ τῇ Βάαλ» καὶ ἅπας ὁ λαὸς τοῦ Ἰσραὴλ δι᾽ αὐτῶν ἐσώθη. (2) οὕτω καὶ τότε ἐν τῷ καιρῷ ἐκείνῳ **τῆς** τότε **ἀποστασίας** καὶ τῆς παιδείας τῶν υἱῶν Ἰσμαὴλ ὀλίγοι εὑρεθήσονται χριστιανοὶ ἀληθεῖς, καθάπερ αὐτὸς ὁ σωτὴρ ἡμῶν ἐν τοῖς ἁγίοις εὐαγγελίοις ἀπεφήνατο·«ἆρα ἐλθὼν ὁ υἱὸς τοῦ ἀνθρώπου εὑρήσει τὴν πίστιν ἐπὶ τῆς γῆς;»

— For the holy apostle says, «Not all who are of Jerusalem, these are the sons of Israel». Therefore not all who are called Christians hit the mark of Christians. For as the Scriptures state, «Seven thousand were saved among the sons of Israel, who had not bowed the knee to Baal», and all the people of Israel were saved through them. So also in that time, even that time of **the apostasy** and chastizement of the sons of Israel, few true Christians shall be found, even as our Saviour himself declared in the holy gospels. «Therefore, when the Son of man comes, shall he found faith on the earth?»

— Greek text — A.C. Lolos. *Die Apokalypse des Ps.-Methodios* [*Beiträge zur klassischen Philologie 83*]. Hain, 1976. Retrieved from Thesaurus Linguae Graecae (stephanus.tlg.uci.edu).

— English translation — The translation is my own as I could find none available.

— The context is the apostasy of the last days. Methodius associated the apostasy of the last days with the discipline of the sons of Israel and with few true Christians being found.

— RELIGIOUS APOSTASY

(187) Nilus of Ancyra, Epistles (Letters), 210

— Ὅτι πρὸς τὴν ῥοπὴν ἕκαστος τὴν ἐπὶ φαύλῳ, ἢ ἐπὶ κρείττονι κρίνεται, πειθέτωσάν σε, ὁ μὲν Ἰούδας διὰ μιᾶς νυκτὸς ἀλλοτριωθεὶς τῆς ζωῆς, προδεδωκὼς τὸν Διδάσκαλον, ὁ δὲ λῃστὴς ἐν στιγμῇ χρόνου οἰκειωθεὶς τῇ ζωῇ. Οὐ μὴ γὰρ μνησθῶσιν αἱ ἀνομίαι τοῦ μὴ παντελῶς **ἀποστασίαν** τοῦ Θεοῦ νοσήσαντος ἀνθρώπου, μηδὲ καρδίαν πονηρὰν ἀπιστίας τε καὶ ἠλιθιότητος ἀναλαβόντος·

— Because with an influence each decides for worse or for better. They persuade themselves. Judas, on the one hand, in one night alienated himself from life, having delivered the teacher. The thief, on the other hand, in a moment domiciled himself in life. Let not the lawless crimes of the diseased man be remembered, lest they take up utter **apostasy** from God or an evil heart of unbelief and folly.

— Greek text — J.P. Migne. *Patrologiae cursus completus* (*series Graeca 79*). Migne, 1857-1866. Retrieved from Thesaurus Linguae Graecae (stephanus.tlg.uci.edu).

— The English translation is my own as I could find none readily available.

— The context points out the danger of thinking about lawless things because that could lead to apostasy from God. Notice the association of apostasy with an evil heart of unbelief, folly, and betraying Jesus.

— RELIGIOUS APOSTASY

(188) Origen, Commentary on Matthew, 14.18

— Μετὰ ταῦτα διαληψόμεθα τὸν τῶν Φαρισαίων λόγον ὃν εἶπον τῷ Ἰησοῦ· τί οὖν Μωσῆς ἐνετείλατο δοῦναι βιβλίον ἀποστασίου καὶ ἀπολῦσαι; εὖ λόγως δ᾽ εἰς τοῦτο παραληψόμεθα τὴν ἀπὸ τοῦ Δευτερονομίου λέξιν περὶ τοῦ **τῆς ἀποστασίας** βιβλίου ἔχουσαν οὕτως· «ἐὰν δὲ λάβῃ τις γυναῖκα καὶ συνοικήσῃ αὐτῇ, καὶ ἔσται ἐὰν μὴ εὕρῃ χάριν ἐναντίον αὐτοῦ ὅτι εὗρεν ἐν αὐτῇ ἄσχημον πρᾶγμα» καὶ τὰ ἑξῆς ἕως τοῦ «καὶ οὐ μιανεῖτε τὴν γῆν ἣν κύριος ὁ θεὸς ὑμῶν δίδωσιν ὑμῖν ἐν κλήρῳ».

— After this we will discuss the saying of the Pharisees which they said to Jesus, «Why then did Moses command to give a bill of divorcement and put her away?» And with good reason we will bring forward for this purpose the passage from Deuteronomy concerning the bill of **divorcement**, which is as follows: «But if a man takes a wife and cohabit with her, and it shall be, if she do not find favour in his sight because he has found in her a thing unseemly,» etc., down to the words, «and you shall not pollute the land which the Lord your God gives you for an inheritance.»

— Greek text — E. Klostermann. *Origenes Werke, vol. 10.1-10.2*; [*Die griechischen christlichen Schriftsteller*]. Teubner, 10.1:1935; 10.2:1937. Retrieved from Thesaurus Linguae Graecae (stephanus. tlg.uci.edu).

— English translation — John Patrick. *Ante-Nicene Fathers, Vol. 9*. Christian Literature Publishing, 1896. Revised and edited for New Advent by Kevin Knight. Accessed at New Advent (newadvent. org/fathers).

— The context is divorce. Origen's use of τῆς ἀποστασίας in *bill of divorce* constructions, e.g. τοῦ βιβλίου τῆς ἀποστασίας and τὸ τῆς ἀποστασίας βιβλίον, is rare. Normally τοῦ ἀποστασίου is employed.

— DIVORCE

(189) Origen, Commentary on Matthew, 14.19

— Μεμνημένοι δὲ τῶν ἀνωτέρω ἡμῖν λελεγμένων εἰς τὸ τοῦ Ἡσαΐου περὶ τοῦ βιβλίου **τῆς ἀποστασίας** ῥητὸν φήσομεν ὅτι ἑαυτὴν ἀπέστησεν ἀνδρὸς τοῦ Χριστοῦ ἡ μήτηρ τοῦ λαοῦ, μὴ λαβοῦσα τὸ **τῆς ἀποστασίας** βιβλίον. ὕστερον δέ, ὅτε εὑρέθη ἐν αὐτῇ «ἄσχημον πρᾶγμα» καὶ οὐχ εὗρε «χάριν ἐναντίον αὐτοῦ», ἐγράφη αὐτῇ βιβλίον ἀποστασίου. δυνάμει γὰρ ἡ καινὴ διαθήκη, τοὺς ἀπὸ τῶν ἐθνῶν καλοῦσα εἰς τὴν οἰκίαν τοῦ τὴν προτέραν γυναῖκα ἀποβεβληκότος, τὸ βιβλίον τοῦ ἀποστασίου δέδωκε τῇ προτέρᾳ ἀποστάσῃ τοῦ ἀνδρὸς νόμου καὶ λόγου.

— Now, keeping in mind what we said above in regard to the passage from Isaiah about the bill **of divorcement**, we will say that the mother of the people separated herself from Christ, her husband, without having received the bill **of divorcement**, but afterwards when there was found in her an unseemly thing, and she did not find favour in his sight, the bill of divorcement was written out for her; for when the new covenant called those of the Gentiles to the house of Him who had cast away his former wife, it virtually gave the bill of divorcement to her who formerly separated from her husband — the law, and the Word.

— Greek text — E. Klostermann. *Origenes Werke, vol. 10.1-10.2*; [*Die griechischen christlichen Schriftsteller*]. Teubner, 10.1:1935; 10.2:1937. Retrieved from Thesaurus Linguae Graecae (stephanus. tlg.uci.edu).

— English translation — John Patrick. *Ante-Nicene Fathers, Vol. 9.* Christian Literature Publishing, 1896. Revised and edited for New Advent by Kevin Knight. Accessed at New Advent (newadvent. org/fathers).

— The context is divorce. Origen's use of τῆς ἀποστασίας in *bill of divorce* constructions, e.g. τοῦ βιβλίου τῆς ἀποστασίας and τὸ τῆς ἀποστασίας βιβλίον, is rare. Normally τοῦ ἀποστασίου is employed.

— DIVORCE

(190) Origen, Commentary on Matthew, 14.19

— διὸ καὶ αὐτὸς αὐτῆς ἀποστὰς ἔγημεν (ἵν᾽ οὕτως ὀνομάσω) ἑτέραν, δοὺς «εἰς τὰς χεῖρας» τῆς προτέρας τὸ τοῦ ἀποστασίου βιβλίον· διὸ μηκέτι δύνανται πράσσειν τὰ κατὰ τὸν νόμον αὐτοῖς προστεταγμένα διὰ τὸ βιβλίον τοῦ ἀποστασίου. καὶ σημεῖον τοῦ εἰληφέναι αὐτὴν βιβλίον ἀποστασίου τὸ Ἱερουσαλὴμ μὲν καθῃρῆσθαι μετὰ τοῦ κληθέντος ὑπ᾽ ἐκείνων ἁγιάσματος καὶ τῶν ἐν αὐτῷ πεπιστευμένων γεγονέναι σεμνῶν καὶ τοῦ θυσιαστηρίου τῶν ὁλοκαυτωμάτων καὶ πάσης τῆς παρ᾽ αὐτῷ λατρείας. σημεῖον δὲ τοῦ βιβλίου **τῆς ἀποστασίας** καὶ τὸ μήτε ἑορτάζειν αὐτοὺς δύνασθαι κἂν κατὰ τὸ γράμμα, τοῦ βουλήματος τοῦ νόμου προστάξαντος «ἐν τῷ τόπῳ ᾧ ἂν ἐκλέξηται κύριος ὁ θεὸς» ἑορτάζειν αὐτούς. ἀλλὰ καὶ τὸ πᾶσαν τὴν συναγωγὴν λιθοβολεῖν τοὺς τάδε ἢ τάδε ἡμαρτηκότας γενέσθαι μὴ δυνάμενον καὶ ἄλλα δὲ μυρία τῶν προστεταγμένων, σημεῖόν ἐστι τοῦ βιβλίου **τῆς ἀποστασίας**, καὶ ὅτι «οὐκ ἔστιν ἔτι προφήτης», καὶ ὅτι λέγουσι· «σημεῖα οὐκ εἴδομεν» ἔτι· ἀφεῖλε γὰρ (φησὶ) κύριος «ἀπὸ τῆς Ἰουδαίας καὶ ἀπὸ τῆς Ἰερουσαλὴμ (κατὰ τὸν τοῦ Ἡσαΐου λόγον) ἰσχύοντα καὶ ἰσχύουσαν, γίγαντα καὶ ἰσχύοντα» καὶ τὰ λοιπὰ μέχρι «συνετοῦ ἀκροατοῦ».

— Therefore he, also, having separated from her, married, so to speak, another, having given «into the hands» of the former the bill of divorcement; wherefore they can no longer do the things enjoined on them by the law, because of the bill of divorcement. And a sign that she has received the bill of divorcement is this, that Jerusalem was destroyed along with what they called the sanctuary of the things in it which were believed to be holy, and with the altar of burnt offerings, and all the worship associated with it. And a further sign of the bill **of divorcement** is this, that they cannot keep their feasts, even though according to the letter of the law designedly commanded them, «in the place which the Lord God appointed» to them for keeping feasts; but there is this also, that the whole synagogue has become unable to stone those who have committed this or that sin; and thousands of things commanded are a sign of the bill **of divorcement**; and the fact that «there is no more a prophet», and that they say, «We no longer see signs»; for the Lord says, He has taken away «from Judæa and from Jerusalem, according to the word of Isaiah, Him that is mighty, and her that is mighty, a powerful giant,» etc., down to the words, «a prudent hearer».

— Greek text — E. Klostermann. *Origenes Werke, vol. 10.1-10.2*; [*Die griechischen christlichen Schriftsteller*]. Teubner, 10.1:1935; 10.2:1937. Retrieved from Thesaurus Linguae Graecae (stephanus.tlg.uci.edu).

— English translation — John Patrick. *Ante-Nicene Fathers, Vol. 9*. Christian Literature Publishing, 1896. Revised and edited for New Advent by Kevin Knight. Accessed at New Advent (newadvent. org/fathers).

— The context is divorce. Origen's use of τῆς ἀποστασίας in *bill of divorce* constructions, e.g. τοῦ βιβλίου τῆς ἀποστασίας and τὸ τῆς ἀποστασίας βιβλίον, is rare. Normally τοῦ ἀποστασίου is employed.

— DIVORCE

(191) Origen, Commentary on Matthew, 14.20

— Καὶ ταῦτα μὲν κατὰ μίαν διήγησιν λελέχθω εἰς τὸν περὶ τοῦ βιβλίου **τῆς ἀποστασίας** νόμον.

— And let these things be said according to our interpretation [the sole interpretation] of the law in regard to the bill of divorcement.

— Greek text — E. Klostermann. *Origenes Werke, vol. 10.1-10.2*; [*Die griechischen christlichen Schriftsteller*]. Teubner, 10.1:1935; 10.2:1937. Retrieved from Thesaurus Linguae Graecae (stephanus. tlg.uci.edu).

— English translation — John Patrick. *Ante-Nicene Fathers, Vol. 9*. Christian Literature Publishing, 1896. Revised and edited for New Advent by Kevin Knight. Accessed at New Advent (newadvent. org/fathers). The comment in square brackets is my own clarification.

— The context is divorce. Origen's use of τῆς ἀποστασίας in *bill of divorce* constructions, e.g. τοῦ βιβλίου τῆς ἀποστασίας and τὸ τῆς ἀποστασίας βιβλίον, is rare. Normally τοῦ ἀποστασίου is employed.

— DIVORCE

(192) Origen, Commentary on Matthew, 14.22

— Τίς οὖν οὐκ ἂν εὐλόγως ἐπαπορήσαι, τί δήποτε ζητουμένου τοῦ ἄρξοντος τῆς ἐκκλησίας τὸν μὲν τοιόνδε δίγαμον οὐ καθίσταμεν διὰ τὰς περὶ τοῦ γάμου λέξεις, τὸν δὲ μονόγαμον καὶ (εἰ τύχοι) μέχρι γήρως συμβιώσαντα τῇ γυναικὶ κρατοῦμεν ἄρχοντα, ἔσθ' ὅτε μηδὲ γυμνασά μενον εἰς ἀγνείαν καὶ σωφροσύνην; ἐκ δὴ τῶν εἰρημένων εἰς τὸν περὶ τοῦ βιβλίου **τῆς ἀποστασίας** νόμον ἐφίστημι μή ποτε, ἐπεὶ σύμβολόν ἐστι καὶ ὁ ἐπίσκοπος καὶ ὁ πρεσβύ τερος καὶ ὁ διάκονος ἀληθινῶν κατὰ τὰ ὀνόματα ταῦτα πραγμάτων, ἐβουλήθη αὐτοὺς συμβολικῶς μονογάμους καταστῆσαι, ἵν' ὁ δυνάμενος ἐπιστῆσαι τοῖς πράγμασιν εὕρῃ ἐκ τοῦ πνευματικοῦ νόμου ἀνάξιον ὄντα ἀρχῆς ἐκκλησιαστικῆς ἐκεῖνον, οὗ ἡ ψυχὴ οὐχ «εὗρε χάριν ἐναντίον» τοῦ ἀνδρὸς αὐτῆς τῷ εὑρῆσθαι «ἐν αὐτῇ ἄσχημον πρᾶγμα» καὶ ἀξίαν αὐτὴν γεγονέναι τοῦ τῆς ἀποστάσεως βιβλίου. δευτέρῳ γὰρ συνοική σασα ἡ τοιαύτη ψυχὴ καὶ παρὰ τῷ τοιούτῳ μισηθεῖσα οὐκέτι δύναται μετὰ τὸ δεύτερον βιβλίον τοῦ ἀπο στασίου ἐπανελθεῖν ἐπὶ τὸν πρότερον ἄνδρα. εἰκὸς μὲν οὖν καὶ ἄλλους παρὰ τοῖς πολλῷ ἡμῶν σοφωτέροις καὶ μᾶλλον βλέπειν τὰ τηλικαῦτα δυναμένοις εὑρεθήσεσθαι λόγους, εἴτε εἰς τὸν περὶ τοῦ **τῆς ἀποστασίας** βιβλίου νόμον εἴτε εἰς τὰ ἀποστολικὰ κωλύοντα διγάμους ἄρχειν τῆς ἐκκλησίας ἢ προκαθέζεσθαι προτετιμημένους ἐν αὐτῇ.

— Who, then, would not naturally be perplexed why at all, when a ruler of the church is being sought for, we do not appoint such a man, though he has been twice married, because of the expressions about marriage, but lay hold of the man who has been once married as our ruler, even if he chance to have lived to old age with his wife, and sometimes may not have been disciplined [exercised] in chastity and temperance? But, from what is said in the law about the bill **of divorcement**, I reflect whether, seeing that the bishop and the presbyter and the deacon are a symbol of things that truly exist in accordance with these names, he wished to appoint those who were figuratively once married, in order that he who is able to give attention to the matter, may find out from the spiritual law the one who was unworthy of ecclesiastical rule, whose soul did not find favour in the eyes of her husband because there had been found in her an unseemly thing, and she had become worthy of the bill of divorcement; for such a soul, having dwelt along with a second husband, and having been hated by such an one, can no longer, after the second bill of divorcement, return to her former husband. It is likely, therefore, also, that other arguments will be found by those who are wiser than we, and have more ability to see into such things, whether in the law about the bill **of divorcement**, or in the apostolic writings which prohibit those who have been twice married from ruling over the church or being preferred to preside over it.

— Greek text — E. Klostermann. *Origenes Werke, vol. 10.1-10.2*; [*Die griechischen christlichen Schriftsteller*]. Teubner, 10.1:1935; 10.2:1937. Retrieved from Thesaurus Linguae Graecae (stephanus. tlg.uci.edu).

— English translation — John Patrick. *Ante-Nicene Fathers, Vol. 9*. Christian Literature Publishing, 1896. Revised and edited for New

Advent by Kevin Knight. Accessed at New Advent (newadvent. org/fathers).
— The context is divorce. Origen's use of τῆς ἀποστασίας in *bill of divorce* constructions, e.g. τοῦ βιβλίου τῆς ἀποστασίας and τὸ τῆς ἀποστασίας βιβλίον, is rare. Normally τοῦ ἀποστασίου is employed.
— DIVORCE

(193) Origen, Commentary on Matthew, 17.26
— ἀποστέλλουσι τοὺς ἑαυτῶν μαθητὰς οἱ Φαρισαῖοι, ἀποστέλλουσι δὲ καὶ τοὺς Ἡρωδιανοὺς πευσομένους περὶ τοῦ φόρου. ποία γὰρ παγὶς ἦν ἐν τῷ ἀποκρίνεσθαι τὸν Ἰησοῦν, εἴτε βούλεται κῆνσον δίδοσθαι Καίσαρι εἴτε μή, εἰ μὴ (ὡς ἀποδεδώκαμεν) κωλύοντος μὲν αὐτοῦ διδόναι κῆνσον Καίσαρι, ἔμελλον Ἡρωδιανοὶ παραδιδόναι αὐτὸν Ῥωμαίοις, ὡς **ἀποστασίαν** διδάσκοντα.
— The Pharisees sent their own disciples, and they also sent Herodians, to probe [Jesus] on the poll tax. For it would be a snare no matter what he answered, whether he advised giving the tax to Caesar or not. If he said no (as we have rendered), banning paying the tax to Caesar, the Herodians were prepared to deliver him to the Romans as one teaching **sedition**.
— Greek text — E. Klostermann, *Origenes Werke, vol. 10.1-10.2*; [*Die griechischen christlichen Schriftsteller*]. Teubner, 10.1:1935; 10.2:1937. Retrieved from Thesaurus Linguae Graecae (stephanus. tlg.uci.edu).
— English translation — The translation is my own, as I could find no available translation for Origen's commentary on Matthew beyond the 14th chapter.
— The context is the wily effort of the Pharisees to snare Jesus on the burning question of whether Jews should pay the tax to Caesar. They figured they could condemn him no matter how he answered. If he opposed paying the tax to Caesar, the Herodians would deliver him to the Romans as teaching sedition against Roman authority.
— POLITICAL SEDITION OR REBELLION.

(194) Origen, Against Celsus, 6.45-46
— Εἶτ' ἐπεὶ τότε μάλιστα τὸ φαῦλον ἐν τῇ χύσει τῆς κακίας καὶ τῇ ἀκρότητι αὐτῆς εἶναι χαρακτηρίζεται, ὅτε ὑποκρίνεται τὸ κρεῖττον,

διὰ τοῦτο περὶ τὸν χείρονα γίνεται ἐκ συνεργίας τῆς τοῦ πατρὸς αὐτοῦ διαβόλου σημεῖα καὶ τέρατα καὶ δυνάμεις ψεύδους. Ὑπὲρ γὰρ τὰς εἰς τοὺς γόητας γινομένας ἀπὸ δαιμόνων συνεργίας πρὸς τὰ φαυλότατα τῶν ἀνθρώπους ἀπατώντων γίνεται συνεργία ἀπ᾽ αὐτοῦ τοῦ διαβόλου ἐπὶ ἀπάτῃ τοῦ γένους τῶν ἀνθρώπων. Λέγει δὲ ὁ Παῦλος περὶ τούτου τοῦ καλουμένου Ἀντιχρίστου διδάσκων καὶ παριστὰς μετά τινος ἐπικρύψεως, τίνα τρόπον ἐπιδημήσει καὶ πότε τῷ γένει τῶν ἀνθρώπων καὶ διὰ τί· ... λέγει δὲ οὕτως· «Ἐρωτῶμεν δὲ ὑμᾶς, ἀδελφοί, ὑπὲρ τῆς παρουσίας τοῦ κυρίου ἡμῶν Ἰησοῦ Χριστοῦ καὶ ἡμῶν ἐπισυναγωγῆς ἐπ᾽ αὐτόν, εἰς τὸ μὴ σαλευθῆναι ὑμᾶς ἀπὸ τοῦ νοὸς μηδὲ θροεῖσθαι, μήτε διὰ πνεύματος μήτε διὰ λόγου μήτε διὰ ἐπιστολῆς ὡς δι᾽ ἡμῶν, ὡς ὅτι ἐνέστηκεν ἡ ἡμέρα τοῦ κυρίου. Μή τις ὑμᾶς ἐξαπατήσῃ κατὰ μηδένα τρόπον, ὅτι, ἐὰν μὴ ἔλθῃ **ἡ ἀποστασία** πρῶτον καὶ ἀποκαλυφθῇ ὁ ἄνθρωπος τῆς ἁμαρτίας, ὁ υἱὸς τῆς ἀπωλείας, ὁ ἀντικείμενος καὶ ὑπεραιρόμενος ἐπὶ πάντα λεγόμενον θεὸν ἢ σέβασμα, ὥστε αὐτὸν εἰς τὸν ναὸν τοῦ θεοῦ καθίσαι, ἀποδεικνύντα ἑαυτὸν ὅτι ἐστὶ θεός. ... οὗ ἐστιν ἡ παρουσία κατ᾽ ἐνέργειαν τοῦ Σατανᾶ ἐν πάσῃ δυνάμει καὶ σημείοις καὶ τέρασι ψεύδους καὶ ἐν πάσῃ ἀπάτῃ ἀδικίας τοῖς ἀπολλυμένοις, ἀνθ᾽ ὧν τὴν ἀγάπην τῆς ἀληθείας οὐκ ἐδέξαντο εἰς τὸ σωθῆναι αὐτούς. Καὶ διὰ τοῦτο πέμπει αὐτοῖς ὁ θεὸς ἐνέργειαν πλάνης εἰς τὸ πιστεῦσαι αὐτοὺς τῷ ψεύδει, ἵνα κριθῶσιν ἅπαντες οἱ μὴ πιστεύσαντες τῇ ἀληθείᾳ ἀλλ᾽ εὐδοκήσαντες ἐν τῇ ἀδικίᾳ.»

— And, in the next place, since evil is especially characterized by its diffusion, and attains its greatest height when it simulates the appearance of the good, for that reason are signs, and marvels, and lying miracles found to accompany evil, through the co-operation of its father the devil. For, far surpassing the help which these demons give to jugglers (who deceive men for the basest of purposes), is the aid which the devil himself affords in order to deceive the human race. Paul, indeed, speaks of him who is called Antichrist, describing, though with a certain reserve, both the manner, and time, and cause of his coming to the human race. ... It is thus that the apostle expresses himself: «We beseech you, brethren, by the coming of our Lord Jesus Christ, and by our gathering together unto Him, that you be not soon shaken in mind, or be troubled, neither by word, nor by spirit, nor by letter as from us, as that the day of the Lord is at hand. Let no man

274

deceive you by any means: for that day shall not come , except there come a **falling away** first, and that man of sin be revealed, the son of perdition; who opposes and exalts himself above all that is called God, or that is worshipped; so that he sits in the temple of God, showing himself that he is God. … whose coming is after the working of Satan, with all power, and signs, and lying wonders, and with all deceivableness of unrighteousness in them that perish; because they received not the love of the truth, that they might be saved. And for this cause God shall send them strong delusion, that they should believe a lie; that they all might be damned who believed not the truth, but had pleasure in unrighteousness.»

— Greek text — M. Borret. *Origène. Contre Celse,* 4 vols. [*Sources chrétiennes* 132, 136, 147, 150]; Éditions du Cerf, 1:1967; 2:1968; 3-4:1969. Retrieved from Thesaurus Linguae Graecae (stephanus. tlg.uci.edu).

— English translation — Frederick Crombie. *Ante-Nicene Fathers, Vol. 4.* Christian Literature Publishing, 1885; repr. Hendrickson Publishers, 1995.

— The context is the antichrist who shall appear at the end of the age. Origen associates the falling away with the efforts of the antichrist to deceive the world, efforts enhanced by the supernatural power of the devil in signs and wonders.

— RELIGIOUS APOSTASY

(195) Origen, Fragments in Luke, fragment 236

— (236) Τοῦ μὲν γὰρ πλήθους τῶν μαθητῶν μεγάλη αἰνούντων φωνῇ τὸν θεὸν σιωπῶσιν οἱ λίθοι· σιωπησάντων δὲ τοῦ πλήθους τῶν μαθητῶν, ὅπερ, ἐὰν ἔλθῃ **ἡ ἀποστασία**, γίνεται, οἱ λίθοι κεκράξουσιν.

— When the multitude of the disciples praised God with a loud voice, the stones were silent. But when the multitude of disciples is silenced, as if **the apostasy** should come, it will happen [that] the stones shall cry out.

— Greek text — M. Rauer, *Origenes Werke, vol. 9, 2nd ed.* [Die griechischen christlichen Schriftsteller 49 (35)]. Akademie Verlag, 1959. Retrieved from Thesaurus Linguae Graecae (stephanus. tlg.uci.edu).

— English translation — The translation is my own as I could find no translation available.

—The context is the relationship between the church praising and the stones crying out. When the church is ultimately silenced by the apostasy, then the stones shall cry out.

— RELIGIOUS APOSTASY

(196) Origen, Fragments in Psalms, Psalm 119:118 (LXX 118:119)

— Καὶ πάλιν. Τί τὸ αἴτιον, ὅτι ἐξουδένωσας αὐτούς; ὅτι ἄδικον τὸ ἐνθύμημα αὐτῶν. Περὶ αὐτῶν φησιν ὁ προφήτης· «Οὐαὶ, τέκνα ἀποστάται!» Καὶ ἐν ἄλλοις· «Οὐαὶ αὐτοῖς ὅτι ἀπεπήδησαν ἀπ᾽ ἐμοῦ.» Τοὺς οὖν τοιούτους οὐ παιδεύει, οὐ μαστίζει κατὰ τοὺς ἀγαπημένους υἱοὺς παρ᾽ αὐτοῦ, ἀλλὰ ἐξουθενεῖ, φάσκων πρὸς ἕκαστον·Παιδεύσει σε **ἡ ἀποστασία** σου, καὶ ἡ κακία σου ἐλέγξει σε.

— And again. What is the reason that they were despised? Because their minds were bent on unrighteousness. Concerning them the prophet says, «Woe to the apostate children!» And in another place, «Woe unto them! for they have fled from me.» He does not discipline such children. He does not whip [them] like the beloved sons with him but despises [them], affirming to each one, «Your **apostasy** shall discipline you, and your evil shall reprove you.»

— J.B. Pitra. *Analecta sacra spicilegio Solesmensi parata, vols. 2 and* 3. Tusculum, 2:1884; 3:1883. Retrieved from Thesaurus Linguae Graecae (stephanus.tlg.uci.edu).

— English Translation — The translation is my own as I could find none available.

—The context is Israel's apostasy from God. Note that ἀποστασία (apostasia) *apostasy* is associated with κακία (kakia) *evil.*

— RELIGIOUS APOSTASY

(197) Origen, Homilies in Psalms, Psalm 77 (LXX 78), Homily 2, chapter 3

— Λέγει οὖν ἐκεῖ ὁ κύριος «ἐν τῷ ἐπιστρέφειν με τὴν αἰχμαλωσίαν τοῦ λαοῦ μου, ἐν τῷ ἰᾶσθαί με τὸν Ἰσραήλ. Καὶ ἀποκαλυφθήσεται ἡ ἀδικία Ἐφραὶμ καὶ ἡ κακία Σαμαρείας, ὅτι ἠργάσαντο ψευδῆ· καὶ κλέπτης πρὸς αὐτὸν εἰσελεύσεται, ἐκδιδύσκων λῃστὴς ἐν τῇ ὁδῷ αὐτοῦ, ὅπως συνᾴδωσιν ὡς ᾄδοντες ἐν ταῖς καρδίαις αὐτῶν.» Τί οὖν βούλεται ταῦτα περὶ τοῦ Ἐφραῒμ ἐν τῷ Ὠσηέ, ἵνα νοήσωμεν ὑψηλότερον παρὰ τὰ εἰρημένα τὸ «υἱοὶ Ἐφραῒμ ἐντείνοντες καὶ βάλλοντες τόξοις»; Ἀπὸ τῆς φυλῆς Ἐφραΐμ, ἀποστήσαντος τὰς δέκα φυλὰς τοῦ Ἱεροβοάμ, οὐκ ἠρκέσθη τῷ **τὴν ἀποστασίαν** πεποιηκέναι, ἀλλὰ εὐλαβηθεὶς μήπως ἐπανέλθωσι προφάσει τοῦ ναοῦ καὶ τῆς φατρίας πρὸς τὸν Ῥοβοάμ, ἀνέπλασεν ἑορτὰς ἀπὸ τῆς καρδίας αὐτοῦ ἑτέρας παρὰ τὰς ἑορτὰς τοῦ θεοῦ, ἐποίησέ τε καὶ δύο δαμάλεις χρυσὰς καὶ ἔθηκεν αὐτὰς ἐν τῇ κληρονομίᾳ τῶν δέκα φυλῶν.

— The Lord says there: «When I turned the captivity of my people, when I healed Israel, both the injustice of Ephraim and the evil of Samaria were revealed, because they carried out lied, and a thief shall enter him, and bandit shall rob on his road, whenever they are singing together as singers in their hearts.» What, then, do these things in Hosea intend concerning Ephraim, so that we may understand in a loftier way the saying, «sons of Ephraim stretching with bows and shooting arrows»? From the tribe of Ephraim, when the ten tribes separated from Jeroboam, he did not just make a **separation**, but, making sure that they did not have the temple and its association with Rehoboam as a motive to return, he made up out of his heart feasts that differed from the feasts of God and also made two golden calves and place them in the allotment of the ten tribes.

— Greek text — L. Perrone (with M. Pradel; E. Prinzivalli; A. Cacciari). *Origenes Werke, vol. 13, Die neuen Psalmenhomilien. Eine kritische Edition des Codex Monacensis Graecus 314*; [*Die griechischen christlichen Schriftsteller der ersten Jahrhunderte. Neue Folge 19*]. De Gruyter, 2015. Retrieved from Thesaurus Linguae Graecae (stephanus.tlg.uci.edu).

— Joseph W. Trigg. *Origen: Homilies on the Psalms: Codex Monacensis Graecus 314; [The Fathers of the Church]*. The Catholic University of America Press, 2020.

— The context is the apostasy of the ten tribes under the leadership of Jeroboam. Notice the association of apostasy with rejecting God's chosen leadership (Rehoboam), rejecting God's temple, inventing new feasts in opposition to God's feasts, and making the golden calves.

— RELIGIOUS APOSTASY

(198) Origen, Scholia on Revelation, scholion 38

— Ὁρμῇ ὁ δράκων πολεμήσας μετὰ τῶν ἀγγέλων καὶ θλιβείς, βληθεὶς κάτω ἐκ τοῦ οὐρανοῦ ἔσυρεν πίπτων τὸ τρίτον τῶν ἀστέρων, ἅτινα ἄστρα θείας δυνάμεις οὔσας συναπεστατηκέναι αὐτῷ καὶ συγκατενεχθῆναι τῷ δράκοντι, ὡς Ἡσαΐας φησίν· «πῶς ἐξέπεσεν ὁ ἑωσφόρος ἐξ οὐρανοῦ». καὶ ἐστάθη ἐπὶ τὴν ἄμμον τῆς θαλάσσης ὁ ἀπόστολός φησιν· «ἀνθ᾽ ὧν τὴν ἀγάπην τοῦ θεοῦ οὐκ ἐδέξαντο εἰς τὸ σωθῆναι αὐτούς, διὰ τοῦτο πέμπει αὐτοῖς ὁ θεὸς ἐνέργειαν πλάνης εἰς τὸ πιστεῦσαι αὐτοὺς τῷ ψεύδει.» τοῦ μὲν γὰρ ἐρχομένου καὶ γνώμῃ τὴν **ἀποστασίαν** ἀνακεφαλαιουμένου πρὸς ἑαυτὸν καὶ αὐτεξουσίου πράξαντος ὅσα καὶ πράξει καὶ «εἰς τὸν ναὸν τοῦ θεοῦ καθήσαντος», ἵνα ὡς Χριστὸν αὐτὸν προσκυνήσωσιν οἱ πλανώμενοι ὑπ᾽ αὐτοῦ, διὸ καὶ δικαίως «εἰς τὴν κάμινον βληθήσονται τοῦ πυρός».

— Once the dragon had waged a fiery war against the angels, and was afflicted and cast down from heaven, he drew the third part of the stars down along with his fall. These stars, which are divine powers, he made rebel along with him and be cast down [from heaven] with him, as indeed Isaiah says, «How is Lucifer fallen from heaven?» And he stood upon the sand of the sea, the Apostle says: «Because they received not the love of God, that they might be saved. And for this cause God sends them a strong delusion, that they should believe a lie.» For, on the one hand, he [sc. the Antichrist] comes, and of his own accord he recapitulates [sums up] all the **apostasy** in his own person, and accomplishes whatever he shall do according to his own free will, and «is seated in the temple of God», so that his dupes may adore him as the Christ [the annointed], which is why they shall deservedly «be cast into the furnace of fire».

— Greek text — C.I. Dyobouniotes and A. von Harnack. *Der Scholien-Kommentar des Origenes zur Apokalypse Johannis; [Texte und Untersuchungen 38.3]*. Hinrichs, 1911. Retrieved from Thesaurus Linguae Graecae (stephanus.tlg.uci.edu).

— English translation — P. Tzamalikos. *An Ancient Commentary on the Book of Revelation: A Critical Edition of the Scholia in Apocalypsin*. Cambridge University Press, 2013. Kindle Edition. Comments in square brackets are my own clarifications.

— The context is the tribulation when Satan is cast to earth and introduces the apostasy and delusion associated with the antichrist.

Notice that apostasy from God is summed up in the antichrist. Notice that apostasy is associated with adoring the antichrist as Christ.
— RELIGIOUS APOSTASY

(199) Origen, Scholia on Revelation, scholion 38

— οὗ τὴν παρουσίαν Ἰωάννης ἐνταῦθα οὕτως ἐμήνυσεν. ἵνα οὖν μή τις αὐτὸν θεϊκῇ δυνάμει δόξῃ ποιεῖν τὰ σημεῖα, ἀλλὰ μαγικῇ ἐνεργείᾳ, ἔφη· καὶ πλανᾷ τοὺς κατοικοῦντας ἐπὶ τῆς γῆς. καὶ οὐδέν γε καὶ θαυμαστὸν εἰ τῶν δαιμονίων καὶ ἀποστατικῶν πνευμάτων ὑπουργούντων αὐτῷ δι' αὐτῶν ποιῇ σημεῖα, ἐν οἷς πλανήσῃ τοὺς κατοικοῦντας ἐπὶ τῆς γῆς. καὶ τὸν ἀριθμὸν δὲ τοῦ ὀνόματος αὐτοῦ φησιν καὶ ἄλλα τινὰ καὶ εἶναι τὸν ἀριθμὸν χξϛ΄, ὅ ἐστιν ἑκατοντάδες ἓξ καὶ δεκάδες ἓξ καὶ μονάδες ἓξ εἰς ἀνακεφαλαίωσιν πάσης τῆς ἐν τοῖς ἑξακισχιλίοις ἔτεσιν γεγονυίας **ἀποστασίας**.

— Whose coming John has thus described at this point. And in order that no one should believe that he (sc. the Antichrist) performs these wonders by divine power, but by the working of magic, he (sc. John) said: And he deceiveth them that dwell on the earth. And it is no surprise that if, since the daemons and apostate spirits are at his service, he, by means of them, performs wonders, by which he leads astray those that dwell on earth. He further declares the number of his name, and certain other things; indeed he says that this number is six hundred and sixty-six; that is, six times a hundred, six times ten, and six units. This is a summing up of the whole of that **apostasy** which has taken place during six thousand years.

— Greek text — C.I. Dyobouniotes and A. von Harnack. *Der Scholien-Kommentar des Origenes zur Apokalypse Johannis*; [*Texte und Untersuchungen 38.3*]. Hinrichs, 1911. Retrieved from Thesaurus Linguae Graecae (stephanus.tlg.uci.edu).

— English translation — P. Tzamalikos. *An Ancient Commentary on the Book of Revelation: A Critical Edition of the Scholia in Apocalypsin*. Cambridge University Press, 2013. Kindle Edition.

— The context is the antichrist: his coming, his signs, his powers, and his number. The number according to Origen sums up all the apostasy for the past six thousand years.
— RELIGIOUS APOSTASY

(200) Origen, Scholia on Revelation, scholion 38

— εἰ γὰρ ἡμέρα κυρίου ὡς χίλια ἔτη, ἐν δὲ ἓξ ἡμέραις συνετελέσθη τὰ γεγονότα, φανερὸν ὅτι ἡ συντέλεια αὐτῶν τὸ ἑξακισχιλιοστὸν ἔτος. καὶ διὰ τοῦτο ἐν παντὶ τούτῳ τῷ χρόνῳ πλασθεὶς ἐν ἀρχῇ ὁ ἄνθρωπος διὰ τῶν χειρῶν τοῦ θεοῦ, τουτέστιν υἱοῦ καὶ πνεύματος, γίνεται κατ᾽ εἰκόνα καὶ ὁμοίωσιν θεοῦ, τοῦ μὲν ἀχύρου ἀποσκευαζομένου, ὅπερ ἐστὶν **ἡ ἀποστασία**, τοῦ δὲ σίτου εἰς ἀποθήκην ἀναλαμβανομένου, ὅπερ ἐστὶν οἱ πρὸς θεὸν πίστει καρποφοροῦντες.

— For if «one day is with the Lord as a thousand years», and in six days [the] created things were completed, it is evident that the sixth thousandth year marks the consummation of them. And therefore throughout all this time, man, who was moulded at the beginning by the hands of God, that is, of the Son and of the Spirit, is made after the image and likeness of God. The chaff, which is **the apostasy**, is cast away; but the wheat, that is, all those whose faith in God brings forth fruit, is gathered into the barn.

— Greek text — C.I. Dyobouniotes and A. von Harnack. *Der Scholien-Kommentar des Origenes zur Apokalypse Johannis*; [*Texte und Untersuchungen 38.3*]. Hinrichs, 1911. Retrieved from Thesaurus Linguae Graecae (stephanus.tlg.uci.edu).

— English translation — P. Tzamalikos. *An Ancient Commentary on the Book of Revelation: A Critical Edition of the Scholia in Apocalypsin*. Cambridge University Press, 2013. Kindle Edition. Comments in square brackets are my own clarifications.

— The context is the sifting and sorting of men at the end of the age. Notice that *apostasia* is the sin of the ungodly who will perish in eternal punishment.

— RELIGIOUS APOSTASY

(201) Origen, Scholia on Revelation, scholion 38

— καὶ διὰ τοῦτο εἰς τὸ θηρίον τὸ ἐρχόμενον ἀνακεφαλαίωσις γίνεται πάσης τῆς ἀδικίας καὶ παντὸς δόλου, ἵνα ἐν αὐτῷ συνρεύσασα πᾶσα δύναμις ἀποστατικὴ εἰς τὴν κάμινον βληθῇ τοῦ πυρός. καταλλήλως οὖν καὶ τὸ ὄνομα αὐτοῦ ἕξει τὸν ἀριθμὸν χξς΄, ἀνακεφαλαιούμενον ἐν ἑαυτῷ τὴν πρὸ τοῦ κατακλυσμοῦ πᾶσαν τῆς κακίας ἐπιμιξίαν ἐξ ἀγγελικῆς **ἀποστασίας** γεγενημένης·

— This is why in this beast, when he comes, a recapitulation of all sorts of iniquity and of every deceit takes place, in order that all rebellious power, which converges in him, may be thrown into the furnace of fire. Fittingly, therefore, shall his name have the number six hundred and sixty-six. For in his own person, all wickedness [the whole mixture of wickedness] which took place previous to the deluge due to the **apostasy** of the angels, will be recapitulated [summed up].
— Greek text — C.I. Dyobouniotes and A. von Harnack. *Der Scholien-Kommentar des Origenes zur Apokalypse Johannis*; [*Texte und Untersuchungen 38.3*]. Hinrichs, 1911. Retrieved from Thesaurus Linguae Graecae (stephanus.tlg.uci.edu).
— English translation — P. Tzamalikos. *An Ancient Commentary on the Book of Revelation: A Critical Edition of the Scholia in Apocalypsin*. Cambridge University Press, 2013. Kindle Edition. The comments in square brackets are my own clarifications.
— The context is the antichrist. He is the summing up of the whole mixture of wickedness which took place in the apostasy of the angels prior to the flood.
— RELIGIOUS APOSTASY

(202) Origen, Selections in Deuteronomy, (Migne 12.808)
— Ὁ Θεὸς τοὺς αὐτὸν προσκυνοῦντας οὐ συγχωρῶν δαίμοσι συνάπτεσθαι, ἀλλὰ τοὺς ἅπαξ αὐτὸν ἐγνωκότας ἐκτὸς εἶναι κελεύων τῆς πρὸς ἐκείνους διαθέσεως, καὶ παραζηλῶν ἐν **τῇ ἀποστασίᾳ** τῶν λαῶν, τὰς μελλούσας αὐτοῖς προλέγει τιμωρίας διὰ τὴν πονηρίαν τῶν ἐπιτηδευμάτων αὐτῶν.
— God disallows those worshipping him to be joined to demons, indeed commands those who have once come to know him to be separate from any disposition with them, fumes with jealousy for those of his people involved in **apostasy**, and foretells coming retribution on account of their evil practices.
— Greek test — J.P. Migne. *Patrologiae cursus completus* (*series Graeca 12*). Migne, 1857-1866. Retrieved from Thesaurus Linguae Graecae (stephanus.tlg.uci.edu).
— English translation — The translation is my own as I could find none available.

— The context is Israel's apostasy. Notice the association of apostasy with evil doings and concourse with demons.
— RELIGIOUS APOSTASY

(203) Origen, Selections in Psalms, Psalm 132 (133) (Migne 12.1652)
— Ἐν τῷ Δευτερονομίῳ Μωϋσῆς μὲν τὸ ὄρος τοῦτο ὀνομάζει Ἀερμών· οἱ Φοίνικες δὲ καλοῦσιν αὐτὸ Σανιώρ, οἱ δὲ Ἀμορραῖοι Σανείρ. Ἔστι δὲ πέραν τοῦ Ἰορδάνου. Λόγος δὲ τοὺς ἀποστατήσαντας τῶν ἀγγέλων ἐπὶ τοῦτο τὸ ὄρος ἐσκέφθαι περὶ **τῆς ἀποστασίας** αὐτῶν καὶ συνθήκας πεποιηκέναι.
— In Deuteronomy Moses named the mountain Hermon. The Phoenicians called it Sanior, and the Amorites called it Senir. It is on the other side of the Jordan. There is a tale that it was upon this mountain that the apostate angels plotted their **apostasy** and made a covenant.
— Greek test — J.P. Migne. *Patrologiae cursus completus* (*series Graeca 12*). Migne, 1857-1866. Retrieved from Thesaurus Linguae Graecae (stephanus.tlg.uci.edu).
— English translation — The translation is my own as I could find none available.
— The context is mount Hermon. It speaks of a tradition associating Mt. Hermon with the apostasy of the angels.
— RELIGIOUS APOSTASY

(204) Palladius of Galatia, The Dialogue of Palladius on the Life of Chrysostom, Chapter 20
— Ἐνεὸς δὲ γενόμενος ἐπὶ πολὺ ὁ Θεόδωρος εἶπεν· <Ὁ ΔΙΑΚ.> Τί οὖν ἐροῦμεν πρὸς ταῦτα, πάτερ; μὴ ἄρα ἐσχάτη ὥρα ἐστίν, καὶ **ἡ ἀποστασία**, κατὰ τὸν Παῦλον, διὰ τούτων λαμβάνει τὴν εἴσοδον, «ἵνα λοιπὸν ἀποκαλυφθῇ ὁ υἱὸς τῆς ἀπωλείας ὁ ἀντικείμενος»; τὸ γὰρ τοὺς κακοὺς εὐημερεῖν καὶ δια πράττεσθαι ταῦτα καὶ χρονίζειν καὶ ἰσχύειν, καὶ τοὺς καλοὺς θλίβεσθαι καὶ λεηλατεῖσθαι, εἰς φρίκην με ἄγει τοῦ πλησιάζειν ἐκεῖνον.
— Long was Theodorus speechless with distress, and at last said <Deac.> What shall we say to all this, father? Can it be that it is the last hour, and **the falling away** of which Paul speaks is being ushered

in by these events, «that the son of perdition, who opposeth, may be revealed»? The thought of the wicked prospering, and succeeding in their aims, and going on for so long, and having such power, while the good are being persecuted and pillaged, fills me with dread that this person is near at hand.

— Greek text — P.R. Coleman-Norton. *Palladii dialogus de vita S. Joanni Chrysostomi.* Cambridge University Press, 1928. Retrieved from Thesaurus Linguae Graecae (stephanus.tlg.uci.edu).

— English translation — Herbert Moore. *The Dialogue of Palladius Concerning the Life of Chrysostom; [Translations of Christian Literature, Series 1, Greek Texts].* Society for Promoting Christian Knowledge, Macmillan, 1921. Transcribed by Roger Pearse for the Tertullian Project, 2006. Accessed at tertullian.org/fathers.

— The context is the apostasy of the last days. Palladius clearly regards the apostasy as the necessary precursor to the son of perdition.

— RELIGIOUS APOSTASY

(205) Palladius of Galatia, Lausiac History, Letter to Lausum

— ὧν πρωτεύουσιν εἰς ἀπώλειαν οἱ τῷ αὐτῷ πάθει τῆς οὐρανίου διαγωγῆς ἐκπεσόντες, οἱ ἐν ἀέρι πετόμενοι δαίμονες τῶν ἐν τοῖς οὐρανοῖς ἀποδράσαντες διδασκάλων. ... δεῖ γὰρ τὴν κατὰ θεὸν ἀσκουμένην ψυχὴν ἢ μανθάνειν πιστῶς ἃ οὐκ οἶδεν, ἢ διδάσκειν σαφῶς ἃ ἔγνω. εἰ δὲ ὁπότερον μὴ βούληται εἰ δύναται, μανίαν νοσεῖ. ἀρχὴ γὰρ **ἀποστασίας** διδασκαλίας κόρος καὶ ἀνορεξία λόγου, ὃν ἀεὶ πεινᾷ ἡ ψυχὴ τοῦ φιλοθέου. ἴσχυε οὖν καὶ ὑγίαινε καὶ ἀνδρίζου, καὶ χαρίσηταί σοι ὁ θεὸς τὸ μεταδιώκειν τὴν γνῶσιν τοῦ Χριστοῦ.

— Their leaders on the road to destruction are those who have fallen from the heavenly life, the demons who fly in the air having fled from their teachers in heaven. ... For the soul that is being trained according to God's purpose must be either learning faithfully what it does not know, or teaching clearly what it knows. But if it wants to do neither, though able to do them, then it is mad. For to be sated with teaching and unable to bear the word, for which the soul of him who loves God is always hungry, is the beginning of **apostasy**. Be strong then and of sound mind and play the man, and may God grant you to pursue closely the knowledge of Christ.

— Greek text — A.C. Butler. *The Lausiac History of Palladius, vol. 2.* Cambridge University Press, 1904 (repr. Olms, 1967). Retrieved from Thesaurus Linguae Graecae (stephanus.tlg.uci.edu).
—English translation — W.K. Lowther Clarke. *The Lausiac History of Palladius;* [*Translations of Christian Literature, Series 1, Greek Texts*]. Society for Promoting Christian Knowledge, Macmillan, 1918.
— The context is an observation on the root of apostasy, which is having no heart for the teaching of the Lord and his word.
— RELIGIOUS APOSTASY

(206) Polychronius bishop of Apamea, Commentary in Ezekiel, Fragments, section 2, chapter 29
— Σημαίνει δὲ τὴν ἐπὶ τοῦ Ἰωακεὶμ βοήθειαν ὑπὸ τοῦ Αἰγυπτίου γενομένην Ἰουδαίοις, κατὰ τὸ τέταρτον ἔτος τῆς τούτου βασιλείας, ἡνίκα ὁ μὲν Ἰωακεὶμ ὑπὸ φόρον τυγχάνων τῷ Ναβουχοδονόσορ, ἀποστατῶν ὡμολογημένων, ὁ δὲ Αἰγύπτιος ὑπισχνεῖτο τὴν αὐτοῦ βοήθειαν· καὶ ἡττηθεὶς ἀνεχώρησεν, ὡς κἂν ταῖς Βασιλείαις εἴρηται, καὶ σαφέστερον ὁ Ἱερεμίας ἐν τοῖς οἰκείοις διδάσκει λόγοις· τὸ οὖν «ἐγενήθης ῥάβδος καλαμίνη τῷ οἴκῳ Ἰσραήλ», ἀντὶ τοῦ ὑποσχόμενος τὴν βοήθειαν, ὠφέλησας μὲν οὐδέν, ἔβλαψας δέ, δίκην καλάμου περιπαρεὶς τοῖς ἐπιστηριζομένοις. —Ἀντὶ τοῦ ὅτ᾽ ἂν παρὰ γνώμην ἐμὴν τὴν σὴν ἐπικαλεσάμενοι βοήθειαν, ἔγνωσας ἐκ τοῦ τέλους **τῆς ἀποστασίας** τὸ ἐπιβλαβές.
— The aid which came to the Jews from the Egyptians in the days of Jehoiakim became evident in the fourth year of his kingship, when Jehoiakim came under tribute to Nebuchadnezzar, as a result of his confessed sedition. The Egyptian had promised him aid, but when he was defeated, he retreated as if he would speak with the kings. And this Jeremiah plainly taught (foretold) with his own words, «you shall be a staff of reed to the house of Israel» instead of supporting him with aid. You profited nothing, but rather injured them, the judgment of the reed piercing those who leaned on it. — Whenever you summoned your own aid beyond my counsel, you have learned to the utmost degree the pain of **apostasy**.
— Greek text — E. Moutsoulas. *Πολυχρόνιος Ἀπαμείας (Μέρος Α΄)* [*Βιβλιοθήκη Ἑλλήνων Πατέρων καὶ Ἐκκλησιαστικων Συγγραφέων*

(*ΒΕΠΕΣ*) *88*]. Ἀποστολικὴ Διακονία τῆς Ἐκκλησίας τῆς Ἑλλάδος, 2007. Retrieved from Thesaurus Linguae Graecae (stephanus. tlg.uci.edu).

— English translation — The translation is my own as I could find none available.

— The context is Jehoiakim becoming a tributary of Nebuchadnezzar because he sought the aid of Egypt agreeing with her in sedition against Babylon. Israel's sedition against Babylon was apostasy against God. Ultimately, Israel learned the pain of apostasy.

— RELIGIOUS APOSTASY

(207) Proclus, Mystagogy on Baptism, chapter 2, section 10

— Ἀποτάσσομαί σοι. Ὡς ἐξ ἀλλοτρίου σοι, τὰ σκεύη μετένεγκε· οὐ γίνομαί σοι σπήλαιον ἀτοπίας, οὐ τηρῶ σῆς ἐν ἐμοὶ κακίας τὰ ὄργανα, οὐ γίνομαί σοι λειτουργὸς καθ' ἑαυτοῦ πρὸς ἀπώλειαν, οὐ διακονοῦμαί σοι πρὸς μοιχείαν, οὐχ ὑπηρετοῦμαί σοι πρὸς φθόνον, οὐ λειτουργῶ πρὸς τὴν μέθην, εἰς κλοπὴν οὐ προσέπομαι. (10) Ἄν ψεῦδος ἐπιτάξῃς, οὐ πείθομαι· ἂν πορνείαν, ἀναίνομαι· ἂν ὡς πρὸς ὑγίειαν ἐπῳδὴν ὑπογράψῃς, οὐ δέχομαι. Μισῶ σου καὶ τὴν δοκοῦσαν εὐεργεσίαν ὡς δέλεαρ· οὐχ ὡς ἰατρὸς θεραπεύεις ἀλλ' ὡς ἐχθρὸς ἐκτιτρώσκεις, οὐχ ὡς συμπαθής μοι τὴν ὑγίειαν προσάγεις ἀλλ' ὡς κακὸς **τὴν ἀποστασίαν** διδάσκεις.

— I renounce you. As a foreigner to you, I have transferred my goods. I will not be for you a grotto of disorderly conduct. I will not keep the instruments of your evil in myself. I will not be your servant against myself unto perdition. I will not serve you with adultery. I will not serve you with envy. I will not serve you with drunkenness. I will not accompany you in thievery. If you command a lie, I will not submit. If fornication, I will refuse. If you would underwrite me with the charm of health, I will not receive it. I hate your seeming advantages as bait [for your snare]. You do not heal like a doctor but as an enemy you bring to miscarriage. You do not bring health as my sympathizer, but you teach **apostasy** as an evil man.

— Greek text — F.J. Leroy. *L'homilétique de Proclus de Constantinople*; [*Studi e Testi 247*]. Biblioteca Apostolica Vaticana, 1967.

— English translation — The translation is my own. There is a translation available by Juliette Day, but the copy I ordered from Book Depository US, an Amazon subsidiary, has been in "On the way, but running late" status for weeks. It did not arrive in time for me to use her translation in this book.

— The context is the rejection of Satan, including his lies and false blessings. Satan pretends to sympathize with our needs and seek our wholeness, but he is actually evil and teaches apostasy from God.

— RELIGIOUS APOSTASY

(208) Procopius of Gaza, Commentary in Isaiah, (Migne 87.2, 1993)

— ἢ περὶ τῶν τῆς ὄντως ἐκπεπτωκότων ζωῆς, ὁποῖοι διὰ **τῆς ἀποστασίας** οἱ δαίμονες, μὴ ἔχοντες ἐν ἑαυτοῖς τὸν ζῶντα τοῦ Θεοῦ λόγον· ἢ καὶ ὅτι ἄτοπον περὶ τῶν ἔτι ζώντων ἐπερωτᾶν τοὺς ἐν τῇ γῇ κειμένους.

— Or concerning those who have truly fallen from life. As the demons [who fell] through **their apostasy,** not having in themselves the living word of God. Or also that it is out of place to inquire of those laying in the ground for information concerning those yet living.

— Greek text — J.P. Migne. *Patrologiae cursus completus* (*series Graeca 87.2*). Migne, 1857-1866. Retrieved from Thesaurus Linguae Graecae (stephanus.tlg.uci.edu).

— English translation — The translation is my own as I could find none available.

— The context is the errors men fall into. One of the errors mentioned is a full-blown fall from life, which is compared to the apostasy of the demons. Notice that *falling away* and *apostasia* are used synonymously.

— RELIGIOUS APOSTASY

(209) Severianius, Fragments in Hebrews, Prologue

— Οἱ αἱρετικοί φασι μὴ εἶναι Παύλου τὴν ἐπιστολήν, καὶ τούτου πρώτην ἀπόδειξιν προφέρουσι τὸ μὴ προτετάχθαι αὐτοῦ τὸ ὄνομα ὡς ἐν ταῖς ἄλλαις ἐπιστολαῖς· δεύτερον τὸ τὴν φράσιν ἄλλην εἶναι, τοῦτ' ἔστι ξένην παρὰ τὴν Παύλου καὶ τὴν κατασκευήν. δεῖ τοίνυν εἰδέναι ὅτι Παῦλος ἐμισεῖτο ὑπὸ Ἰουδαίων ὡς **ἀποστασίαν** νόμου διδάσκων, διὰ τοῦτο καὶ κινδυνεύσας ἐν Ἱεροσολύμοις καὶ μόλις διαφυγὼν ἐπέμφθη εἰς Ῥώμην.

— The heretics assert that the epistle is not of Paul, The first argument they present is that his name is not attached as in his other epistles. The second is that the speech is distinct, that is, it is foreign from the diction and arrangement of Paul. Accordingly, it ought to be understood that Paul was hated by the Jews as teaching **apostasy** from the law, therefore his life was in danger in Jerusalem, and having barely escaped, he was sent to Rome.

— Greek text — K. Staab. *Pauluskommentar aus der griechischen Kirche aus Katenenhandschriften gesammelt.* Aschendorff, 1933. Retrieved from Thesaurus Linguae Graecae (stephanus.tlg.uci.edu).

— English translation — The translation is my own as I could find none available.

— The context answers the non-Pauline authorship argument by pointing out that Paul was rejected as a heretic who taught apostasy from the law and was worthy of death. In other words, it would be counterproductive to put his name on the document.

— RELIGIOUS APOSTASY

(210) Severianus, On the Prodigal Son, (Migne p. 631)

— πολλοὺς μὲν ἔχει τοὺς πόνους, μικρὰν δὲ τὴν ἀπόλαυσιν. Αὐτὴ πᾶσα ἡ ζωὴ ἡμῶν πλείονι κόπῳ μᾶλλον ἢ εὐφροσύνῃ συνέζευκται. «Αἱ ἡμέραι γὰρ τῶν ἐτῶν ἡμῶν ἐν αὐτοῖς ἑβδομήκοντα ἔτη. · καὶ τὸ πλεῖον αὐτῶν, κόπος καὶ πόνος». τὸ δὲ λοιπόν, ἡ ἔνδεια αὐτὸν ἐπαιδαγώγησε, καὶ ἡ θλίψις ἐπέστρεψε. «Παιδεύει σε γὰρ **ἡ ἀποστασία** σου καὶ ἡ κακία σου ἐλέγξει σε».

— Many are the sorrows of life, few the enjoyments. This whole life of ours is yoked more with much pain than with gladness. «For the days of our years are seventy years. And the majority of them is labor and sorrow.» As for the rest, lack instructs a man, and tribulation corrects him. «For your **apostasy** shall educate you and your evil shall reprove you.»

— Greek text — J.P. Migne. *Patrologiae cursus completus* (*series Graeca* 59). Migne, 1857-1866. Retrieved from Thesaurus Linguae Graecae (stephanus.tlg.uci.edu).

— English translation — The translation is my own as I could find none available.

— The context is the hardships of life, with a particular focus on those hardships we bring on ourselves when we stray into evil and apostasy.

— RELIGIOUS APOSTASY

(211) Severianus, Fragments in 2 Thessalonians, 2:1-4, section 332-334

— Παραινεῖ αὐτοὺς μὴ θορυβεῖσθαι ἀκαίρως πρὸ τῆς ἐπιφανείας τοῦ κυρίου, μήτε εἰ προφῆται λέγοιεν εἶναι ἐν οἷς πνεῦμα πλάνης ἐστίν, μήτε εἰ λόγοι καὶ φῆμαι περὶ τοῦ κυρίου κατασπείροιντο, μήτε εἰ ἐπιστολήν τινες πλασάμενοι κομίζοιεν ὡς ἡμετέραν. «ὅτι ἐὰν μὴ ἔλθη **ἡ ἀποστασία** πρῶτον καὶ ἀποκαλυφθῇ ὁ ἄνθρωπος τῆς ἁμαρτίας, ὁ υἱὸς τῆς ἀπωλείας, ὁ ἀντικείμενος καὶ ὑπεραιρόμενος ἐπὶ πάντα λεγόμενον θεὸν ἢ σέβασμα.» μὴ προσδοκᾶτε, φησί, τὸν σωτῆρα πρὸ τοῦ πλάνου ὃν δεῖ πρότερον ἐλθεῖν, καθὼς ἔφην. «ὑπὲρ πάντα θεὸν ἢ σέβασμα ὑπεραιρόμενον», οἷον ὑπὲρ πᾶσαν εἰδωλολατρείαν … περὶ δὲ τῆς ἐσομένης πλάνης τῶν ἀνθρώπων καὶ αὐτὸς ὁ σωτὴρ προεῖπεν ὅτι δυσχερὲς ἐλθόντα αὐτὸν εὑρεῖν τὴν πίστιν ἐπὶ τῆς γῆς. ὁ ἄνθρωπος τῆς ἁμαρτίας, τοῦτ' ἔστι ὁ ἀντίχριστος· ἥξει γὰρ εἰς Ἱεροσόλυμα ὡς ἀνοικοδομήσων τὸν ναόν, καὶ στήσεται ἐν τῷ ἁγίῳ τόπῳ θεὸν ἑαυτὸν ἀναγορεύσων. ὁ ἀντικείμενος καὶ ὑπεραιρόμενος ὑπὲρ πάντα μὲν λεγόμενον θεόν, ἀντὶ τοῦ ὑπὲρ πᾶσαν εἰδωλολατρείαν· ὑπὲρ δὲ πᾶν σέβασμα, ἀντὶ τοῦ πᾶσαν αἵρεσιν ἣν ἀντέθηκε τῷ λόγῳ τῆς ἀληθείας.

— He warns them not to be disturbed unseasonably before the appearance of the Lord, not if men claim to be prophets in whom there is a spirit of error, not if messages and reports concerning the Lord are widespread, not if some fabricators provide an epistle as from us. «Because that day shall not come, except there come **a falling away** first, and the man of sin be revealed, the son of perdition; who opposes and exalts himself above all that is called God, or that is worshipped.» Do not expect, he says, the Saviour before the deceiver, who must come first as he stated. «Who exalts himself over every god and object of worship». For example, over all idolatry … Concerning the coming deception of man, the Saviour himself foretold that when he comes it will be hard to find faith on earth. For the man of sin, that is the antichrist, shall come into Jerusalem as the builder of the temple, and

288

he shall stand in the holy place calling himself god. He opposes and exalts himself above all that is called god instead of over every form of idolatry, above all that is worshiped instead of over every heresy which is opposed to the word of truth.

— Greek text — K. Staab. *Pauluskommentar aus der griechischen Kirche aus Katenenhandschriften gesammelt.* Aschendorff, 1933. Retrieved from Thesaurus Linguae Graecae (stephanus.tlg.uci.edu).

— English translation — The translation is my own as I could find none available.

— The context concerns Paul's admonition that the apostasy and the man of sin shall come before the coming of the Lord. Severianus associates the Son of man's difficulty with finding faith on earth when he returns with the antichrist and the apostasy that he causes.

— RELIGIOUS APOSTASY

(212) Socrates Scholasticus, Ecclesiastical History, 1.6

— Ἐν τῇ ἡμετέρᾳ τοίνυν παροικίᾳ, ἐξῆλθον νῦν ἄνδρες παράνομοι καὶ Χριστομάχοι, διδάσκοντες **ἀποστασίαν**, ἣν εἰκότως ἄν τις πρόδρομον τοῦ Ἀντιχρίστου νομίσειε καὶ καλέσειε. Καὶ ἐβουλόμην μὲν σιωπῇ παραδοῦναι τὸ τοιοῦτον, ἵν' ἴσως ἐν τοῖς ἀποστάταις μόνοις ἀναλωθῇ τὸ κακόν, καὶ μὴ εἰς ἑτέρους τόπους διαβὰν, ῥυπώσῃ τινῶν ἀκεραίων τὰς ἀκοάς.·

— Know therefore that there have recently arisen in our diocese lawless and anti-christian men, teaching **apostasy** such as one may justly consider and denominate the forerunner of Antichrist. I wished indeed to consign this disorder to silence, that if possible the evil might be confined to the apostates alone, and not go forth into other districts and contaminate the ears of some of the simple.

— Greek text — P. Maraval and P. Périchon. *Socrate de Constantinople, Histoire ecclésiastique (Livres I-VII).* Éditions du Cerf, 2004-2007. Retrieved from Thesaurus Linguae Graecae (stephanus.tlg.uci.edu).

— English translation — A.C. Zenos. *Nicene and Post-Nicene Fathers, Second Series, Vol. 2.* Christian Literature Publishing, 1890. Revised and edited for New Advent by Kevin Knight. Accessed at New Advent (newadvent.org/fathers).

— The context associates *apostasia* with teaching errors that boil down to lawlessness and contending against Christ, and regards those who engage in this practice as forerunners of the antichrist. Notice that he regards apostasy as a necessary precursor to the antichrist.
— RELIGIOUS APOSTASY

(213) Tatian, Oration to the Greeks, chapter 8
— Ὑπόθεσις δὲ αὐτοῖς **τῆς ἀποστασίας** οἱ ἄνθρωποι γίνονται. διάγραμμα γὰρ αὐτοῖς ἀστροθεσίας ἀναδείξαντες ὥσπερ οἱ τοῖς κύβοις παίζοντες, τὴν εἱμαρμένην εἰσηγήσαντο λίαν ἄδικον. ὅ τε γὰρ κρίνων καὶ ὁ κρινόμενος καθ᾽ εἱμαρμένην εἰσὶν γεγονότες, καὶ οἱ φονεύοντες καὶ οἱ φονευόμενοι καὶ οἱ πλουτοῦντες καὶ οἱ πενόμενοι τῆς αὐτῆς εἱμαρμένης ὑπάρχουσιν ἀπογεννήματα, πᾶσά τε γένεσις ὥσπερ ἐν θεάτρῳ τερπωλὴν παρέσχε τούτοις, παρ᾽ οἷς, ὥς φησιν Ὅμηρος, ἄσβεστος δ᾽ ἄρ᾽ ἐνῶρτο γέλως μακάρεσσι θεοῖσιν.
— But men become the cause of their own **apostasy**. For they take up charts of star positions, like they were playing with dice, and propose Fate, a flagrant injustice. Both the judge and the judged are made so by Fate. Both the murderers and the murdered, the wealthy and the impoverished are the offspring of the same Fate. Every birth is regarded as a theatrical entertainment by those beings of whom Homer says — Among the gods, rose laughter irrepressible.
— Greek text — E.J. Goodspeed. *Die ältesten Apologeten.* Vandenhoeck & Ruprecht, 1915. Retrieved from Thesaurus Linguae Graecae (stephanus.tlg.uci.edu).
— English translation — The translation is my adaptation of Kevin Knight's adaptation of the translation by J.E. Ryland in *Ante-Nicene Fathers, Vol. 2*, Christian Literature Publishing, 1885. Accessed at New Advent (newadvent.org/fathers).
— The context is men departing from God by regarding their lives as dictated by Fate and the patterns of the stars in the heavens.
— RELIGIOUS APOSTASY

(214) Theodore of Mopsuestia, Commentary in John, fragment 100
— Ἐάν, φασί, πολλοὶ πιστεύσωσιν εἰς αὐτόν, κίνδυνος ἡμῖν οὐκ ὀλίγος ἐκ τούτων ἀναφανεῖται· εὐπρόσωπον δὲ ἠβουλήθησαν

ἀφορμὴν τῇ ἐπιβουλῇ ἐπιθεῖναι. Ἐπειδὴ γὰρ ὑπόφοροι ἐσμὲν Ῥωμαίοις, ἐὰν ἴδωσι πολλοὺς συναγομένους πρὸς αὐτόν, ὑποπτεύσουσιν ὅτι βασιλέα αὐτὸν θέλομεν στῆσαι, καὶ ὡς **ἀποστασίαν** μελετώντων ἐπιστρατεύσουσι καθ' ἡμῶν καὶ ἀπολέσουσιν ἡμᾶς. Τοῦτο δὲ γέγονε διὰ τὸ τούτων κατὰ Κυρίου τόλμημα.

— If, they allege, many believe in him, there is a danger for us that not a few of them shall be a spectacle. That will give them a fair occasion for their counsel. Since we are Roman subjects, if they see that many are gathering to him, they shall suspect that we want to install him as king, and they shall war against us as ones considering **rebellion**, and they shall destroy us. This did come to pass because of their boldness [audacity] against the Lord.

— Greek text — R. Devreesse. *Essai sur Théodore de Mopsueste*; [*Studi e Testi 141*]. Biblioteca Apostolica Vaticana, 1948. Retrieved from Thesaurus Linguae Graecae (stephanus.tlg.uci.edu).

— English translation — The translation is my own as I could find none available.

— The context is fear that if the Romans see many coming to Christ, they might suspect that his disciples want to install him as king, and they shall war against them as men minded toward sedition and destroy them.

— POLITICAL SEDITION OR REBELLION

(215) Theodoret, Compendium of the Fables of the Heretics, Book 5, Chapter 23 — Concerning the Antichrist, (Migne 83.529)
— «Μή τις ὑμᾶς ἐξαπατήσῃ κατὰ μηδένα τρόπον, ὅτι ἐὰν μὴ ἔλθῃ **ἡ ἀποστασία** πρῶτον, καὶ ἀποκαλυφθῇ ὁ ἄνθρωπος τῆς ἁμαρτίας, ὁ υἱὸς τῆς ἀπωλείας, ὁ ἀντικείμενος καὶ ὑπεραιρόμενος ἐπὶ πάντα λεγόμενον θεὸν, ἢ σέβασμα, ὥστε αὐτὸν καὶ εἰς τὸν ναὸν τοῦ θεοῦ ὡς θεὸν καθίσαι, ἀποδεικνύοντα ἑαυτὸν ὅτι ἔστι θεός.» **Ἀποστασίαν** αὐτὴν τοῦ Ἀντιχρίστου καλεῖ τὴν παρουσίαν. Πολλοὶ γὰρ ὑπὸ τῶν ἐσομένων τεράτων ἐξαπατώμενοι τῆς ἀληθείας ἀποστήσονται, καὶ τὸ ψεῦδος ἀσπάσονται.

— «Let no man deceive you by any means: for that day shall not come, except there come **a falling away** first, and the man of sin be revealed, the son of perdition; Who opposes and exalts himself above all that is called God, or that is worshipped; so that he as God sits in the temple of God, proclaiming himself God.» He calls the coming of the antichrist **apostasy** itself. For many, being deceived by the coming signs, shall apostatize from the truth and greet [welcome] the lie.

— Greek text — J.P. Migne. *Patrologiae cursus completus* (*series Graeca* 83). Migne, 1857-1866. Retrieved from Thesaurus Linguae Graecae (stephanus.tlg.uci.edu).

— English translation. — The translation is my own as I could find no available English translation.

— The context is the coming of the antichrist. Notice that Theodoret regards the coming of the antichrist as the apostasy. He likely means that the antichrist is the cause of the apostasy.

— RELIGIOUS APOSTASY

(216) Theodoret, Letters, 63, (Festal)

— Τῶν μὲν ἄλλων τῆς ἑορτῆς ἀγαθῶν συνήθως ἀπελαύσαμεν. Καὶ γὰρ τὴν τῶν σωτηρίων παθημάτων ἑωρτάσαμεν μνήμην, καὶ διὰ τῆς Δεσποτικῆς ἀναστάσεως ἐδεξάμεθα τὰ τῆς κοινῆς ἀναστάσεως εὐαγγέλια, καὶ τὴν ἄρρητον τοῦ Θεοῦ καὶ Σωτῆρος ἡμῶν φιλανθρωπίαν ὑμνήσαμεν· ἡ δὲ τῶν Ἐκκλησιῶν ζάλη καθαρᾶς μεταλαχεῖν εὐφροσύνης οὐκ εἴασεν. Εἰ γὰρ ἑνὸς μέλους ἀλγοῦντος ὅλον κοινωνεῖ τῆς ὀδύνης τὸ σῶμα, παντὸς ταραττομένου τοῦ σώματος πῶς ἔνεστι μὴ θρηνεῖν; Ἐπιτείνει δὲ ἡμῖν τὴν ἀθυμίαν τὸ νομίζειν εἶναι ταῦτα **τῆς** παντελοῦς **ἀποστασίας** προοίμιον. Εὐξάσθω τοίνυν ἡ θεοσέβειά σου, εἰ μὲν ταῦτα οὕτως ἔχει, τῆς θείας ἡμᾶς ἐπικουρίας τυχεῖν, «ἵνα δυνηθῶμεν ἀντιστῆναι», κατὰ τὸν θεῖον Ἀπόστολον, «τῇ ἡμέρᾳ τῇ πονηρᾷ». Εἰ δέ τις χρόνος ὑπολέλειπται τῇ τοῦδε τοῦ βίου συστάσει, λυθῆναι τὸν κλύδωνα, καὶ τὴν προτέραν γαλήνην τὰς Ἐκκλησίας ἀπολαβεῖν· ἵνα μὴ ἐπιπλεῖστον οἱ τῆς ἀληθείας ἐχθροὶ ταῖς ἡμετέραις ἐπαγάλλωνται συμφοραῖς.

— We have enjoyed the wonted blessings of the Feast. We have kept the memorial Feast of the Passion of Salvation; by means of the resurrection of the Lord we have received the glad tidings of the resurrection of all, and have hymned the ineffable loving kindness of our God and Saviour. But the storm tossing the churches has not suffered us to take our share of unalloyed gladness. If, when one member is in pain the whole body is partaker of the pang, how can we forbear from lamentation when all the body is distressed? And it intensifies our discouragement to think that these things are the prelude of the general [full-blown, complete] **apostasy**. May your piety pray that since we are in this plight we may get the divine succour, that, as the divine Apostle phrases it, we may "be able to withstand the evil day." But if any time remain for this life's business, pray that the tempest may pass away, and the churches recover their former calm, that the enemies of the truth may no more exult at our misfortunes.

— Greek text — Y. Azéma. *Théodoret de Cyr. Correspondance II*; [*Sources chrétiennes 98.*] Éditions du Cerf, 1964. Retrieved from Thesaurus Linguae Graecae (stephanus.tlg.uci.edu).

— English translation — Blomfield Jackson. *Nicene and Post-Nicene Fathers, Second Series, Vol. 3*. Christian Literature Publishing, 1892, repr. Hendrickson Publishers, 1999. The clarifying comment in square brackets is my own.

— The context is the storm tossing the church in Theodoret's time which he believed was a prelude to the apostasy of the last days.

— RELIGIOUS APOSTASY

(217) Theodoret, Letters, 125 (147 English), (To John, Bishop of Germanicia)

— Τὰ μὲν πρότερα γράμματα τῆς σῆς ὁσιότητος εὐθὺς δεξάμενος ἀντιγέγραφα. Περὶ δὲ τῶν προκειμένων οὐδέν ἐστιν ἐλπίσαι χρηστόν. **Τῆς** γὰρ παντελοῦς **ἀποστασίας** ὑπολαμβάνω ταῦτα εἶναι προοίμια. Τὸ γὰρ τοὺς θρηνοῦντας τὰ κατὰ βίαν, ὥς φασιν, ἐν Ἐφέσῳ γεγενημένα μὴ μεταμέλεσθαι, ἀλλ' ἐπι μένειν τοῖς παρανόμως παρ' αὐτῶν τολμηθεῖσιν, καὶ ἐποικοδομεῖν κατὰ ταὐτὸν τήν τε ἀδικίαν καὶ τὴν ἀσέβειαν, καὶ τὸ τοὺς ἄλλους μήτε συμβουλεύειν, ἵνα αὐτοῖς ἐξαρνηθῇ τὰ τολμηθέντα, μήτε ἐπιμενόντων οἷς παρανόμως ἔδρασαν φεύγειν τὴν κοινωνίαν, τί τῶν χρηστῶν ἐλπίζειν ἐᾷ;

— Immediately on receipt of your holiness' former letter I replied. About the present state of affairs, it is impossible to entertain any good hope. I apprehend that this is the beginning of the general [full-blown, complete] **apostasy**. For when we see that those who lament what was done as they say, by violence, at Ephesus, show no signs of repentance, but abide by their unlawful deeds and are building up a superstructure at once of injustice and of impiety; when we see that the rest take no concerted action to deny their deeds and do not refuse to hold communion with men who abide by their unlawful action, what hope of good is it possible for us to entertain?

— Greek text — Y. Azéma. *Théodoret de Cyr. Correspondance II*; [*Sources chrétiennes 98.*] Éditions du Cerf, 1964. Retrieved from Thesaurus Linguae Graecae (stephanus.tlg.uci.edu).

— English translation — Blomfield Jackson. *Nicene and Post-Nicene Fathers, Second Series, Vol. 3*. Christian Literature Publishing, 1892, repr. Hendrickson Publishers, 1999. The clarifying comment in square brackets is my own.

— The context is the violence, injustice, and impiety in Theodoret's day which he regarded as the beginning of the full-blown apostasy of the last days.

— RELIGIOUS APOSTASY

(218) Theodoret, On the Incarnation of the Lord, Chapter 15 (some editions 16), (Migne 75.1444)

— ὅτι εἰ ὁ Θεὸς Λόγος ἦν ἀντὶ νοῦ ἐν τῷ ληφθέντι, καὶ ὁ διάβολος δικαιολογίαις χρήσαιτο ἂν εὐλόγοις, καὶ εἴποι ἂν εἰκότως· Ἐγώ, Δέσποτα καὶ ποιητὰ τῶν ὅλων, οὐ πρὸς σὲ τὴν μάχην ἀνεδεξάμην· οἶδα γάρ σου τὴν ἀξίαν, ἐπίσταμαι τὴν ἐξουσίαν, γινώσκω τὴν δεσποτείαν. Ὁμολογῶ τὴν δουλείαν, εἰ καὶ **ἀποστασίαν** νοσῶ. ·

— If the God-Word replaced the mind in that which was assumed, even the devil could find some justified excuses, and might reasonably say: Ruler and Creator of the universe, I did not begin the fight against you, because I know your dignity, I am aware of your might, and recognise your dominion. I acknowledge my servitude even being an **apostate** [even if I am sick with apostasy].

— Greek text — J.P. Migne. *Patrologiae cursus completus* (*series Graeca 75*). Migne, 1857-1866. Retrieved from Thesaurus Linguae Graecae (stephanus.tlg.uci.edu).

— English translation — István Pásztori-Kupán. *Theodoret of Cyrus*; [*The Early Church Fathers*]. Routledge, 2006.

— The context is erroneous views of the incarnation which give Satan room to excuse the fact that he was sick with apostasy against God.

— RELIGIOUS APOSTASY

(219) Theodoret, Commentary on the Letters of Paul, 2 Thessalonians, 2:3, (Migne 82.664)

— «Ὅτι ἐὰν μὴ ἔλθῃ **ἡ ἀποστασία** πρῶτον, καὶ ἀποκαλυφθῇ ὁ ἄνθρωπος τῆς ἁμαρτίας, ὁ υἱὸς τῆς ἀπωλείας· ὁ ἀντικείμενος καὶ ὑπεραιρόμενος ἐπὶ πάντα λεγόμενον θεὸν, ἢ σέβασμα, ὥστε αὐτὸν εἰς τὸν ναὸν τοῦ Θεοῦ ὡς θεὸν καθίσαι, ἀποδεικνύντα ἑαυτὸν ὅτι ἔστι θεός.» **Ἀποστασίαν** αὐτὸν ἐκάλεσε τὸν Ἀντίχριστον, ἀπὸ τοῦ πράγματος αὐτῷ τοὔνομα τεθεικώς. Ἀποστῆσαι γὰρ ἅπαντας τῆς ἀληθείας πειρᾶται. Ἄνθρωπον δὲ αὐτὸν ἁμαρτίας προσηγόρευσεν, ἐπειδὴ ἄνθρωπός ἐστι τὴν φύσιν, πᾶσαν ἐν ἑαυτῷ τοῦ διαβόλου δεχόμενος τὴν ἐνέργειαν· υἱὸν δὲ ἀπωλείας, ὡς καὶ αὐτὸν ἀπολλύμενον, καὶ ἑτέροις πρόξενον τούτου γινόμενον.

— «Because unless **the defection** comes first, and the man of sin is revealed, the son of perdition, who opposes and exalts himself above every so-called god or object of worship so that he takes his seat as God in the temple of God, proclaiming himself to be God». By **defection** he referred to the Anti-Christ in person [he called the antichrist apostasy], making a title out of the event [assigning the description of the event to the man himself]. [(For he tries to make all men apostatize from the truth)]. He called him the man of sin since he is a man by nature, receiving all the devil's activity [capacity, ability] in himself, and son of perdition as being ruined himself and proving the source of ruin to others.

— Greek text — J.P. Migne. *Patrologiae cursus completus* (*series Graeca 82*). Migne, 1857-1866. Retrieved from Thesaurus Linguae Graecae (stephanus.tlg.uci.edu).

— English translation — Robert C. Hill. *Theodoret of Cyrus: Commentary on the Letters of St. Paul, Vol. 2*. Holy Cross Orthodox Press, 2001. The portions in square brackets are my own clarifying translations. The sentence enclosed in both square brackets and parentheses is my translation of a line which Robert Hill left out of his translation. Whether he did so because it wasn't in his text or because he felt it was redundant, being repeated a few sentences later, I don't know.

— The context is the apostasy at the end of the age that is associated with the antichrist. Theodoretus identifies the antichrist as the

apostasy since the event is traced to the person. The antichrist shall attempt to persuade all of mankind to apostatize from the truth.
— RELIGIOUS APOSTASY

(220) Theodoret, Commentary on Daniel, 7:7, (Migne 81.1421)
— Μικρὸν δὲ αὐτὸ κέρας καλεῖ, ὡς ἀπὸ μικρᾶς φυλῆς τῶν Ἰουδαίων φυόμενον· θεωρητὸν δὲ, ὡς ἐπίσημον μετὰ ταῦτα γινόμενον. Διὰ δὲ τῶν ὀφθαλμῶν τὴν φρόνησιν καὶ πανουργίαν ἠνίξατο, ᾗ χρώμενος ἐξαπατήσει πολλούς. Ἀλλὰ «καὶ στόμα», φησὶ, «λαλοῦν μεγάλα», τουτέστιν, ἀλαζονικὰ καὶ ὑπέρογκα. Σαφῶς δὲ ἡμᾶς ὁ μακάριος Παῦλος τοῦτο διδάσκει, λέγων· «Μή τις ὑμᾶς ἐξαπατάτω κατὰ μηδένα τρόπον, ὅτι ἐὰν μὴ ἔλθῃ ἡ **ἀποστασία** πρῶτον, καὶ ἀποκαλυφθῇ ὁ ἄνθρωπος τῆς ἁμαρτίας ὁ υἱὸς τῆς ἀπωλείας, ὁ ἀντικείμενος, καὶ ὑπεραιρόμενος ὑπὲρ πάντα λεγόμενον Θεὸν, ἢ σέβασμα, ὥστε καὶ εἰς τὸν ναὸν τοῦ Θεοῦ εἰσελθόντα καθίσαι, ἀποδεικνύοντα ἑαυτὸν, ὅτι ἐστὶ Θεός.» Τοῦτο αἰνιττόμενος καὶ ὁ μακάριος ἔφη Δανιήλ· «Καὶ στόμα λαλοῦν μεγάλα, καὶ ἐποίει πόλεμον μετὰ τῶν ἁγίων.» Πάντα γὰρ, φησὶ, πραγματεύεται, κοινωνοὺς τῆς πονηρίας καὶ τῆς τιμωρίας ἅπαντας ἀνθρώπους λαβεῖν ἐφιέμενος.

— Now, he calls the horn itself little as springing up from the little tribe of the Jews, and conspicuous as becoming famous afterwards; by the eyes he suggested the cleverness and trickery he employed in trampling many underfoot. He also says «a mouth speaking lofty words», that is, arrogant and haughty; blessed Paul gives a wise lesson in this in saying, «Let no one deceive you in any way, because unless **the rebellion** comes first, and the sinful one is revealed, the child of ruin, the adversary who is lifted up over every so-called god or object of worship so as to enter and take a seat in God's temple, presenting himself as God». Hinting at this, blessed Daniel also said, «a mouth speaking lofty words, and it made war on the holy ones»: it tries every stratagem in its desire to make all human beings sharers in wickedness and retribution.

— Greek text — J.P. Migne. *Patrologiae cursus completus* (*series Graeca 81*). Migne, 1857-1866. Retrieved from Thesaurus Linguae Graecae (stephanus.tlg.uci.edu).

— English translation — Robert C. Hill. *Theodoret of Cyrus: Commentary on Daniel*; [*Writings From the Greco-Roman World, No. 7*]. Society of Biblical Literature, 2006.

— The context is the apostasy or rebellion of the last days. Theodoret here traces this to the working of the antichrist who tries every conceivable stratagem to get men to join him in his wickedness and rebellion.

— RELIGIOUS APOSTASY

(221) Theodoret, Interpretations in Jeremiah, 2:17, (Migne 81.509)

— Εἶτα τῆς ἀσθενείας τὴν αἰτίαν διδάσκει· «Οὐχὶ ταῦτα ἐποίησέ σοι τὸ καταλιπεῖν σε ἐμέ; λέγει Κύριος ὁ Θεός σου.» Ἔπειτα καὶ σημαίνει τὴν ἀρχὴν **τῆς ἀποστασίας**. «Ἐν τῷ καιρῷ ἄγοντός σε ἐν τῇ ἐρήμῳ.» Εὐθὺς γὰρ Αἰγυπτίων ἀπαλλαγεὶς, ἐμὲ μὲν ἐγκατέλιπες, τὸν δὲ μόσχον ἐθεοποίησας.

— Then he explains the reason for the weakness. «Was it not your forsaking me that brought this upon you? says the Lord your God.» Then he indicates also the beginning of **the revolt**. «At the time I was guiding you through the desert»: as soon as you were freed from Egypt you abandoned me and made a god of a calf.

— Greek text — J.P. Migne. *Patrologiae cursus completus* (*series Graeca) 81*. Migne, 1857-1866. Retrieved from Thesaurus Linguae Graecae (stephanus.tlg.uci.edu).

— English translation — Robert Charles Hill. *Theodoret of Cyrus: Commentaries on the Prophets, Vol. One*. Holy Cross Orthodox Press, 2006.

— The context is Israel's apostasy. Notice that *apostasia* is associated with forsaking the Lord, making an image of a bull, and regarding it as god.

— RELIGIOUS APOSTASY

(222) Theodoret, Interpretations in Jeremiah, 2:18-19, (Migne 81.509)

— Καὶ νῦν τί σοι καὶ τῇ ὁδῷ Αἰγύπτου, τοῦ πιεῖν ὕδωρ Γηῶν; Καὶ τί σοι καὶ τῇ ὁδῷ Ἀσσυρίων, τοῦ πιεῖν ὕδωρ ποταμῶν; Ἡνίκα ὑπὸ Σύρων ἐπολεμοῦντο, τοὺς Ἀσσυρίους εἰς συμμαχίαν ἐκάλεσαν· ὅτε δὲ Ἀσσύριοι αὐτοῖς ἐπεστράτευσαν, πρὸς Αἰγυπτίους κατέφυγον· Γηῶν γὰρ τὸν Νεῖλον καλεῖ. «Παιδεύσει σε **ἡ ἀποστασία** σου, καὶ ἡ κακία σου ἐλέγξει σε· καὶ γνῶθι, καὶ ἴδε, ὅτι πικρὸν καὶ πονηρόν σοι τὸ καταλιπεῖν σὲ ἐμὲ, λέγει Κύριος ὁ Θεός σου.» Καὶ οὐκ εὐδόκησα ἐπὶ σοὶ, λέγει Κύριος ὁ Θεός σου. Ἐμὲ, φησὶν, εἰς συμμαχίαν οὐκ ἐκάλεσας, ἀλλ' ἐκείνους. Διὰ τοῦτο ἐκείνοις σε παρέδωκα. Τοιοῦτό τι πεπόνθασι καὶ οἱ τὸν Σωτῆρα σταυρώσαντες· ἀρνηθέντες γὰρ αὐτὸν, ἔλεγον μὴ ἔχειν βασιλέα εἰ μὴ Καίσαρα, οὗ δὴ χάριν αὐτοὺς Καίσαρι παραδέδωκεν.

—«What good to you now is the way to Egypt, to drink water of Gihon? What good to you is the way of Assyrians, to drink water of the rivers?» When you were attacked by Syrians, they called on the Assyrians for assistance; and when Assyrians assailed them, they had recourse to Egyptians (referring to the Nile as Gihon). «Your **revolt** will chastise you, and your wickedness will censure you. Know and see that your forsaking me is harsh and bad for you, says the Lord your God; I was not pleased with you, says the Lord your God.» You did not call on me for assistance, but on them—hence I handed you over to them. Those who crucified the Savior also suffered something like this: denying him they said they had no king but Caesar—hence he handed them over to Caesar.

— Greek text — J.P. Migne. *Patrologiae cursus completus (series Graeca 81)*. Migne, 1857-1866. Retrieved from Thesaurus Linguae Graecae (stephanus.tlg.uci.edu).

— English translation — Robert Charles Hill. *Theodoret of Cyrus: Commentaries on the Prophets, Vol. One.* Holy Cross Orthodox Press, 2006.

— The context is Israel's apostasy. Instead of leaning on the Lord, she leaned on the arm of the flesh, namely Assyria and Egypt. Notice the association of *apostasia* with forsaking the Lord, not calling on the Lord, and seeking the aid of the nations.

— RELIGIOUS APOSTASY

(223) Theodoret, Interpretations in Jeremiah, 2:24, (Migne 81.513)

— Ἃ γὰρ ἀκούειν ἠβούλοντο, ταῦτα οἱ ψευδοπροφῆται προλέγειν προσεποιοῦντο. ... Μετὰ ταῦτα διδάσκει, ὅτι πολλάκις συμβουλευθεῖσα τῆς βλαβερᾶς ἀποστῆναι πορείας, ἐθρασύνετο ἄντικρυς, **τὴν ἀποστασίαν** ὁμολογοῦσα. Ἀλλὰ διὰ τοῦτο αἰσχύνῃ αὐτοὺς, φησὶ, περιβαλῶ πάντας ὁμοῦ, καὶ βασιλέας, καὶ ἄρχοντας, καὶ ἱερέας, καὶ τοὺς τὰ ψευδῆ προφητεύοντας· καὶ ἀπεικασθήσονται κλέπτῃ ἐπ᾽ αὐτοφώρῳ ἁλόντι, καὶ σφόδρα ἐρυθριῶντι. Τοὺς μὲν γὰρ ἐκ ξύλου καὶ λίθου κατασκευαζομένους θεοὺς, πατέρας ὠνόμαζον καὶ γεννήτορας· ἐμοὶ δὲ τὰ νῶτα ἔδωκαν, καὶ ὡς ἐχθρὸν ἀπεστράφησαν.

— What they wanted to hear the false prophets made it their business to prophesy … After this he teaches that, though often advised to desist from their harmful ways, they were bold and blatant in professing **their revolt**. For that reason, however, he says, I shall envelop all equally in shame—kings, rulers, priests, and the prophets of falsehood; they will be like a thief caught in the act of theft, utterly crestfallen. After all, while calling the gods made from wood and stone fathers and parents, they turned their back on me and avoided me like an enemy.

— Greek text — J.P. Migne. *Patrologiae cursus completus* (*series Graeca 80*). Migne, 1857-1866. Retrieved from Thesaurus Linguae Graecae (stephanus.tlg.uci.edu).

— English translation — Robert Charles Hill. *Theodoret of Cyrus: Commentaries on the Prophets, Vol. One.* Holy Cross Orthodox Press, 2006.

— The context is Israel's apostasy. Notice the association of apostasy with false prophets, turning one's back on God, manufacturing gods out of wood and stone, and treating God like an enemy.

— RELIGIOUS APOSTASY

(224) Theodoret, Questions in the book of the Kings and Chronicles, Question 45, (Migne 80.716)

— Τί γὰρ τὸν Ἰούδαν καὶ τὸν Βενιαμὶν ὤνησε τὸ τὸν θεῖον ἔχειν νεών; Τὴν γὰρ αὐτὴν καὶ οὗτοι παρανομίαν ἐτόλμων· «Ὠκοδόμησαν γὰρ», φησὶν, «αὐτοῖς ὑψηλὰ καὶ στήλας, καὶ ἄλση, ἐπὶ πάντα βουνὸν ὑψηλὸν, καὶ ὑποκάτω παντὸς ξύλου ἀλσώδους. Καὶ σύνδεσμος ἐγένετο ἐν τῇ γῇ.» Τὸν δὲ σύνδεσμον ἀντὶ τῆς ἀποστάσεως τέθεικε. Καὶ γὰρ ἡ Ἰεζάβελ τοῦ Ἰωρὰμ μεμαθηκυῖα τὴν τελευτήν, καὶ τὸν Ἰοὺ τῆς βασιλείας τὴν χειροτονίαν δεξάμενον, ἐβόησε, Σύνδεσμος, σύνδεσμος, τουτέστιν **ἀποστασία** καὶ τυραννίς. Τοῦτο δὲ καὶ τὰ ἑξῆς δηλοῖ· «Καὶ ἐποίησαν ἀπὸ πάντων βδελυγμάτων τῶν ἐθνῶν, ὧν ἐξώρισε Κύριος ἀπὸ προσώπου τῶν υἱῶν Ἰσραὴλ.» Οὐ τοίνυν διὰ τὴν τῆς βασιλείας διαίρεσιν ἐξώκειλαν εἰς ἀσέβειαν αἱ δέκα φυλαί, ἀλλὰ διὰ τὴν οἰκείαν παρανομίαν.

— What did having the holy temple profit Judah and Benjamin? For they were emboldened in the same transgression. «For they built themselves», he says, «high places, and images, and groves on every high hill and under every green tree. And there was conspiracy in the land.» For he employed "conspiracy" instead of "apostasy." For when Jezebel had learned of the death of Jehoram and that Jehu had been selected king, she cried "conspiracy, conspiracy," that is, **apostasy** and tyranny. This and the following context makes that clear. «And they did according to all the abominations of the nations which the LORD cast out before the children of Israel.» Therefore, it was not because of the division of the kingdom that the ten tribes ran aground in ungodliness, but because of their own transgression.

— Greek text — J.P. Migne. *Patrologiae cursus completus* (*series Graeca 80*). Migne, 1857-1866. Retrieved from Thesaurus Linguae Graecae (stephanus.tlg.uci.edu).

— English translation — The translation is my own as I could find none available.

— The context is apostasy. There is an interesting contrast here between Jezebel's cry of conspiracy (against the line of Ahab) and the ten tribes falling into apostasy (against God). Apostasy is associated with abominations, idolatry, ungodliness, and transgression.

— RELIGIOUS APOSTASY

APPENDIX G
Byzantine Era

Each of these three passages from the early Byzantine era has been included for different reasons.

The first because it is the *departure* passage cited in Liddel & Scott which is pointed to as evidence that *apostasia* can bear the sense of human *departure* for a trip, the sense necessary to uphold the rapture interpretation of *apostasia* in 2 Thessalonians 2:3.

The second because it involves the only definition for *apostasia* given in Liddel & Scott that isn't covered elsewhere in this volume.

The third because it is the earliest reference that I could find of *apostasia* being used in the sense of human *departure* for a trip, whether mundane or glorious—the sense that the rapture-theory advocates need to support their doctrine.

A candid investigation reveals that none of these three passages shed light on the interpretation of *apostasia* in 2 Thessalonians 2:3. Two of them employ *apostasia* in a scientific sense which has no bearing on the passage in question. And all of them—being centuries beyond the penning of 2 Thessalonians— are far too late to have any bearing on the interpretation of *apostasia* in the passage in question.

Olympiadorus, Commentary on Aristotle's Meteorology, p 320
— Τὸ περὶ πηκτοῦ καὶ τηκτοῦ πάλιν ὁ φιλόσοφος ἐπανακεφαλαιοῦται, οὐχ ὥς τινες ᾠήθησαν βουλόμενος ἐπιτομὴν ποιήσασθαι τῶν ἀνωτέρω περὶ αὐτῶν ἐργωδῶς εἰρημένων· ἀλλὰ τοῦτο ποιεῖ χάριν τοῦ ἐπανορθώσασθαι τὸ παχυμερῶς εἰρημένον ἐν τοῖς προλαβοῦσι, ταὐτὸν δ᾽ εἰπεῖν ὅτι ἔλεγε τοὺς ἅλας καὶ τὸ νίτρον θερμῷ πήγνυσθαι καὶ ψυχρῷ λύεσθαι. ἔστι δὲ ἡ ἐπανακεφαλαίωσις τοιαύτη· τῶν πηγνυμένων τὰ μὲν ὕδατός ἐστι, τὰ δὲ γῆς. καὶ ὅσα μὲν ὕδατός ἐστιν, ἐκεῖνα ψυχρῷ πήγνυται, ἀπουσίᾳ δ᾽ ὑγρῶν πήγνυται, τουτέστι ξηρῷ. ἀλλ᾽ ἵνα τὸ μὴ ποιεῖν ὑλικῇ αἰτίᾳ ἀπονέμῃ ὁ Ἀριστοτέλης, τουτέστι τὴν πῆξιν, τῇ ξηρότητι τὴν αἰτίαν **τῆς ἀποστασίας** τοῦ ὑγροῦ παρατίθεται καὶ ταύτῃ δίδωσι τὴν πῆξιν, τουτέστι τὴν θερμότητα.

— Concerning solidifying and melting, the philosopher once again sums it up, not as some have opined, epitomizing the things addressed above in general terms, but he does this for the sake of establishing what had been less than ideally addressed earlier, that is to say, that he said that salt and soda congeal in heat and loose in cold. Of things congealing, some are liquids, others are solids. Anything that is a liquid will congeal with cold. But in the absence of moisture it congeals, that is with dryness. But that he might not make matter the cause of the congealing, Aristotle assigned dryness as the cause of the **departure [evaporation]** of the moisture and heat as the cause of the congealing.

— Greek text — G. Stüve. *Olympiodori in Aristotelis meteora commentaria*; *Commentaria in Aristotelem Graeca 12.2*. Reimer, 1900. Retrieved from Thesaurus Linguae Graecae (stephanus.tlg. uci.edu).

— English translation — The translation is my own as I could find none available.

— Here *apostasia* is used in a mid-sixth century scientific treatise in the sense of *evaporation*, that is, water departing under the influence of heat. There is nothing in this scientific usage that offers support for the sense of human *departure* for trips, be they mundane or glorious. Furthermore, this passage—the first instance of *apostasia* in this sense (scientific senses were normally covered by *apostasis*)—appears five centuries after Paul penned 2 Thessalonians, so this unique sense has no bearing on the sense of *apostasia* in the passage under consideration. To import into the New Testament any sense that first appeared centuries after the penning of that precious volume would be an anachronistic mistake.

— Scientific sense of EVAPORATION

Elias, Commentary on Aristotle's Categories, 119

— καὶ εἰ ἦν ἐν τοῖς Πλάτωνος χρόνοις ἡ διαλεκτική, οὐκ ἂν ἐπέγραψεν ὁ Πλάτων πρὸ τοῦ οἰκείου μουσείου 'ἀγεωμέτρητος μηδεὶς εἰσίτω', ὁπότε καὶ οὗτος ἐνεδείξατο τὴν δύναμιν αὐτῆς ἐν τῷ Σοφιστῇ λέγων οὕτως 'γύμναζε σαυτὸν διὰ τῆς καλουμένης παρὰ πολλοῖς ἀδολεσχίας, ἕως ἔτι νέος εἶ, ἐπεὶ διαφεύξεταί σε τἀληθές', ἀδολεσχίαν καλέσας **τὴν ἀποστασίαν** τῶν πραγμάτων ἤγουν τὴν λογικήν. καὶ γὰρ Ἀριστοτέλης ἐν τῇ λογικῇ ἀντὶ τῶν πραγμάτων εἰσφέρει ταῦτα τὰ στοιχεῖα, ἄλφα βῆτα γάμμα, καὶ διὰ τούτων διδάσκει τὰς συμπλοκὰς τῶν συλλογισμῶν.

— And if the dialectic method [the Aristotelian version] had existed in Plato's time, Plato would not have engraved before his own school [inscribed on his door] "Let no one ignorant of geometry enter." Since he also demonstrated great ability in it [in philosophy] in his professorship, speaking in this manner, "exercise yourself through that which is maligned as useless knowledge by many, while you are yet young, because truth shall truly preserve you." The **distinction** between concepts, so-called useless knowledge, is properly called logic. For Aristotle introduced the three elements: alpha, beta, gamma, to be used in the field of logic rather than concepts, and through these he taught the connections of the syllogism. [The modern treatment of the syllogism calls these elements the major premise, the minor premise, and the conclusion.]

— Greek text — A. Busse. *Eliae in Porphyrii isagogen et Aristotelis categorias commentaria*; *Commentaria in Aristotelem Graeca 18.1.* Reimer, 1900. Retrieved from Thesaurus Linguae Graecae (stephanus.tlg.uci.edu).

— English translation — Translation is my own as I could find none available.

— Here *apostasia* is used in a scientific publication in a scientific sense of *difference* or *distinction*, which one can readily see is derived from the scientific sense of *distance*. This instance, because it is a scientific usage rather than a common usage, and because it is five centuries after the penning of 2 Thessalonians, has no bearing whatsoever on the interpretation of *apostasia* in 2 Thessalonians 2:3.

— Scientific sense of DISTINCTION

The Assumption of the Virgin, 32-33

— 32) ἀναστάντες οὖν εὐθέως οἱ ἀπόστολοι ἐξῆλθον ἐκ τοῦ οἴκου, βαστάζοντες τὴν κλίνην τῆς δεσποίνης Θεοτόκου, καὶ τὴν ὁρμὴν ἐποιοῦντο ἐπὶ τὰ Ἱεροσόλυμα. εὐθέως δέ, καθὼς εἶπεν τό πνεῦμα τὸ ἅγιον, διὰ νεφέλης ἀρθέντες εὑρέθησαν εἰς Ἱεροσόλυμα εἰς τὸν οἶκον τῆς δεσποίνης. καὶ ἀναστάντες ἐπὶ πέντε ἡμέρας ἐποιοῦμεν ἄπαυστον ὑμνῳδίαν. 33) ὅτε δὲ ἔφθασεν ὁ χιλίαρχος ἐπὶ τὴν Βηθλεὲμ καὶ οὐχ εὗρεν ἐκεῖ τὴν μητέρα τοῦ κυρίου οὔτε τοὺς ἀποστόλους, ἐκράτησεν τοὺς Βηθλεεμίτας, λέγων πρὸς αὐτούς. οὐχ ὑμεῖς ἤλθατε λέγοντες τῷ ἡγεμόνι καὶ τοῖς ἱερεῦσιν ἅπαντα τὰ γενόμενα σημεῖα καὶ θαύματα, καὶ ὡς παρεγένοντο οἱ ἀπόστολοι ἀπὸ πάσης χώρας; ποῦ οὖν εἰσίν; δεῦτε εἰσέλθατε εἰς τὸν ἡγεμόνα εἰς Ἱερουσαλήμ, ἠγνόει γὰρ ὁ χιλίαρχος **τὴν** τῶν ἀποστόλων καὶ τῆς μητρὸς τοῦ κυρίου **ἀποστασίαν** τὴν εἰς ἱερουσαλήμ. λαβὼν οὖν ὁ χιλίαρχος τοὺς Βηθλεεμίτας εἰσῆλθεν πρὸς τὸν ἡγεμόνα φάσκων μηδένα εὑρηκέναι.

— The apostles therefore rose up immediately, and went forth from the house, carrying the bed of the Lady the mother of God, and directed their course to Jerusalem; and immediately, as the Holy Spirit had said, being lifted up by a cloud, they were found in Jerusalem in the house of the Lady. And they stood up, and for five days made an unceasing singing of praise. And when the tribune came to Bethlehem, and found there neither the mother of the Lord nor the apostles, he laid hold of the Bethlehemites, saying to them: Did you not come telling the procurator and the priests all the signs and wonders that had come to pass, and how the apostles had come out of every country? Where are they, then? Come, go to the procurator at Jerusalem. For the tribune did not know of **the departure** of the apostles and the Lord's mother to Jerusalem. The tribune, then, having taken the Bethlehemites, went in to the procurator, saying that he had found no one.

— Greek text — Constantinus Tischendorf. *Apocalypses apocryphae Mosis, Esdrae, Pauli, Iohannis: item Mariae dormitio, additis Evangeliorum et actuum Apocryphorum supplementis*. Hermann Mendelssohn, 1866. Accessed at Internet Archive (archive.org).

— English translation — *Ante-Nicene Fathers, vol. 8*, Christian Literature Publishing Company, 1886, repr. Hendrickson Publishers, 1994.

— Though this piece of Marian apocryphal literature was published in the Ante-Nicene collection, it certainly doesn't belong there. This work doesn't just cover the apocryphal account of Mary's dormition, it also includes the apocryphal account (fable) of her bodily ascension. The earliest fables of the bodily assumption of Mary date from the fifth and sixth centuries, some four to five hundred years after Paul wrote his second epistle to the Thessalonians. This particular document is generally dated to the sixth or seventh century. One of the manuscripts, in fact, claims John Archbishop of Thessalonica of the seventh century as the author.

— This is the earliest instance I have found of *apostasia* being used in the sense of general *departure*, that is of human beings departing to travel from one location to another. Its sixth- or seventh-century dating makes it far too late to be regarded in any conversation on the interpretation of *apostasia* in 2 Thessalonians 2:3. Even if someone argued for a fourth-century date—which would make it the earliest Marian ascension document—it would still be a couple centuries too late to consider this sense as a potential sense for *apostasia* in 2 Thessalonians 2:3.

— I would also point out that were *apostasia* capable of bearing the sense of *rapture*, using it for Mary's bodily ascension to heaven would have been an ideal place to use it. Instead, the author used it for simple departure to Jerusalem.

— DEPARTURE

ENDNOTES

[1] While it is altogether likely that a few instances may have slipped through the cracks, nobody can accuse me of making a selective use of the evidence or doing a haphazard job.

[2] See Richard Reiter, "A History of the Development of the Rapture Positions," in Gleason Archer, Paul Feinberg, Douglas Moo, *The Rapture:Pre-, Mid-, or Post-Tribulational?* Zondervan, 1984.

[3] *The Coming Kingdom of Christ*, Sword of the Lord, 1954. In chapter 13, "The Great Falling Away—Sin and Worldliness Among Christians," he writes, "Second Thessalonians 2:3 says, 'That day shall not come, except there come a falling away first.' I believe that this refers to the rapture of the saints, when the invisible ties of gravity will be broken and we will suddenly fall away into the air to meet Jesus."

[4] *Rethinking the Rapture*, Loizeaux Brothers, 1954. See his remarks in chapter 7, "That Day Shall Not Come Except—" pp. 67-71.

[5] *The Rapture Question*, Dunham Publishing, 1957, pp. 71-72.

[6] H. G. Liddell and R. Scott, *Greek-English Lexicon, 9th ed, With a Revised Supplement*, Clarendon Press, 1996. Orig. ed. Oxford Univ. Press, 1843; 9th ed. 1940; New Supplement 1996.

[7] Ken Wuest says, "But then *hee apostasia* of which Paul is speaking, precedes the revelation of Antichrist in his true identity, and is *to katechon* that which holds back his revelation (2:6). The *hee apostasia*, therefore, cannot be either a general apostasy in Christendom which does precede the coming of Antichrist, nor can it be the particular apostasy which is the result of his activities in making himself the alone object of worship. Furthermore, that which holds back his revelation (v. 3) is vitally connected with *hoo katechoon* (v. 7), He who holds back the same event. The latter is, in my opinion, the Holy Spirit and His activities in the Church. All of which means that I am driven to the inescapable conclusion that the *hee apostasia* (v. 3) refers to the Rapture of the Church which precedes the Day of the Lord, and holds back the revelation of the Man of Sin who ushers in the world-aspect of that period." [Kenneth S. Wuest, *Letter to E. Schuyler English*, published in "Let the Prophets Speak," *Our Hope*, (vol. LVI, num. 12; June 1950), p. 731.]

[8] *Exegetical Fallacies*, D.A. Carson, Baker Book House, 1984, p. 26. The entire section, pp. 26-32, is worth reading.

[9] It also bears numerous technical senses like *asyndeton* (grammar), *distance* (astronomy, geometry, military), and *abscess* (medicine).

[10] Of the rare forms: ἀποστάτις (sedition, apostasy) is found only in the Apocrypha and Cyril of Alexandria, ἀποστάτεσις (rebellion) is known only from Xenophon's *Cyropaedia*, and ἀπόστασης (sedition, apostasy) is a Doric and Aeolic form of ἀπόστασίς.

[11] In Greek these are: ἀπόστασίς (sedition, rebellion, apostasy), ἀποστασία (sedition, rebellion, apostasy), ἀποστάτης (rebel, apostate, deserter, runaway), ἀποστάσιον (divorce), ἀποστάτις (sedition apostasy), ἀποστάτεσις (rebellion), ἀπόστασης (rebellion, apostasy), ἀποστατικός (rebellious), ἀποστατέω (to rebel), ἀποστασιάζω (cause to rebel), ἀποστατέον (rebelling), and ἀποστατικῶς (rebelliously).

[12] Such words were taken up from earthly and pagan-religion contexts and employed in the glorious context of God's program of eternal redemption, now invested with a God-centric, eternity-centric, and truth-centric focus that they had lacked.

[13] See Archimedes, *Arenarius* (*The Sand Reckoner*) on pp. 84-85 in Appendix A — Pre-Roman Era.

[14] See Galen, *On the Constitution of the Art of Medicine* and his other references on pp. 93-94 in Appendix C — Late-Roman Era.

[15] See in Appendix F — Church Fathers: (1) *Acts of Xanthippe and Polyxena*, p. 108; (72) Cyril of Alexandria, *Commentary on Isaiah the Prophet*, chapter 50, pp. 162-163; (188) Origen, *Commentary on Matthew*, 14.18, p. 268; (189) Origen, *Commentary on Matthew*, 14.19, pp. 268-269; (190) Origen, *Commentary on Matthew*, 14.19, pp. 269-271; (191) Origen, Commentary on Matthew, 14.20, p. 271; (192) Origen, Commentary on Matthew, 14.22, pp. 271-273.

[16] See (152) Evagrius of Pontus, *On the Vices Opposed to the Virtues*, chapter 4, in Appendix F — Church Fathers on pp. 237-238.

[17] For the sake of simplication, I have included slave *revolt* and military *mutiny* under the heading of political *sedition* or *rebellion*. While these disruptions weren't always politically motivated, they were generally intertwined with the boiling political issues of the day. Moreover, I didn't see any significant gain in adding two smaller categories.

[18] Asyndeton is the omission of a conjunction between parts of a sentence where conjunctions are normally employed. The Latin phrase "veni, vidi, vici" and its English translation "I came, I saw, I conquered" are examples.

[19] Paul Feinberg, in the appendix of his chapter "2 Thessalonians 2 and the Rapture," pp. 309-310, in *When The Trumpet Sounds*, edited by Thomas Ice and Timothy Demy, Harvest House, 1995.

[20] Archimedes, *Arenarius* (*The Sand Reckoner*) on pp. 84-85 in Appendix A — Pre-Roman Era.

[21] See (152) Evagrius of Pontus, *On the Vices Opposed to the Virtues*, chapter 4, in Appendix F — Church Fathers on pp. 237-238.

[22] It first appeared in the sixth or seventh century in *The Assumption of the Virgin*, a classic example of the Mariolatry literature of the early Catholic Church. See the entry in Appendix G — Byzantine Era, pp. 303-305.

[23] See the article "Jubilees, Book of" by James VanderKam in the *Encyclopedia of the Dead Sea Scrolls, Vol. 1*, Oxford University Press, 2000.

[24] See "The Influence of the Septuagint on the New Testament Vocabulary" by Everett F. Harrison in *Bibliotheca Sacra 113 (Jan 1956)*, pp. 37-45, Dallas Theological Seminary.

[25] See the relevant material in Josephus, *The Jewish War*, 12.6 and 2 Maccabees 6:1-12.

[26] Many of the advocates of the apostasia-rapture theory are throwing around the mistaken date of 1576. Every source I examined gives 1582 as the date of the publication of the New Testament. The Old Testament portion was published in two volumes in 1609 and 1610.

[27] A.L. Mayhew and W. W. Skeat, *A Concise Dictionary of Middle English From AD 1150 to 1580*, Clarendon Press, 1888. I accessed the HTML eBook version provided by Project Gutenberg at https://www.gutenberg.org/cache/epub/10625/pg10625-images.html

[28] The basic sources for the *Online Egymology Dictionary* at etymonline.com, according to their own statement are, "Weekley's *An Etymological Dictionary of Modern English*, Klein's *A Comprehensive Etymological Dictionary of the English Language*, *Oxford English Dictionary* (second edition), *Barnhart Dictionary of Etymology*, Holthausen's *Etymologisches Wörterbuch der Englischen Sprache*, and Kipfer and Chapman's *Dictionary of American Slang*. The full list of scholarly sources employed is an impressive list of 83 titles.

[29] *The Oxford English Dictionary*, Clarendon Press, 1933.

[30] The derivation of the verb *depart* itself throws fascinating light on the subject. The *Online Egymology Dictionary* at etymonline.com gives the following entry — **depart (v.)**-- mid-13c., departen, "part from each other, part company;" late 13c., "separate into parts," original senses now archaic or obsolete, from Old French departir (10c.) "to divide, distribute; separate (oneself), depart; die," from Late Latin departire "to divide" (transitive), from de- "from" (see de-) + partire "to part, divide," from pars (genitive partis) "a part, piece, a share, a division." Based on this information, one can well see why *departure* and *departing* regularly bore senses as *division*, *separation*, and *turning away* in the 1500s and 1600s.

[31] This marginal note was first pointed out to me by Joseph Kerr of I Am A Watchman who kindly sent me a photo of the relevant page from a Bible in his personal collection.

[32] J.N. Darby, who generally tried to rigorously correlate his translations with the Greek, renders this verse, "because lawlessness shall prevail, the love of the most shall grow cold."

[33] Heinrich Bullinger, *A commentary vpon the seconde epistle of S Paul to the Thessalonians*. Printed in Southwarke: In S. Thomas hospytall by Iames Nicolson, 1538.

[34] His original English runs as follows: "And fyrste we wyll speake of the departynge. Departynge is here taken after suche a maner, as whan a man doth slyde backe or fayle from hys author or prynce. Saynt Ambrose doth expounde it of the diuydynge of the kyngdome of ye Romaynes, and of the departyng of other kyngdomes frō it. Other haue interpreted it of the departyng of fayth, of the whiche the Apostle spake, i. Timo. iiii. sayenge: The sprete speaketh euydentlye, that in the

latter dayes some shall depart from the fayth, geuyng hede vnto spretes of erroure and deuelyshe doctrynes, &c."

[35] *Commentaries on The Epistle of Paul to the Philippians, Colossians, and Thessalonians by John Calvin: Translated and edited from the original Latin and colated with the French version* by John Pringle. Reprinted by Christian Classics Ethereal Library, 1999.

[36]It should be noted that Calvin's comments are based on the familiar Latin translation, "Ne quis vos decipiat ullo modo; quia nisi prius venerit *discessio*, et nisi revelatus fuerit sceleratus ille filius perditus." This tells us that he understood *discessio* to mean *apostasy* or *revolt* and to have reference to the treacherous departure from God associated with the antichrist.

[37] Accessed at Early English Books Online Text Creation Partnership, Univ. of Mich. Library (quod.lib.umich.edu).

[38] This is the Wyclif reading in *The English Hexapla*, Samuel Bagster and Sons, 1841, which derived its Wyclif text from a very early Wyclif manuscript.

[39] This is the earlier version in Forshall and Madden's critical edition published by Oxford in 1850. It was based on four early manuscripts and carefully collated with nineteen other early manuscripts.

[40] This is the later version in Forshall and Madden's critical edition published by Oxford in 1850. It was based on a single later manuscript, 1 C 8 in the Old Royal Collection, and carefully collated with thirty-four others.

[41] The full entry in *The Oxford English Dictionary*, Clarendon Press, 1933 reads— **discencioun**: "Dissension. Forms: dissensiun, -sion; disc-, dys-, des-, -ciun, -cioun, -cion, -tion, also discencion, etc. ... 1. Disagreement ... as produces strife or contention; discord."

[42] Wyclif's Bible reads, "Forsoth *dissencioun* is maad, so they thei departiden atwyny."

[43] In the original English it read, "First sal be *dissensiun* er ante-christ sal cum in land."

[44] The *Deutsches Wörterbuch* von Jacob Grimm und Wilhelm Grimm says, "MISZHELLUNG, f. uneinigkeit, mhd. missehellunge, in der ältern sprache bis ins 17. jahrh. für miszhelligkeit: dissonantia missehellung Dief. 187a; miszhällung, discrepantia, discordia, peccatum." The *Mittelhochdeutsches Handwörterbuch* von Matthias Lexer says, "misse-hëllunge stf., mishelligkeit, dissonantia, dissonus." If we look up *Mißhelligkeit* in a modern German lexicon, such as Cassel's, we see that it means *disagreement, dissension, discord*.

[45] *Misshellung* and the alternate spelling *Missehellung* were used for urban revolts as those in Worms in 1301-1303 and in Rottweil in 1378-79. See *The Routledge History Handbook of Medieval Revolt*, edited by Justine Firnhabe-Baker with Dirk Schoenaers, Routledge, 2017, p. 249.

[46] *Cassel's German-English, English-German Dictionary*, rev. Harold Betteridge, , MacMillan Publishing, 1978.

[47] This translation was made with the help of both *A Comparative Glossary of the Gothic Language With Especial Reference to English and German*, G.H. Balg, Westermann (New York), Truebner (London), Niemeyer (Germany), 1887-1889 and *Kurzgefasstes Etymologisches Wörterbuch des Gotischen Sprache*, C.C. Uhlenbeck, Johannes Müller, 1900.

[48] *Kurzgefasstes Etymologisches Wörterbuch des Gotischen Sprache*, C.C. Uhlenbeck, Johannes Müller, 1900. The entry in the original German reads, "trennung, scheidung, zu afstandan sich eutfernen, sich abwenden, s. standan." This lexicon is available online at the Internet Archive (https://archive.org/details/ KurzgefasstesEtymologischesWrterbuchDerGotischenSprache). The translations of the German words in the definition, except for the last one, are from the Deutsch-English Wörterbuch available at dict.cc.

[49] *A Comparative Glossary of the Gothic Language With Especial Reference to English and German*, G.H. Balg, Westermann (New York), Truebner (London), Niemeyer (Germany), 1887-1889. An online version can be found at Hathi Trust (https://catalog.hathitrust.org/Record/001210721).

[50] *Cassel's Latin Dictionary*, D.P. Simpson, Cassel & Company, 1968. Orig. Publ. 1959.

[51] C. T. Lewis and C Short, *A Latin Dictionary*, Clarendon Press, 1945; 1st ed. 1879. An online version is available at Internet Archive (https://archive.org/details/ in.ernet.dli.2015.147309).

[52] *Oxford Latin Dictionary*, Clarendon Press, 1968. An online version is availabel at Internet Archive (https://archive.org/details/aa.-vv.-oxford-latin-dictionary-1968/mode/2up).

[53] Jerome's collected Letters, "Letter 121 (Ad Algasium de quaestionibus xi)," Question 11, Sancti Eusebii Hieronymi Stridonensis Presbyteri Epistolae Secundum Ordinem Temporum Ad Amussim Digestae Et In Quatuor Classes Distributae: Quarta Classis: Complectens Epistolas Ab Ineunte Anno 401, Usque AD 420. Sive Hieronymi Vitae Finem. Accessed in the original language at patrologia-lib.ru. The original Latin reads, "Nisi, inquit, venerit *discessio* primum, quod dicitur *apostasia*, ut omnes gentes quae Romano imperio subjacent, recedant ab eis, et revelatus fuerit, id est, ostensus, quem omnia Prophetarum verba praenuntiant, homo peccati, in quo fons omnium peccatorum est."

[54] *Biblia Sacra iuxta Vulgatam Clementinam*, *Nova Editio*, Bibliotheca De Autores Cristianos, 1965.

[55] Hermann Roensch. *Das Neue Testament Tertullian's Aus den Schriften des Letzteren möglichst vollständig, reconstruirt mit Einleitungen und Anmerkungen*. Fues' Verlag, 1871. The Latin reads, "Ne quis vos seducat ullo modo. Quoniam nisi veniat abscessio primo et reveletur delinquentiae homo, filius perditionis." The reading *abscessio* doesn't change the sense. It has essentially the same meaning as *discessio*. Cassel's Latin Dictionary says, "**abscessio**. a going away, a separation."

[56] Same volume as above. The phrase in question in the Old Latin version used by Tertullian is "nisi veniat abscessio primo." His two comments on the passage are: "huius utique regni" and "nisi Romanus status, cuius abscessio in decem reges dispersa antichristum superducet."

[57] The Latin reads "Ne quis seducat vos vllo modo: quoniam nisi venerit *dissensio* primum: et reuelatus fuerit homo peccati: filius perditionis."

[58] *Cassel's Latin Dictionary*, D.P. Simpson, Cassel & Company, 1968. Orig. Publ. 1959.

[59] The Latin reads, "quoniam nisi venerit *dissensio* primus."

[60] **Beza (1565)**: Column 2 — Nequis vos seducat vllo modo. Non enim adveniet dies Christi quin venerit *defectio* prius, & retectus fuerit homo ille sceleratus, filius, inquam, ille perditionis. Column 3 — Nequis uos seducat ullo modo: quoniam nisi uenerit *discessio* primum & reuelatus fuerit homo peccati, filius perditionis. **Beza (1598)**: Column 2 — Nequis vos seducat yllo modo. Nisi enim adveniet dies Christi quin venerit *defectio* prius, & reuelatus fuerit homo ille peccati, filius, inquam, ille perditionis. Column 3 — Nequis vos seducat ullo modo: quoniam nisi venerit *discessio* primum & reuelatus fuerit homo peccati, filius perditionis.

[61] *He has fallen away* is ἐξέπεσε and *to apostasy* is πρὸς ἀποστασίαν. The passage can be found at (29) Basil of Caesaria, *Exposition of the Prophet Isaiah*, in Appendix F — Church Fathers on pp. 128-129.

[62] The phrase used for *falling away* is πάντως ἔξω πεσοῦνται (pantōs exō pesountai) *utterly falling away*. The phrase ἔξω πεσοῦνται (the adverb ἔξω and the future of πίπτω (pipto) fall is essentially equivalent to ἐκπίπτω (ekpiptō) fall away. The passage can be found at (81) Cyril of Alexandria, *Commentary on the Twelve Minor Prophets*, Hosea 6:7 in Appendix A — Church Fathers on pp. 171-172.

[63] The Greek here is ἢ περὶ τῶν τῆς ὄντως ἐκπεπτωκότων ζωῆς, ὁποῖοι διὰ τῆς ἀποστασίας οἱ δαίμονες. The word ἐκπεπτωκότων is the genitive plural perfect participle of ἐκπίπτω (ekpiptō) *to fall* away. The passage can be found at (208) Procopius of Gaza, *Commentary in Isaiah*, in Appendix A — Church Fathers on p. 286.

[64] The Greek terms here are τῆς τῶν κρειττόνων ἀποστασίας and ἐκπεπτωκότα. The passage can be found at (149) Eusebius of Caesarea, *Preparation for the Gospel*, in Appendix A — Church Fathers on pp. 234-235.

[65] The Greek phrase here is εἰς παντελῆ ἐξέπιπτον ἀποστασίαν. The passage can be found at (128) Eusebius of Caesarea, *Commentary on Psalms*, 18:17ff (LXX 17:18) in Appendix A — Church Fathers on p. 216.

[66] The Greek terms here are ἐξέπεσον and ἀποστασία. The passage can be found at (47) Chrysostom, *Expositions on Psalms*, 13.2-3 (LXX 12.3-4) in Appendix A — Church Fathers on pp. 141-142.

[67] The Greek terms here are ἐξέπεσον and ἀποστασία. The passage can be found at (46) Chrysostom, *Forty-Eight Excerpts from Diverse Homilies*, in Appendix A — Church Fathers on pp. 140-141.

[68] Cassel's German dictionary says *Abfall* means *defection, secession, backsliding, revolt, rebellion.*

[69] Thomas, Tymme, *The figure of Antichrist with the tokens of the end of the world, most plainly disciphered by a Catholike and diuine exposition of the seconde epistle of Paul to the Thessalonians, collected out of the best and most approued diuines, both olde and new, very profitable for all men in this age to reade,* imprinted at London by T. Dawson for Fraunces Coldocke, 1586. Can be accessed at the Online Books Page of the Univ. of Penn, (onlinebooks.library.upenn.edu/webbin/book/lookupname?key=Tymme%2C%20Thomas%2C%20%2D1620).

[70] *Commentaries on The Epistle of Paul to the Philippians, Colossians, and Thessalonians by John Calvin: Translated and edited from the original Latin and colated with the French version* by John Pringle. Reprinted by Christian Classics Ethereal Library, 1999.

[71] Links for all five of these editions of Beza's Latin translation can be found at vuntblog.blogspot.com/2012/11/bezas-new-testament-editions-online.html.

[72] The Anglo-Norman Dictionary says, "Apostasie: eccl. *apostasy, renunciation of one's faith*; (c. 1305), "L'un si est apostata de mal apostasye", Boz Char 474 [Le Char d'Orgueil, by Nicholas Bozon].

[73] The Oxford English dictionary gives examples of *apostasy* in the works of Wyclif (c. 1380) and in Purvey (1395). The former wrote, "*Apostasye* þat goiþ evene aȝen þe ordre of Crist." In modern English this would read, "*Apostasy* that goes even against the order of Christ." [Wyclif, De Dot. Eccl. Wks. 1871, III.438]. The latter wrote, "*Apostasie*, either goinge abak fro cristene feith." In modern English this would read, "*Apostasy*, each going back from the Christian faith." [Purvey, Remonstr. (1851)24.] There is not a doubt in my mind that historians of the English language could trace the examples even farther back. *Apostasy* likely came into the English language via the French influence in the court and the Latin influence in the church.

[74] The Lewis and Short Lexicon says, "**apostasia**, ae, f., = ἀποστασία, a departure from one's religion, apostasy, Salv. Gub. Dei, 6, [Salvian, *On the Government of God*, 6]." Salvius was a sixth-century theologian.

[75] See (152) Evagrius of Pontus, *On the Vices Opposed to the Virtues*, chapter 4, in Appendix F — Church Fathers on pp. 237-238.

[76] (37) Basil of Caesaria, *Letters*, To the Alexandrians, 139 in Appendix A — Church Fathers on p. 133.

[77] (40) Basil of Caesaria, *Letters*, To Barses the Bishop of Edessa, 264 in Appendix A — Church Fathers on pp. 136-137.

[78] (42) Basil of Caesaria, *Sermons on Manners: Collected by Symeon Metaphrastes*, Message 12, in Appendix A — Church Fathers on pp. 137-138.

[79] (15) Athanasius, *Deposition of Arius*, section 1, [The Decisions of the Synod of Nicea, section 35, Opitz], in Appendix A — Church Fathers on pp. 118-119.

[80] (18) Athanasius, *History of Arianism*, section 77, in Appendix A — Church Fathers on pp. 120-121.

[81] (107) Cyril of Jerusalem, *Catechetical Lectures*, 15.9, in Appendix A — Church Fathers on pp. 197-199.

[82] (181) Justin Martyr, *Dialogue with Trypho*, 110, in Appendix A — Church Fathers on pp. 262-263.

[83] (219) Theodoret, *Commentary on the Letters of Paul*, 2 The ssalonians, 2:3, in Appendix A — Church Fathers on pp. 295-296.

[84] (215) Theodoret, *Compendium of the Fables of the Heretics*, Book 5, Chapter 23 — Concerning the Antichrist, in Appendix A — Church Fathers on pp. 291-292.

[85] (198) Origen, *Scholia on Revelation*, scholion 38, in Appendix A — Church Fathers on pp. 278-279.

[86] (181) Justin Martyr, *Dialogue with Trypho*, 110, in Appendix A — Church Fathers on pp. 262-263.

[87] (60) Chrysostom, *Homilies on 2 Thessalonians*, Homily 3, in Appendix A — Church Fathers on pp. 152-153.

[88] Because of their sufferings, they feared that they might already be in the day of the Lord. This was likely a spiritualized version of that day that exploited texts like "judgment begins in the house of God." Paul corrected the error by revisiting the literal understanding of the day of the Lord. It is a literal day that will not come until the world sees the literal dawning of that day. The dawning of that day will feature the literal antichrist and the literal apostasy that he foments. The church won't see any of this day, not the day proper when the Lord descends from heaven, and not the dawning of that day when the antichrist is revealed, the great persecution begins, and the falling away happens. They are going up in the rapture at the morning star— the crack of dawn—before the approaching day is noticeable to the dwellers on the earth. So there is no need to worry about the day of the Lord.

[89] That these things happen prior to the day of the Lord is problematic for those who hold that the technical sense of the day of the Lord is the seventieth week. But there is no problem for those who understand that the day of the Lord, technically speaking, is the day that the Lord descends in judgment and that the seventieth week is the day of the Lord approaching, i.e. dawning on the world. Notice the time characteristics that the following passages give us. The day of the Lord is still at hand when the nations are gathered for Armageddon (Joel 3:9-14, Zeph. 1:7-17, Rev. 15:1). The signs which herald the arrival of the day of the Lord come after the three and a half years of great tribulation (Matt. 24:29-31). The day of the Lord will be one literal day (Zech. 14:7), when the sun will go down at noon and darken the land (Amos 8:9), during which time it will be neither day nor night (Zech 14:7), but in the evening it will be light again (Zech 14:7). The Lord alone will be glorified in the day of the Lord (Is. 2:11). This is not true during the 70th week when the world is worshipping the antichrist and the devil. But it will be true when the Son of man descends from heaven in righteous indignation.

[90] Some teachers might classify the usage patterns a little differently, but this treatment has sufficient breadth and precision to get the point across.

[91] See §268 (p. 140) in Blass and Debrunner, *A Greek Grammar of the New Testament and Other Early Christian Literature*, Univ. of Chicago Press, 7th impress., 1974; publ. 1961. See also §916 (p. 257) in Herbert Weir Smyth, *A Greek Grammar*, repr. Benediction Classics, 2014; orig. publ. American Book Company, 1920. See also p. 206 in Moulton, *A Grammar of New Testament Greek*, Vol. III Syntax, by Nigel Turner, T&T Clark, 1993, orig. publ. 1963.

[92] See §270 (p. 141) in Blass and Debrunner, *A Greek Grammar of the New Testament and Other Early Christian Literature*, Univ. of Chicago Press, 7th impress., 1974; publ. 1961. See also §§1154-1167 in Herbert Weir Smyth, *A Greek Grammar*, repr. Benediction Classics, 2014; orig. publ. American Book Company, 1920. See also pp. 185-186 in Moulton, *A Grammar of New Testament Greek*, Vol. III Syntax, by Nigel Turner, T&T Clark, 1993, orig. publ. 1963.

[93] See pp. 182-184 in Moulton, *A Grammar of New Testament Greek*, Vol. III Syntax, by Nigel Turner, T&T Clark, 1993, orig. publ. 1963. See also §§1168-1171 (p. 295) in Herbert Weir Smyth, *A Greek Grammar*, repr. Benediction Classics, 2014; orig. publ. American Book Company, 1920.

[94] See pp. 221-222 in Moulton, *A Grammar of New Testament Greek*, Vol. III Syntax, by Nigel Turner, T&T Clark, 1993, orig. publ. 1963.

[95] See §412 (p. 212) in Blass and Debrunner, *A Greek Grammar of the New Testament and Other Early Christian Literature*, Univ. of Chicago Press, 7th impress., 1974; publ. 1961. See also pp. 151-153 in Moulton, *A Grammar of New Testament Greek*, Vol. III Syntax, by Nigel Turner, T&T Clark, 1993, orig. publ. 1963.

[96] See pp. 172-174 in Moulton, *A Grammar of New Testament Greek*, Vol. III Syntax, by Nigel Turner, T&T Clark, 1993, orig. publ. 1963. See also §1120b in Herbert Weir Smyth, *A Greek Grammar*, repr. Benediction Classics, 2014; orig. publ. American Book Company, 1920.

[97] The supposed referring noun *apostasia* is in verse 3. The supposed referents *coming* and *gathering* are in verse 1. Between them we have "the day of Christ" at the end of verse 2 and "through an epistle" shortly prior. Day is ἡ ἡμέρα in Greek and epistle is ἡ ἐπιστολή.

[98] Daniel 9:26, καὶ μετὰ **τὰς ἑβδομάδας τὰς ἑξήκοντα δύο** ἐξολεθρευθήσεται χρῖσμα. Daniel 9:27, καὶ δυναμώσει διαθήκην πολλοῖς, ἑβδομὰς μία· καὶ **ἐν τῷ ἡμίσει τῆς ἑβδομάδος** ἀρθήσεταί μου θυσία καὶ σπονδή. Revelation 11:6, οὗτοι ἔχουσιν τὴν ἐξουσίαν κλεῖσαι τὸν οὐρανόν, ἵνα μὴ ὑετὸς βρέχῃ **τὰς ἡμέρας τῆς προφητείας αὐτῶν**. Luke 2 2:2, **αὕτη ἡ ἀπογραφὴ πρώτη** ἐγένετο ἡγεμονεύοντος τῆς Συρίας Κυρηνίου.

[99] See the remarks on the generic use of the article in §263 (p. 138) in Blass and Debrunner, *A Greek Grammar of the New Testament and Other Early Christian Literature*, Univ. of Chicago Press, 7th impress., 1974; publ. 1961. See also the

remarks in §1118 (pp. 286-287) and §§1122-1124 (pp. 287-288) in Herbert Weir Smyth, *A Greek Grammar*, repr. Benediction Classics, 2014; orig. publ. American Book Company, 1920.

[100] I have here assumed that the common understanding of the restrainer is correct—it is the Holy Spirit restraining iniquity (not the mystery of iniquity restraining truth). I have also assumed the common understanding of the Greek phrase ἐκ μέσου γένηται—it is an out-coming that is a *removal* of the Holy Spirit in the church (rather than an out-coming that is a *revealing* of the antichrist). According to the common understanding, the Holy Spirit will be removed with the rapture of the church, and then the antichrist will be revealed.

[101] Kenneth S. Wuest, Letter to E. Schuyler English, published in "Let the Prophets Speak," *Our Hope*, (vol. LVI, num. 12; June 1950), p. 731.

[102] J.N. Darby, who generally tried to rigorously correlate his translations with the Greek, renders this verse, "because lawlessness shall prevail, the love of the most shall grow cold."

[103] It is also found in Luke 11:24-26.

[104] According to Zechariah 13:7-9, two-thirds of Israel will perish in the judgment and one-third will come through the refiner's fire. This is an amazing percentage of salvation in any society or nation.

Made in the USA
Thornton, CO
01/20/24 09:47:04

e9fb816a-0ee8-452a-8991-53c5773c2789R01